RULE OF LAW AND RIGHT TO INFORMATION

About the Authors

Abhishek Shukla is a practising lawyer at Punjab and Haryana High Court at Chandigarh. He has the experience of pursuing legal practice through District Courts, Punjab State Commission, Haryana State Commission and Debt Recovery Tribunal where various aspects of law were used for social and legal engineering. The author Advocate Abhishek Shukla has acquired acumen at arguing cases, vetting legal drafts, client counselling and general administration.

His grasp over procedural law, stages of trial and cross-examination skills were enhanced by working with Mr. Rohit Sapra, a leading legal practitioner at District Courts, Chandigarh.

Having worked as Assistant Lawyer to Mr. Rajeev Atma Ram, Senior Advocate Punjab and Haryana High Court, the author further honed his skills in Criminal Law, Service Law, Law of Contract, Negotiable Instruments Act and Constitutional Law.

Surinder K. Shukla, after doing masters from Punjab University in 1976, became the recipient of Doctoral Research Fellowship from University Grants Commission. She has published extensively in journals of national and international repute besides writing books and contributing chapters to several books, some of which have been cited in International Political Science Abstracts, Paris, France. Travelled extensively in India and abroad. Dr. Shukla has been elected Board Member of various Research Committees of International Political Science Association since 1994. Besides being a prolific reader, teacher and writer, the author is a proud home-maker. Currently she is Professor of Political Science at Punjab University, Chandigarh.

Rule of Law and Right to Information

Abhishek Shukla
Surinder K. Shukla

CONCEPT PUBLISHING COMPANY PVT. LTD.
NEW DELHI-110 059

ISBN-13 : 978-81-8069-859-0

First Published 2012

Published and Printed by

Concept Since 1974

Concept Publishing Company Pvt. Ltd.
A/15-16, Commercial Block, Mohan Garden
New Delhi-110059 (India)
T: 25351460, 25351794, *F*: 091-11-25357109
E: publishing@conceptpub.com, W: www.conceptpub.com
Editorial Office: H-13, Bali Nagar, New Delhi-110 015, India.

Cataloging in Publication Data--*Courtesy:* D.K. Agencies (P) Ltd. <docinfo@dkagencies.com>

Shukla, Abhishek.
Rule of law and right to information / Abhishek Shukla, Surinder K. Shukla.
p. cm.
Includes bibliographical references (p.) and index.
ISBN 9788180698590

1. Rule of law—India. 2. Freedom of information—India. I. Shukla, Surinder K. (Surinder Kler), 1954-, joint author. II. Title.

DDC 340.110954 23

Preface

The main challenge facing India's legal and judicial systems is delivering justice to the poor people. Although the Constitution of India grants rights to people of India but a large section have little access to courts. As the cost of good quality legal services is escalating, the ability of citizens to get effective and high quality legal assistance and access to justice is diminishing. The legal system is in danger of becoming further alienated from the citizens. New and innovative solutions are needed to ensure that the citizens have access to justice. Right to Information Act is one such solution whereby citizen's reach is extended for a greater access to justice.

Rule of Law in its most basic form is the principle that no one is above Law. But is there an indiscriminatory Rule of Law? The book explores these problems and navigates the reader through legal philosophy and fundamental concepts, concerns and controversies.

If Rule of Law is state-centric, Right of Information Act is people-centric. While the one protects and ensures egalitarianism from the legal point of view, the other empowers citizen to have greater access to state information. Both the Rule of Law and Right to Information Act aim intrinsically towards protection of citizen for whom the state exists. Both are constructs of human mind and focus on rights of citizen.

From the perspective of the citizen and citizen friendly governance the Right to Information Act 2005 remains the most revolutionary breakthrough after the 73rd and 74th Constitutional Amendments. The Act has the potential to develop into a most effective weapon in the hands of ordinary citizen to get the grievances addressed. In **S.P. Gupta** v. **Union of India (1982),** Justice Bhagwati observed that even if a document is confidential, it must be produced, not withstanding its confidentiality, if it is necessary for fairly disposing of the case, unless it can be shown that its disclosure would otherwise be injurious to public interest.

The main stumbling block in the way of implementing citizen right to information *vis-à-vis* government has been the **Official Secrets Act, 1823,** which is a British legacy as far as administration is concerned. The Act fosters a 'culture of secrecy' thereby enhancing an aura of mistrust between officials and the ordinary citizen. The National Commission to Review the Working of the Constitution recommended that Article 19(1) (a) of the Constitution should be amended *inter alia* to specifically include freedom to seek and receive information. The Commission said "Much of the common man's distress and helplessness could be traced to his lack of knowledge of decision-making process. He remains ignorant and unaware of the processes which virtually affect his interest. Government procedures and regulation shrouded in a veil of secrecy do not allow the clients to know how their cases are being handled".

Further the Commission said 'They (citizens) shy away from questioning officers handling their cases because of the latter's snobbish attitude and bow-wow style'. Right to information should, therefore, be guaranteed and needs to be given real substance. In this regard, government must assume a major responsibility and mobilize skills to ensure flow of information to citizens. The traditional insistence on secrecy should be discarded. In fact we should have an oath of transparency in place of an oath of secrecy. Administration should become transparent and participatory.

Commenting on the benefits of Right to Information the **National Commission to Review the Working of the Constitution** observed:

Right to information can usher in many benefits, such as speedy disposal of cases, minimizing manipulative and dilatory tactics of the *babudom*, and, last but most importantly, putting a considerable check on graft and corruption.

It is hoped that Right to Information Act will strengthen Rule of Law thereby empowering the citizen of India and provide depth to India's democracy.

Acknowledgements

We are grateful to our family and extended family as also to friends and colleagues at the Bar and at the University who have directly and indirectly contributed towards the writing of this volume. We are grateful to personnel of libraries at the Bar Council and at Panjab University who helped in locating material for this work. We are grateful to Professor A.D. Mishra, Director Gandhi Smarak, Rajghat for his support for this publication. Contexts of Law were discussed with Professor Gordon Woodman, Emeritus Professor of Comparative Law, Birmingham Law School, Professor Anne Griffiths, University of Edinburgh and Professors Franz and Keebet Benda-Beckmann, founder of International Commission on Folk Law and Plural Law, Germany, to whom we owe our gratitude.

We are thankful to Shri Sandeep for typing the manuscripts diligently.

We are grateful to Shri Ashok Kumar Mittal of Concept Publishing Company Pvt. Ltd., who was instrumental in ensuring an early publication. Although we are grateful to all those individuals and friends and students who remain unnamed, we alone are responsible for any errors.

Abhishek Shukla
Advocate,
Punjab and Haryana High Court,
Chandigarh

Surinder K. Shukla
Professor
Political Science,
Panjab University, Chandigarh.

आ नो भद्राः ऋतवो यान्तु विश्वतः

Let noble thoughts come to us from every side.

Rigveda 1-89

Outside, beyond what is right and wrong,
There exists a vast field.
We will find each other there.

Mevlana Jalaluddin Rumi
(Thirteenth Century)

The mood and temper of the public with regard to the treatment of crime and criminals is one of the most unfailing tests of the civilization of any country.

Sir Winston Churchill

Fallen cherub; to be weak is to be miserable.

(From Paradise Lost, Book I)
John Milton

Not even thousand years of joy can justify seven days of repression.

Persian poet Hafez

My mom still believes
That good is always rewarded
Honesty still pays
That there is always light
At the end of a tunnel.

Bela Nibedita Sen (2005)

Abbreviations

AA	Appellate Authorities
AIR	All India Reporter
APIO	Assistant Public Information Officer
CEC	Chief Election Commissioner
CERC	Consumer Education Research Council
CHRI	Commonwealth Human Rights Information
CMP	Common Minimum Programme
DoPT	Department of Personnel and Training
EFoIA	Electronic Freedom of India Act
EPA	Environ Protection Agency
FoIA	Freedom of Information Act
MKSS	Mazdoor Kisan Shakti Sangathan
MRIA	Maharashtra Right to Information Act
NCPRI	National Campaign for Right to Information
PIO	Public Information Officer
RTI	Right to Information
TCIL	Telecommunications Consultants India Ltd.
UNCITRAL	United Nations Commission on International Trade Law
UPSC	Union Public Service Commission
YASHADA	Yashwantrao Academy of Development Administration

List of Cases

Curtis Publishing Co.	*v.*	Butts
S.P. Gupta	*v.*	Union of India, AIR 1982, SC 149
Smith	*v.*	East India
Beatson	*v.*	Skene
Davpack Systems Pvt. Ltd.	*v.*	India
Bihar	*v.*	Kripalu Shankar
Keshavananda Bharti	*v.*	State of Kerala 1973, SC 1641
Minerva Mills	*v.*	The Union of India 1980, SC 1787
Shankari Prasad	*v.*	The Union of India, AIR 1951, SC 458

Cases Referred to PIL

People's Union	*v.*	Union of India, AIR SC 1473 (para 1)
State of WB	*v.*	Sampat, AIR 1985, SC 195 (para 10)
Chaitanya	*v.*	State of Karnataka, AIR 1986, SC 825 (para 10)
Raunaq International Ltd.	*v.*	IVR Construction Ltd., AIR 1999, SC 303 (para 12)

1

Rule of Law

Law consists of a set of general, public and enforceable rules, usually regarded as binding in the society to which it applies. It is valued as the principal means through which liberty and order are maintained. This is usually achieved through the rule of law, the belief that all behaviour should conform to a framework of law. This doctrine is closely linked with constitutionalism and limited government.

Contexts of Law

Legal contexts may be clear, but they are often diffused, contested and they change over time due to the change in systemic character of legal systems. Depending on this systemic character, contexts of law differ in geographical and in substantive scope. The contents of law differ in the institutions and types of actors involved. They differ in permeability and in the density and scope of which parts or clusters within legal systems are linked together and are nested in the larger system (Benda-Beckmann, 2001). The different parts of a legal system are linked, become intertwined, respond to each other and are recombined over time. This happens within one legal system and between legal systems. Situations of legal pluralism are particularly conducive to such linking.

Gordon Woodman (1998) while formulating his critique in a theoretical discussion about law points out that the assumption that legal systems can be clearly distinguished is becoming less and less convincing. This has implications for the way legal contexts are formed and used in interaction. In this changed scenario, Woodman suggests that to bring clarity, there is need for 'mapping of law' or cartography of law.

The systemic properties of legal systems seem to have important social consequences. To a large extent they determine what the relevant legal contexts are in which people operate. Systemic changes in law have an impact on legal contexts and these are constraining and enabling factors in the social behaviour of persons and groups.

Blurred Boundaries

Much work on legal pluralism has been done in which component parts are clearly defined as customary law, religious law, state law etc. In the 1950s and 1960s much effort was made to show that local customs could be usefully regarded as law. The basis of legitimization differed from that of state law, but there was no fundamental difference between state law and customary law.

Under the term 'making of customary law' scholars have pointed that much of what was taken as part of authentic customary law, was in fact a creation by the colonial state, or at least a reaction to the colonial state (Chanock, 1982; Moore 1978). These later studies from the colonial experience made it clear that there was not such a neat separation of these systems, that interaction created hybrid legal forms all along the colonial period. And Woodman (1998) remarks that the difference between what can be considered as State Law and what falls outside that scope is no longer clear.

Moral Justification of Breaking the Law

Mroal justification of law breaking lies in two explanations. **One** is based on the question, 'Why should I obey the law'? This raises the issue of political obligation. Political obligation denotes not a duty to obey a particular law but rather the citizens' duty to respect and obey the state itself.

The *other* argument is based on the question "What justification is there for breaking the law"? This raises the issue of what is called civil disobedience law breaking which is justified by reference to religious, moral or political principles. Civil disobedience has a long and respectable history. Under Mahatma Gandhi's influence, non-violent civil disobedience became a powerful weapon in the campaign for India's independence which took place in 1947. In the early 1960s Martin Luther King adopted similar political approval in the struggle for Black Civil Rights in the American South.

Mahatma Gandhi's philosophy of non-violent resistance, *satyagraha,* reinforced by his ascetic lifestyle gave an enormous moral authority to the movement for independence and provided a model for later civil rights activists. First outlined in *Hind Swaraj* (1909) Home Rule was based on a philosophy ultimately derived from Hinduism in which the universe is regulated by the primacy of truth or *Satya.* As mankind is 'ultimately one', love, care, and a concern for others is the natural basis for human relations. Gandhi, in fact, described love as the 'law of our being'. For Gandhi, non-violence not only expressed the proper moral relationship among people, but also, when linked with self-sacrifice or *tapasya,* constituted a powerful social and political programme. Gandhi condemned Western civilisation for its materialism and moral weakness, and regarded it as the source of violence and injustice.

Gandhi, a lawyer by profession developed his philosophy of civil disobedience while working in South Africa where he organised protests against discrimination. On return to India in 1915 he became the leader of national movement. He employed civil disobedience as an overt and public act: it aims to break a law in order to 'make a point' rather than an attempt to get away with it. Civil disobedience is this distinguished from other criminal acts by its motives. Indeed, it is the willingness to accept penalties for law-breaking, which gives civil disobedience its moral authority and emotional power.

In some cases, civil disobedience may involve the breaking of laws which are unjust, its aim being to protest against the law in question and achieve its removal. In his famous 'march to the sea', popularly known as *'Dandi March'*, Gandhi sought to protest against the law banning Indians from making salt by making a symbolic amount of salt from seawater and thus courting arrest, but only as a part of a larger campaign for national independence.

Whether it is designed to attack a particular law or advance a wider cause, all acts of civil disobedience are justified by asserting a distinction between law and justice. At the centre of civil disobedience stands the belief that the individual rather than government is the ultimate moral authority.

Perhaps the most important application of the rule of law is the principle that governmental authority is legitimately exercised only in accordance with written, publicly disclosed laws adopted and enforced in accordance with established procedural steps that are referred to as due process. The principle is intended to be a safeguard against arbitrary governance, whether by a totalitarian leader or by mob rule. Thus, the rule of law is hostile both to dictatorship and to anarchy. Samuel Rutherford was one of the first modem authors to give the principle theoretical foundations, in **Lex Rex** (1644), and later Montesquieu in **The Spirit of the Laws (1748).**

In continental Europe and legal thinking, the rule of law has frequently, but not always, been associated with a **Reichtsstaat.** According to modem Anglo-American thinking, hallmarks of adherence to the rule of law commonly include a clear separation of powers, legal certainty, the principle of legitimate expectation and equality of all before the law.

The concept is not without controversy, and it has been said that the phrase: The Rule of Law has become debatable due to ideological abuse and general over-use.

In his treatise: *Law of the Constitution* (10th Ed., 1959), pp. 187, *et seq.*, Dicey identified three principles which together establish the rule of law: "(1) the absolute supremacy or predominance of regular law as opposed to the influence of arbitrary power; (2) equality before the law or the equal subjection of all classes to the ordinary law of the land administered by the ordinary courts; and (3) the law of the constitution is a consequence of the rights of individuals as defined and enforced by the courts"

Halsbury's *Laws of England*, Vol: Law and Human Rights, paragraph 6, footnote 1:

... every official, from the Prime Minister down to a constable or a collector of taxes, is under the same responsibility for every act done without legal justification as any other citizen. The Reports abound with cases in which officials have been brought before the courts, and made, in their personal capacity, liable to punishment, or to the payment of damages, for acts done in their official character but in excess of their lawful authority. [Appointed government officials and politicians, alike] ... and all subordinates, though carrying out the commands of their official superiors, are as responsible for any act which the **law** does not authorise as is any private and unofficial person. [*Law of the Constitution* (London: MacMillan, 9th ed., 1950), 194].

Another definition can be found at Halsbury's *Laws of England,* Vol: Constitutional Law and Human Rights, paragraph 6.

The legal basis of government gives rise to the principle of legality, sometimes referred to as the rule of law. This may be expressed as a number of propositions, as described below:

(1) The existence or non-existence of a power or duty is a matter of law and not of fact, and so must be determined by reference either to the nature of the legal personality of the body in question and the capacities that go with it, or to some enactment or reported case. As far as the capacities that go with legal personality are concerned, many public bodies are incorporated by statute and so statutory provisions will define and limit their legal capacities. Individuals who are public office-holders have the capacities that go with the legal personality that they have as natural persons.

(2) The argument of state necessity is not sufficient to establish the existence of a power or duty which would entitle a public body to act in a way that interferes with the rights or liberties of individuals. However, the common law does recognize that in case of extreme

urgency, when the ordinary machinery of the state cannot function, there is a justification for the doing of acts needed to restore the regular functioning of the machinery of government.

(3) If effect is to be given to the doctrine that the existence or non-existence of a power or duty is a matter of law, it should be possible for the courts to determine whether or not a particular power or duty exists, to define its ambit and provide an effective remedy for unlawful action. The independence of the judiciary is essential to the principle of legality. The right of access to the courts can be excluded by statute, but this is not often done in express terms. A person whose civil or political rights and freedoms as guaranteed by the Convention for the Protection of Human Rights and Fundamental Freedoms (the European Convention on Human Rights) have been infringed is entitled under the Convention to an effective right of access to the courts and an effective national remedy. On the other hand, powers are often given to bodies other than the ordinary courts, to decide questions of law without appeal to the ordinary courts, and sometimes in such terms that their freedom from appellate jurisdiction extends to their findings of fact or law on which the existence of their powers depends.

(4) Since the principal elements of the structure of the machinery of government, and the powers and duties which belong to its several parts, are defined by law, its form and course can be altered only by a change of law. Conversely, since the legislative power of Parliament is unrestricted, except where European Community law has primacy, its form and course can at any time be altered by Parliament.

In American law, the most famous exposition of the same principle was drafted by John Adams for the constitution of the Commonwealth of Massachusetts, in justification of the principle of separation of powers :

> In the government of this commonwealth, the legislative department shall never exercise the executive and judicial powers or either of them: the executive shall never exercise the legislative and judicial powers, or either of them: the judicial shall never exercise the legislative and executive powers, or either of them: to the end it may be a government of laws and not of men. Massachusetts Constitution. Part The First, Art. XXX (1780).

The last phrase, "to the end it may be a government of laws and not of men", has been quoted with approval by the U.S. Supreme Court and every state Supreme Court in the United States.

A similar concept is found in Common Sense by Thomas Paine:

> *. . . the world may know, that so far as we approve of monarchy, that in America THE* ***LAW*** *IS KING. For as in absolute governments the King is* ***law****, so in free countries the* ***law*** *OUGHT to be King; and there ought to be no other.*

The concept "rule of law" is generally associated with several other concepts, such as :

- Nullum crimen. nulla voena sine praevia lese poenali—No *ex post facto* laws.
- Presumption of innocence—All individuals are "presumed innocent until proven otherwise".
- Legal equality—All individuals are given the same rights without distinction to their social stature, religion, political opinions, etc. That is, as Montesquieu would have it, "law should be like death, which spares no one".
- *Habeas corpus*—in full *habeas corpus ad subjiciendum*, a Latin term meaning "you must have the body to be subjected (to examination)". A person who is arrested has the right to be told what crimes he or she is accused of, and to request that his or her custody be reviewed

by judicial authority. Persons unlawfully imprisoned have to be freed.

The concept of "rule of law" *per se* says nothing of the "justness" of the laws themselves, but simply how the legal system upholds the law. As a consequence of this, a very undemocratic nation or one without respect for human rights can exist with or without a "rule of law", a situation which many argue is applicable to several modern dictatorships. However, the "rule of law" or Rechtsstaat is considered a prerequisite for democracy, and as such, has served as a common basis for human rights discourse between countries such as the People's Republic of China and the West.

The rule of law is an ancient ideal, first posited by Plato as grounded in divine reason and so inherent in the natural order. It continues to be important as a normative ideal, even as legal scholars struggle to define it. The concept of impartial rule of law is found in the Chinese political philosophy of legalism, but the totalitarian nature of the regime that this produced had a profound effect on Chinese political thought which at least rhetorically emphasized personal moral relations over impersonal legal ones. Although Chinese emperors were not subject to law, in practice they found it necessary to act according to regular procedures for reasons of statecraft.

In the Anglo-American legal tradition, rule of law has been seen as a guard against despotism and as enforcing limitations on the power of the government. In China, the discourse around rule of law centres on the notion that laws ultimately enhance the law power of the state and the nation, which is why the Chinese government adopts the principle of rule by law rather than rule of law.

More recently, the rule of law has been considered as one of the key dimensions that determines the quality and good governance of a country. Researches, like the Worldwide Governance Indicators, defines the rule of law as: "the extent to which agents have confidence and abide by the rules of society, and in particular the quality of contract enforcement, the police and the courts, as well as the likelihood of crime or violence.

Declaration of Delhi

In 1959 an international gathering of over 185 Judges, lawyers, and law professors from 53 countries, held meeting in New Delhi and speaking at the International Committee of Jurists, made a declaration regarding the fundamental principle of the rule of law.

Lord Bingham's Sub-Rules

In his speech on November 16, 2006, for the Sir David Williams Lecture in the Law Faculty of Cambridge University, Lord Bingham of Corntule postulated eight sub-rules of the rule of law. Taking a strongly substantive view on the rule of law, the sub-rules are as follows :

- The law must be accessible and so far as possible intelligible, clear and predictable;
- Questions of legal right and liability should ordinarily be resolved by application of the law and not the exercise of discretion;
- The laws of the land should apply equally to all, save to the extent that objective differences justify differentiation;
- The law must afford adequate protection of fundamental human rights;
- Means must be provided for resolving, without prohibitive cost or inordinate delay, *bona fide* civil disputes which the parties themselves are unable to resolve;
- Ministers and public officers at all levels must exercise the powers conferred on them reasonably, in good faith, for the purpose for which the powers were conferred and without exceeding the limits of such powers;
- Adjudicative procedures provided by the state should be fair and the state must comply with its obligations in international law, the law which, whether deriving from treaty or international custom and practice, governs the conduct of nations; and

- The state must comply with its obligations under international law.

Marxist theory asserts the capitalist state is an instrument of oppression of the proletariat at the hands of the bourgeoisie, which set the laws to suit itself. Following this, some critical theorists analyze the "rule of law" as a judicial fiction which aims at disguising the reality of violence and, in Marxist terminology, "class struggle". This theory presumes that the "bourgeoisie" holds the power to set the laws.

Law, Order and Justice

Law is found in all modern societies, and is usually regarded as the bedrock of civilized existence. Law commands citizens, telling them what they must do; it lays down prohibitions indicating what citizens cannot do; and it allocates entitlements defining what citizens have right to do. Although it is widely accepted that law is a necessary feature of any healthy and stable society, there is considerable debate about the nature and role of law. Opinions, for instance, conflict about the origins and purpose of law. Does it liberate or oppress? Do laws exist to safeguard all individuals and promote the common good, or do they merely serve the interests of the select few? Moreover, there is controversy about the relationship between law and morality. Does law enforce moral standards; should it try to? How much freedom should the law allow the individual, and over what issues?

Such questions also relate to the need for personal security and social order. According to the politicians, the concepts of order and law often appear to be fused into the composite notion of law-and-order. Rolling these two ideas together sees law as the principal device through which order is maintained, but raises a series of further problems. In particular, is order only secured through a system of rule-enforcement and punishment or can it emerge naturally through the influence of social solidarity and rational good sense? Finally, there is the **complex problem of the relationship between law and justice**. Is the purpose of law to see that justice is done, and, anyway what would that entail? Furthermore, how is it possible to distinguish between just and unjust laws, and, in particular, does the distinction suggest that in certain circumstances it may be justifiable to break the law?

Law

The term 'law' has been used in a wide variety of ways. In the **first** place, there are scientific laws or what are called descriptive laws. These describe regular necessary patterns of behaviour found in either natural or social life. The most obvious examples are found in the natural sciences; for instance, in the laws of motion and thermodynamics advanced by physicists. But this notion of law has also been employed by social theorists, in an attempt to highlight predictable, even inevitable, patterns of social behaviour. This can be seen in Engels's assertion that Marx uncovered the 'laws' of historical and social development, and in the so-called 'laws' of demand and supply which underlie economic theory. An **alternative** use, however, treats law generally as a means of enforcing norms or standards of social behaviour. **Sociologists** have thus seen forms of law at work in all organised societies, ranging from informal processes usually found in traditional societies to the formal all legal systems typical of modern societies. By contrast, **political theorists** have tended to understand law more specifically, seeing it as a distinctive social institution clearly separate from other social rules or norms and only found in modern societies.

In a general sense, law constitutes a set of rules, including commands, prohibitions and entitlements. However, what is it that distinguishes law from other social rules? **First,** law is made by the government and so applies throughout society. In that way, law reflects the 'will of the state' and, therefore, takes precedence over all other norms and social rules. For instance, conformity to the rules of a sports club, church or trade union does not provide citizens with immunity if they have broken the 'law of the land'. **Secondly,** law is compulsory; citizens are not allowed to choose which laws to obey and which to ignore, because law is backed up by a system of coercion and punishment. **Thirdly,** law has a 'public' quality in that it consists of published and recognised rules. This is partly, achieved by enacting law through a formal, legislative process. Moreover, the punishments handed down for law-breaking are predictable and can be anticipated, whereas arbitrary arrest or imprisonment has a random and dictatorial character. **Fourthly,** law is usually recognised as binding upon those to whom it applies, even if particular laws may be regarded as 'unjust' or 'unfair'. Law is, therefore, more than simply a set of enforced commands; it also embodies moral claims, implying that legal should be obeyed.

The Rule of Law

The rule of law is a constitutional principle respected with almost devotional intensity in liberal democratic states. At heart, it is quite simply the principle that **the law should 'rule'**, that it should provide a framework within which all citizens act and beyond which no one, neither private citizen nor government official, should go. The principle of the rule of law developed out of a long-established liberal theory of law. From John Locke onwards, liberals have regarded law not as a constraint upon the individual but, as an essential guarantee of this liberty. Without the protection of law, each person is constantly under threat from every other member of society. As indeed they are from him. The danger of unrestrained individual conduct was graphically represented by the barbarism of the 'state of nature'. The fundamental purpose of law is, therefore, to protect individual rights, which in Locke's view meant the right to life, liberty and property.

The supreme virtue of the rule of law is, therefore, that it serves to protect the individual citizen from the state; it ensures a "government of laws and not of men". Such an idea was enshrined in the German concept of the Rechtsstaat a state based on law, which came to be widely adopted throughout continental Europe and encouraged the development of codified and professional legal systems. The rule of law, however, has a distinctively Anglo-American character. In the United States, the supremacy of law is emphasised by the status of the US Constitution, by the checks and balances it establishes and the individual rights outlined in the Bill of Rights. This is made clear in the Fifth and Fourteenth Amendments, which specifically forbid federal or state government from denying any person life, liberty and property without due process of law. The doctrine of 'due process' not only restricts the discretionary power of public officials but also enshrines a number of individual rights, notably the right of a fair trial and to equal treatment under the law. Nevertheless, it also vests considerable power in the hands of judges who, by interpreting the law, effectively determine the proper realm of government action.

By contrast, the British conception of the rule of law has seen it as typical of unmodified constitutional systems, within which rights and duties are rooted in common law, laws derived from long-established customs and traditions. The classic account of such a view is found in A.V. Dicey's Introduction to the Study of the Law of the Constitution [(1885) (1939)]. In Dicey's view, the rule of law embraces four separate features. **First,** no one should be punished except for breaches of law. This is the most fundamental feature of the rule of law because it distinguishes between "rule-bound government" and "arbitrary government", suggesting that where the rule of law exists government cannot simply act as it pleases; for instance, it cannot punish citizens merely because it objects to their opinions or disapproves of their behaviour. **Secondly,** the rule of law requires what Dicey called 'equal subjection' to the law, more commonly understood as equality before the law. Quite simply, the law should be no respecter of persons, it should not discriminate against people on grounds of race, gender, religious creed, social background and so forth, and it should apply equally to ordinary citizens and to government officials. **Thirdly,** when law is broken there must be a certainty of punishment. The law can only 'rule' if it is applied at all times and in all circumstances; the law rules only selectively when some law-breakers are prosecuted and punished, while others are not. **Finally,** the rule of law requires that the rights and liberties of the individual are embodied in the "ordinary law' of the land. This would ensure. Dicey hoped, that when individual rights are violated citizens can seek redress through the courts.

Although Dicey believed that the rule of law was typical of the British system of government and those modelled upon it, in a number of respects Britain offers a particularly poor example of the rule of law. For instance, though Dicey strove to reconcile the two, it can be argued that parliamentary sovereignty, the central principle of Britain's uncodified constitution, violates the very idea of a rule of law. It is difficult to suggest that the law 'rules' if the legislature itself is not bound by any external constraints. This problem has been exacerbated by the growth of executive power and the effective control which the government of the day exercises over Parliament, made possible by party discipline. This encouraged Lord Hailsham (1976) to describe the British system of government as an 'elective dictatorship'. Moreover, in the absence of a Bill of Rights, individual rights and liberties often enjoy little protection, meaning that grievances cannot be redressed through the courts. The establishment of a meaningful rule of law in Britain may, therefore, require far-reaching constitutional reform, including the codification of the constitution, the introduction of a Bill of Rights and the construction of a clear separation of powers between legislature and executive.

In its broad sense, the rule of law is a core liberal democratic principle, embodying ideas, such as constitutionalism and limited government to which most modern states aspire. In particular, the rule of law imposes significant constraints upon how law is made and how it is adjudicated. For example, it suggests that all laws should be 'general' in the sense that they apply to all citizens and do not select particular individuals or groups for special treatment, good or bad. It is, further, vital that citizens know 'where they stand' laws should, therefore, be precisely framed and accessible to the public. Retrospective legislation, for example, is clearly unacceptable on such grounds, since it allows citizens to be punished for actions that were legal at the time they occurred. In the same way, the rule of law is usually thought to be irreconcilable with cruel and inhuman forms of punishment. Above all, the principle of rule of law implies that the courts should be impartial and accessible to all. This can only be achieved if the judiciary, whose role it is to interpret law and adjudicate between the parties to a dispute, enjoys independence from government. The independence of the judiciary is designed to ensure that judges are 'above' or 'outside' the machinery of government. Law, in other words, must be kept strictly separate from politics.

Nevertheless, the rule of law also has its critics. Some have, for instance suggested that it is correct to say that the law 'rules' may acknowledge nothing more than that citizens are compelled to obey it. In this narrow sense, the rule of law is reduced to the statement that 'everybody must obey the law'. Others have argued that the principle pays little attention to the content of law. Some have, therefore, argued that the rule of law was observed in the Third Reich and in the Soviet Union simply because oppression wore the cloak of legality. Even its keenest defenders will acknowledge that although the rule of law may be a necessary condition for just government, it is not in itself a sufficient one. Marxist critics go further, however. Marxists have traditionally regarded law not as a safeguard for individual liberty but as a means for securing property rights and protecting the capitalist system. For Marx, law, like politics and ideology, was part of a 'superstructure' conditioned by the economic 'base', in this case the capitalist mode of production. Law thus protects private property, social inequality and class domination. The formal equality which the rule of law proclaims contrasts, Marxists argue, with social and economic inequalities that, for instance, restrict access to law and to effective legal advice. Furthermore, class biases operate within a judiciary that is drawn disproportionately from the ranks of the propertied and the privileged, whose interpretation of law is conditioned by their class origins.

Natural and Positive Law

The relationship between law and morality is one of the most complex thorniest problems in political theory. Philosophers have long been taxed by questions related or the nature of law, its origins and purpose. Does law, for instance, merely give effect to a set of higher moral principles, or is there a clear distinction between law and morality? How far does, or should, the law of the community seek to enforce standards of ethical behaviour? Such questions go to the heart of the distinction between two contrasting theories of law: natural law and positive law.

On the surface, law and morality are very different things. Law refers to a distinctive form of social control backed up by the means of enforcement; it, therefore, defines what can and what cannot be done. Morality, on the other hand, is concerned with ethical questions and the difference between 'right' and 'wrong'; it thus prescribes what should and what should not be done. In one important respect, however, law is an easier concept to grasp than morality. Law can be understood as a social fact, it has an objective character that can be studied and analysed. In contrast, morality is by its very nature a subjective entity, a matter of opinion or personal judgement. For this reason, it is often unclear what the term 'morality' refers to. Are morals simply the customs and conventions which reign within a particular community, its mores? Need morality be based upon clearly defined and well-established principles, rational or religious, which sanction certain forms of behaviour while condemning others? Are moral ideals those that each individual is entitled to impose on himself or herself; is morality, in short, of concern only to the individual?

Those thinkers who insist that law is, or should be, rooted in a moral system subscribe to some kind of theory of 'natural law. Theories of natural law date back to Plato and Aristotle. Plato believed that behind the ever-changing forms of social and political life lay unchanging archetypal forms, the Ideas, of which only an enlightened elite, the philosopher-kings, had knowledge. A 'Just' society was, therefore, one in which human laws conformed as far as possible to this transcendental wisdom. This line of thought was continued by Aristotle, who believed that the purpose of law and organized social life was to encourage humankind to live in accordance with virtue. In his view, there was a perfect law, fixed for all time, which would provide the basis for citizenship and all other forms of social behaviour. Medieval thinkers such as Thomas Aquinas also took it for granted that human laws had a moral basis. Natural law, he argued, could be penetrated through our God given natural reason and guides us towards the attainment of the good life on earth.

The demands of natural law came to be expressed through the idea of natural rights. Natural rights were thought to have been invested in humankind either by God or by nature. Thinkers such as Locke and Thomas Jefferson proposed that the purpose of human-made law was to protect these God-given and inalienable rights. However, the rise of rationalism and scientific thought served by the nineteenth century to make natural law theories distinctly unfashionable. Nevertheless, the twentieth century has witnessed a revival of such ideas, precipitated, in part, by the cloak of legality behind which Nazi and Stalinist terror took place. The desire to establish a higher set of moral values against which national law could be judged was, for example, one of the problems which the Nuremberg Trials (1945-49) had to address. Under the auspices of the newly created United Nations, major Nazi figures were prosecuted for war crimes, even though in many cases they had acted legally in the eyes of the Nazi regime itself. This was made possible by reference to the notion of natural law, albeit dressed up in the modern language, of human rights. Indeed, it is now widely accepted that both national and international laws should conform to the higher moral principle set out in the doctrine of human rights.

The central theme of all conceptions of natural law is the idea that law should conform to some prior moral standards, that the purpose of law is to enforce morality. This notion, however, came under attack in the nineteenth century from what John Osborne called 'the science of positive law'. The idea of positive law sought to free the understanding of law from moral, religious and mystical assumptions. Many have seen its roots in **Thomas Hobbes's** command theory of law: 'law is the word of him that by right hath command over others'. In effect, law is nothing more than the will of the sovereign. By the nineteenth century, **John Austin (1790-1859)** had developed this into the theory of 'legal positivism', which saw the defining feature of law not as its conformity to higher moral or religious principles, but in the fact that it is established and enforced by a political superior, a 'sovereign person' or body. This boils down to the belief that law is law because it is obeyed. One of its implications is, for instance, that the notion of international law is highly questionable. If the treaties and UN resolutions that constitute what is called 'international law' cannot be enforced, they should be regarded as a collection of moral principles and ideals, and not a law. A modern attempt to refine legal positivism was undertaken in H.L.A. Hart's *The Concept of Law* (1961). Hart was concerned to explain law not in terms of moral principles but by reference to its purpose within human society. Law, he suggested, stems from the 'union of primary and secondary rules', each of which serves a particular function. The role of **primary rules** is to regulate social behaviour these can be thought of as the 'content' of the legal system, for instance, criminal law. **Secondary rules**, on the other hand, are rules which confer powers upon the institution of government; they lay down how primary rules are made, enforced and adjudicated, and so determine their validity.

While natural law theories are criticised as being hopelessly philosophical, positive law theories threaten to divorce law entirely from morality. The most extreme case of this was Hobbes, who insisted that citizens had an obligation to obey all laws, however oppressive, since to do otherwise would risk a descent into the chaos of the state of nature. However, other legal positivists allow that law can, and should, be subject to moral scrutiny, and perhaps that it should be changed if it is morally faulty. Their position, however, is simply that moral questions do not affect whether law is law. In other words, whereas natural law theorists seek to run together the issues 'what the law is' and 'what the law ought to be', legal positivists treat these matters as strictly separate. An alternative view of law, however, emerged in the early part of the century, associated with the ideas of the famous

American jurist, Oliver Wendell Holmes (1809-94). This is **legal realism,** the theory that it is really judges who make law because it is they who decide how cases are to be resolved. In this sense, all Laws can be thought to be judge-made. However, as Judges are non-elected, this view has disturbing implications for the prospect of democratic government.

Law and Liberty

While political philosophers have been concerned about broad questions such as the nature of law itself, everyday debates about the relationship between law and morality have tended to focus upon the moral content of specific laws. Which laws are morally justified, and which ones are not? How far, if at all, should the law seek to 'teach morals'? Such questions often arise out of the moral controversies of the day, and seek to know whether the law should permit or prohibit practices such as abortion, prostitution, pornography, television violence, surrogate motherhood, genetic engineering and so forth. At the heart of these questions is the issue of individual liberty and the balance between those moral choices that should properly be made by the individual and those that should be decided by society and enforced through law.

In many ways the classic contribution to this debate was made in the nineteenth century by **John Stuart Mill** who, in *On Liberty* [(1859); 1972], asserted that, "The only purpose for which power can rightfully be exercised over any member of a civilised community against his will is to prevent harm to others." Mill's position on law was libertarian: he wanted the individual to enjoy the broadest possible realm of freedom. 'Over himself', Mill proclaimed, 'over his own body and mind the individual is sovereign'. However, such a principle, often referred to as the 'harm principle', implies a very clear distinction between actions that are **'self-regarding'**, whose impact is largely or entirely confined to the person in question, and those that can be thought of as **'other-regarding'**. In Mill's view, the law has no right to interfere with 'self-regarding' actions; in this realm individuals are entitled or exercise unrestrained liberty. Law should, therefore, only restrict the individual in the realm of **'other-regarding'** actions, and then only in the event of harm being done to others. The strict application of this principle would clearly challenge a wide range of laws currently in existence, notably those that are paternalistic, for instance, laws prohibiting suicide and prostitution are clearly unacceptable, since their primary intent is to prevent people damaging or harming themselves. The same could be said of laws prohibiting drug-taking or enforcing the use of seat-belts or crash-helmets, to the extent that these reflect a concern about the individuals concerned as opposed to the costs (harm) imposed on society.

Mill's ideas reflect a fierce commitment to individual liberty, born out of a faith in human reason and the conviction that only through the exercise of personal choice would human beings develop and achieve 'individuality'. His ideas, however, raise a number of difficulties. In the **first** place, what is meant by 'harm'? Mill clearly understood harm to mean physical harm, but there are at least grounds for extending the notion of harm to include psychological, mental, moral and even spiritual harm. For example, although blasphemy clearly does not cause physical harm it may, nevertheless, cause 'offence'; it may challenge the most sacred principles of a religious group and so threaten its security. Just such an argument was used by Muslim fundamentalists in their campaign against the publication of Salman Rushdie's *The Satanic Verses.* In the same way, it could be argued that in economic life price agreements between firms should be illegal because they both the interests of consumers, who end up paying higher prices, as well as those of competitor firms. **Secondly,** who counts as the 'others' who should not be harmed? This question is most obviously raised by issues like abortion and embryo research where it is the status of the unborn which is in question. If a human embryo is treated as an 'other', interfering with it or harming it in anyway is morally reprehensible. However, if the embryo remains part of the mother until it is born she has a perfect right to do with it what she pleases.

A **third** problem relates to individual autonomy. Mill undoubtedly wanted people to exercise the greatest possible degree of control over their own destinies, but even he recognized that this could not always be achieved, as, for instance, in the case of children. Children, he accepted, possessed neither the experience nor the understanding to make wise decisions on their own behalf; as a result, he regarded the exercise of parental authority as perfectly acceptable. However, this principle can also be applied on grounds other than age, for example, in relation to alcohol consumption and drug-taking. On the face of it, these are 'self-regarding' actions, unless, of course, the principle of 'harm' is extended to include the distress caused to the family involved or the healthcare costs incurred by society. Nevertheless, the use of addictive substances raises the additional problem that they rob the user of free will and so deprive him or her of the capacity to make rational decisions. Paternalistic legislation may well be justifiable on precisely these grounds. Indeed, the principle could be extended almost indefinitely. For example, it could perhaps be argued that smoking should be banned on the grounds that nicotine is physically and psychologically addictive, and that those who endanger their health through smoking must either be poorly informed or be incapable of making wise judgements on their own behalf. In short, they must be saved from themselves.

An alternative basis for establishing the relationship between law and morality is by considering not the claims of individual liberty but the damage which unrestrained liberty can do to the, fabric of society. A classic statement of this position was advanced in **The Enforcement of Morals (1968)** by Patrick Devlin, which argues that there is a 'public morality' which society had a right to enforce through the instrument of law. Devlin's concern with this issue was raised by the legalization of homosexuality and other pieces of so-called 'permissive' legislation in the 1960s. Underlying his position is the belief that society is held together by a 'shared' morality, a fundamental agreement about what is 'good' and what is 'evil'. Law, therefore, has the right to 'enforce morals' when changes in lifestyle and moral behaviour threaten the social fabric and the security of all citizens living within it. Such a view, however, differs from paternalism in that the latter is more narrowly concerned with making people do what is in their interests, though in cases like banning pornography it can be argued that paternalism and the enforcement of morals coincide. Devlin can be said to have extended Mill's notion of harm to include 'offence', at least when actions provoke what Devlin called 'real feelings of revulsion' rather than simply dislike. Such a position has also been adopted by the conservative New Right since the 1970s in relation to what it regards as theory of 'moral pollution'. This is reflected in anxiety about the portrayal of sex and violence on television and the spread of gay and lesbian rights. Against the twin threats of permissiveness and multi-culturalism, conservative thinkers have usually extolled the virtues of 'traditional morality' and 'family values'.

The central theme of such arguments is that morality is simply too important to be left to the individual. Where the interests of 'society' and those of the 'individual' conflict, law must always take the side of the former. Such a position, however, raises some serious questions. **First,** is there any such thing as a 'public morality'? Is there a set of 'majority' values which can be distinguished from 'minority' ones? Apart from acts like murder, physical violence, rape and theft, moral views in fact diverge considerably from generation to generation, from social group to social group, and indeed from individual to individual. This ethical pluralism is particularly evident in those areas of personal and sexual morality homosexuality, abortion, violence on television and so on with which the moral New Right is especially concerned. **Secondly**, there is a danger that under the banner of traditional morality, law is doing little more than enforcing social prejudice. If acts are banned simply because they cause offence to the majority, this comes close to saying that morality comes down to a show of hands. Surely, moral judgements must always be critical, at least in the sense that they are based upon clear and rational principles rather than just widely held beliefs. Do laws persecuting the Jews, for instance, become morality acceptable simply because anti-Semitic ideas are widely held in society? **Finally,** it is by no means clear that a healthy and stable society can only exist where a shared morality prevails. This belief, for example, calls the very idea of a multi-cultural and multi-faith society into question. This issue, however, is best pursued by an analysis of social order and the conditions that maintain it.

Order

Fear of disorder and social instability has been perhaps the most fundamental and abiding concern of Western political philosophy. Daring back to the social contract theories of the seventeenth century, political thinkers have grappled with the problem of order and sought ways of preventing human existence degenerating into chaos and confusion. Without order and stability, human life would, in Hobbes's words, be **'Solitary, poor, nasty, brutish and short'.** Such fears are also evident in the everyday use of the word 'anarchy' to imply disorder, chaos and violence. For these reasons, order has attracted almost unqualified approval from political theorists, at least in so far as none of them are prepared to defend 'disorder'. At the same time, however, the term order conjures up very different images for different political thinkers. At the extreme, traditional conservatives believe that order is inseparable from notions like control, discipline and obedience; at the other, anarchists have suggested that 'order' is related to natural harmony, equilibrium and balance. Such ideological divisions reflect profound disagreement not only about the concept of order but also about how it can be established and how it should be maintained.

While there may be competing conceptions of order, certain common characteristics can nevertheless be identified. Order, in everyday language, refers to regular and tidy patterns, as when soldiers are said to stand **'on order'** or the universe is described as being. In social life, order describes regular, stable and predictable forms of behaviour, for which reason social order suggests continuity, even permanence.

Social disorder, by contrast, implies chaotic, random and violent behaviour, that is by its very nature unstable and constantly changing. Above all, the virtue that is associated with order is personal security, both physical security, freedom from intimidation and violence and the fear of such, and psychological security, the comfort and stability which only regular and familiar circumstances engender.

Justice in Liberal Societies

Almost everyone at every stage of life is somehow conscious of the term 'justice'. Political thinkers since the earliest times have been trying to formulate definitions regarding the concept of justice. Right from the time of Socrates, justice has been one of the most heated topic of debate.

The concept of justice in liberal world emphasizes on liberal perspective and liberal dimensions of justice, historic origin and development of the conception of justice. As a concept, justice has been subject to moral, philosophical, legal and theological influences throughout history. It continues to be the centre of much of the discussion in the context of the academic discipline of social science.

Meaning of Justice

The word 'justice' has been derived from Latin—word Justice meaning the idea of joining or fitting; it is the idea of bond or tie (Barker, 1951: 102).

Idea of justice, signifies the quality of being just and reasonable. Justice is concerned with the proper ordering of things and persons within the society. It is related with 'right' and is the basis of distinguishing between right and wrong. The notion of what is just and what is unjust, what is right and wrong, is different in different societies. Therefore, the meaning of justice in history varies from person to person, from society to society and from time to time. As different philosophers have defined the concept of justice in different ways, it is impossible to give it a specific meaning.

Justice is a Relative Concept

The concept of justice cannot be studied independently: it is a relative concept and is closely related with set of values, morals and behaviour, prevailing in various societies at different periods of time. With the change in time and circumstances, the values of society undergo changes. This in turn brings changes in conception of justice. Our social consciousness is ever growing and changing process, something that was regarded 'just' some centuries ago may not be regarded so, today. For example, slavery and serfdom were widely justified in ancient and medieval Europe, untouchability was justified in India few decades ago. But these conditions are now widely accepted as unjust.

So for proper understanding and analysis of justice, it is essential to study the prevailing values, morals and circumstances in different social systems.

Different ideologies have produced different conceptions of Justice. Greek philosopher Plato tried to define justice as virtue. Under philosophy, the base of justice lies in liberty and under egalitarian theory, justice is linked to equality. Socialists relate justice with basic needs and economic equality. Utilitarian thought related justice with acts providing greatest happiness to members of society. John Rawls theory of justice relates justice with distribution of goods in society. So different ideologies have different bases of justice. For clear understanding of different perceptions of justice, we need to study historical origin of idea of justice.

Origin of Idea of Justice

The first clear conception of justice can be traced back to the great Greek philosopher Plato. The Greek word for justice is 'diakousine', which has a broader meaning than English word 'justice' is meaning, is similar to that of morality; it is based on interdependence and well-being of society. Greeks defined Justice as something which is essential for harmony. 'Platonic Justice' has its roots in morality. It neither has any external force nor any legal force, it is something internal of human soul. The source of justice for all idealist thinkers like Plato, Aristotle, Kant, Green, Hegel, etc., lies in ethics. For them the moral values which are sanctioned by the community, constitute the major source of justice.

During the medieval period in Europe, there was dominance of Christianity and supremacy of Church. Religion became the guiding force behind the notion of Justice. The medieval and Roman Catholic Church propagated the view that it is God, who gives the notion of justice and his notion of justice is preserved and propagated by the church. In the medieval Europe, the religious values as propagated by church were major source of notion of justice. After the separation of church from state in modern times, religion has lost its importance as the source of justice.

The natural right theorists of early modern Europe advocated the rule of reason. Locke and his followers, held the view that every human being is a rational being and, therefore, should be self-governing in his actions. Therefore, for Locke, justice was in conformity to natural law, i.e. universal human reason. This conception of human reason as source of notion of Justice was a bridge between ethical and religious notions of Justice. For Rousseau, justice was in accordance to general will and injustice was opposition to this will.

The liberalism of seventeenth and eighteenth centuries supported the idea of open competition and free market. The negative liberalists of this era, accepted private property in accordance with economic justice and state was entrusted with minimum functions. J.S. Mill and Jeremy Bentham stressed upon civil society as dispenser of justice in which market plays dominating role. Market has no favourites and is equal for all.

With the development of industry and commercial revolutions of nineteenth century, the idea of Justice came to be related with economics. Under the conditions of free market and open competition, economic inequalities increased which led to unjust human relations. Positive liberalists held the view that it was increase in liberty that increased inequality. Private property became the major source of exploitation and divided society into classes, due to increasing economic inequalities. The state (under positive liberalism) was entrusted with positive economic function. The positive liberalists like Green and Laski advocated the system of welfare state and progressive taxation as the precondition for establishing just economic society. They stressed upon social equality as the fundamental basis of Justice. In twentieth century, it has been accepted that personal liberties are justified only if they are not opposed to social justice.

Marxism advocated the abolition of private property and establishment of communism as preconditions of economic justice. The Marxian theory held the view that capitalism through its source of private property, divided the society into classes (rich and poor). Marxian conception of economic justice could be achieved only in exploitation free socialist society. The Marxian theory advocates that an individual can enjoy justice only when his basic needs are fulfilled and he is free from the fear of state.

So with changes in time, values and circumstances the conception of justice underwent changes. Different ideologies have produced radically different theories of Justice.

Historical Perspective on Conception of Justice

Originally, the political theory and the conception of Justice is related with European thinkers—Historically, the different conceptions of Justice can be studied under following headings: (a) ancient Europe, (b) medieval Europe, and (c) modern Europe. Ancient Europe—Ancient Greek philosophers, like Plato and Aristotle, dominated western thought with their everlasting influences on whole philosophy of man, including the conception of Justice.

(a) Ancient Europe

(i) Plato's Conception of Justice

The great Greek philosopher Plato conceptualized justice in his masterpiece work, *Republic* which is a Socratic dialogue by

Plato written approximately 360 B.C. It is a comprehensive work on philosophy of man and political theory. The fundamental problem in *Republic* is about searching the meaning and nature of justice. That is the reason that Plato gave an alternate name to his book *Concerning Justice* (Barker, 1918: 204).

Platonic justice is inseparable from his ideal state. For Plato that state is ideal, where justice exists, justice is the soul of his ideal state. Plato saw in his 'justice', as the only remedy to save morally and politically decayed Athenian society.

Platonic justice is based on morality; it is moral bond which joins men together in his ideal state. Plato defined justice as part of human virtue. Human virtue is that quality which makes a man a good man. Human virtue according to Plato, has four categories—wisdom, courage, temperance and justice (Foster, 1942: 37).

Plato further divides the human soul into three qualities which is an idea borrowed from Pythagoreans. These are qualities of reason, spirit and appetite; these all three motivating forces are present in every individual in varying amounts. In a society individuals will groove themselves according to the quality predominant in them (Mukherjee & Ramaswamy, 1999: 69).

The quality of reason guides the right path and creates bonds of union among the members of society. It is the quality which develops the spirit of knowing, understanding and loving others.

The quality of spirit represents honour, pride and courage. It inspires individual to fight against injustice and is the source of ambition and competition. Third element is that of appetite which is irrational, it is the supporter of pleasure and satisfaction. Appetite gives birth to desires like love, hunger, thirst etc.

On the basis of these qualities or motivating forces Plato divided the society in three classes—rulers, warriors and artisans or workers. Every individual has better aptitude for certain things and they show greater efficiency in those things, depending upon the predominance of that particular element in their soul. Individuals with their rational faculty predominant would constitute the ruling class and the venture of such a soul was wisdom. This rational element increases the learning capacity of individual and enable him to follow the right path. Individuals in whom the element of spirit was predominant quality, constituted the auxiliary or warrior class. The venue of such soul was courage; this quality constitutes the military force for state. Together soldiers and rulers would constitute the guardian class. Individual in whom the element of appetite, was predominant, constituted the artisan or producing class. The virtue of such soul was temperance. This class is lover of gain and money (Barker, 1959: 106).

Plato's division of individuals is based on his scheme of education. In Plato's ideal state scheme of education is such that it develops the individual to his fullest capacity. Individuals on the basis of quality (reason, spirit or appetite) predominant in them get the specific form of education and training. This education and training helps them to emerge into three classes—rulers, soldiers and artisans (Barker, 1959: 119).

Just State

State in which all these three classes perform their functions without interfering in each others affairs is a just state. In a just state (Plato's ideal state), there prevails harmonious balance of life among all three classes.

Just Individual

Just individual is that who lives the life in which his predominant quality (reason, spirit or appetite) is made to serve the community. Individual is just, if he sticks to job for which he is best suited for. Any interference by an individual in affairs of other classes, would make him unjust. A just person would not allow three elements of his soul to trespass each other's spheres. Platonic justice means "the will to concentrate in one's own sphere of duty and not to meddle with the sphere of others and its habitation, therefore, it is in heart of even citizen who does his duty in his appointed place" (Barker, 1918: 204).

So we see that, 'Platonic Justice' is inseparable quality of moral life of community. It is the harmonious bond which holds society together. Plato's conception of justice is moral not legal, emphasis is on duties not rights, it is the way of attaining goodness.

(ii) Aristotle's Conception of Justice

Aristotle emphasized on distributive conception of justice, he advocated that proportional equality and distributive justice would promote harmony in the society. Aristotle divided justice into two categories—complete justice and distributive justice.

(a) Complete Justice

Complete justice is related to moral virtue and regulates social relations among individuals. It is the virtue in action or excellence of character. Complete justice is related to the Greek view of state as an ethical society. Justice as complete virtue lies in living according to moral laws of community. According to this conception, laws are based on morality and justice lies in conformity to these laws. So a citizen who is law abiding is also a just citizen. Law abiding person is a virtuous person because the law is in conformity to morality. But it is only in ideal state that Justice is absolute and can be identified with absolute virtue.

(b) Particular Justice

Aristotle's conception of particular Justice is further divided into two categories—Distributive Justice and Corrective Justice.

(1) Distributive Justice

Distributive justice is much more realistic and practicable concept, it aims at promoting common good. This conception of justice is based on treating equals equally and unequal unequally. Distributive justice means distribution of wealth, honour or rewards according to merit. Thus distributive Justice exists in accordance to rules of proportional equality. As guiding principle of proportionate equality is that those who contribute more should receive more, so under distributive justice, awards are distributed according to the contribution of the individuals to the society. But standards of measuring contributions differ from society to society. For example, for a democrat freedom of birth and equality, for an oligarch wealth is the criteria for measuring contributions to society.

According to Aristotle, contributions by an individual to the society should be measured in form of wealth and virtue, awards should be distributed in proportion to these contributions (Barker, 1918: 338).

(2) Corrective Justice

Corrective Justice deals with legal aspects of justice and checks the violation of individual rights. This aspect of justice provides for remedies to imperfections in existing law it deals with both civil and criminal law.

Thus we see that Aristotle's conception of distributive justice is related with distribution of goods in the society. His conception of distributive justice is much more realistic and related with actual states.

(b) Medieval Europe

In the Medieval Europe, there existed supremacy and domination of the church. State was under the control of church for the governance of temporal thing. In the Middle Ages, church was a well organized institution and presented itself as the interpreter of the divine law. Claiming itself as the representative of God's will, church also defined the notion of Justice.

(i) Saint Augustine

St. Augustine was a very influential Christian thinker of the medieval period. He was a pupil and a convert of Saint

Ambrose. He related the idea of justice with religion. According to him Just state was one in which religion was taught under law and authority. To him, justice was to establish right relationship between man and God. It was the way to restore peace in society and end conflicts.

Saint Augustine emphasized that human salvation was possible only through Christian state; it was only in Christian state that justice could exist. According to him Justice could not be created through civil authority, but by church as it represented the will of God. Justice, for St. Augustine, laid in obeying the Will of God. This Will of God is vested in the universal order. So Justice can be attained only when the whole society conforms to this universal order or Will of God (Foster, 1942: 204).

(ii) Saint Thomas Aquinas

St. Thomas Aquinas was the most influential philosopher of thirteenth century and represents the medieval thought in totality. He was a firm believer in Christian theology and regarded religion superior to state. St. Aquinas was the champion of papal supremacy and upheld the supremacy of church over the state. St. Aquinas held the view that all true laws are manifestations of eternal law which is based on divine reason. All laws which are based on divine reason (reason of God) are just laws as they aim at the welfare of whole community. St. Aquinas talked about four kind of laws—eternal law, natural law, divine law and human law (Suda, 1989: 290).

According to Aquinas, eternal law is the supreme. It is the reason in the mind of God that governs the whole universe. Natural law is reflection of Divine reason in human beings, it enables the individual to follow the right path and avoid evils. It enables the person to distinguish good from bad. Divine law consists of special code of morals which are communicated to man be divine agency. For example, special code of laws which God gave to the Jews legislation given through scriptures or Church, constitutes Divine law. Human laws are man-made laws for the regularization of the human conduct. St. Aquinas advocates that human laws must be in accordance to reason. Human law is Just only if it conforms to natural law and subordinates to the eternal Law of God. Also the laws to be just, should aim at harmony and common good; therefore, they must be based on popular support. As St. Aquinas says, "Law is an ordinance of reason for the common good promulgated by him who has the care of community" (Rao, 1986: 225).

According to Aquinas, justice is fixed and perpetual will to give everyone his own rights. In this regard Justice, is moral virtue, it means to always respect the rights of others. Rights are contained in common law and customs of the society, to implement these rights constitute justice (*www.googfe.com*).

Thus we see that, religion and morality were the basis of justice in the medieval and or the dark ages. Christianity and the role of Church were strongly influential in defining the notion of justice.

(c) Modern Europe

(i) Liberal Perspective on Justice

The secularization of justice was accomplished only after the liberating effects at Renaissance, Reformation, and Commercial industrial revolution in Europe. Early liberals like Locke, Rousseau and Kant associated justice with synthesis of liberty, equality and positive law. Liberal perspective on justice, regards institutions such as feudalism, absolute monarchy and caste privileges as unjust and illegal.

Liberal perspective on Justice treats liberty as the central problem of justice. It is particularly concerned with substantive liberty, for which it seeks to accommodate the principles of equality and fraternity in the broader framework of liberty. This perspective is chiefly represented by John Rawls' Theory of Justice.

(a) Utilitarian Theory of Justice

The first comprehensive liberal notion of justice was provided by David Hume, Jeremy Bentham and J.S. Mill, known as utilitarian theory of justice. According to Hume, 'the public utility is the sole origin of justice'. Although there were elements of utilitarianism in the works of Hume, its sustained and detailed development was provided by Bentham. According to the utilitarian thought, the greatest happiness of the greater number was the measure of right and wrong or justice and injustice. Utilitarianism in its simplest formulation claimed that the morally right act or just policy is that which produces the greatest happiness for the members of society. The utilitarian theory valued justice as the most important and most privileged of social utilities. Mill associated justice with rights, the affirmation of liberty of every individual and with those rules and acts which most crucially affect human welfare.

As compared with previous theories of Justice utilitarianism had utilitarian thought and had no link with religion. The goals that it sought to promote were not dependent upon God.

(i) Utilitarian thought had no link with religion. The goals that it sought to promote were not dependent upon God.
(ii) It believed that all customs, rules, laws and actions should be tested against the standard of human development, i.e., how far they increased the happiness of the individual.

Utilitarian theory was a strong weapon against prejudices and superstitions. It challenged those who claimed authority on the name of morality and religion.

However, this utilitarian conception of Justice was challenged in the twentieth century on a number of grounds. It did not consider the gross inequalities arising out of capitalist property relations as unjust. The utilitarian principle threatened to oppress some members of society in the interest of greatest good of the greatest number. It justified the sacrifices of weaker sections of society for the benefit of the majority. Utilitarian thought violates the principle of justice and can sanction acts which can be unjust (Vermani, 1996: 302).

(b) John Rawls' Theory of Justice

As there were number of loopholes and contradictions within the utilitarian conception of Justice, it was replaced by alternate theory of Justice, by an American philosopher John Rawls. John Rawls laid down his theoretical foundations of justice in his masterpiece work *A Theory of Justice* (1971). It has been one of the most famous and influential book of twentieth century. Its impact has been so huge that it has been translated into many, European, Chinese, Japanese and Korean, languages.

Rawls outlined the features of his 'justice' in an article published in 1957 entitled "Justice as Fairness". The revised version of Rawls' theory was published in *Distributing Justice* (1967), but his most elaborate and comprehensive work on Justice was presented in *A Theory of Justice* (1971). The clarification of theory continued through a series of his two books—*Political Liberalism* and *The Law of Peoples* (1999).

Rawls' theory of Justice was very well timed theory; it gave a new spirit to liberalism when it was facing serious challenges. It was the time, when utilitarianism proved incapable of protecting the interests of weaker sections of society. In U.S.A., various moments lead by blacks, students and anti-Vietnam activities, etc., questioned dominant political values and institutions of that time (Jain, 1989:300). Contract as the Basis of Theory.

Rawls' theory of justice justifies that state was built as contract among individuals. Then he tries to prove that contract was built on the basis of equality and liberty. 'Original Position' is the most important concept that he has used in his theory of justice.

Original Position

It is a situation or position where the contract takes place. The key ingredient of this contract is 'veil of ignorance'. This is a situation in which there is no awareness about present and future. It is a situation of complete ignorance in which all are unaware of their skills, abilities and outcomes of their efforts.

So, in this way Rawls' social contract is, similar to that of Hobbes, Locke and Rousseau.

After the social contract—when state comes into existence, nobody knows his position, status and there are no principles of justice. According to Rawls, justice is the first virtue of a good society. So for building a good state, people form the principles of justice. As nobody in state knows his position and outcomes, the principles and rules made for Justice are fair. But later on when these rules of justice come into practice, they prove to be advantageous to some and disadvantageous to others—These rules and principles of justice bring gains for some and loss for others—Rawls' theory on justice tries to overcome or solve this complex problem. In his theory, he forms governing principles of just-society. His theory on justice states that Justice is a concept related with problem of just distribution of primary goods in society. In Rawls' theory, these primary goods are of two types:

(a) Social goods such as income, wealth, opportunities, powers, rights and liberties.
(b) Natural goods like health, intelligence, vigour, imagination, natural talents which are affected by social institutions but are not directly distributed by them. Rawls Principles of Distributive Justice are:

(a) First Principle

Each person to have an equal right to most extensive basic liberties, compatible with similar liberties of others.

In this principle, lies the opportunity to maximize the gains of liberty. Their is provision that everyone would have basic liberties. So people would enjoy freedom of speech and expression, property, freedom of forming associations, freedom from poverty, etc. According to Rawls' theory of justice, these types of freedoms are absolute and must not be violated at any time. There is, no clarity regarding the priority of one liberty over the other. There is, therefore, plurality of all liberties. All liberties must exist at the same time.

(b) Second Principle

Social and economic inequalities are to be arranged, so that both are: (i) to the greatest benefit to the least advantaged; and (ii) these inequalities are attached to offices and positions open for all under conditions of fair equality of opportunity.

According to this principle, those who are weakest in society, should get the maximum benefit. The distribution of social and economic needs leads to inequalities in society. So the distribution should be arranged in such a manner that inequalities are in favour of weaker sections of society. The distribution of primary social goods (rights, liberties, opportunities, income, etc.), should be in such manner, that weaker sections or least advantageous get maximum benefits. Such distribution is according to norms of Justice (Asirvatham, 1936: 356).

Conflicting interests exist in the society and every individual is interested in greater share, so this theory deals with distributive patterns.

This theory is a combination of liberty, equality and utility in the capitalist world. It lays emphasis on equality of opportunity to compete and it has its base in culture of constitutional democracies. This theory provides moral depth to liberalism which it always lacked. As development of one is inseparable from development of all, this theory signifies moral interdependence of all individuals in the society (maximum benefits to lowest sections). So it is equality of opportunity which is the cornerstone of Justice. According to John Rawls proper function of government is not only to maintain social order, but the achievement of distributive justice by according highest value to the needs of neediest. In its proper sense, justice calls not for rewarding those with superior ability but compensating those endowed with lesser ability. Rawls' theory of justice is in consonance with the requirements of liberal democratic state (Hawkesworth & Kogan; 1992: 286).

(ii) Socialist Perspective on Justice

The Socialist movement in nineteenth century, which arose out of the criticism of capitalist society produced its own ideas of liberty, equality and justice. The major focus of socialist perspective was on search for a more profound justice, not only formal but substantial which would provide an alternative to the capitalist economic system.

Under the socialist perspective we will study Anarchist, Marxist and Democratic Socialist conceptions of Justice. Though all of them are not socialists of same shade, yet they are socialists in their own light. There are notable differences among Anarchists, Marxists and Democratic Socialists regarding their objectives and strategy. But still there is some similarity among them so far as some aspects of socialism are concerned. They are similar in their view, that justice is impossible in exploitative capitalist world. They want to end the capitalist—system or reform it in such a way that justice can exist. The chief concern of all socialists has been injustice meted out to the workers, peasants, poor, unemployed and other weaker sections of society. Socialist idea of justice springs out from the realms of injustice, which exists in the society (Jain, 1989: 293). Let us briefly study important Socialist Conceptions on Justice.

(a) Anarchist Conception

The word Anarchism has been derived from Greek word *anarchia* meaning 'without chief or head or without top authority'. Anarchists are apposed to state; they regard state as unnecessary evil. State for Anarchists is something negative exploitative, oppressive and unjust. They regard stale as unjust because it is based on coercion and authority. This perspective believes that it is an instrument of wealth, property and privileges. State is biased in favour of rich and, therefore, cannot solve problems of common man. According to Anarchists, state curtails both individual as well as collective liberty. They hold the view that justice is impossible in state as both state and government are evils. So state must be completely abolished.

Thinkers like P.J. Proudhon {French), Bakunin, Peter Kropotkin, Tolstoy (Russians) and Mahatma Gandhi (Indian) are the chief exponents of Anarchism. They are of the view that people can organize themselves into just society through voluntary agreements and co-operation.

According to Anarchist perspective, justice lies in free-society where "an individual enjoys maximum freedom". A just society is a voluntary built society where material goods are fairly distributed and common tasks are carried out by voluntary agreements.

So we can conclude by saying that Anarchist conception of justice lies in absence of any force, political coercion and political authority. Justice lies in free society voluntarily built by individuals.

(b) Marxian Conception of Justice

According to Marxian perspective, justice is possible only in communist society, which is based on the principle of "to each according to his need, from each according to his capacity." It is only in socialist society that an individual can enjoy just and rightful place. Karl Marx (1818-83) and his followers were of the view that Justice is impossible in capitalist state. It is the instrument of private property which is the source of exploitation and hence injustice. As open competition, free market and institution of private property dominates the capitalist world, society becomes a class-divided society (rich and poor, exploiters and exploited). Economically, society gets divided into classes and it is this economic inequality, which creates injustice.

In the capitalist state, industrialized class exploits the working class to the fullest extent, to maximize their benefits. This richer and influential class due to their control over economic power, also monopolizes the political power. They use this political power or state power, to increase that benefits and exploit the poor working class.

Marx did not see any reforms in capitalism; he advocated entire transformation of the system. Marxian ideology emphasizes that abolition of private property is a prerequisite for creating just society. According to Marx and Engels, in socialist society, there would be no private property and so no class divisions. This will further lead to social equality and hence Justice will prevail.

According to Marxian perspective Justice is not an eternal or divine idea, it is related with economic system and nature of society. The Marxian "Just society" is a classless and stateless society, which is based on cooperation and mutual relations among workers. Unlike capitalist notion of justice, which is related to liberty, Marxian notion of justice is related to equality. In classless and stateless society, basic-needs of individuals will be fulfilled, there would be no fear of state and hence justice can be enjoyed.

(c) Social Democratic Perspective

Social-democratic perspective aims at achieving socialism through democratic means, it is a reformist approach in capitalism and Marxism. This is related with regulative, restrictive and controlled capitalism. Social-democratic theory aims at establishing just society through peaceful and constitutional reforms. Unlike Anarchists and Marxists, it entrusts state with some positive welfare functions. For Social democrats, state is an instrument for creating justice.

This approach provides for decentralization of political and economic power. It emphasizes on provisions like mixed economy, redistribution of wealth, nationalization of basic industries, fair distribution of property, etc., to remove economic inequalities. Social democrats seek to establish justice, not only by reducing economic inequalities, but also by moral, intellectual and emotional development of an individual. Thus, this approach provides facilities for higher education and important rights, which are fundamental for development of one's personality. Thinker's like Harold J. Laski and Durbin are chief exponents of this approach.

(iii) Types of Justice in Liberal Societies

(a) Legal Justice

Legal Justice is related with Laws and making of laws in the society. It is related with functioning of judicial system. In strict sense, justice lies in conforming to laws. Thus simplest definition of justice lies in legal Justice.

Requirements for Legal Justice:

(i) Laws should be reasonable and equitable. Rationality of law depends upon the social requirements of the society which are associated with human values. A law may be reasonable in one society and unreasonable in other society, depending upon social requirements (Arora & Awasthy, 2004: 432).

(ii) There should be equality before law and equal protection before law.

(iii) Laws should not be based upon outdated practices, reactionaries and conservatives. Laws should contain human values, according to prevailing social conditions.

(iv) Any discrimination made in laws should be on rational grounds. The aim of every law should be welfare of the whole community.

(v) In order to have just and rational laws, law making institutions should also be just. Laws should be made by legitimate and rational law making institutions liberal democracies, there is provision of elected representatives and responsible legislatures, which are necessary conditions for making just and equitable laws (Gauba, 2003 : 376).

(vi) Liberal constitutions emphasize on independent and impartial Judiciary, which is a prerequisite of legal justice. Independent judicial system acts as the watch dog of people's rights and liberties.

(vii) Justice should not be beyond the economic reach of common man, it should not be expensive. Their should be easy accessibility to courts. Justice delayed is justice denied and delayed justice is always in favour of culprit. In this sense, legal justice is related with efficiency of law and law courts.

(b) Economic Justice

Economic justice is related with satisfaction of economic needs and reduction in economic inequalities. Economic justice deals with recording of human relations in economic sphere. It aims at ending economic exploitation and dignity of individual in economic sphere. In liberal sense, economic justice is related with right to private property and right to free market. Liberalism of seventeenth and eighteenth century was in favour of open competition and free market. It supported the capitalist made of production. Negative liberalism (seventeenth and eighteenth century) considered private property as the fruit of labour. So it was in accordance with economic justice.

Due to widespread economic inequalities, positive liberalism of nineteenth century introduced important economic reforms necessary for economic justice. Nineteenth century liberalism gave importance to protection of economic interests of weaker sections of society, it advocated concepts of welfare state and progressive taxation for enlistment of poor and reduction of inequalities. Present day liberal constitutions provide various important economic rights considered necessary for economic justice. For example, right to work, fixed hours of work, etc.

Marxian Conception of Economic Justice

For Marxian's justice lies only in socialist society, it is impossible to enjoy economic justice in capitalist society. Marxian theory advocates abolition of private property as necessary pre-conditions for securing economic justice. For Marx economic justice lies in exploitation free communist society, i.e., classless and stateless society. Thus we see that Marxian conception of economic justice is related with abolition of private property and establishment of communism.

(iii) Political Justice

Political Justice is based on the principle of political equality. Political equality stands for equal opportunity in affairs of state. Political justice is possible only in democratic society; only democratic processes and democratic institutions can deliver political justice. Political justice stands for care of the interests of whole society and not of privileged class only. Political justice can be delivered only if governing institutions of society are representative institutions and political power is exercised by representatives of people. So it is essential that people enjoy universal adult franchise. Independent judiciary, rule of law, constitutional government, "responsible government, free and fair elections, etc., are certain basic prerequisites of political justice."

Political justice is related with equality in rights and liberties. Political rights like right to contest elections, right to form political parties and associations, right to criticize government policies, freedom of thought and expression, etc., should be available to citizens, without any discrimination on basis of caste, sex, creed, religion, etc. There should be provisions for free and independent channels of communications, between government and people, therefore, press and media should be impartial. Thus we see that political justice is closely related with liberal democratic provisions.

(iv) Social Justice

Social Justice means availability of equal social opportunities for the development of personality of all the people in society, without any discrimination on the basis of caste, colour, sex or race. Everyone without any discrimination, should be able to enjoy the basic social conditions, necessary for social development. Thus the issue of social justice is related with social equality and social rights. Social equality and social rights are dependent upon economic equality. Social life of community cannot be made just unless economic relations are suitably transformed. The conception of social justice, in its wider sense, refer to re-ordering of social life in such a manner, that material and moral benefits of social efforts are not cornered by a small privileged class. The benefits of society should be used to ensure the enlistment of lower and weaker sections of society. Social justice can exist only in exploitation free society.

In comprehensive sense, term social-justice aims at establishing economic justice as well as restoring dignity of human beings who have lost it due to lower economic, educational and cultural status. It is generally thought of a society which affords individuals and groups fair treatment and just share of the benefits of society. Social justice is both a philosophical problem and an important issue in politics, religion and civil society. The terms social justice is often employed by political left to describe a society with a greater degree of economic egalitarianism, which may be achieved through progressive taxation, income redistribution or property redistribution. The right wing also uses the term social justice but generally believes that just society is best achieved through the operation of free market, which they believe provides equality of opportunity and promotes philanthropy and charity. Both right and left tend to agree on the importance of rule of law human rights and some form of safety net.

(v) Analysis of Justice

The quest for justice began with the beginning of human thinking. Different philosophers have analysed the concept in different ways. The concept of justice have not remained static, rather it has changed with the change of time and circumstances. It is closely related with religion morality, equality, liberty, property, law, politics and economics. Thus any discussion of justice has to take into account, the multi-dimensional characters of the concept. Justice is a relative concept.

Right to Development as a New Human Right

The Declaration on Right to Development was adopted by General Assembly of United Nations on 4th December, 1986 Resolution 41/128, in which it stated the right to development as a human right. Right to development began to evolve since 1981, Commission on Human Rights formed a working group, which proposed various new rights and right to development was one of them. Many discussions and deliberations were held and right to development began to evolve gradually. Though it has been declared as a human right yet the major task of implementing and enhancing the Declaration remains to be performed. There can be many interpretations of the Declaration like all constitutional documents, the need of the hour is to find true meaning and essence of right to development and to implement it for the development of mankind.

Evolution of Right to Development

Human rights movement in the post-Second World War period considered both civil and political and economic, social and cultural rights as constituents of human rights. Both were conceded, without any doubt as integrated and interrelated. But with the beginning of Cold War, this consensus over integrity of political and economic rights was broken. Two separate covenants, one on civil and political rights and other on economic, social and cultural rights were formed as international treaties in 1966 and came into force in 1976. For many years deliberations were held to develop the original concept of integrated and indivisible human rights. With the emergence of balance of power, an opening for progress of human rights was created. In 1960s the newly independent, poor, non-Western states became members of UN and introduced a new emphasis on economic rights into international debate. In 1974, number of texts concerning New International Economic Order (NIEO) were approved. These texts tried to draw attention towards global economic inequality as cause of human rights violation, and demanded for equitable distribution of resources. In 1972, Mr. Keba M'Baye a senior judge of Senegal argued in a public lecture that everyone had a right to development and 'right to live better'.

Chairman, Human Rights Commission in 1977, played a key role in adoption of a resolution so that the UN should undertake a study of right to development as a human right. After many years of deliberations and negotiations. Declaration on Right to Development was adopted. It integrated economic, social and cultural rights with civil and political rights.

Right to Development as Third Generation Right

The third generation of human rights can be divided into two broad categories—first category includes right to development, right to self-determination and right to the ownership of the common heritage of mankind, which are based on demands of Third World countries; and the second category includes right to peace and right to a healthy environment, which are of general character and are equally important to everybody and to every country. The Third World countries became members of UN. They were mainly concerned with the problems, such as racial discrimination and apartheid, colonization and underdevelopment. So they demanded the need for such rights which would eradicate these problems. As a result of the demands of Third World countries and emerging general problems of mankind a new concept of 'third generation rights' has emerged. According to this new concept, civil and political rights were first generation of 'liberty' rights; economic, social and cultural right were second generation of 'equality' rights and now there was a need for a third generation of 'solidarity' rights.

According to the right to self-determination, people can freely choose their political status and economic policies. Self-determination under this right means political freedom as well as economic sovereignty over natural resources of the country.

Right to peace means to avoid wars as well as to overcome hunger and miseries of all people of the world and to remove wide gap between living conditions of rich and poor. Right to healthy environment stands for man's right to healthy environment for living life of dignity and well-being. Right to development stands for development of all human beings politically, economically as well as biologically.

Right to Development is linked to all other rights of third generation as well as to the rights of first and second generation. It aims at creating favourable environment for attainment of all other human rights.

Nature of Right to Development

Text of the Declaration on the Right to Development states that right to development is inalienable human right. It aims at the realization of fundamental freedoms and all human rights. Human person is central subject of development. It also aims at all-round development, i.e., social, economic, cultural and political. The benefits of development are to be meant for all and they can be realized only with participation and contribution of all human beings. It seeks to ensure "equality of opportunity for all". According to the Declaration, it is primary responsibility of states to create favourable conditions for realization of right to development. International cooperation should be maintained by states operating at international level.

Right to Development and the Contextual Debates

Since the declaration on right to development, many controversies and debates started emerging regarding. Dichotomy between Collective and Individual Rights with the beginning of Cold War, ambiguity regarding civil and political rights as equal to economic, social and cultural rights started emerging. Western bloc was upholder of the civil and political rights and socialist bloc favoured economic, social and cultural rights. Though with the adoption of right to development this controversy was resolved on formal plane yet still some differences remained inside and were complicated when Third World countries started demanding that right to development is a collective right of a group of countries to bring development of all countries with NIEO. Western countries supported civil and political rights along with political and cold war because they considered human rights as individual rights and they should be justiciable. Moreover, each right holder must have corresponding duty holder. Identification of human rights in terms of individual rights implies that they are based on negative freedom such as right to life prohibits others from killing. Economic and social rights are associated with positive freedoms which the state has to secure and protect by taking positive actions. On this basis, they are collective rights and not considered as human rights. As right to development is linked to collective rights and economic and social rights so it is usually criticized as human right. But it is superficial to identify civil and political rights with negative rights and economical, social and cultural rights with positive rights because both require negative as well as positive action. So, both civil and political rights and economic and cultural rights are human rights.

Right to development was promoted both by Third World protagonists and first world critics as a collective rights of states and of peoples for development. Many legal institutional agreements and convents have recognized and built upon collective rights. In collective rights, the right holder can be collective such as nation, but the beneficiary of the exercise of the right has to be individual. In many cases individual rights can be satisfied only in a collective context and the right of a state or nation to develop is a necessary condition for fulfilment of the rights and realization of the development of individuals. The Human Rights approach to development is that development is collective right of a nation or a state and the exercise of these rights must lead to realization of rights of all individuals to development. In this way, the right to development correlated collective and individual rights. It has been argued that the declaration mixed up the individual rights and collective rights which are different and should be kept distinct. Collective rights holders are not physical persons, they require an institutional person to exercise their rights. They are exercised by state. All human rights are primarily held against the state and here state is placed in a position to use its human rights to deny the individual human rights while still plausibly claiming to be pursuing human rights. But the declaration does not provide any notion of human rights of states. It articulates responsibilities of states to create an environment so that human beings can exercise their human rights.

Earlier there were many criticisms put on individual that they do not have corresponding duties and unless there is no corresponding duty-holder a right-holder cannot enjoy his rights. The Right to Development entails duties on all human beings, states, groups and world community to create such conditions in which human rights can be realized and their violations are prevented.

The main theme of Declaration is that human person is central subject of development. He should be an active participant and beneficiary of right to development. States are entitled to right and duty to formulate such policies so as to achieve the well-being of all individuals and people. It demands for active, free and meaningful participation of all individuals. The right to development puts responsibility on all human beings for development. This responsibility is towards all human rights as well as duties to promote and protect appropriate political, social and economic order for development. The right to participation is assured by the Declaration and it imposes duties in expanded form.

1. It entails a duty that speech should not be criminalized, i.e., all the forms of communication like speaking, writings, etc., should not be offences punishable by law.
2. The right to speech must entail a duty to hear, listen and respond.
3. The right to freedom of speech and expression, as a participatory right not only bears the responsibility on individuals but on collectivities also.

4. Development of all human beings is the duty of all the states.
5. All states have the responsibility to provide facilities to all humans so that they may develop properly.
6. The participatory rights require access to relevant information in languages.
7. Participatory rights lay stress on participation in decision making.

Participation is essential to develop the right to development. Right to participation in reactive form, means collective articulation of the response to development policies. In its proactive form it emphasizes the responsibility of the people in initiation of the articulation of development policies. Participatory rights assume a logic of collaboration for development in both the forms. The final aim of these rights is to strive towards the goals of appropriate development. The rights to freedom of speech and expression, and of mass media have, therefore, to be recognized as prerequisites of the right to development.

The Declaration on Right to Development is a charter of duties for human beings everywhere to struggle, to create and maintain conditions where all sorts of development is possible. It is the central duty of all human beings to animate all the formulations of Declaration and performance of this duty justifies their having right to establishing such a world order which is free of massive violations of human rights and maintains peace and favourable environment for human survival (Upendra Baxi, 'The Development of the Right to Development" in Janus *Symonides* (ed), *Human Rights: New Dimensions and Challenges,* Ashgate Publishing Limtied, England, 1998, p. 102).

The Declaration also refers to the duties of state [in Article 8(2)] to encourage participation of all human beings in all spheres for the sake of development and to fully realize all the human rights. It can be assumed that this article intends participation in governance. It declares that governance must be based on the consent of the governed. In this sense, it may also entail rights of referendum and recall. Right to participation further extends to that legal and extralegal repression of acts of participation in all spheres of life which hinder the development of right to development.

The declaration also lays down that along with states, international community and non-governmental organizations (NGOs) also have the duty to promote human rights and to create an environment in which right to development is fully realized. Universalism *versus* Relativism Scholars of Human Rights generally group them into three competing perceptions—those of Western, Socialist and Third World. Each perception is associated with one of the three generations of Human Rights; Western with Civil and Political Rights, Socialist with Economic, Cultural and Social Rights and Third World with People's Right. Some scholars argue that idea of human rights is derived from the Western liberal democratic world and it has little relevance to other parts of the world. Others suggest that human rights should be applicable anywhere regardless of place or time. As a result of these different views the question which generally arises is that 'Are the language of human rights and the context of human rights as embodied in the Universal Declaration of Human Rights or International Covenant on Civil and Political Rights universal? Or are the values incorporated in them relative to given cultures and states? The two major competing schools of thought regarding this are universal and relativist.

Universalism lays emphasis on the universality of human rights and their applicability everywhere. They consider human rights as basic rights. Universal rights are those rights which should be enjoyed by everybody regardless of any other considerations. So, universal human rights cannot be based on some conditions which are to be met. In order to enjoy them there is no need to qualify some conditions and they cannot be renounced. They are held by everybody because of mere fact of being human and their basis is moral, not political. The findings of some anthropologists suggest that some values can travel cross culturally. Some practices like torture and killings are condemned everywhere. The Universal Declaration on

Human Rights has come to be accepted universally. The ratification of two international covenants by growing number of countries also suggests the universality of human rights. The socialist concept of human rights much before the end of communist rule, began to incorporate the liberal definition of human rights. The end of cold war helped the universal arguments. Many Western countries have started giving value to economic and social rights.

The other approach is of relativism, which stresses on diversity and difference of human rights. Relativists argue that human rights are a social and historical phenomenon and, therefore, cannot be explained outside their specific environment. They concede that there is diversity of cultures and subsequently a great diversity of ideas on rights because rights and rules about morality and human behaviour depend upon cultural contexts. Therefore, there cannot be one transcendental or transcultural notion of rights and, therefore, no culture is justified in imposing on others what are essentially its own ideas.

Though in the past half century, the world has witnessed the rise of number of universal standards in the form of treaties and declarations on human rights, e.g., the 1948 Universal Declaration on Human Rights and the 1966 International Covenant on Civil and Political Rights, the International Covenant on Economic, Social and Cultural Rights and the two optional protocols to the first covenant. However, there are still inconsistencies between universal standard setting and national implementation. A number of countries especially in Asia have not acceded to the International Covenants and other international treaties on human rights. Those who have become members of international instruments on human rights, there are many differences at national level, many laws and practices conflict with international standards. Cultural relativism is becoming a main challenge to the universality of human rights.

But in modern world, cultures are not isolated. They interact peacefully and influence each other. With globalization the intercultural dynamics are set in motion which lead to emergence and consolidation of specific culture and ethical values common to the various cultural areas.

Vienna Conference of 1993 rejected the cultural relativism. Many states considered universality and cultural specificity as fully compatible notions. In its first paragraph, the Declaration reaffirms the solemn commitment of all states to fulfil their obligations to promote universal respect for and observance and protection of all human rights and fundamental freedoms for all. Though in paragraph 5, the problem of national and regional peculiarities is mentioned but it emphasises as on duty of states to promote and protect all human rights and fundamental freedoms regardless of their political, economic and cultural systems. The existence of cultural differences should not lead to the rejection of any part of universal human rights. Fundamental principle like equality between men and women cannot be rejected by any culture. All cultures can contribute to the promotion of human rights. Development and Globalization with the beginning of modern world, it is observed that globalization has affected human rights strongly. Globalization is the term used to characterize the processes of growing interconnection and interdependence in the modern world. The concept of globalization is multi-dimensional such as economic, cultural, political, military and social, but economic dimension of globalization is most evident and observed. Under it, international trade is widening. As a result of human mobility it seems that world is shrinking. With the reduction in trade barriers, artificial barriers have been removed. A homogeneous worldwide culture is developing in the process of globalization which is sometimes referred to as creation of global village.

Human rights declaration imposes obligations on states to implement human rights. Declaration on Right to Development entails a responsibility on them to create favourable environment so that all human beings may realize all the human rights. But the new concept of economic globalization is opposed to strong states.

END NOTES

Benda-Beckmann, Keebet Von, 'The Contexts of Law', Paper presented at XIII International Congress of Commission on Folk Law and Legal Pluralism at Dhulikhel, Nepal, 10-13 December, 2001.

Chanock, M. (1982), 'Making Customary Law: Men, Women and Courts in Northern Rhodesia' in *African Women and Law—Historical Perspectives* (ed.), M.J. Hary and M. Wright, Boston, Boston University, pp. 63-67.

Fitzpatrick, P. (1983), 'Law Plurality and Underdevelopment' in *Legality, Ideology and the State,* edited by D. Sugarmann, London, Academic Press, pp. 159-182.

Moore, S.F. (1978), *Law as Process,* London, Routledge and Kegan Paul.

Woodman, G.R. (1998), Ideological Combat and Social Observation: Recent Debate about Legal Pluralism, *Journal of Legal Pluralism,* 42: 21-59.

2

Rule of Law and Equality before Law

Rule of law principle is one of the key components of liberal democracy, the other is universal suffrage. On the one hand, government's range of discretion can be limited by instituting the rule of law principle, on the other it can be held responsible to the electorate through universal suffrage. Both these components of liberal democracy effectively control the inclinations of governing powers to impose unfair burdens and limitations of freedom upon citizens. To an extent the rulers are deprived of their powers of arbitrary and self-serving rule. An independent judiciary furthers that process which is originally based on trust.

Link between Rule of Law-Citizen-Judiciary

Rule of law is a legal doctrine according to which no individual is above law and everyone must answer to it. An independent judiciary gives credibility to the system and confidence to the citizen in the capability of the system to render justice in any eventuality. Judiciary gives credence to the trust reposed by citizen in the governing powers.

Rule of Law and Independence of Judiciary

Independent Judiciary is an essential part of Rule of Law. Non-arbitrationness is a necessary concomitant of the rule of law [**AP Aggarwal** ***v.*** **Govt. of NCT of Delhi** (2000) 1 SCC 600 (para 12) : AIR 2000 SC 205].

Credibility in the functioning of justice delivery system and the reasonable perception of the affected parties are the relevant considerations to ensure the continuance of public confidence in the credibility and impartiality of the judiciary [**PK Ghosh *v.* JG Rajput** (1995)6 SCC 744, (para 10) : AIR 1996 SC 513].

Justice and Law

The Constitution of the Republic of India guarantees, besides other rights, protection of life and personal liberty and provides adequate safeguards against the arbitrary deprivation thereof by the State.

Adoption of a Constitution by India in 1950 did not disturb continuity of existing laws and unified structure of courts. Unity and uniformity of the judicial structure were preserved by placing such areas of law as criminal law and procedure, civil procedure, will, succession, contract including special form of contract, but not including contract relating to agricultural land, registration of deeds and documents, evidence, etc., in the Concurrent List.

Sources of Law

The main sources of law in India are the Constitution, statutes (legislation), customary law and case law. Statutes are enacted by Parliament, State legislatures and Union Territory legislatures. Besides, there is a vast body of laws known as subordinate legislation in the form of rules, regulations as well as bye-laws made by Central, State governments and local authorities like municipal corporations, municipalities, gram panchayats and other local bodies. This subordinate legislation is made under the authority conferred or delegated either by Parliament or State or Union Territory legislatures concerned. Judicial decisions of superior courts like Supreme Court and High Courts are important sources of law—Decisions of Supreme Court are binding on all courts within the territory of India. Local customs and conventions which are not against statute, morality, etc., are also recognised and taken into account by courts while administering justice in certain spheres.

Enactment of Laws

Parliament is competent to make laws on matters enumerated in the Union List. State legislatures are competent to make laws on matters enumerated in the State List. Parliament alone has power to make laws on matters not included in the State or Concurrent List. On matters enumerated in the Concurrent List, laws can be made by both Parliament and legislatures. But in the event of repugnancy, law made by Parliament shall prevail and law made by State legislature, to the extent of repugnancy, be void unless the latter law having been reserved for consideration of President, has received his assent, and in that event it shall prevail in that state.

Judiciary

At the apex of the entire judicial system exists Supreme Court of India with a High Court for each state or group of states, and under High Courts, there is a hierarchy of subordinate courts Panchayat courts also function in some states under various names like Nyaya Panchayat, Panchayat Adalat, Gram Kachehri, etc., to decide civil and criminal disputes of petty and local nature. Different state laws provide for jurisdiction of these courts.

Each state is divided into judicial districts presided over by a district and sessions judge, who is the principal civil court of original jurisdiction and can try all offences including those punishable with death. He is the highest judicial authority in a district. Below him, there are courts of civil jurisdiction, known in different states as munsifs, sub-judges, civil judges and the like. Similarly, criminal judiciary comprises chief judicial magistrate and judicial magistrates of first and second class.

Rule of Law

Equality before law is correlative to the concept of rule of law for all-round evaluation of healthy social order. A basic postulate of the rule of law is that "justice should not only be done but it must also be seen to be done." If there be a basis which cannot be treated as unreasonable for a litigant to expect that his matter should not be heard by a particular Judge and there is no compelling necessity, such as the absence of an alternative, it is appropriate that the learned Judge should recluse himself from the Bench hearing that matter. This step is required to be taken by him not because he is likely to be influenced in any manner in doing justice in the cause, but because his hearing the matter is likely to give rise to a reasonable apprehension in the mind of the litigant that his mind—may be subconsciously—has been influenced by some extraneous factor in making the decision, particularly if it happens to be in favour of the opposite party. Credibility in the functioning of justice delivery system and the reasonable perception of the affected parties are the relevant considerations to ensure the continuance of public confidence in the credibility and impartiality of the judiciary [P.K.G, Rajput, (1995) 6 SCC 744, (para 10) : AIR 1996 SC 513].

Right to Equality

The right to equality, a necessary corollary of the concept of rule of law, has been incorporated in the Constitution (Articles 14 to 18). Article 14 guarantees equality in general whereas under articles 15, 16, 17 and 18 discrimination is prohibited on specific grounds. Article 14 envisaged 'equality before the law and equal protection of the laws with the object to secure to all persons, citizens or non-citizens, the equality of status and opportunity referred to in the preamble of the Constitution'. Article 15 outlaws discrimination on grounds of religion, race, caste, sex or place of birth; Article 16 provides for equality of opportunity in matters of public employment; Article 17 abolishes untouchability; and Article 18 prohibits the state from conferring any title except a military or academic distinction. Equality before the law is a negative concept whereas 'equal protection of the laws is a positive one'. The former declares that everyone is equal before the law that on one can claim special privileges and that all classes are equally subject to the ordinary law of the land; the latter postulates an equal protection to all alike in the same situation and under like circumstances.

It is important to note that though discrimination is prohibited, reasonable classification founded on intelligible, differentia which distinguishes persons, transaction of things grouped together from others left out of the group, is permitted. Such a differentia, the Supreme Court has held, must a rational to the objective sought to be achieved by the Act. In other words, there must be a nexus between the basis of classification and the objective of the Act. The Supreme Court has avoided doctrinaire approach and has liberally interpreted this article. The court in fact has emphasised on the presumption of constitutionality and has upheld classification on one ground or another. In the **Bank Nationalization case,** however, the Supreme Court rejected the earlier Judicial theory that it was enough to concentrate on the powers of the state and object of state and action to the exclusion of its effects on person or party whose interests were affected. In the present case, the Court declared the nationalization of fourteen banks as violative of article the Government of India contended that the nationalization of the said banks was done because the policy of the government was to control the concentration of private economic resources to ensure the achievement of the Directive Principles of State Policy and only such banks were selected, the acquisition of which was conducive to the national policy. The Supreme Court, however, declared that the nationalization of fourteen banks was a flagrantly hostile discrimination, and was *ultra vires* of the Constitution.

This decision was clearly a departure from the earlier policy of the Supreme Court and it caused a great embarrassment to the ruling party, for it came a moment when the split in the Congress party had taken place and ruling

Congress was reduced in strength. Soon the Lok Sabha was dissolved and after the elections, the Parliament enacted the Constitution (Twenty-fifth) Amendment, whereby it provided that if a law was made to secure implementation of the Directive Principles specified in Clause (b) or Clause (c) of Article 39, such a law would not be challenged in any court of law on the ground that it violated any of the Fundamental Rights conferred by Article 14, Article 19 or Article 31. Twenty-fifth Amendment will be discussed at length on later stage).

Right to Freedom

Article 19(1) which guarantees right embodies six freedoms (originally seven) to the citizen, namely freedom of speech and expression, of peaceful assembly, of association, of movement, residence freedom to practice any profession, to carry on trade or occupation. These freedoms can be enjoyed by citizens only. Further, these freedoms can be enjoyed only if a person is free. In other words, if a citizen is lawfully deprived of his freedom as a punishment of committing a crime or breaking a law, there can be no question of his exercising or involving the rights, that is to say he can within certain units speak what he likes, from any association or union.

Again as already pointed out the freedoms embodied in Article 19 can be enjoyed only:

When the proclamation of emergency is not in operation, for Article 19 is automatically suspended when emergency is proclaimed under Article 358 of the Constitution.

Further the restrictions are envisaged under Clauses (2) to (6) of Article 19. The word 'restriction' has, however, been qualified by the words, reasonable, which contemplated the role of the Court to determine the reasonability.

A citizen, however, is entitled to enjoy each and every freedom without being made to sacrifice one's freedom for the sake of another. One's freedom cannot be preferred to another.

Right to Freedom of Speech and Expression: This is a right, which may be said to provide the basis of democratic life. The freedom of speech and expression implies that the individual has a right to think, express himself freely according to his convictions, to advocate any philosophy or ideology he believes in. This has been rightly called the 'boast of democracy for the principle of the consent of the governed'.

Freedom of speech and expression implies communication, dissemination, propagation of ideas, opinions freely expressed by mouth, writing, printing, etc. It thus, includes the freedom of press, movies, radio and television. Article 19, however, does not expressly provide for these freedoms but the Supreme Court has ruled in numerous cases that the freedom of speech and expression includes the freedom of the press.

There is hardly any need to emphasise the importance of the freedom of the press as a free press is one of the great interpreters between the government and the people and is one of the significant means to the end of a free society. It lays the foundation of all democratic organizations and is essential for the proper functioning of the process of popular government. Jefferson once remarked that if he had to choose between a free government and free press, any free government would soon perish, while with a free press, a free government would soon emerge.

The freedom of speech and expression, however, is not of absolute nature. Reasonable restriction can be imposed by legislation in the interest of sovereignty and integrity of India, the security of the state, friendly relations with foreign states, public order, decency or morality or in relation to contempt of court, defamation or incitement to an offence.

Freedom to Assembly: Under Article 19(1)(b) all citizens have the freedom to assemble peacefully and without arms and the state is empowered under Article 19 (3) to impose reasonable restrictions in the interests of sovereignty and integrity of India or public order.

Freedom to form Association or Unions: This freedom is guaranteed by Article 19 (1) subject to the reasonable restriction, that the state may impose in the interest of sovereignty of India, public order or morality. This right again like the right to free speech and expression lies at the foundations of a free society.

The Supreme Court, however, gave a very narrow interpretation of the freedom in **P. Balakrishnan** v. **Union of India.** In this case, the petitioners claimed that the order terminating their services, because they were communists or trade unionists, violated the freedom to form association guaranteed under Article 19(1)(c). The Court, however, rejected their petition and held the appellants have no doubt a fundamental right to form association but they have no right to be continued employment by the state.

Freedom of Movement, Residence and Settlement: Article 19(1) and (e) guaranteed the freedom of movement throughout the territory of India, to reside or settle in any part of the territory of India, subject to reasonable restrictions in the interest of the general public or for the protection of the interests of any Scheduled Tribe.

Freedom of Trade and Occupation: The citizens under Article 19(1)(g) have the freedom to practice any profession, carry any occupation, trade or business, subject to reasonable restrictions in the interests of the general public under Clause (6) of Article 19. This clause was amended in 1951 to empower the state to make laws relating to (i) professional or trade or technical qualifications necessary for practicing any profession or carrying on any occupation or trade or business, or (ii) carrying on by the state or by a corporation owned or controlled by the state, or any trade, business, industry or service whether to the exclusion, complete or partial, of citizens or otherwise. The effect of this amendment is that a state can create a monopoly in its favour in respect of any trade or business.

Protection in respect of conviction for offences: Article 20 guarantees protection in respect of conviction for offences. It prohibits conditions and sentence under *'ex post facto'* law providing against double jeopardy (that a person shall not be prosecuted and punished twice for the same offence) and self incrimination.

Right to Life and Personal Liberty

The framers of Constitution of India did not feel satisfied with the scope of freedom guaranteed under Article 19.

Consequently, they specifically 'incorporated the right to life' and 'personal liberty' in Article 21 of the Constitution, which reads: "No person shall be deprived of his life or personal liberty except according to the procedure established by law". It is a modified version of the rights guaranteed under the Fifth and Fourteenth Amendments of the Constitution of the United States. In these two amendments, words "due process of law" are used in place of procedure established by law. The 'due process' clause which has been described by Justice Frankfurter as the 'most majestic' concept, has been interpreted very vaguely and it is alleged that in the guise of interpreting the clause the American Courts have gradually arrogated to themselves the powers to revise all legislation. It is further alleged that the opinions of the Supreme Court on 'due process' have confused rather than clarified the subject. Keeping in view its impression and other drawbacks, the framers of the Constitution of India preferred to use the words 'procedure established by law' an expression borrowed from Article 31 of the Constitution of Japan of 1961.

Thus the right to life and personal liberty is not an absolute right but is a qualified right which is circumscribed by the possibility to risk of being lost according to procedure established by law. In **A.K. Gopalan** v. **State of Madras,** the Majority interpreted the word law as enacted law. This interpretation was widely criticized in the juristic circles as it placed the liberty of the citizen at the mercy if the party in power. It is interesting to note that a retired judge of the Supreme Court who while on the bench concurred unfortunate, observes the judge, "that the Supreme Court has decided that the "procedure established by law" meant the same things as procedure prescribed by law. The Supreme Court has framed the interpretation which was not consistent with the nature of Fundamental Rights and was contrary to the very essence of Fundamental Rights. The Supreme Court has, however, consistently conformed to its decision given in *Gopalan case.* 86th Constitution Amendment Act (2002) adds Article 21-A and providing right to free and compulsory education to children between 6 to 14 years of age by law. *Protection against*

Arrest and Detention : Clauses (1) and (2) of Article 22 provide certain safeguards in respect of arrest and detention, in the first place, no person who is arrested shall be detained without being informed, as soon as may be, of the grounds of his arrest; secondly, he has the right to consult and to be defended by a legal practitioner of his choice; thirdly, such a person must be produced before the nearest magistrate within twenty-four hours and he shall not be detained in custody beyond this period without the authority of the magistrate.

Preventive Detention

The above noted safeguards are not applicable to enemy aliens and to persons who are under preventive detention. There is a constitutional sanction for the law of preventive detention. It is difficult to reconcile the idea of preventive detention with democratic concepts, but with accumulative evidence of domestic subversion and other such disruptive activities reconciliation of liberty and security becomes a recurring necessity in every country. "This sinister looking feature" observed Justice Palanjali Sastri, "so strongly out of place in a democratic Constitution which invests personal liberty with sacrosanctity of Fundamental Right and so incompatible with the promises of its preamble, is without doubt designed to prevent the use of freedom by any anti-social elements which might imperil the national welfare of the infant republic.

The distinguishing feature of the preventive detention law is that to enforce it: condition of emergency is not required as a condition precedent. India is 'the only democratic country in the world where fundamental law sanctions detention without trial in time of peace and in situation which is not in the nature of any emergency'.

The Constitution, however, provides for certain procedural safeguards against preventive detention which are embodied in Clauses (4) to (7) of Article 22. No person be detained for more than two months, unless an advisory board approved that there is sufficient cause for a detention longer than this period [22(4)]. Further the grounds of detention must be communicated to the defence except when disclosure is against public interest [22(5)] the defence must be given an earliest opportunity to represent against the order of detention. [22(6)]. Clause (7) of Article 22, however, confers sweeping powers on the parliament which in effect tantamount to negative the procedural safeguards guaranteed by the preceding clauses of the same Article. The present clause empowers to make any law to determine the procedure to be followed in advisory board and the maximum period of detention. The Act of Preventive Detention was passed by the Parliament by virtue of legislative power conferred on it under List I, Entry 9 and List III, Entry 3 of Schedule 7 on February 25, 1950, for one year but extended from time to time till December 31, 1969. The Act was, however, under constant fire till it expired on December 31, 1969. It was described black spot on the Constitution. Slur on self rule and India's capacity to run a democratic government in spite of the criticism from all sections of the society the party in power kept the Act in force till it had comfortable majority to life to it.

After a lapse of two years, the Congress government which got the adequate majority in the 1971 Lok Sabha Elections, again passed two laws of preventive detention (a) the maintenance of Internal Security Act 1971 and (b) the Conservation of Foreign Exchange and Prevention of Smuggling Activities Act 1971. By the Constitution (39th Amendment) Act 1975. Both these Acts were placed in the Ninth Schedule so as to give them immunity from being challenged in the courts on the ground of contravention of any of the fundamental rights. Any provision in these Acts could not, therefore, be declared invalid by the court on the ground that it had deprived the detenu of his rights to be informed of the ground that it has deprived the detenu of his rights to be informed of the ground of detention [Article 23(5)] of that has rendered illusory the jurisdiction of the Supreme Court under Article 32 as happened in *Gopalan's case*. Even the limited safeguards provided in these two Acts were suspended during the operation of the Proclamation of Internal Emergency (June 1975 to March 1977) and the two Acts were amended for this purpose.

During the Janata regime, the Maintenance of Internal Security Act (MISA) 1971 was repealed in August 1978, but the other Act COFEPOSA was retained. Again in 1980, with the installation of Congress Government headed by Mrs. Gandhi at the Centre, the government passed the National Security Act 1980, and the Prevention of Black Marketing and Maintenance of Supplies of Essential Commodities Act 1980, providing for preventive detention. In 1984 certain changes were made in the N.S.A. making it more rigid. The Judicial Review of Preventive Detention Laws was reduced. In 1985, the government passed the Terrorist and Disruptive Activities (Prevention) Act, known as TADA in the context of terrorism in Punjab. The Act remained in force for 10 years and lapsed on May 23, 1995 due to its widespread criticism and because of its misuse and stringent provisions. After a lapse of six years the NDA government promulgated the Prevention of Terrorism Ordinance (POTO) on October 24, 2001. As it could not be tabled in the forthcoming Parliament session it was repromulgated in January 2002. Finally, it was tabled in Parliament in March but was rejected in Rajya Sabha and the Government passed it in a joint sitting of Parliament as Prevention of Terrorism Act (POTA) on March 26, 2002.

Judicial review of administrative action is an essential part of rule of law [**State of Bihar** v. **Subhash Singh,** (1997) 4 SCC 430 (para 3) : AIR 1997 SC 1390] and so is independence of judiciary [**High Court of Judicature at Bombay** v. **Shirish Kumar Rangarao Patil**], (1997) 6 SCC 339 (para 13)]. Non-arbitrariness is a necessary concomitant of the rule of law. **Style (Dress Land)** v. **Union Territory, Chandigarh, (1999)** 7 SCC 89 (para 12). Also see **A.P. Aggarwal** v. **Govt. of NCT of Delhi,** (2000) 1 SCC 600 (para 12): AIR 2000 SC 205.

When the High Court itself became conscious that the decision regarding admission of an ineligible student was wrong and the precedent was not worth repeating, still it was repeated time and again, it amounted to a mockery of "Rule of Law" and promotes rather than the "Rule of Man". **Central Board of Secondary Education** v. **Nikhil Gulati,** (1998) 3 SCC 5 : AIR 1998 SC 1205.

Classification authorised by other provisions of the Constitution.—1. Article 14 is a general provision and has to be read subject to the other provisions included within the Part on Fundamental Rights. Hence, any law making special provision for women (or children) under Article 15(3) cannot be challenged on the ground of contravention of Article 14. **(Yusuf Abdul Aziz** v. **State of Bombay,** 1954 SCR 930 : AIR 1954 SC 321.)

Thus, Section 54(4) of the Representation of the People Act 1951, which confers a double advantage upon members of the Scheduled Castes or Tribes to be returned to the general seats even though seats have been reserved for them under the Constitution, being sanctioned by Article 15(4), cannot be held to be void for contravention of Article 14. **(Giri V.V.** v. **Dora Suri D.**, AIR 1959 SC 1318 (1325): 1960 (1) SCR 321).

2. Where the Constitution itself makes a classification, the charge of discrimination cannot be levelled against such separate treatment. **[Sainik Motors (M/s.)** v. **State of Rajasthan,** AIR 1961 SC 1480 (I486) : 1962 (1) SCR 517].

Thus, the special treatment of government servants in the matter of their tenure [Art. 310(1)], **(Raj Kishore** v. **State of U.P.,** AIR 1954 All 343) or an order made by the President under Article 311(2), Proviso (c) **(Jagadish Dajiba** v. **Accountant General,** AIR 1958 Bom. 283: 60 Bom. LR. 241), or the taxation by a State of road transport [Entry 56, List II], cannot be challenged as violative of Article 14.

But, the special treatment authorized by these other provisions must be kept within reasonable limits and should not be made so excessive as to render nugatory the general equality professed to the members of ail communities by Article 14 **[Devadasan T.** v. **Union of India.** AIR 1964 SC 179 (780) : 1964 (4) SCR 680]. Hence, the special provision for the advancement of the backward classes or Scheduled Castes and Tribes under Article 15(4) **[General Manager, Southern Railway** v. **Rangachari,** 1962 (2) SCR 586: AIR 1962 SC 36], or the reservation of posts for the backward classes under Article 16(4) will be unconstitutional because of contravention of

Article 14, if it is carried to an unreasonable extent. (**Balaji M.R.** v. **State of Mysore** AIR 1963 SC 649).

Reasonableness

In the sphere of contractual relations, the state, its instrumentalities, public authorities or those whose acts bear insignia of public element, action to public duty or obligation are enjoined in a manner that is fair, just and equitable, after taking objectively all the relevant options into consideration and in a manner that is reasonable, relevant and germane to effectuate the purpose for public good and in general public interest and it must not take any irrelevant or irrational factors into consideration or appear arbitrary in its decision [**L.I.C. of India** v. **Consumer Education & Research Centre,** 1995) 5 SCC 482, (para 27): AIR 1995 SC 1811]. The award to punish maternally to a Government servant in a disciplinary proceeding, if unreasonable, Article 14 would be attracted [**B.C. Chaturvedi** v. **Union of India** (1995) 6 SCC 749, (para 24) : AJR 1996 SC 484]. Where the provision in the Executive instructions denying the benefit of service rendered by a deputations on an equivalent post in his parent department was contradictory) to the law declared by the Supreme Court, the offending portion was declared unreasonable and was struck down [**Sub-Inspector Rooplal** v. **Lt. Governor, (2000) :** 1 SCC 644 (para 23)]. Determination and fixation of standard rent by freezing or pegging down of rent as on 1-9-1940 or as on the date of first letting is arbitrary and unreasonable in view of constant escalation of prices due to inflation and corresponding fall in money value with the passage of time [**Malpe Vishwanath Acharya** v. **State of Maharashtra,** (1998) 2 SCC 1 (paras 2(1-27) : AIR 1998 SC 72]. Rent control legislation should be just both to the tenants and the landlords, striking a balance between their rival interests [**Malpe Vishwanath Acharya** v. **State of Maharashtra,** (1998) 2 SCC 1 (para 29 and 30): AIR 1998 SC 602]. Where a corporation handed over a park of historical importance to a builder to build a Palika Bazar without following the proper procedure and keeping in mind the public purpose, the act of the corporation was held to be unreasonable, arbitrary, unfair, opposed to public policy, public interest and public trust doctrine. The construction was directed to be demolished [**M.I. Builders Pvt. Ltd.** v. **Radhey Shyam Saku,** (1999) (i) SCC 464 [(paras 69, 71, 72, 73, 74, 80 and 81) : AIR 1999 SC 2468].

The period of three years continuous service of an *ad hoc* appointee for regularization of his services as prescribed under Regularization Rules has been held to be reasonable [**Khagesh Kumar** v. **Inspector General of Registration,** 1995 [Supp. 182, (para 19): AIR 1996 SC 417]. Implementation of Tikoo Committee report recommending new and more beneficial criterion of eligibility for promotion of specialists in Central Health Services from a date almost one year later from its date of submission has been held to be reasonable as the report is only recommendatory and the final decision rests with Government, besides it involves huge financial implication and sorting out of service problems [**V.P. Malik (Dr.)** v. **Union of India,** (1996) 1 SCC 456, (para 4): AIR 1996 SC 1048]. Procedure of making promotion and fixing seniority according to roster points is just and reasonable [**Jadish Lal** v. **State of Haryana,** (1997) 6 SCC 538 (para 4): AIR 1997 SC 2366]. An employee with a low seniority in his cadre, in view of his qualifications and experience was promoted on an *ad hoc* basis in a post specially created for him on the condition that he would not be entitled to claim seniority over his seniors in the general category or preference for the next promotion. Similar conditions were placed while giving him the next promotion which were held to be fair and reasonable [**Mohan Dutt Sharma** v. **Chief Justice, Punjab and Haryana High Court,** [(1997) 8 SCC 445 (paras 9-12) : AIR 1997 SC 3094]. Rule 89-A(2) of the Rules framed under the Bengal Finance (Sales Tax) Act, 1941, placing a statutory obligation upon the consignor/vendor to issue and the consignee/purchaser to carry the declaration form is neither unreasonable nor oppressive [**Calcutta Iron Merchant's Association** v. **Commissioner of Commercial Taxes,** (1996) SCC 537 (para 9-12): AIR 1997 SC]. Time specified for exchange of high denomination bank notes under the High Denomination Bank Notes (Demonetization) Act, 1978, having regard to the purpose sought to be achieved by the Act, has been held to be not unreasonable **[Jayantilal Ratanchand Shah** v. **Reserve Bank of India** (1996) 9 SCC 650 (Para 10)]. Three months cut-off period given to the government employees sent on deputation to Corporation for giving notice of option to Government against being absorbed in the Corporation service is appropriate and reasonable **[State of U.P.** v. **Roadways Ministerial Staff Association U.P.** (1996) 9 SCC 479 (Para 5)]. The Supreme Court held that the Government proposal to permit the 'archakas' (*pujaris*) to retain the lands in their possession in lieu of remuneration for rendering services, to determine cadre strength on case to case basis as in case of other religious institutions taking into account all the parameters like income, activity level, the actual needs of the *'mutt,'* etc. and to pay additional remuneration for extra services rendered by *'Archakas'* during *Brahmotsavams* and special festivals in temples having no fixed scales on the basis of circumstances of each case and when such remuneration was paid to secular staff, was reasonable.—Mere possibility of abuse of a statutory provision by those in charge of administering it, cannot be a ground for holding it procedurally or substantively unreasonable. It would amount to just, fair and reasonable procedure to remove the encroachment by pavement dwellers but if they are well-settled for a long time action can be taken by giving two weeks'/ten days' notice—Procedure of removal of Gram Pradhan by Gram Panchayat, a smaller body, instead of by Gaon Sabha which elects him, is not unreasonable as the Gram Panchayat is the representative body of Gaon Sabha. The provision for different period of exemption for restaurants/eating houses and hotels is neither irrational or arbitrary.

After receiving an application for grant of licence for import/export the authorities require a reasonable time to process the application and what is a reasonable time depends on the facts of each case. The reasonableness of a provision depends upon the circumstances obtaining at a particular time and the urgency of the evil sought to be controlled. The possibility of the power being abused is no ground for declaring a provision violative of Article 14. A legislation which was initially justified may become arbitrary and unreasonable with the passage of time. In the absence of rules, the action of the government is required to be fair and reasonable. The Central Government has statutory power to sell, lease or otherwise transfer any land or building belonging to it in Chandigarh on such terms and conditions as it may think fit. Such terms and conditions could be regulated by rules made by the Central Government. However, failing to make rules would not render the transfer illegal, void or inoperative. Laying of criteria to shortlist a large number of candidates is permissible but the criteria must be reasonable and not arbitrary having regard to the post for which recruitment is made.

How far Reasonableness may be Determined with Reference to Other Laws

1. For the purpose of application of Article 14, laws made by different Legislatures cannot be taken together for the purpose of comparison or contrast to show that the provisions of the one are discriminatory when read with the provisions of the other. Each law must be dealt with specifically.
2. Of course, when the same Legislature enacts a number of connected laws, their combined operation may be taken into consideration for determining whether the provisions of any one of them are discriminatory law. But the same process cannot be applied where similar laws on the same subject are enacted by different Legislatures.

What Classification is Reasonable

1. What Article 14 prohibits is class legislation and not reasonable classification for the purpose of legislation. If the Legislature takes care to reasonably classify persons for legislative purposes and if it deals equally

with all persons belonging to a well-defined class it is not open to the charge of denial of equal protection on the ground that the law does not apply to other persons. The classification of power generation into "power project" for generation and distribution of electricity generally and "power plant" set up by industrial units to generate electricity for captive consumption, has been held to be well-defined; so also the classification of carriages into inter-State and intra-State contract carriages and the classification of the residents of Andaman and Nicobar Islands into settlers prior to 1942 and settlers after 1942 as the former had to suffer much and the latter were brought under rehabilitation schemes. The government servants absorbed in public sector undertakings and commuting 100 per cent of their pension will not be entitled to dearness relief on full pension like those commuting only one-third of the pension as they form a separate category.

2. In order, however, to pass the test of permissible classification **two** conditions must be fulfilled, namely, (i) that the classification must be founded on an intelligible differential which distinguishes persons or things that are grouped together from others left out of the group; and (ii) that, that differential must have a rational relation to the object sought to be achieved by the statute in question. The amendment in the Rent Control Act precluding the landlords of non-residential buildings from seeking eviction on the ground of *bona fide* requirement having no nexus with the object sought to be achieved by the principal Act, is violative of Article 14. The classification may be founded on different basis; such as, geographical, or according to objects or occupation or the like. What is necessary is that there must be a nexus between the basis of classification and the object of the Act under consideration. Those who joined the Army as a sacrifice during the external aggression and those who did so as a career opportunity form two different categories,

giving them benefits on different principles is not discriminatory. Quantum of fee for licence can be fixed for running a lodging house or eating house, etc.—on the basis of the rent payable for the premises concerned—Fixing a cut-off date for passing a certain test for the entitlement of advance increments, is proper classification. Offences under Section 3 of the Scheduled Castes and Scheduled Tribes (Prevention of Atrocities) Act 1989 constitute a separate class and cannot be compared with other offences. A mere possibility of a better classification is no ground to strike down the classification made by the statutory authority.

3. (a) Article 14 does not insist that legislative classification should be scientifically perfect or logically complete. The Court would not interfere unless the classification results in pronounced inequality. On the other hand, it would not uphold mini-classification where the differences between the classes or categories are inconsequential.

   A classification would be justified if it is not palpably arbitrary. The class of similar persons who availed the right and remedy but were unsuccessful are treated as a distinct class. It can by no means be said to be arbitrary. If there is equality and uniformity within each group, the law will not be condemned as discriminative, though due to some fortuitous circumstance arising out of a peculiar situation some included in a class get an advantage over others, so long as they are not singled out for special treatment.

   (b) The difference which will warrant a reasonable classification need not be great. What is required is that it must be real and substantial and must bear some just and reasonable relation to the object of the legislation. But classification having regard to microscopic differences is not good. "To overdo classification is to undo equality."

4. When a law is challenged as denying equal protection; the question for determination by the Court is not

whether it has resulted in inequality, but whether there is some difference which bears a just and reasonable relation to the object of legislation. Mere differentiation or inequality of treatment or inequality of burden does not *per se* amount to discrimination within the inhibition of the equal protection clause. To attract the operation of the clause it is necessary to show that the selection or differentiation is unreasonable or arbitrary; that it does not rest on any rational basis having regard to the object which the Legislature has in view.

When the Legislature enacts a statutory presumption in respect of certain acts or a burden of proof upon certain persons, the statute cannot be challenged as discriminatory if the rule of evidence has a rational relation to the object to be achieved by the Act.

5. When, therefore, a law is challenged as offending against the guarantee in Article 14, the first duty of the Court is to examine the purpose and policy of the Act and then to discover whether the classification made by the law has a reasonable relation to the object which the Legislature seeks to obtain—The purpose or object of the Act is to be ascertained from an examination of its "title, preamble and provisions".
6. A law which was non-discriminatory at its inception may be rendered discriminatory by reason of external circumstances which take away the reasonable basis of classification. This happened after the merger of different territories with differential laws and a number of Indian State laws have been held to be discriminatory since the commencement of the Constitution, on the ground that these laws differed from the laws which governed the rest of the territory of the State with which the Indian State in question merged.
7. But—(i) The reasonableness is to be judged with reference to the object of the legislation and not moral considerations, of course, there may be cases where gross immorality of measure may condemn the legislation as arbitrary or irrational.

(ii) The law of one State cannot be held to be discriminatory by contrasting it with the law prevailing in another State. If the sources of authority for the two statutes be different, Article 14 has no application.

8. A manufacturer of motor vehicles sent the vehicles to its Regional Sales of once in other States and delivered them there to the State Transport Undertakings and other purchasers. Subsequently, the State where the vehicles were manufactured, sought to reopen the assessment on the ground that such sales were inter-state sales—However, reopening of assessment only in respect of sale to the undertakings and not in respect of other sales, was held to be valid.

Classification of a Single Individual and Ad Hoc Legislation

1. A classification may be reasonable even though a single individual (or object) is treated as a class by himself (or itself), if there are some special circumstances or reasons applicable to him (or it) alone and not applicable to others.
2. But even though it is permissible for the Legislature to classify a single individual where he possesses real and substantial features different from other individuals in relation to the object of the legislation in question, Article 14 would not tolerate any discriminatory legislation against a single named individual or individuals which simulates a "Bill of Attainder", and no reasonable basis for the classification appears on the face of the legislation nor is deducible from the surrounding circumstances or matters of common knowledge.
3. Where a law is of general application, it cannot be challenged as discriminatory merely because the object of its enactment was to benefit a particular individual.
4. On the other hand—In the name of classifying individuals on the ground of special features, the Legislature cannot assume the jurisdiction to adjudicate disputes regarding private rights and thus deprive

named individuals of their right to go to the duly constituted courts a right of access to which for the determination of private legal rights belongs to every person.

END NOTES

AIR 1950 SC 27.

A.K. Gopalan v. *State of Madras,* AIR 1957 SC 27.

A.K. Gopalan v. *State of Madras,* AIR 1950 SC 27.

Anand J. Haridas & Co. *v.* S.P. Kastur, AIR 1968 SC 567, State of Mysore *v.* P. Nara Singh Roy AIR 1968 SC 349 RC *Copper* v. *Union of India,* AIR 1970 SC 564.

Article 22 (3).

Bashesher Nath *v.* Income Tax Commissioner. AIR 1959 SC 149.

Before the dissolution of Lok Sabha in December 1970, Congress (R) did not have sufficient time to give life.

Brij Bhushan *v.* State of Delhi AIR 1950 SC 129.

Charanjit Lal *v.* Union of India AIR 1951 SC 41: State of West Bengal *v.* Anwar Ah., 1952 SC 75. Budhan Chowdhry *v.* State of Bihar, AIR 155 SC 191, Ram Krishan Dalmia *v.* Justice Tendolikar AIR 1958 TC 539; State of J & K *v.* Bakshi Gulam Mohd., AIR 1967 SC 122.

Express Newspapers Ltd. v. *Union of India,* AIR 1958 SC 578.

Justice Fazi Ali who gave a dissenting opinion observed that the words Procedure established by law, must include four essentials (i) notice, (ii) an opportunity, (iii) an impartial notice, and (iv) an orderly course of procedure (*A.K. Gopalan* v. *State of Madras,* AIR 1957 SC 27 (60-61).

M.S.M. Sharma v. *Sri Krishna Sinha,* AIR 1959 SC 395.

Munro writes due process clause has become a sort of palladium covering all manner of individual rights. See W.B. Munro. *The Government of United States* (1947), p. 520.

N.C. Chaterjee, *Lok Sabha Debates,* December 11,1954.

P.B. Gajendragadkar. *Law, Liberty and Social Justice,* (1962) p. 89.

Per Justice Patanjali Sastri, *Thapar* v. *State of Madras,* AIR 1950 SC 124.

Ramesh Thapar *v.* Sate of Madras, AIR 1950 SC 129.

Sagir Ahmad v. *State of U.P.* AIR 154 SC 728. *Akadshi* v. *State of Orissa,* AIR 1963 SC 1047.

Sakal Papers, (p) Ltd. v. *Union of India,* AIR 1962 SC 303.

See *Indian Civil Liberties Bulletin,* August 1967. p. 310.

See Ray A. Brown. Due Process Police powers and the Supreme Court, *Harvard Law Review,* Vol. 40, 1926. J.P. 1943 (1966).

S. Mohan Kumaramanglam suggests that the amendment of Article 21 is vitally necessary if that article is to have any meaning (p. 42).

S. Mohan Kumaramanglam, *Person Liberty,* AIR 1956, 39.

States have passed their own legislation for preventive detention. The States have concurrent jurisdiction in this matter.

The expressions equality before the law and equal protection of law have been borrowed from the English doctrine of rules of law and the American Constitution respectively.

The Supreme Court was under severe attack for its decision in the Bank Nationalization Case. The Judges who sat on the bench were described as reaction arise and leftist members of Parliament demanded the impeachment of those judges who had shares in the Banks and sat on the bench of the Court to hear the case. See *The Tribune,* April 14,1970 8:3.

This amendment was made to negative fee effect of the Allahabad High Court decision in *Moti Lal* v. *U.P.* (AIR 1951 ALL 257). Which had defeated the *'Policy of Nationalization of Road Transport Service'* initiated by the U.P. Government.

V.C. Deshpande, *Lok Sabha Debates,* 10 December, 1954.

3

Rule of Law and Judicial Review

Judicial review of administrative action is an essential part of rule of law. Supreme Court is the Guardian of the Fundamental Rights.

Supreme Court has also played a significant role as the guardian of fundamental rights. The Supreme Court shares with the High Court the jurisdiction to try all cases involving Fundamental Rights, in other words, all cases where fundamental rights have been infringed upon can go straight to the Supreme Court. It can issue various writs under Article 32 for the protection of rights such as *habeas corpus, mandamus, prohibition, quo warranto* and *certiorari.* The Supreme Court has unequivocally protected the fundamental rights. It can be rightly described as the champion of the fundamental rights.

The fundamental rights enshrined in our Constitution are full of ambiguities and there is hardly any right which does not carry the clause of reasonable restrictions. That is to say that on every right mentioned in the chapter on fundamental rights (Chapter III) reasonable restrictions can be imposed. The Supreme Court has brought within its purview the reasonableness of such restrictions. So much so that by its interpretation it has done away with the restrictions and clear and sound fundamental rights have emerged.

Power of Judicial Review

Like the Supreme Court of America, the Supreme Court of India has also the power of Judicial Review. Judicial review means the power to review the laws by Judiciary, i.e. the court can judge the validity of laws and can declare them valid or invalid. The Supreme Courts of Britain, France and Switzerland do not enjoy the power of Judicial review because in these countries the supremacy of Parliament is established and the courts cannot declare the laws made by Parliament as invalid on the basis that they are inconsistent with the Constitution. Although India also adopted the British institutions but the principle of Parliamentary sovereignty has not been accepted fully. The reason is that in India, federal form of government has been established. In federal form, the constitution is the supreme law of the land and Supreme Court is the Custodian of Constitution as well as its interpreter. Hence, it is vested with the power of Judicial review. But the power is not so broad as that of the Supreme Court of America. The Supreme Court in America has the power to declare any law unconstitutional on the ground of its not being in accordance with the "due process of law" which can be interpreted in any manner. While in India the phrase "procedure established by law" is used which means that the Supreme Court in India can declare law void if it is found to have transgressed constitutional limitations. In other words, a law to be valid must in all cases be in conformity with the constitutional requirements. The Parliament and the State legislatures in India are supreme in their respective legislative fields and courts have no authority to question the wisdom or policy to the law duly made by them. Chief Justice Mehar Chand Mahajan pronounced that the Constitution gives a certain field of action to the parliament in which the Supreme Court cannot interfere. Thus, in India neither the Parliament is supreme nor the Judiciary but Constitution is the supreme law of the land.

The power of judicial review is not clearly defined in any article of the Constitution, but it is implied in various provisions of the Constitution. Article 246 describes the legislative powers of Union and States. If the Parliament or the State Legislature transgress their powers, the Supreme Court as the custodian of Constitution can review their Acts. As a protector of Fundamental rights, the Supreme Court also enjoys this power under Article 13 which declares that every law inconsistent with fundamental rights shall be void. Supreme Court can also exercise the power of judicial review while deciding the disputes between the Centre and States or among States themselves in its original jurisdiction. Besides these provisions while assuming their offices, the judges of Supreme Court take an oath to uphold the Constitution and laws. Hence, it is their duty to uphold the Constitution against attacks from executive or legislature.

The Supreme Court has the power to review the laws enacted by parliament and by State legislature, the constitutional amendments as well as the ordinances issued by Union executive or State executive. But the Supreme Court cannot use this power by itself. It can review the laws or ordinances only when they are challenged in the Supreme Court by some person or institution. The Supreme Court has at various occasions exercised this power. It declared the Bank Nationalisation Act of 1969 and Ordinance regarding Abolition of Privileges of Rulers, invalid in 1970. While protecting the fundamental rights, it declared even some of the constitutional amendments as invalid on many occasions and to overcome the difficulties caused by its decision, government had to again amend the Constitution. Such as in **Golak Nath Case** (1967) while considering the validity of Seventh Amendment Act, it held that fundamental rights cannot be amended by Parliament. After such a judgement the government could not enact any legislation which affected the fundamental rights. To overcome this difficulty the government passed 24th Constitutional Amendment Act (1971) by which Parliament was vested clearly with the power to amend the fundamental rights. As the parliament got the power to amend the fundamental rights, it further amended the right to property by 25th Amendment and abolished the privy purses of Indian Rulers by 26th Amendment. But again the amending power of parliament was challenged in the Supreme Court in **Keshvanand Bharti case** in 1973.

The Indian Supreme Court has used the power of judicial review to preserve the fundamental rights. But by the judgement in the **Keshvanand Bharti case** (Constitutional Amendment Case) it decided that the Supreme Court shall use this power for preserving the basic structure of the

Constitution, because while giving to the Parliament the power to amend any part of the Constitution, the Supreme Court has held that this power cannot be used to destroy the basic structure of the Constitution. This is to say that whether a certain law or amendment destroys the fundamentals of the Constitution or not is subject to the review by the Supreme Court.

In its historic judgement the Supreme Court has permitted the implementation of Articles 39(b) and (c) of Directive Principles of State Policy even against Article 14, 19 and 31 of the Constitution as provided in the 25th Amendment. But whether a certain law is really intended to give effect to the Directive Principles is with the purview of Supreme Court. That is to say that the Supreme Court has permitted the implementation of Directive Principles, even against three fundamental rights (mentioned in the Articles 14, 19 and 31) but the Court has to see to it that no government takes away the fundamental rights in the garb of implementation of Directive Principles. But **42nd Amendment** curtailed the powers of judiciary through provisions which are as follows:

(1) It gave primacy to Directive Principles.
(2) It deprived courts of the power to look into the validity of a Constitutional Amendment Act. For this it added clause (4) to Article 368.
(3) It laid down that the Supreme Court could look into the Constitutional validity of Central law only (Article 131A) and not of the State law unless there was some conflict between the Central and the State laws (Article 132A). It also laid down that High Courts could look into the validity of only State Laws (Article 226A).
(4) It provided that for looking into the constitutional validity of laws special benches in Supreme Court and High Courts would be formed. In case of Supreme Court it would consist of 7 judges and in case of High Court 5 judges and 2/3 majority would be necessary to strike down the law. If the total strength of a High Court was less than 5, then the bench would consist of

all judges and a decision by unanimous vote was necessary to strike down the law.

(5) It restricted the power to issue writs of the High Courts. The High Courts were deprived of the power to issue writs 'for any other purpose' under Article 226.

These provisions of the 42nd Amendment were criticized severely. Janta Government restored the powers of the Judiciary by 43rd and 44th Amendment Acts. 43rd Amendment provided the Supreme Court and the High Courts the powers to look into the validity of any law, Central or State, as the courts enjoyed before the 42nd Amendment. It also abolished the provisions of constituting special benches and the special majority for constitutional cases. In this matter also the original position was restored, 44th Amendment restored the powers of High Courts to issue writs, 'for any other purpose'. But the provisions establishing the precedence of all the directive principles over the fundamental rights could not be deleted. Moreover, the courts were not given the powers to review the Constitution Amended Acts. But in **Minerva Mills case** (May 1980), Supreme Court struck down these two clauses of the 42nd Amendment, it has held that the Parliament cannot amend the basic structure of the Constitution. Thus, the decision in **Keshvanand Bharti case** (Constitutional Amendment case) 1973 has been restored by the Supreme Court. The Supreme Court has held that all amendments by which the ninth schedule was amended from time to time before April 24, 1973 (date of decision in **Keshvanand Bharti case**) were valid. But the amendments to ninth schedule made after this date are open to challenge on the ground that some them destroy the basic structure of the Constitution.

Supreme Court and Political Process : Judicial Activism

Besides its traditional defined role as Interpreter of Constitution and protector of fundamental rights, Supreme Court has played a crucial role in the political process of the country. In the recent years (during the last decade) this role has been quite assertive especially its role in **Hawala Cases** concerning corruption in high places which is termed as 'Judicial Activism'. The Supreme Court has tried to cleanse the political system which has been rapidly deteriorating without accountability to the people—The real sovereigns of the land. To many legal observers, however, the Supreme Court's assertive role in **Jain Hawala Case** was not the first instance of judicial activism. The first phase of Supreme Court's active role was after the declaration of internal emergency in the country. The Supreme Court came up with the device of public interest litigation (PIL), a tool meant to ensure justice for the underprivileged and marginalized. During this period many PIL cases that were entertained by Supreme Court were confined to mainly the issues of human rights and the environment. In the nineties, (there have been many cases of judicial intervention) such as fixing quotas and even fees for medical colleges, abolishing capitation fees for various professional courses. But with increasing awareness of legal redress and the growth of activist groups, the PIL movement started focusing on corruption in high places which involved politicians, businessmen and bureaucrats working in alliance with each other. Several such cases have been entertained by the highest court in the recent past and the **Jain Hawala case** was one of them. According to Supreme Court advocate R.K. Jain "the judges were always responsive to corruption allegations against political leaders. It is just that more such cases are coming before them these days. The important cases in this context are as follows:

Jain Hawala case was filed by two journalists and two lawyers in October 1993. Not much headway was made regarding the entries made in the Jain diaries which included the names of senior politicians of the country (at least 115) who were alleged to have received pay-offs up to Rs. 65 crore from S.K. Jain, the Bhilai based industrialist. The diaries were discovered during a sporadic CBI raid on Hawala operators in Delhi in 1991 from S.K. Jain's employee J.K. Jain. CBI which was probing the matter was alleged to have been sitting in for over two years. The Supreme Court's response was also slow for a year. It was in November 1994 when a new bench headed by Justice J.S. Verma began castigating the government and its agencies for not following up the diary entries vigorously that the case began to move further. The Court made CBI Director Vijya Rama Rao personally responsible for the Hawala probe requiring him to report periodically to the court. The Supreme Court virtually dictated terms to the CBI, in this case. In other words telling the executive how to do its job. It was the assertive role played by Supreme Court and especially by Justice J.S. Verma that in early 1996 explosion charge sheets were filed against ministers and senior politicians which rocked the nation and the political establishment. Parliament remained paralyzed for several days as opposition demanded the Prime Minister P.V. Narasimha Rao should resign.

Supreme Court also played the same assertive role in **Chandraswami case.** On a PIL filed by lawyer Anukul Pradhan, the Court stopped Chandraswami from going abroad in October 1993. The petition was filed against the backdrop of the Union Minister Rajesh Pilot's controversial letter asking the CBI to arrest Chandraswami in connection with the Bombay blasts case following Babloo Srivastava's allegation that the god man had met mafia don Dawood Ibrahim in Dubai. The petition also served to focus attention on the inaction of the CBI and Enforcement Directorate in cases pending against. Chandraswami for years including the **St. Kitts Forgery case** in which Prime Minister P.V. Narasimha Rao figured prominently. Ultimately, Chandraswami and his associate Kailash Nath were arrested on May 2, 1996 by CBI officials in pursuant to a non-bailable warrant by CMM (Delhi) for cheating NRI Lakhubhai Pathak of one million American Dollars in 1983.The accused had been on bail since February 17,1988 in this case. Former Prime Minister Narasimha Rao was also issued summons on June 9, 1996 in this case under Sections 420 and 120(8) of IPC on an evidence given by Pathak that he had given the said money to Chandraswami on the assurance of P.V. Narasimha Rao, then Union Foreign Minister that his 'work would be done' (contract for a supply of newsprint). Mr. Pathak had lodged a complaint at the Indian High Commission in London in 1987. Commenting on the filing of this case as observation was made in an editorial article in *Tribune* dated June 11, 1996. The case would have never seen the light of day but for the judicial activism of the Apex Court in making the CBI and other investigating agencies directly answerable to it.

Another act of judicial activism was pronounced on June 11, 1996 in the **Jharkhand Mukti Morcha MPs Pay Off case** when a two judges vacation bench of the Supreme Court comprising Judges A.S. Anand and Majumdar upheld the Delhi High Court order asking the CBI to file a fresh F.I.R. in the bribery case relating to four JMM MPs (Suraj Mandal, Shibu Soren, Shalindra Mahato and Simon Marandi) of the Lok Sabha (the complaint was that Rs. 1.10 crore was given to the four JMM MPs to save Rao's government on July 28, 1993, for the vote of confidence). The Supreme Court's dismissal of the CBI's special leave petition stating that "at this stage we find no need to intervene" was a bold step dictating terms to CBI to mention all the names referred to in a complaint filed as PIL before Delhi High Court. Among the names which figured were former PM Narasimha Rao; Congress leader, V.C. Shukla; Satish Sharma; Ajit Singh; and Bhajan Lal; and industrialist Lalit Suri. In yet another case of large scale corruption in the allotment of subsidized housing in Delhi to Government employees Supreme Court intervened. Eviction notices were served to 72 VIPs and the then Urban Development Minister Sheela Kaul was dropped from the Cabinet.

In yet another **Income Tax PIL case** filed by consumer rights activist H.D. Shourie, the Supreme Court directed all the political parties to fulfil their statutory requirement to maintain audited accounts and file annual returns—disclosing the quantum and sources of income. If they do not respond to the courts order, they run the risk of getting their properties attached, or worse, being barred from contesting elections. All these cases are expected to have a bearing on the political process. The former Secretary General of Lok Sabha Subhash Kashyap says, **"The Income Tax case** against political parties will ensure that the question of accountability is not confined to individuals/being prosecuted in connection with the **Hawala case.** Thanks to the Supreme Court's actions even those who never thought about the sources of political funds will now start questioning". By subjecting the political process to a judicial scrutiny more intense than ever before, the Supreme

Court, in the process, has also begun to get a fresh agenda for political reform. A noted social worker Anna Hazarre says "This will be an important step in cleansing the system and ultimately forcing the unholy trinity of politicians, businessmen and bureaucrats to be more transparent and display greater accountability in their decisions and dealings".

But on the other hand some legal experts say that the judiciary cannot forever bear the burden of systemic inadequacy, i.e., the lack of autonomous investigating agencies. The various corruption cases highlight the urgent need to correct the systemic flaw. As long as the investigating agencies like the CBI remain government controlled, the Supreme Court may have to intervene to give legitimacy to the Indian polity and the world's democracy. However, the United Front government intended to limit this judicial activism (PIL cases) through a legislation or by adding a new chapter to the Civil Procedure Code which would define admissibility (parameters) of PIL cases. This has not been possible because of opposition from left and BJP. In June 1996, the government was seriously considering to introduce such a bill. The government views that the Judiciary has transgressed from its traditional role. But the Supreme Court continues to actively participate in the political process. It has heard several PIL cases and has given valuable directions. Recently (September 12, 2003) the Chief Justice of India V. N. Khare reminded the Narendra Modi Government of Gujarat of its "Raj Dharama" in **Best Bakery Kand case** and directed the Government to punish the guilty and do justice to the riot victims or it should quit. In yet another historic judgement (September 16, 2003) the Supreme Court told the Union Government that it could not sell BPCL and HPCL (Oil Undertakings) without the approval of Parliament thus paralyzing the government's policy of disinvestment.

Supreme Court is the final interpreter of the Constitution and thus, can take the Constitution to the side it likes. In the words of Alladi Krishna Swami Ayyar, "The future evolution of the Constitution will thus depend to large extent upon the work of the Supreme Court and the direction given to it by the court". The former Attorney General of India Shri M.C. Seetalvad had observed that, "The writ of the Supreme Court will run over the territory of over two million square miles, inhabited by a population of 330 million (now 960 million). It can truly be said that the jurisdiction and powers of this court in their nature and extent are wider than those exercised by the highest court of any country in the Commonwealth or by the Supreme Court of U.S.A."

In India the Supreme Court has the power of Judicial Review under which it sees that the laws passed by the Parliament and the State Legislatures and the executive orders and ordinances issued by Union and State executives are in consonance with the Constitution or not and in case these are not, it can declare them unconstitutional. Thus, it maintains the supremacy of the Constitution.

For the first time, the interpretation of the power of judicial review was made by Justice Marshall of American Supreme Court in 1803 in the case of **Marbury** v. **Madison.** According to Justice Marshall, "Judicial review is examination by the courts in cases actually brought before them of Legislative statutes and executive and administrative acts to determine whether or not they are prohibited by a written constitution or are in excess of powers granted by it".

Basis of the Power of Judicial Review in India

So many articles of the Constitution of India indirectly give the power of the judicial review to the judiciary such as—

1. ***Protection of Fundamental Rights***: Article 13 (2), makes the provision that the state shall not make any law which takes away or abridges the rights conferred in the Chapter of Fundamental Rights and any law made in contravention of this clause shall to the extent of contravention be void. Article 32 of the Constitution provides to the citizens the right to constitutional remedies and the Supreme Court can issue writs for the protection of Fundamental Rights.
2. ***Original Jurisdiction of the Supreme Court***: Article 13 of the Constitution enunciates the original jurisdiction of the Supreme Court under which it has the power to

settle disputes between the Centre and the States and the Supreme Court decides such disputes according to the articles of the Constitution.

3. ***Legislative Jurisdiction of the Centre and the States* :** Article 146, fixes the legislative jurisdiction of the Centre and the States and the division of subjects is made in the Seventh Schedule of the Constitution. The Supreme Court ensures that there is no arbitrary encroachment by both Centre and the States in the legislative jurisdiction of each other.
4. ***Limitation to alter the Basic Structure of the Constitution*:** In 1973, in the judgement of the **Case of Keshwanand Bharti** v. **The State of Kerala,** the Supreme Court put a limitation on the power of the Parliament that it cannot amend the basic structure of the Constitution. In 1980, the Supreme Court while giving judgement in the **Case of Minerva Mills** v. **The Union of India** rejected clauses 4 and 45 of 42nd Constitutional Amendment Act on the ground that it violates the basic structure of the Constitution.
5. ***Oath by the Judges to Protect the Constitution*:** Under Article 124 (6) of the Constitution while assuming office, the judges take an oath to uphold the Constitution. Therefore, the judges are bound to reject any such law which goes against the Constitution.

Scope of the Judicial Review

The following subjects come under the scope of the judicial review:

(i) Constitutional Amendments,

(ii) Laws passed by the Union Parliament and the State Legislatures,

(iii) Ordinances issued by the State and Union Executive,

(iv) Executive orders issued by the State and Union Executive, and

(v) The treaties entered into by the Union Government with other countries.

Limitations of the Powers of Judicial Review : The Supreme Court cannot make use of its power of judicial review in the following subjects—

(i) Laws included in the 9th Schedule of the Constitution,
(ii) Decision of the Speaker on Money Bill,
(iii) The detention of a person according to the procedure established by law,
(iv) The contracts made with the Princes of Princely States which were kept beyond the jurisdiction of the Supreme Court,
(v) Laws passed on the delimitation of the constituencies,
(vi) Political controversies between the Centre and the States,
(vii) Disputes related to the distribution of the water of inter-State rivers.

Power of the Judicial Review is the Part of the Basic Structures of the Constitution— In March 1997, in a judgement the Supreme Court made it clear that the powers of Judicial Review of the Supreme Court and High Courts under the Articles 32, 226 and 227 are part of the structure of the Constitution and these cannot be amended even by constitutional amendment.

Use of the Power of Judicial Review

The Supreme Court has made use of its power of judicial review in many cases such as:

1. ***Judicial Review and Disputes between Centre and the States***: To settle the disputes between Centre and the States is the jurisdiction of the Supreme Court. While giving its judgement in the case of **The State of West Bengal** v. **The Union of India**, the Chief Justice Sinha made it very clear that the division of the legislative and executive powers between the Centre and the States did not mean that the State Government were independent and the Parliament had no right to pass

law to acquire the property of the States. In this case the Bengal Government had contended that the Union Government could not acquire the land where coal mines were situated. But the Supreme Court had rejected this contention of the Bengal Government.

On April 30, 1977, the Acting President Shri B.D. Jatti dissolved the State Legislatures of nine States. The State governments of the six States challenged decision in the Supreme Court. But the Supreme Court rejected their plea on the ground that to remain the members of Legislative Assembly was not their Fundamental Right. It is their political right and the Article 356 of the Constitution makes the provision to impose President's Rule in the States.

2. ***Judicial Review and Fundamental Rights*:** The Supreme Court had made use of the power of judicial review many times for protection of the Fundamental Rights. The Supreme Court rejected the Bank Nationalisation Act 1970 and the executive order to abolish the Privy Purses on the ground that both these violated the fundamental rights. Through its judgement given in April 1973, the Supreme Court declared unconstitutional Clause 17 (A) of the Internal Security Act 1971. This clause had made the Provision to detain a person from three months to two years without getting the advice of the advisory board.. .

   The Supreme Court through an important judgement delivered on April 29, 1973 rejected some parts of Article 31(c) which was included by 25th Amendment.This amendment had made provision to keep certain laws passed with the view to enforce Directive Principles, beyond the purview of the judicial review. While giving its judgement on the writ petitions filed by St. Xavier College Society and other minority managed institutions, the Supreme Court rejected six clauses of the Gujarat University Act 1949 (amended in 1973) on the ground that these violated the Cultural and Educational Right of the minorities granted under Articles 29 and 30 of the Constitution.

3. ***Judicial Review and the Basic Structure of the Constitution***: In 1973, while giving judgement in the case of **Keshwanand Bharti** v. **The Kerala State,** the Supreme Court accepted the right of the Parliament to amend the Fundamental Rights, but it put a limitation on the Parliament not to amend the basic structure of the Constitution. In 1980, in the judgement of the case of **Minerva Mills** v. **The Indian Union,** the Supreme Court rejected clauses 4 and 55 of 42nd Amendment on the ground that these violated the basic structure of the Constitution.
4. ***Judicial Review and Right to Property***: In 1951, according to the decision of the **Shankri Parsad** v. **The Government of India case** the Supreme Court justified the First Amendment of the Constitution which was made with a view to abolish *zamindari.* But in the famous **Golak Nath case** of 1967, the Supreme Court again put a limitation on the Parliament and prohibited it from making any amendment in Fundamental Rights. This limitation was abolished in 1973 through the judgement in **Keshwanand Bharti case.** In 1979, through 44th Amendment, the right to property was made an ordinary legal right and this has ended all the controversies related with right to property.
5. ***Judicial Review and Anti-Defection Law***: In 1985 after reviewing the constitutional validity of the Anti-Defection Law (52 Constitutional Amendment), the Supreme Court through its judgement delivered on November 12, 1992 upheld the law. But the Supreme Court rejected the article of the Anti-Defection Law under which the decision of the Speaker declaring any member ineligible from being the member of the house, was kept beyond the jurisdiction of the Supreme Court.
6. ***Judicial Review and Reservation***: On November 16, 1992 in a historic decision the Supreme Court upheld the legitimacy of the ordinance issued by V.P. Singh Government on August 13, 1990 reserving 27 per cent seats in government services for other backward classes. But along with, the Supreme Court put a

condition that the socially advanced persons of other backward classes shall not get this benefit. The Supreme Court also said that the advantage of reservation shall be given only at the time of recruitment and not at the time of promotion.

7. ***Judicial Review and Constitutional Emergency***: The Supreme Court in its judgement delivered on March 11, 1904 upheld the dismissal of the governments of Madhya Pràdesh, Himachal Pradesh and Rajasthan. We must remember that these State governments were dismissed after the demolition, of disputed site of Babri Masjid and Ram Janam Bhoomi in December 1992. But before this dismissal of the Nagaland Government in 1988, Karnataka Government of Janta Dal in 1989 and Meghalaya Government in 1991 was declared unconstitutional. On February 21, 1998 Shri Romesh. Bhandari the Governor of Uttar Pradesh dismissed the government of Shri Kalyan Singh and appointed Shri Jagdambika Pal the Chief Minister of Uttar Pradesh, but both claimed majority support in Legislative Assembly. To resolve this constitutional crisis, the Supreme Court through an extraordinary judgement asked, to 'hold composite floor test' to ascertain the majority support in a specially convened session of the Legislative Assembly.

8. ***Judicial Review and Poll Reforms Act***: Through a judgement delivered on March 13, 2003, the three judges bench of the Supreme Court while declaring unconstitutional the Representation of People (Amendment) Act 2002 said that the voters have Fundamental Right to know about the criminal antecedents of their candidates. The Bench further held that the Right to Information of voters was vitally linked to their Right to Freedom of Expression guaranteed under Article 19 of the Constitution and the amendment of People's Representation Act curtailed it, the bench also observed that the Legislature cannot declare that the law declared by the Supreme

Court was not binding. While justifying valid its order of May 2, 2002, the Supreme Court directed the Election Commission to issue fresh order for the implementation of these for all the coming elections.

So, from time to time, the Supreme Court has made use of the power of judicial review to protect the Constitution.

Utility of Judicial Review

The utility or the use of Judicial Review can be divided as follows:

1. ***Check on the Misuse of Power*** : This power of the Supreme Court has made it difficult for the executive and legislature to misuse their powers as it can declare unconstitutional their wrong actions.
2. ***Helpful to maintain the Supremacy of the Constitution***: With the use of the power of judicial review, the Supreme Court also acts as watch dog and guardian of the Constitution and thus maintains its supremacy.
3. ***Helpful in the Growth of the Constitution***: With the use of this power, the Supreme Court has made the Constitution adaptable according to the changing situations and has also brought dynamism in the Constitution.
4. ***Protection of Federal System***: The judiciary has also checked the arbitrary interference of both, the Centre and the States in each others jurisdiction and this way has saved the federal system in India.
5. ***Balance among different organs of Government***: With the use of this power, the Supreme Court has also maintained balance among the different organs of the government by not allowing unnecessary interference.
6. ***Protection of Fundamental Rights and Liberties***: Many times with the use of this power of judicial review the Supreme Court has ensured the fundamental rights and liberties of the citizens.

7. ***Proper interpretation of the Constitution***: From time to time the Supreme Court has given the proper interpretation of the constitution.

However, detractors of Judicial Review criticise it on the following grounds :

1. ***No clear mention in the Constitution***: The critics are of the opinion that the very use of the power of the judicial review by the Supreme Court is unconstitutional as the Constitution of India does not make clear mention of this power anywhere.
2. ***Against Democratic Principles***: To reject the laws made by the people's representatives, by the judges nominated by executive, is against the democratic principles. In democracy the supreme power lies with the people and the Parliament is their representative body.
3. ***It lowers the Prestige of the Parliament*** : This power of the judiciary lowers the prestige of the Parliament and State Legislatures as the laws passed by these bodies can be rejected by the judiciary.
4. ***It makes the Parliament and State Legislatures Irresponsible***: The power of the judicial review makes the Parliament and the State Legislatures irresponsible also as they know that even correct laws made by them can be declared unconstitutional by the judiciary.
5. ***It causes Delay***: This power also causes delay in making the evaluation of the constitutional amendments and the laws. For example, the Clauses 4 and 55 of the 42nd Amendment were declared unconstitutional by the Supreme Court in 1980. So, this causes delay in the enforcement of a particular law.
6. **Deadlock between Judiciary and Executive.** In India, the use of the power of judicial review by the judiciary, has become the cause of confrontation between the executive and the judiciary which famous journalist Shri Kuldip Nayyar has called 'Unfortunate

Confrontation'. Such a confrontation proves harmful for the administration and the nation.

7. **It is Reactionary.** The critics are of the opinion that the judges of the Supreme Court come from a particular background and they are not aware of the interests of a common man. So, many decisions given by them are reactionary. For example, their judgements in *Golak Nath* (1967), **Abolition of Privy Purses** (1969) and **Bank Nationalisation** (1970) cases were reactionary.
8. **Possibility of Judicial Despotism.** Critics are also of the opinion that the use of the power of judicial review by the judiciary also encourages judicial despotism, which is not right.
9. **One Man's Dictatorship.** In India, the decisions are made with majority and generally the decisions have been made with the majority of one judge. For example, the judgements in the **Golak Nath case** and in the Transfer of Judges were made with the proportion of 6 : 5 and 4 : 3. So, it is clear that the judgements are based on the majority of one judge and some people term it "One Judge's Dictatorship." Shri Nath Pai a former Member of Parliament has said, "The destiny of India depends upon one Judge and that is my quarrel".

After giving arguments for and against the use of the power of the judicial review, we come to the conclusion that its use can be both useful as well as harmful. So, the judiciary should make use of this power with great care keeping in mind the general welfare of the people.

Suggestions for Future: While making use of this power, the judiciary should keep in mind the following points:

(i) Constitutional Amendment is a political matter and like the American Supreme Court, the Indian Supreme Court should also make use of this power after great contemplation and with great care,

(ii) The decisions should be made with 2/3 majority,

(iii) While making use of this power the judges should keep in mind the changing social and economic conditions, and

(iv) The Parliament should have the right to amend such laws on which the power of judicial review has been used.

Independence of Judiciary

Independence of Judiciary is one of the cornerstones of democratic political system because only an independent judiciary:

(i) can protect the rights and liberties of the individuals,
(ii) can maintain the supremacy of the Constitution,
(iii) can rightly interpret the Constitution,
(iv) can maintain the faith of the people in the administration,
(v) can maintain balance between the Centre and the States, and
(vi) can make the administration responsible.

The independence of judiciary implies three essential conditions. **First,** the judiciary must be free from the encroachments of other departments of government. **Second,** the judgements of judiciary must be free from the onslaughts of executive and legislative interference. Last, the judges must be free to do justice without fear or favour. In a representative form of government, it is required that the judges must remain aloof from the influence of party politics that has its full and unrestricted sway in the spheres of executive and legislative departments. L.S. Amery has rightly said, "The independence of judiciary loses all meaning if any judicial decision unpleasing to the party leaders can at once be reversed by fresh or even retrospective legislation". The Constitution of India has made the following arrangements to maintain the independence of the judiciary—

Impartial Method of Appointment: Of all the methods of appointments, the appointment of the judges by executive on the basis of fixed qualifications, is considered the best. According to Article 24 of the Constitution of India, the judges of the Supreme Court are appointed by the President out of the persons who fulfil the qualifications mentioned in the Constitution. Apart from this, in the appointment of the Chief Justice, the President consults the judges of the Supreme Court and High Courts and in the appointment of the judges, he consults the Chief Justice of India.

Judicial Review

In India according to David Selbourne: "The Judiciary is attacked in the name of the sovereignty of Parliament, while sovereignty of Parliament is attacked in the name of democracy and the people; while 'democracy and people' are being attacked in the name of 'national discipline' and the struggle against conspiracy and subversions"

Meaning of Judicial Review

"Judicial Review" indicates institutional arrangements by which courts can declare the constitutional validity of the laws passed by the legislature or the actions taken by the administrative and the executive authorities. It is essentially an American institution and is based on the simple logic that the Constitution is supreme and confers limited powers to the executive and the legislature and if they overstep their limitations then the judiciary must restrain them.

Judicial Review in India

Though there was a Judicial Review in India under the Government of India Act 1935, yet its scope was quite limited. At that time the scope of Judicial Review was limited to the interpretation of the provision of the Government of India Act 1935 which provided for the distribution of powers between the Centre and the Provinces. Since the present Constitution not only provides for the distribution of powers between the

Union and the States but also has a chapter on Fundamental Rights, hence, the scope of Judicial Review has been widened under the present Constitution. Now it extends to three principal areas, that is (i) it preserves the constitutional balance between the Union and the State governments; (ii) it maintains the balance between Executive and the Legislature; and (iii) it defends the Fundamental Rights under the present Constitution. Moreover, the courts have been given the power of Judicial Review in unmistakable terms. The Constitution prohibits legislation which violates Fundamental Rights, and also empowers the Supreme Court and High Courts to issue various types of writs in order to ensure that the Fundamental Rights are not vitiated, and the Union and the State Government do not overstep the jurisdiction prescribed by the Constitution for them by the Seventh Schedule. In a way the Judicial Review in India has a more direct basis than in USA because in USA Judicial Review has been "inferred" but in India it has been "conferred"

Restrictions on Judicial Review

While providing for a Judicial Review in the Constitution the framers were very cautious and keeping in view the "Judicial activism" of the Supreme Court in USA on the basis of 'due process clause', which resulted in a headlong clash between Franklin D. Roosevelt and the Court, and the Court packing controversy they replaced this phrase by "except according to the procedure established by law", or "save by authority of law". This phrase has been used in Article XXXI of the Japanese Constitution of 1946 and is more specific and exact? This shows that keeping in view the American experience, there was some element of distrust in the judiciary right from the beginning. They were not certain about the attitude of the Judiciary towards the socioeconomic justice promised to the people by the Preamble and the Directive Principles of the State Policy. Hence, they wanted to restrict the scope of Judicial Review. For this purpose certain restrictions on Judicial Review were incorporated in the Constitution itself. The matters such as the advice of the Council of Ministers to the President and the

Governor, the manner of authentication and execution of orders of the President and the Governor, Privileges of members of Parliament and State Legislatures, validity of the proceedings and conduct of proceedings in Parliament and State Legislatures, delimitation of constituencies, publication of substantially true report of the proceedings of Parliament and State Legislatures are beyond the purview of the Judicial Review. Even the President and the Governors so long as they are in office are beyond the purview of Judicial Review for the exercise of their powers.

Efforts to Curb Judicial Review

Because of the rigid attitude of the Supreme Court towards property rights in general and Fundamental Rights *vis-á-vis* Directive Principles of State Policy in particular, the Constitution has been amended a number of times and some of these amendments curbed the power of Judicial Review. For example, the statutes placed in the Ninth Schedule were excluded from the purview of Judicial Review by the First Constitution Amendment Act of 1951. By May 1988, there were as many as 202 enactments in this Schedule. In the **Minerva Mill case,** however, the Supreme Court held that any act included in the Ninth Schedule after its judgement in the Fundamental Rights case on April 24, 1973 would not get the protection of Article 3B and can be struck down if it violated the basic structure of the Constitution. As many as 59 Acts were either added or amended in this Schedule after 1973.

After the decisions of the Supreme Court in the Golak Nath (1967), Bank Nationalisation and in Privy Purses (1970) cases, the Supreme Court was under attack and when Mrs. Indira Gandhi came into power after the Fifth Lok Sabha elections of 1971, the Constitution was amended frequently and three of these amendments tried to curb the powers of Judicial Review. For example, the 24th Amendment of the Constitution withdrew Constitutional Amendments from the purview of Judicial Review. This was done by providing that the word "law" in Article 13 does not include "Constitutional Amendments". This was done in order to nullify the decision of the Supreme Court in the **Golak Nath case** in which the Supreme Court declared that the constitutional amendment is a "law" as mentioned in Article 13 and, hence, Fundamental Rights cannot be amended.

The Twenty-fifth Constitution Amendment Act 1971 further restricted the powers of the Judicial Review. This amendment added Article 31C which excluded Judicial Review about the laws containing declaration giving effect to the implementation of Directive Principles of State Policy mentioned in clauses (b) and (c) of Article 39. A part of this Amendment was, however, declared as null and void in 1973 in the **Keshvanand Bharti case.** In this case the Supreme Court declared that the basic structure of the Constitution cannot be amended.

Thereafter the Constitution was again amended in 1975 and the 39th Amendment excluded from the Judicial purview, the election of the President, Vice President, Prime Minister and the Speaker. Clauses (4) and (5) of this Amendment were again declared as null and void in the **Indira Gandhi** v. **Raj Narain** on the ground that it violated the principle of equality before law.

Since the Supreme Court was not prepared to accept curbs on Judicial Review which were against the basic scheme of the Constitution, hence, during the Emergency Parliament passed the 42nd Amendment of the Constitution which drastically curbed the powers of Judicial Review. These curbs were as follows:

(a) the Fundamental Rights mentioned in Articles 14, 19, 31 were made subordinate to all the Directive Principles of State Policy by amending Article 31C and Judicial Review was excluded by providing that no law giving effect to the policy of State towards Directive Principles of State Policy shall be void on the ground that it is inconsistent with, or takes away, or abridges, any of the Rights conferred by Articles 14, 19 and 31;

(b) the constitutional validity of the State laws was not to be considered by the Supreme Court under Article 32, (Article 32A);

(c) the Supreme Court was to have exclusive jurisdiction. Only with regard to questions as to the constitutional validity of Central laws (Article 131A);

(d) the constitutional invalidity of the Central. or State laws was to be decided by a minimum number of seven judges, by a majority of not less than two-thirds of the judges sitting for the purpose (Article 144A);

(e) powers of the High Court to issue writs of various types for the redressal of grievances were to be exercised if the injury was of a substantial nature or if there was a substantial failure of justice;

(f) constitutional validity of Central laws was not to, be considered by the High Court under Article 226;

(g) the minimum number of judges of the High Court to determine the constitutional validity of the State law was to be five and they should declare the law invalid by two-thirds of the judges sitting for the purpose. If the number of judges in the High Court was less than five, then all the judges must sit together and unanimously hold it constitutionally invalid;

(h) the satisfaction of the 'President to declare internal/external Emergency, failure of constitutional machinery in a State, and Financial Emergency under Articles 352, 356 and 360 respectively was excluded from the purview of Judicial Review;

(i) constitutional amendments, including amendments of the Fundamental Rights made in the past or to be made in the future was also excluded from the Judicial Review and Parliament was given unlimited power of amending the Constitution. This amendment was made in order to nullify the "Basic structure" decision in **Keshvanand Bharti's case.**

This amendment almost clipped the wings of the High Court and the Supreme Court and drastically reduced their power of Judicial Review. However, when the Janata Government came into power the curbs on Judicial Review mentioned from (b) to (g) were repealed by the 43rd Amendment of the Constitution passed in 1978. The curbs mentioned in (h) was removed by the 44th Amendment of the Constitution. The curbs mentioned in (a) were declared as null and void in the **Minerva Mill case** of 1980, which means Parliament does not have unlimited power of amendment and it cannot change the basic structure of the Constitution.

This shows that right from the **Golak Nath case** in 1967 Parliament has been trying to curb the power of Judicial Review and the Supreme Court has successfully resisted it so far.

Judicial Review of Constitutional Amendment

Just as in USA the decision of the Supreme Court in **Marbury** vs. **Madison** is very important because the origin of Judicial Review in USA is attributed to it; similarly the decision of the Supreme Court in the **Keshvanand Bharti's case** is very important in the judicial history of India because in this case the Supreme Court held that the Constitution has a certain basic structure which cannot be amended. The implication of this 'basic structure' theory is that Parliament has a limited amending power and the constitutional amendments are subject to Judicial Review. Until 1981, the Supreme Court had declared some of the clauses of 17th, 25th, 39th and 42nd Amendments of the Constitution as null and void. These decisions of the Supreme Court were criticized by some Members of Parliament. In a way the Congress Party led by Mrs. Indira Gandhi did not accept the limitation on the amending power of Parliament on the basis of the basic structure decision given by the Supreme Court in the **Keshvanand Bharti's case.** In fact, as early as 1975, when the decision of the election appeal of Mrs. Gandhi had been pending before the Supreme Court after arguments have been concluded, the Attorney General applied that a larger bench should be constituted to reconsider the decision in the **Fundamental Rights case.** The application was granted and a bench of 13 judges was constituted for that purpose. However, after hearing arguments for two days, the bench was dissolved which suggests that the bench was not in favour of reconsidering the **Fundamental Rights case.** The Government, however, may again ask the Supreme Court to constitute another bench of 13 judges to review that case.

The "basic structure" decision of the Supreme Court has created tension between the then ruling group in Parliament and the Supreme Court. It is important to note that in USA, in the **Coleman** v. **Miller case** Justice Black said that the constitutional amendment, process is not subject to Judicial Review, however, in this very case the Supreme Court held that the State cannot rescind its ratification if it has once agreed to the amendment and communicated its decision to the Secretary of State. However, the state can ratify an amendment even if it has rejected it on an earlier occasion. These pronouncements of the Supreme Court prove that even in USA Judicial Review is applicable to constitutional amendments.

Hence, the decision in the **Keshvanand Bharti's case** that the Parliament has a limited powers to amend the Constitution is correct. The temporary majority in Parliament otherwise, would play a havoc with the Constitution. It is important to note that in Italy in 1921 and in Germany in 1933, it was the Parliament that voted the dictators to power. Even in India the 39th Amendment of the Constitution can be cited as a proof in this respect. "Can the repudiation of the accountability go further than the statement of objects and reasons given for 39th Amendment which sought to justify immunity to the acts of the Prime Minister while in office and deprived the courts of their jurisdiction to try the election petition in which she herself was a guilty party in the first instance?"

Commenting on the 39th Amendment of the Constitution, L.M. Seervai observes that "when in the past (Golak Nath) Parliament's unlimited power of Constitutional Amendment was questioned, it was done with the fear that such power might be abused. Even in the **Keshvanand case** this was the basis of attack. But in the election case, the abuse of power was no longer a hypothetical possibility. It was no longer possible to speak of the air of unreality for Article 329(4) supplied the reality".

Hence, in the **Minerva Mill case,** by striking down clauses 4 and 5 of Article 368, the Constitution Bench of the

Supreme Court has rightly restored the doctrine of "Judicial Review" which the Constitution (42nd) Amendment Act 1976, had very substantially curtailed. By returning to the judiciary, the power to examine Constitution Amending Statutes made by Parliament, the Supreme Court has again placed the doctrine of *ultra vires* on a very high judicial pedestal. In sum, the situation is back to where it was when the Supreme Court pronounced on the famous **Keshvanand Bharti** v. **the State of Kerala** case in 1973 and struck down the second part of Article 31C which had been introduced in the Constitution by the 25th Amendment of 1971.

Judicial Review Frequent Cause of Constitutional Amendment

Because of the rigid and inflexible attitude adopted by the Supreme Court in defending Fundamental Rights in general and the Right to Property in particular *vis-à-vis* the Directive Principles of State Policy, the courts came under fire both in Parliament and outside. Immediately after the promulgation of the Constitution on 26th January, 1950, some of the State Legislatures had passed the Zamindari Abolition Legislation which were challenged on the ground that it violated right to property. Some of the State High Courts upheld the Legislation, whereas the other High Courts including the Patna High Court, declared them as null and void, and as a result thereof the First Amendment of the Constitution was passed in 1951 which added Articles 31A and 31B. Article 31B provided that Acts and Regulations specified in the Ninth Schedule shall not be void on the ground that they violate Fundamental Rights. This was done in order to validate certain land laws which abolished Zamindari. Thereafter, the land legislation was questioned on the ground, that the compensation given was not on the market rate and the court upheld this contention. Because of this decision the Fourth Constitution Amendment Act (1955) had to be passed which provided that a law which compulsorily acquired property for a public purpose will not be questioned on the ground that the compensation provided by law is not adequate.

However, in spite of this amendment the court held that compensation means fair compensation which means compensation at market rate and as a result thereof the 25th Amendment of the Constitution was passed in 1972 which deleted the word "compensation" and substituted the word "amount" in its place. It further provided that for the implementation of the Directive Principles mentioned in Clauses (b) and (c) of Article 39 the Fundamental Rights mentioned in Articles 14, 19 and 31 can be violated. After this Amendment was upheld in the **Keshvanand Bharti case,** the 42nd Amendment of the Constitution provided that for the implementation of any of the Directive Principles of State Policy, the Fundamental Rights mentioned in Articles 14, 19 and 31 can be violated. It means Articles 14, 19 and 31 were subordinated to all the Directive Principles of State Policy, and this was a dangerous situation. Hence, the Right to Property has to be deleted from the chapter on Fundamental Rights by the 44th Amendment of the Constitution passed in 1978. It may be mentioned here that changes made in Article 31C by the 42nd Amendment Act were declared as null and void in the **Minerva Mill case.**

This shows that the attitude of the Supreme Court towards Right to Property has been very rigid till 1972. In fact, in order to defend the right to property it even did not observe the doctrine of 'Stare decisis'.

For example, in the **Shankri Prasad** and **Sajjan Singh cases,** the Supreme Court held that the Fundamental Rights are amendable but in the **Golak Nath case** these decisions were overruled by a narrow majority of 6 to 5. The decision of the **Golak Nath case** was again overruled in the **Keshvanand Bharti's case.** In this case, the Supreme Court held that Parliament can amend the Fundamental Rights but not the basic structure of the Constitution. No doubt there is nothing in the Constitution of India which prevents the Supreme Court from changing its earlier decision. This is also the practice of the Supreme Court in USA as well. However, it should be done only if it is convinced that earlier decisions have been wrong and had a harmful effect on the general interest of public.

Judicial Review of Parliamentary Proceedings

The Constitution provides that the proceedings of the Parliament and State Legislature cannot be called in question on the ground of any alleged irregularity of procedure. It means Judicial Review has been excluded if there is an irregularity of the Procedure but not in the case of illegality of the proceedings. For example, whenever a resolution for the removal of the Speaker is to be moved the Constitution provides that a notice of 14 days should be given in order to move a resolution for the removal of the Speaker of the Lok Sabha *v.* Legislative Assembly. However, in Tamil Nadu, when K.A. Mathialagan, the then Speaker was removed in 1972 without giving 14 days notice, it was challenged in Madras High Court on the ground that it violated Article 179 of the Constitution. The Court, however, considered it as an irregularity of the procedure and refused to interfere with the Proceedings of the Assembly. However, if an ordinance is issued at the time when the Assembly is in session it will be illegal and, hence, the Courts would declare it as null and void.

Judicial Review and Parliamentary Privileges

According to the Constitution, the members of Parliament and the State Legislatures have certain privileges and unless they are defined by law, they are those which were enjoyed before the coming into force of Section 15 of the Constitution (Forty-fourth Amendment) Act, 1978. If someone violates these privileges, Parliament and the State Legislatures can punish to the extent of committing him to imprisonment for its contempt. In that case if the imprisoned person approaches the High Court or the Supreme Court that his Fundamental Rights has been violated, the Courts can examine the legality of the case. If the Legislature, while imprisoning a person for the contempt of its privileges, commits certain irregularity in the procedure, the Court will not interfere. However, if the procedure is illegal, then the Courts may interfere. This opinion was given by the Supreme Court in its advisory opinion in the **Keshav Singh case.**

Judicial Review of Ordinary Laws/Ordinances

Ordinary laws (laws other than the Constitutional Amendments) can be declared as null and void by the High Court and the Supreme Court, if:

(a) they violate any of the Fundamental Rights; and
(b) they are not in accordance with the lists mentioned in the Seventh Schedule which demarcate jurisdiction of the Parliament and State Legislatures.

Between 1950 and 1980 Parliament passed 1977 acts excluding Constitutional Amendments and out of them the Supreme Court invalidated laws passed on 22 occasions.

Like ordinary laws, even the ordinances issued by the President or the Governors can also be declared as null, and void if they violate Fundamental Rights or are not in accordance with the lists mentioned in the Seventh Schedule. For example, Bank Nationalization Ordinance was issued by the Vice President, acting as President on July 19, 1969. This ordinance was declared as unconstitutional by the Supreme Court by a majority of 10 to 1 on February 10, 1970.

This shows that the powers of Judicial Review of the Supreme Court are very important in order to keep the rule of law and constitutionalism intact. The 39th and 42nd Constitution Amendment Acts prove this contention. But for the power of Judicial Review the basic structure of the Constitution would have been changed beyond recognition, and the rule of law would have been thrown to the winds. It must, however, be appreciated even those decisions of the Supreme Court which have drastically restricted the powers of the Executive have been so far accepted by the Government under protest but some of them such as Bank Nationalisation, Privy Purses, Golak Nath and Keshvanand Bharti cases have been characterised as reactionary, and used as vote-catching slogans by attacking the judiciary under protest. There has been no precedent until now of the type set by President Andrew

Jackson of the USA who said, "Well, John Marshall has made his decision; now let him enforce it. When that stage comes, the judiciary is helpless because the judiciary is the weakest of the three branches of the government. According to Justice Frankfurter, the judiciary "neither has the purse nor the sword and its authority consists of sustained public confidence in its decisions." Hence, according to Lord Bryce sometimes "to yield a little may be prudent, for the tree that cannot bend to the blast may be broken". But in India the politicians do not want that. In fact, some of the prominent spokesmen of the Congress party which has an absolute majority in Parliament "have made no secret of their aversion for the concept of Judicial Review and of their desire to clip the courts of their powers". They want only persons of pliable conscience to be appointed as judges. Expressing concern at attempts to undermine the judiciary, Mr. Khanna warned that constitutional anarchy and legal chaos could follow, once judges with pliable consciences and subservient to the wishes of the political wing of the State came to the seat of justice. And the first casualty would be the supremacy of the Constitution.

He said judges who inspired confidence must be on the bench so that those who entered court precincts believed that "justice here is administered with an even hand in any legal combat whatever might be the parties arrayed before it.

PIL a Weapon to be used With Care, says Supreme Court

"Easy access to justice no licence for filing frivolous petitions".

The Supreme Court has frowned on the practice of filing public interest litigation (PIL) petitions for personal interest. "Easy access to justice should not be misused as a licence to file misconceived and frivolous petitions", said a Bench consisting of Justices Arijit Pasayat and S.H. Kapadia.

The time had come to weed out petitions which, though titled PIL, were in essence something else. It was shocking that courts were flooded with a large number of the so-called PIL petitions, of which even a minuscule percentage could not legitimately be called PIL.

Writing the judgment, Justice Pasayat said, "though the parameters of PIL have been indicated by this court in a large number of cases, unmindful of the real intentions and objectives. High Courts are entertaining such petitions and wasting valuable judicial time which could otherwise be utilised for disposal of genuine cases".

In the PIL, official documents were being annexed without even indicating how the petitioner came to possess them, the Bench said, "It is depressing to note that on account of such trumpery proceedings initiated before the courts, innumerable days are wasted".

Laudable Concept

The judges said, "We spare no effort in fostering and developing the laudable concept of PIL and extending our long arm of sympathy to the poor, the ignorant, the oppressed and the needy whose fundamental rights are infringed and violated and whose grievances go unnoticed, unrepresented and unheard".

The Bench said: "While [there are] genuine litigants with legitimate grievances relating to civil matters involving properties worth hundreds of millions of rupees and substantial rights and criminal cases in which persons sentenced to death facing the gallows under untold agony and persons sentenced to life imprisonment and kept in incarceration for long years with the fond hope of getting into the courts and having their grievances redressed, the busybodies, meddlesome interlopers, wayfarers or officious interveners having absolutely no real public interest except personal gain or private profit get into courts by filing vexatious and frivolous petitions".

The Bench said, "PIL is a weapon which has to be used with great care and circumspection and the judiciary has to be extremely careful to see that behind the beautiful veil of public interest an ugly private malice, vested interest and, or publicity seeking is not lurking. It is to be used as an effective weapon in the armoury of law for delivering social justice to the citizens.

The attractive brand of PIL should not be allowed to be used for suspicious products of mischief". It should be aimed at redress of a genuine public wrong or injury and should not be publicity-oriented or founded on personal vendetta.

"The court must not allow its process to be abused for oblique considerations by masked phantoms who monitor at times from behind. Often they are actuated by a desire to win notoriety or cheap popularity. The petitions of such busybodies deserve to be thrown out by rejection on the threshold, and in appropriate cases with exemplary costs."

The Bench, in the instant case, allowed an appeal from an affected employee against a Punjab and Haryana High Court judgement entertaining a PIL petition in a service matter.

Parliament's Actions subject to Judicial Review

Status of an exalted constitutional functionary does not stop court from exercising judicial review—J. Venkatesan

The Supreme Court on October 17, 2011 held that the actions of Parliament are subject to Judicial Review and no absolute immunity can be claimed to usurp the jurisdiction of the court.

Writing the judgment upholding the expulsion of MPs in the cash-for-query scan. Chief Justice Sabharwal said: "Parliament is a co-ordinate organ and its news do deserve deference even while its acts are amenable to judicial scrutiny".

A five-judge Constitution Bench said: "Constitutional system of government abhors absolutism and it being the cardinal principal Constitution that no one, howsoever lofty, can claim to be the sole judge of the power given under the Constitution. Mere co-ordinate constitutional status, or even the status of an exalted constitutional functionary, does not disentitle this court from exercising its jurisdiction of judicial review of action which partakes the character of judicial or quasi-judicial decision."

The Bench said, "The fact that Parliament is an august body to co-ordinate constitutional position does not mean that there can be no judicially manageable standards to review exercise of its power. The Judicature is not prevented from scrutinizing the validity of the action of the legislature trespassing on the fundamental rights conferred on the citizens".

Rejecting the arguments of Union Government, the Bench said: "The contention that the exercise of privileges by legislatures cannot be decided against the touchstone of fundamental rights or the constitutional provisions is not correct".

The Bench said: "If a citizen, whether a non-member or a member of the legislature, complains that his fundamental rights under Article 20 or 21 had been contravened, it is the duty of this court to examine the merits of the said contention, especially when the impugned action entails civil consequences. There is no basis to chum of bar of exclusive cognizance or absolute to the parliamentary proceedings in Article 105 (3) of the Constitution".

The Bench said: "Ordinarily, the legislature, as a body, cannot be accused of having acted for an extraneous purpose or being actuated by caprice or malafide intention and that court will nut lightly presume abuse or misuse, giving allowance for the fact that the legislature is the best judge of such matters. But if in a given case, the allegations to such effect are made, the court may examine the validity of the said contention".

It further said, "The Rules which the legislature has to make for regulating its procedure and the conduct of its business have to be subject to the provisions of the Constitution. Mere availability of the Rules of Procedure and Conduct of Business is never a guarantee that they have been duly followed. The proceedings which may be tainted on account of substantive or gross illegality or unconstitutionality are not protected from judicial scrutiny".

On the contention that the Speaker of the Lok Sabha had pre-judged the issue by stating that the guilty would be punished, the Bench said: "It is clear that when he stated that nobody would be spared he was not immediately passing a judgement that the petitioners were guilty. He was only giving vent to his feeling on the subject of the proper course of action in the event of the inquiry confirming the facts that had been projected in the telecast. The guilt would come later. The fact that he had constituted an Inquiry Committee with members drawn also from parties in the Opposition rather goes to show that the resolve at that stage was to find the truth".

The Bench did not agree with the allegation of exercise of power or that the principles of natural justice were violated in the expulsion of the petitioners. On the contention that the quantum of punishment was disproportionate to the charges, it said: "That is a matter which must be left to the prerogative and sole discretion of the legislative body. We are of the considered view that the impugned constitution of the Lok Sabha and the Rajya Sabha cannot be questioned before as on the plea of proportionality".

Nariman Hails Verdict

Eminent jurist and senior lawyer Fali Nariman has welcomed the Supreme Court verdict, upholding the termination of the membership of 11 MPs in December 2005 saying, "the court has showed great judicial statesmanship. The court has delivered a judgment full of wisdom, very bold".

He said that the Judgement showed, "there is no area in the Constitution, which is beyond judicial review. The Constitution reposes final authority on the Supreme Court judicial review on all matters concerning the Constitution can be gone into by the Supreme Court not because it is supreme but the function is entrusted to it by the Constitution. I don't see any friction between the judiciary and the executive or parliament. Even if there is friction it shows a healthy democracy".

"Right to Represent People Not Absolute"

Legal Correspondent at New Delhi reported that the Supreme Court held that representing the people of a particular constituency was not an absolute right, and there could be certain limitations.

The majority judgement by Chief Justice Y.K. Sabharwal said: "Expulsion is related to the conduct of the member that lowers the dignity of the House, which may not have been necessarily known at the time of election. It is not a capricious exercise of the House, but an action to protect its dignity before the people of the country. This is also an integral aspect of our democratic set-up. In our view, the power of expulsion is not contrary to a democratic process. It is rather part of the guarantee of a democratic process".

The Bench said, "Expulsion is not a decision by a single person. It is a decision taken by the representatives of the rest of the country. The power of expulsion does not bar a member from standing for a re-election or the constituency from electing that member once again. We hold that the power of expulsion docs not violate the right of the constituency or any other democratic principles".

It rejected the argument of denial (or justice) imply because the inquiry was completed quickly. "It has become almost fashionable to raise the banner of 'justice delayed is justice denied' in case of protracted proceedings, and to argue 'justice hurried is justice buried' if the results are quick".

Expulsion Power is No Incidental Matter : Dissenting Judge

Legal Correspondent, New Delhi, reported that parliament has no power of cessation of membership by way of expulsion, Justice R.V. Raveendran said in his dissenting judgement in the Supreme Court in the cash-for-query scam case. "The Constitution makers have made detailed and specific provisions regarding the manner in which a person becomes a member of Parliament (elected/nominated), the duration for which he continues as a member and the manner in which he ceases to be a member and his seat becomes vacant. Therefore, neither the question of election or nomination nor is no hidden tenure, nor cessation/termination of membership covered by the express provisions in the Constitution can fall under 'other powers, privileges and immunities' of the House mentioned in Article 105 (3)." By no stretch of imagination could the expulsion power be considered as an incidental matter, said Mr. Justice Raveendran. Had such a power been given, it would have been specifically mentioned. "There is no power of expulsion in Parliament either inherent in or traceable to Article 105(3). Expulsion will be possible only if Article 102 or 101 is suitably amended or if a law is made under Article 102(1)(e) enabling the House an example member found unworthy of continuing as a member."

Justice Raveendran said the appropriate course in case of allegation of corruption against a member was to prosecute him in accordance with the law. Pending such criminal proceedings, the number could be suspended. If he was convicted, he would become disqualified and if acquitted, he would be entitled to continue as member.

Separate Verdict

In a separate judgement, Justice O.K. Thakkar concurred with the majority view and said: "If there is gross advice of power by Parliament/State Legislature, this court will not hesitate in discharging its duty by quashing the order or setting aside unreasonable action".

Effective Discharge of Duties

He said: "By and large, constitutional functionaries in this country have admirably performed their function, exercised their powers and discharged their duties effectively, efficiently and sincerely and there is no reason to doubt that in coming years also, they would continue to act in a responsible manner expected of them".

Key role of law should be to ensure fairness, says Nobel Laureate Stiglitz.

Intellectual property rights cause economic inefficiency by creating monopolies.

The rule of law has to be interpreted with sensitivity if the twin aims of economic efficiency as well as social equity are to be achieved, according to Nobel laureate economist Joseph Stiglitz.

While democracy can act as an incident check on abuses, the key role of law should be to ensure fair pass and not just I concentrate on economic efficiency, he said, addressing the fourth annual K.C. Basu endowment lecture on economics and law, organised by the National University of Juridical Sciences here on Tuesday.

Property Rights

Property rights could not be effective in a democracy unless they were considered legitimate. Prof. Stiglitz said, refuting the simple model propagated by the Chicago school of economists that said that economic efficiency could be enhanced in society by establishing clearly penned property rights.

Citing the example of the states comprising the former Soviet Union as they transitioned from the control economy of the Communist era to a rapid pace of privatizations favoured by the International Monetary Fund (IMF), he said the enormous wealth that the oligarchs seized created discontent in the property rights system as many citizens were denied even the meagre pension to which they were entitled.

The trickle down theory did not work as the absence of good corporate governance laws meant that oligarchs stripped the privatized assets and diverted the capital outside instead of reinvesting. "Monopolists are not interested in passing laws favouring competition."

Laws, such as those on intellectual property rights, created economic inefficiency by their very nature, creating monopolies and restricting the use of knowledge. While its use by the pharmaceutical industry to restrict the production of generic drugs affected the right to life itself, it also meant creation of "patent thickets" in software industries that resulted in innovation getting impeded. Similarly, bankruptcy laws pushed by the IMF were often not sensitive to equity consideration, and thus silted innovation.

Cautioning against the pernicious provisions of bilateral multi-trade investment agreements that were being increasingly resorted to, Prof. Stiglitz said they were responsible for promoting business without responsibility, undermining the Judicial system in the process. While the problem of asymmetry in laws was best exemplified by the failure of Indian authorities to extradite those responsible for the Bhopal tragedy, provisions such as limited liability were often misused to protect irresponsible action on the part of corporate bodies.

Proactive Role of Judiciary

The Judiciary assumed a proactive role as the role of law-making Parliament became subject to indecision due to various political reasons on the Indian political scene. Hence, Judiciary began to assume a role of prominence as also 'wipe the tear' from every citizen's eye.

The main challenge facing India's legal and judicial systems in delivering justice to the poor. Although Constitution guarantees rights to people of India but a large section of people have no access to courts due to high costs involved. As the cost of **good quality legal** services is escalating, the ability of citizen to get effective justice is diminishing.

New and innovative solutions are needed to ensure that citizens have access to justice. **Right to Information Act, 2005** is one such solution whereby citizen's reach is extended for a greater access to justice.

Supreme Court while upholding death sentence to Dara Singh for burning to death Australian Christian Missionary Graham Stuart Staines and his minor sons. On 22nd January, 2011 the Bench noted that 'it is undisputed that there is no justification for interfering in someone's belief by way of 'use of force', provocation, conversion, incitement or upon a flawed premise that one religion is better than the other. It strikes at the very root of the orderly society, which the founding fathers of our Constitution dreamt of.

Judicial Activism has always been with us though differences in styles vary. In that sense, Indian Judicial Activism has not one but several histories. The narrative path could be delineated thus : **Nehruvian era,** the **post-Nehruvian** era, the latter dividing itself into the **Emergency** and **post-Emergency periods.** But we must remember that other narrative paths remain possible. For example, a *dalit* narrative of judicial activism may construct constitution from the time of activism in terms of **pre-Mandal** and **post-Mandal,** whereas a Marxian approach may do so in terms of its relation to practices of state formation. Periodization according to Marxian approach will entail the following categories :

- The formative period of the bourgeois landlord state,
- The rise of parliamentary communism,
- The Naxalite movement.
- The movement of an exceptional situation (such as the Emergency rule),
- The rise of state finance capitalism and contemporary economic globalization. Periodization almost always entails ideological practices.

Judicial Activism believes that developments in law, with all their labyrinth complexity, ought to remain socially legible and intelligible jargon-free style of juridical analysis is in itself an important resource for **human rights**, Rule of Law, and the open future of democracy. Two virtues remain integral to Judicial Activism, and they are :

1. **Clarity of Style**—It remains indispensable to multidisciplinary understanding of the law in books and the law in action.
2. **Integrity**—The second virtue consists of the courage to publically acknowledge the error of one's stated public positions.

Judicial Activism in India is shaped by a motley of factors such as:

- The arrangement of constitutional power especially in the structuring of a relatively autonomous judiciary.
- Social constructions of judicial role and functions.
- The histories of formation of the Bar and its location in the grids of power or resistance.
- The flows of political events, which determine the times of judicial acquiescence with regimes of power.

However **judicial activism** is simply not reducible to merely doctrinal narratives of judicial performance, important as these are. Judicial Activism is not just a matter of serial affirmation of judicial power over other domains and instrumentalities of state power. It is also a narrative of evolution of new constitutional cultures of power.

It offers no panacea for the nation's constitutional ills—it offers only perhaps **therapeutic use** of judicial power change with the changing contexts of domination and resistance. Judicial Activism brings into full view the constitutional conviction of **justices, scholars** and **activists.** Among the examples are: the famous **Golak Nath case** that removed a Fundamental Right in order that larger number of people could benefit.

In fact there are two kinds of judicial activism at work in India—**Reactionary** and **Progressive.** Nehruvian era activism on issues of land reform and right to property, and the pro-Emergency activism manifests **reactionary judicial activism. Progressive judicial activism** commences with **Golak Nath** and **Keshavananda Bharti cases** which culminated in a wholly different genre of social action litigation.

END NOTES

'How Judges Overrule: Speech Act Theory and the Doctrine of Stare Decisis', The Yale Law Journal, Vol. 113, No. 2, November 2003. pp. 493-531.

http://indiankanoon.org

'chum of bar'—terminology is taken from fishes—the physical basis of fish colour and mechanism of controlling colour. A chum line is the trail of bait or scent in the water that attracts game fish.

'Stare-stasis'—stand by decided matters. It is no secret that lawyers have their own unique discipline and approach to resolution of legal problems. Not surprisingly there are laws about determining the law. One of the most important of these laws is law of precedent or 'stare decisis'.

Supremecourtofindia.nic.in

Vishwa-Bharti Annual Report (1923) : The Vishva Bharti Quarterly, January 1924, p. 410.

Tagore, Rabindernath : The function of a Library Address of the Chairman Recetion Committee, All-India Library Conference, Calcutta, December 1928, Kolkata : Vishva Bharti August 1957, p. 1-6.

4

Rule of Law and Economics

RTI : Right to Information Act, 2005

The last forty years or so have seen the passage of freedom of information legislation in several countries beginning with the United States in 1966, Denmark and Norway in 1970, Australia and New Zealand in 1982, Canada in 1983, and Ireland in 1998, and India in 2005. There are several major reasons why the development of freedom of information legislation is a welcome trend. First RTI legislation breaks with the often entrenched tradition of secrecy in several countries and, in doing so, helps empower the citizen *vis-à-vis* the state, thus deepening democracy and enhancing citizen control of political processes. Second, more information helps citizens make better and more reasoned choices about important public policy and electoral issues, and participate in the political process more fully. Third, the capacity to demand information from governments is a powerful deterrent against governmental corruption and graft or plain inefficiency. In this sense, RTI legislation can be a powerful aid to the process of economic development, not just democracy.

Demand for Right to Information is a sign of development. And development cannot take place on empty stomach (Amartya Sen, 2009).

Indian economy is based on the principal of mixed economy. However, capitalism remains the basis. Let us review the situation relating to capitalism before we come to the Indian context.

Capitalism

Capitalism is an economic system in which wealth, and the means of producing wealth, are privately owned and controlled rather than commonly, publicly, or state-owned and controlled. Through capitalism, the land, labour, and capital are owned, operated, and traded by private individuals either singly or jointly, and investments. Distribution, income, production, pricing and supply of goods, commodities and services are determined by voluntary private decision in a market economy.

A distinguishing feature of capitalism is that each person owns his or her own labour and, therefore, is allowed to sell the use of it to employers. In a capitalist state, private rights and property relations are protected by the rule of law in a limited regulatory framework. In the modern capitalist state, legislative action is confined to defining and Portal Politics enforcing the basic rules of the market, though the state may provide some public goods and infrastructure individuals.

Some consider *laissez faire* to be "pure capitalism". *Laissez faire* [French, "leave to do (by itself)"], signifies minimizing or eliminating state interference in economic affairs and the competitive process, allowing the free play of supply and demand. *Laissez-faire* capitalism has never existed in practice. Because all large economies today have a mixture of private and public ownership and control, some feel that the term "mixed economies more precisely describes most contemporary economies. In the "capitalist mixed economy", the state intervenes in market activity and provides many services.

During the last century capitalism has often been contrasted with centrally planned economies. The central axiom of Capitalism is that the best allocation of resources is achieved through consumers having free choice, and producers responding accordingly to meet collective consumer demand. This contrasts with planned economies in which the state directs what shall be produced. A consequence is the belief that privatization of previously state-provided services will tend to achieve a more efficient delivery thereof. Further implications are usually in favour of free trade, and abolition of subsidies. Although individuals and groups must act rationally in any society for their own good, the consequences of both rational and irrational actions are said to be more readily apparent in a capitalist society.

Capitalistic economic practices have incrementally become institutionalized in England between the 16th and 19th centuries, although some features of capitalist organization existed in the ancient world, and early aspects of merchant capitalism flourished during the Late Middle Ages.

Capitalism has been dominant in the Western world sometime at the end of feudalism from Britain, it gradually spread throughout Europe, across political and cultural frontiers. In the 19th and 20th centuries, capitalism provided the main, but not exclusive, means of industrialization throughout much of the world.

Etymology

The etymology of the word *capital* has roots in the trade and ownership of animals. The Latin root of the capital is *capitalis,* from the proto-Indo-European *kaput,* which means "head", this being how wealth was measured. The terms *chattel* and *cattle* itself also derive from this same origin.

According to the Oxford English Dictionary, capitalism was first used by novelist William Makepeace Thackeray in 1854, by which he meant by having ownership of capital. Arthur Young first used the term *capitalist* of his economic surveys in his work *Travels in France* (1792). *Samuel Taylor Coleridge,* an English poet, used capitalist in his work *Table Talk* (1823), and Benjamin Disraeli used capitalist in the 1845 work *Sybil.*\

Pierre-Joseph Proudhon used *capitalist* is his first work *What is Property?* (1840) to refer to the owners of capital. Karl Marx and Friedrich Engels also used *capitalist* (*Kapitalist*) as a private owner of capital in The *Communist Manifesto* (1848), and referred the capitalistic system (kapitalistische system) to the capitalist mode of production (Kapitalistische produktionsform) in *Das Kapital* (1867). Marx's notion of the capitalist mode of production is characterised as a system of primarily private ownership of the means of production in a mainly market economy, with a legal framework on commerce and a physical infrastructure provided by the state.

According to the OED, Carl Adolph Douai, a German-American socialist and abolitionist, used *private capitalism* in 1863. A work entitled *Better Times* (1877) and an unknown author in 1884 of the *Pall Mall Gazette* also used *capitalism.*

However, the first use of capitalism to describe the production system was the German economist Werner Sombart, in his 1902 book *The Jews and Modern Capitalism* (*Die Juden und das Wirtschaflsleben*). Sombart's close friend and colleague, Max Weber, also used capitalism in his 1904 book *The Protestant Ethic and the Spirit of Capitalism* (*Die protestantische Ethik und der Geist des Kapitalismus*).

Perspectives

The concept of capitalism has evolved over time, with later thinkers often building on the analysis of earlier thinkers. Moreover, the component concepts used in defining capitalism—such as private ownership, markets and investment—have evolved along with changes in theory, in law, and in practice. This is a concept that is often compared with labourism.

Classical Political Economy

The classical school economic thought emerged in Britain in the late 18th century. The classical political economists Adam Smith, David Ricardo, Jean-Baptiste, Say, and John Stuart Mill published analyses of the production, distribution and exchange of goods in a market that have since formed the basis of study for most contemporary economists.

In France, 'Physiocrats' like François Quesnay promoted free trade based on a conception that wealth originated from land. Quesnay's *Tableau Economique* (1759), described the economy analytically and laid the foundation of the Physiocrats economic theory, followed by Anne Robert Jacques Turgot who opposed tariffs and customs duties and advocated free trade. Richard Cantillon defined long-run equilibrium as the balance of flows of income, and argued that the supply and demand mechanism around land influenced short-term prices.

Adam Smith's attack on mercantilism and his reasoning for "the system of natural liberty" in *The Wealth of Nations* (1776) are usually taken as the beginning of classical political economy. Smith devised a set of concepts that remain strongly associated with capitalism today, particularly his theory of the "invisible hand" of the market, through which the pursuit of individual self-interest unintentionally produces a collective good for society. It was necessary for Smith to be so forceful in his argument in favour of free markets because he had to overcome the popular mercantilist sentiment of the time period. He criticized monopolies, tariffs, duties, and other state enforced restrictions of his time and believed that the market is the most fair and efficient arbitrator of resources. This view was shared by David Ricardo, second most important of the classical political economists and one of the most influential economists of modem times. In *The Principles of Political Economy and Taxation* (1817) he developed the Law of Comparative Advantage, which explains why it is profitable for two parties to trade, even if one of the trading partners is more efficient in every type of economic production. This principle supports the economic case for free trade. Ricardo was a supporter of Say's law and held the view that full employment is the normal equilibrium for a competitive economy. He also argued that inflation is closely related to changes in quantity of money and credit and was a proponent of the law of diminishing returns, which states that each additional unit of input yields less and less additional output. The values of classical political economy are strongly associated with the classical liberal doctrine of minimal government intervention in the economy, though it does not necessarily oppose the state's provision of a few basic public goods.

Classical liberal thought has generally assumed a clear division between the economy and other realms of social activity, such as the state.

While economic liberalism favours markets unfettered by the government, it maintains that the state has a legitimate role in providing public goods. For instance, Adam Smith argued that the state has a role in providing roads, canals, schools and bridges that cannot be efficiently implemented by private entities. However, he preferred that these goods should be paid proportionally to their consumption (e.g. putting a toll). In addition, he advocated retaliatory tariffs to bring about free trade, and copyrights and patents to encourage innovation.

Weberian Political Sociology

In some social sciences, the understanding of the defining characteristics of capitalism has been strongly influenced by nineteenth century German social theorist Max Weber. Weber considered market exchange, rather than production, as the defining feature of capitalism; capitalist enterprises, in contrast Max Weber in 1917 to their counterparts in prior modes of economic activity, was their rationalization of production, directed towards maximizing efficiency and productivity. According to Weber, workers in pre-capitalist economic institutions understood work in terms of a personal relationship between master and journeyman in a guild, or between lord and peasant in a manor. In his book *The Protestant Ethic and the Spirit of Capitalism* (1904-1905), Weber sought to trace how capitalism transformed these traditional modes of economic activity. For Weber, the 'spirit of capitalism' began with the Puritan understanding of one's 'calling' in life and their labouring for God rather than for men. This is pictured in *Proverbs,* "Seest thou a man diligent in his calling? He shall stand before kings" and in *Colossians,* "Whatever you do, do your work heartily, as for the Lord rather than for men." In the *Protestant Ethic* Weber further stated that "moneymaking — provided it is done legally — is, within the modern economic order, the result and the expression of diligence in one's calling..." Thus in Weber's opinion, it was with a devotion to God in the workplace and seeking assurance of salvation described as the Protestant work ethic that the Puritans helped from the basis to the modern economic order.

This 'spirit' was gradually codified by law; rendering wage-labourers legally 'free' to sell work; encouraging the development of technology aimed at the organization of production on the basis of rational principles; and clarifying the apparent separation of the public and private lives of workers, especially between the home and the workplace. Therefore, unlike Marx, Weber did not see capitalism as primarily the consequence of changes in the means of production.

Capitalism, for Weber, was the most advanced economic system ever developed over the course of human history. Weber associated capitalism with the advance of the business corporation, public credit, and the further advance of bureaucracy of the modern world. Although Weber defended capitalism against its socialist critics of the period, he saw its rationalizing tendencies as a possible threat to traditional cultural values and institutions, and a possible iron case constraining human freedom. This is further seen in his criticism of "specialists without spirit, hedonists without a heart" that were developing, in his opinion, with the fading of the original Puritan 'spirit' associated with capitalism.

German Historical School and Austrian School

From the perspective of the German Historical School, capitalism is primarily identified in terms of the organization of production for markets. Although this perspective shares similar theoretical roots with that of Weber, its emphasis on markets and money lends it different focus. For followers of the German Historical School, the key shift from traditional modes of economic activity to capitalism involved the shift from medieval restrictions on credit and money to the modem monetary economy combined with an emphasis on the profit motive.

In the late nineteenth century the German historical school of economics diverged with the emerging Austrian School of Economics, led at the time by Carl Menger. Later generations of followers of the Austrian School continued to be influential in Western economic thought through much of the twentieth century. The Austrian economist Joseph Schumpeter, a forerunner of the Austrian School of Economics, emphasized the "creative destruction" of capitalism — the fact that market economies undergo constant change. At any moment of time, posits Schumpeter, there are rising industries and declining industries. Schumpeter, and many contemporary economists influenced by his work, argue that resources should flow from the declining to the expanding industries for an economy to grow, but they recognized that sometimes resources are slow to withdraw from the declining industries because of various forms of institutional resistance to change.

The Austrian economists Ludwig von Mises and Friedrich Hayek were among the leading defenders of market capitalism against twentieth century proponents of socialist planned economies. Mises and Hayek argued that only market capitalism could manage a complex, modern economy. Since a modern economy produces such a large array of distinct goods and services, and consists of such a large array of consumers and enterprises, asserted Mises and Hayek, the information problems facing any other form of economic organization other than market capitalism would exceed its capacity to handle information. Thinkers within supply-side economics built on the work of the Austrian School, and particularly emphasize Say's Law: "supply creates its own demand." Capitalism, to this school, is defined by lack of state restraint on the decisions of producers.

Austrian economists claim that Marx failed to make the distinction between capitalism and mercantilism they argue that Max conflated the imperialistic, colonialistic, protectionist and interventionist doctrines of mercantilism with capitalism.

Austrian economics has been a major influence on the ideology of libertarianism, which considers *laissez-faire* capitalism to be the ideal economic system. Murray Rothbard, who founded the Centre for Libertarian Studies and the *Journal of Libertarian Studies,* is referred to as the father of Libertarianism in the United States. He was associated with the 1982 creation of the Ludwig von Mises Institute and later was its academic vice president. In 1987, he started the scholarly "Review of Austrian Economics," now called the Quarterly *Journal of Austrian Economics.* Rothbard coined the term "Anarcho-capitalism".

Keynesian Economics

In his 1937, the General Theory of Employment, Interest, and Money, the British economist John Maynard Keynes argued that capitalism suffered a basic problem in its ability to recover from periods of slowdowns in investment. Keynes argued that a capitalist economy could remain in an indefinite equilibrium despite high unemployment. Essentially rejecting Say's law, he argued that some people may have a liquidity preference which would see them rather hold money than buy new goods or services, which, therefore, raised the prospect that the Great Depression would not end without what he termed in the General Theory "a somewhat comprehensive socialization of investment".

Keynesian economics challenged the notion that *laissez-faire* capitalist economics could operate well on their own, without state intervention used to promote aggregate demand, fighting high unemployment and deflation of the sort seen during the 1930s. He and his followers recommended "pump priming" the economy to avoid recession: cutting taxes, increasing government borrowing, and spending during an economic downturn. This was to be accompanied by trying to control wages nationally partly through the use of inflation to cut real wages and to deter people from holding money. John Maynard Keynes tried to provide solutions to many of Marx's problems without completely abandoning the classical understanding of capitalism. His work attempted to show that regulation can be effective, and that economic stabilizers can reign in the aggressive expansions and recessions that Marx disliked. These changes sought to create more stability in the business cycle, and reduce the abuses of labourers. Keynesian economists argue that Keynesian policies were one of the primary reasons capitalism was able to recover following the Great Depression. The premises of Keynes's work have, however, since been challenged by neoclassical and supply-side economics and the Austrian School.

Another challenge to Keynesian thinking came from his colleague Piero Sraffa, and subsequently from the Neo-Ricardian school that followed Sraffa. In Sraffa's highly technical analysis, capitalism is defined by an entire system of social relations among both producers and consumers, but with a primary emphasis on the demands of production. According to Sraffa, the tendency of capital to seek its highest rate of profit causes a dynamic instability in social and economic relations.

Neoclassical Economics and the Chicago School

Today, most academic research on capitalism in the English speaking world draws on neoclassical economic thought. It favours extensive market coordination and relatively neutral patterns of governmental market regulation aimed at maintaining property rights, rather than privileging particular social actors; deregulated labour markets; corporate governance dominated by financial owners of firms; and financial systems depending chiefly on capital market-based financing rather than state financing.

Milton Friedman effectively took many of the basic principles set forth by Adam Smith and the classical economists and modernized them, in a way. One example of this is his article in the September 1970 issue of *The New York Times Magazine,* where he claims that the social responsibility of business is "to use its resources and engage in activities designed to increase its profits...(through) open and free competition without deception or fraud". This is tantamount to Smith's argument that self-interest in turn benefits the whole of society. Work like this helped lay the foundations for the coming remarketization of capitalism and the supply-side economics of Ronald Reagan and Margaret Thatcher.

The Chicago School of economics is best known for its free market advocacy and monetarist ideas. According to Milton Friedman and monetarists, market economies are inherently stable if left to themselves and depressions result only from government intervention. Friedman, for example, argued that the Great Depression was result of a contraction of the money supply, controlled by the Federal Reserve, and not by the lack of investment as Keynes had argued. Ben Bernanke, current Chairman of the Federal Reserve, is among the economists today generally accepting Friedman's analysis of the causes of the Great Depression.

Neoclassical economists, today the majority of economists, consider value to be subjective, varying from person to person and for the same person at different times, and thus reject the labour theory of value. Marginalism is the theory that economic value results from marginal utility and marginal cost (the marginal concepts). These economists see capitalists as earning profits by forgoing current consumption, by taking risks, and by organizing production.

History

Mercantilism

The period between the 16th and 18th centuries is commonly described as mercantilism. This period was associated with geographic discoveries by merchant overseas traders, especially from England and the Low Countries; the European colonization of the Americas; and the rapid growth.

Mercantilism was a system of seaport from 1638 at trade for profit, although commodities were still at the height of mercantilism largely produced by non-capitalist production methods. While some scholars see mercantilism as the earliest stage of modern capitalism, others argue that modern capitalism did not emerge until later. For example, noting the pre-capitalist features of mercantilism, Karl Polanyi argued that capitalism did not emerge until the establishment of free trade in Britain in the 1830s.

The earliest forms of mercantilism date back to the Roman Empire. When the Roman Empire expanded, the mercantilist economy expanded throughout Europe. After the collapse of the Roman Empire, most of the European economy became controlled by local feudal powers, and mercantilism collapsed there. However, mercantilism persisted in Arabia. Due to its proximity to neighbouring countries, the Arabs established trade routes to Egypt, Persia, and Byzantium. As Islam spread in the seventh century, mercantilism spread rapidly to Spain, Portugal, Northern Africa, and Asia. Mercantilism finally revived in Europe in the fourteenth century, as mercantilism spread from Spain and Portugal.

Feudalism began to lay some of the foundations necessary for the development of mercantilism, a precursor to capitalism. Feudalism took place mostly in Europe and lasted from the medieval period up through the sixteenth century. Feudal manors were almost entirely self-sufficient and, therefore, limited the role of the market. This stifled the growth of capitalism. However, the relatively sudden emergence of new technologies and discoveries, particularly in the industries of agriculture and exploration, revitalized the growth of capitalism. The most important development at the end of Feudalism was the emergence of "the dichotomy between wage earners and capitalist merchants".

Among the major tenets of mercantilist theory was bullionism, a doctrine stressing the importance of accumulating precious metals. Mercantilists argued that a state should export more goods than it imported so that foreigners would have to pay the difference in precious metals. Mercantilists asserted that only raw materials that could not be extracted at home should be imported; and promoted government subsidies, such as the granting of monopolies and protective tariffs, were necessary to encourage home production of manufactured goods. European merchants, backed by state controls, subsidies, and monopolies, made most of their profits from the buying and selling of goods. In the words of Francis Bacon, the purpose of mercantilism was "the opening and well-balancing of trade; the cherishing of manufacturers; the banishing of idleness; the repressing of waste and excess by sumptuary laws; the improvement and husbanding of the soil; the regulation of prices". Similar practices of economic regimentation had begun earlier in the medieval towns. However, under mercantilism, given the contemporaneous rise of the absolutism, the state superseded the local guilds as the regulator of the economy. During that time the guilds essentially functioned like cartels that monopolized the quantity of craftsmen to earn above market wages.

Commercialism

At the period of the eighteenth century, the commercial stage of capitalism transcended from the previous domination of capitalism by merchants. Commercialism, or commercial capitalism, originated from the start of the British and Dutch East India Company. These companies were characterized by its monopoly on trade, granted by the letters patents. Recognized as chartered joint-stock companies by the state, these companies enjoyed a large sum of power, ranging from law-making, military, and treaty-making privileges. Characterized by its colonial and expansionary powers by states, powerful nation-states sought to accumulate precious metals, and military conflicts arose. During this era, merchants, who had traded under the previous stage of mercantilism, invested capital in the East India Companies and other colonies, seeking a return on investment.

Industrialism

By the late eighteenth century, mercantilism was in crisis: mercantile activity could not produce sufficient wealth to pay for the military expenditures of the states that protected, and depended on commerce. This crisis intensified with the Industrial Revolution. Although mercantilist policies endured in European countries with weak industrial bases, such as Prussia and Russia, into the nineteenth century, rapidly industrializing countries began questioning the value of mercantilist policies by the late eighteenth century. This is most evident in Great Britain, the home of the Industrial Revolution, where a new group led by David Hume and Adam Smith, in the mid eighteenth century, challenged fundamental mercantilist doctrines as the belief that the amount of the world's wealth remained constant and that a state could only increase its wealth at the expense of another state.

At the same time that philosophers and politicians were debating the merits of mercantilism, the mid-eighteenth century gave rise to an alternative set of economic relations and practices: industrial (bourgeois) capitalism. Most scholars agree that the emergence of capitalism was made possible by earlier economic developments in England. According to Marxists, it was made possible by the exploitation of wage-labour on a large scale, which English landowners first experimented with after the crisis of the fourteenth century. According to World Systems Theorists like Immanuel Wallerstein, it was made possible by the accumulation of vast amounts of capital under the merchant phase of capitalism.

During the resulting Industrial Revolution, the industrialist replaced the merchant as a dominant actor in the capitalist system and effected the decline of the traditional handicraft skills of artisans, guilds, and journeymen. Also during this period, capitalism marked the transformation of relations between the British landowning gentry and peasants, giving rise to the production of cash crops for the market rather than for subsistence on a feudal manor. The surplus generated by the rise of commercial agriculture encouraged increased mechanization of agriculture and the rise of the bourgeoisie.

Marx dated industrial capitalism from the last third of the eighteenth century, marked the development of the factory system of manufacturing, characterized by a complex division of labour between and within work process and the routinization of work tasks; and finally, established the global domination of the capitalist mode of production. In the midst of this newly developing concept of division of labour came exploitation of labour on a much larger scale than was ever seen before.

Britain also abandoned its protectionist policy, as embraced by mercantilism. In the nineteenth century, Richard

Cobden and John Bright, who based their beliefs on the Manchester School, initiated a movement to lower tariffs. In the 1840s, Britain adopted a less protectionist policy, with the repeal of the Corn Laws and the Navigation Acts. Britain reduced tariffs and quotas, in line with Adam Smith and David Ricardo's advocacy for free trade. As noting the various pre-capitalist features of mercantilism, Karl Polanyi argued that capitalism did not emerge until the establishment of free trade in Britain in the 1830s. Other sources indicate that mercantilism fell after the repeal of the Navigation Acts m 1849, and libertarians argue that the current system is still mercantilist. However, due to companies legislation, British capitalism was not exclusively *laissez-faire.* The British state created charters creating immunities for the corporations under the Limited Liability Act 1855 and the Joint Stock Companies Act 1856. The British East India Company and controls in major industries during that time were also important examples of economic regulations. See List of Acts of Parliament of the United Kingdom Parliament, 1840-1859 and History of labour law in the United Kingdom.

Most of the early proponents of the liberal theory of economics in the United States subscribed to the American School. This school of thought was inspired by the ideas of Alexander Hamilton, who proposed the creation of the First National Bank and the Second National Bank and increased tariffs (e.g. tariff of 1828) to favour northern industrial interests. Following Hamilton's death, more abiding protectionist influence in the ante-bellum period came from Henry Clay and his American System.

In the mid-nineteenth century, the United States followed the Whig tradition of economic liberalism, which included increased state control, regulation and macro-economic development of infrastructure. Public works such as the provision and regulation transportation such as railroads took effect. The Pacific Railway Acts provided the development of the First Transcontinental Railroad. In order to help pay for its war effort in the American Civil the United States government imposed its first personal income tax, on August 5, 1861, as part of the Revenue Act of 1861 (3 per cent of all incomes over US $800; rescinded in 1872).

Following the American Civil War, the movement towards a mixed economy accelerated with even more protectionism and government regulation. In the 1880s and 1890s, significant tariff increases were enacted (see the McKinley Tariff and Dingley Tariff). Moreover, with the enactment of the Inter-state Commerce Act of 1887, the Sherman Anti-trust Act, the federal government began to assume an increasing role in regulating and directing the country's economy.

Monopolism

In the late nineteenth century, the control and direction of large areas of industry came into the hands of financiers. This period has been defined as state capitalism, state monopoly capitalism, or corporate capitalism, characterized by the subordination of processes of production to the accumulation of profits upto a financial system. Major characteristics of capitalism in this period included the establishment of large industrial cartels or monopolies; the ownership and management of industry by fanciers divorced from the production process; and the development of a complex system of banking, an equity market, and corporate holdings of capital through stock ownership. Increasingly, large industries and land became the subject of profit and loss by financial speculators.

From about the American Civil War 1871 to the early twentieth century, capitalism has also been increasingly influenced by large, monopolistic corporations. The oil, telecommunication, railroad, shipping, banking and financial industries are characterized by its monopolistic domination. Inside these corporations, a division of labour separates shareholders, owners, managers, and actual labourers. Although thence of monopoly capitalism originated among Marxist theorists, non-Marxist economic historians have also commented on the rise of monopolies and trusts in the period. Stromberg, Joseph R. (2001) "The Role of State Monopoly

Capitalism in the American Empire (http://mises.org/ joumals/jls) *Journal of Libertarian Studies.*

By the last quarter of the nineteenth century, the emergence of large industrial trusts had provoked legislation in the U.S. to reduce the monopolistic tendencies of the period. Gradually, during this Progressive Era, the U.S. federal government played a larger role in passing antitrust laws and regulation of industrial standards for key industries of special public concern. However, contemporary, non-bourgeois economic historians believe these new laws were in fact designed to aid large corporations at the expense of smaller competitors. By the end of the nineteenth century, economic depressions and boom and bust business cycles had become a recurring problem, although such problems were most likely caused by government intervention, not failures in free markets (Rand, 1967; Friedman, 1962; Bernstein, 2005). In particular, the Long Depression of the 1870s and 1880s and the Great Depression of the 1930s affected almost the entire capitalist world, and generated discussion about capitalism's long-term survival prospects. In the early twentieth century, a succession of U.S. Presidents, beginning with Warren Harding's "Return to Normalcy," the state decreased taxation rates, with the Revenue Act of 1924 and 1926. This allowed for the prosperity of "The Roaring Twenties", but later was said to be largely responsible for the Great Depression. During the 1930s, Marxist commentators often posited the possibility of capitalism's decline or demise, often in alleged contrast to the ability of the Soviet Union to avoid suffering the effects of the global depression.

Keynesianism and Neoliberalism

In the period following the global depression of the 1930s, the state played an increasingly prominent role in the capitalistic system throughout much of the world. In 1929, for example, total U.S. government expenditures (federal, state, and local) amounted to less than one-tenth of GNP; from the 1970s they amounted to around one-third (EB). Similar increases were seen in all bourgeois economies, some of which, such as France, have reached even higher ratios of government expenditures to GNP than the United States. These economies have since been widely described as "mixed economies".

During the post-war boom, a broad array of new analytical tools in the social sciences were developed to explain the social and economic trends of the period, including the concepts of post-industrial society and the welfare State. The phase of capitalism from the beginning of the postwar period through the 1970s has sometimes been described as "state capitalism", especially by Marxian thinkers. This era was greatly influenced by Keynesian economic stabilization policies.

The long post-war boom ended in the late 1960s and early 1970s, and the situation was worsened by the rise of stagflation. Exceptionally high inflation combined with slow output growth, rising unemployment, and eventually recession caused loss of credibility of Keynesian welfare-statist mode of regulation. Under the influence of Friedrich Hayek and Milton Friedman, Western states embraced policy prescriptions inspired by the *laissez-faire* capitalism and classical liberalism. In particular, monetarism, a theoretical alternative to Keynesianism that is more compatible with *laissez-faire,* gained increasing prominence in the capitalist world, especially under the leadership of Ronald Reagan in the U.S. and Margaret Thatcher in the U.K. in the 1980s. Finally, the general public's interest shifted from the collectivist concerns of Keynes's managed capitalism to a focus on individual freedom and choice, called "remarketized capitalism". In the eyes of many economic and political commentators, collapse of the Soviet Union supposedly brought further evidence of superiority of market capitalism over communism.

Globalization

Although overseas trade has been associated with the development of capitalism for over five hundred years, some thinkers argue that a number of trends associated with globalization have acted to increase the mobility of people and capital since the last quarter of the twentieth century, combining to circumscribe the room to manoeuvre of states in choosing non-capitalist models of development. Today, these trends have bolstered the argument that capitalism should now be viewed as a truly world system. However other thinkers argue that globalization, even in its quantitative degree, is no greater now than during earlier periods of capitalist trade. The roots of globalized capitalism can be traced back to the imperialism of the early twentieth century. Imperialistic policies promoted the spread of capitalistic principles, and the doors of trade stayed open in foreign countries even after imperialism had come to an end.

After the abandonment of the Bretton Woods system and the strict state control of foreign exchange rates, the total value of transactions in foreign exchange was estimated to be at least twenty times greater than that of all foreign movements of goods and services. The internationalization of finance, which some see as beyond the reach of state control, combined with the growing ease with which large corporations have been able to relocate their operations to low-wage states, has posed the question of the 'eclipse' of state sovereignty, arising from the growing 'globalization' of capital. Economic growth in the last half-century has been consistently strong. Life expectancy has almost doubled in the developing world since the post-war years and is starting to close the gap on the developed world where the improvement has been smaller. Infant mortality has decreased in every developing region of the world, thanks to the work of a handful of charitable bourgeoisie, but the destitute continue to suffer and die while the bourgeoisie increase their profits. While scientists generally agree about the size of global income inequality, there is a general disagreement about the recent direction of chance of 1981. However, it is growing within particular nations such as China. The book, *The Improving State of the World,* argues that economic growth since the Industrial Revolution has been very strong and that factors such as adequate nutrition, life expectancy, infant mortality, literacy, prevalence of child labour, education, and available free time have improved greatly.

The biggest reason for the increasingly global capitalist economy is the telecommunications revolution that has taken place over the last twenty years. Fax machines, cell phones, and the internet have made it possible for work to be done and transactions to take place from almost anywhere in the world. In 2008, state intervention in global capital markets by the American and other governments was seen by many as signalling a crisis for free-market capitalism. Serious turmoil in the banking system and finical markets due in part to the supreme mortgage crisis reached a critical stage during September 2008, characterized by severely contracted liquidity in the global credit markets and going-concern threats to investment banks and other institutions.

Political Advocacy

Support

Many theorists and policymakers in predominantly capitalist nations have emphasized capitalism's ability to promote economic growth, as measured by Gross Domestic Product (GDP), capacity utilization or standard of living. This argument was central, for example, to Adam Smith's advocacy of letting a free market control production and price, and allocate resources. Many theorists have noted that this increase in global GDP over time coincides with the emergence of the modern world capitalist system. While the measurements are not identical, proponents argue that increasing GDP (per capita) is empirically shown to bring about improved standards of living, such as better availability of food, housing, clothing, and health care. The decrease in the number of hours worked per week and the decreased participation of children and the elderly in the workforce have been attributed to capitalism. Proponents also believe that a capitalist economy offers far more opportunities for individuals to raise their income through new professions or business ventures than do other economic forms. To their thinking, this potential is much greater than in either traditional feudal or tribal societies or in socialist societies.

Milton Friedman has argued that the economic freedom of competitive capitalism is a requisite of political freedom. Friedman argued that centralized control of economic activity is always accompanied by political repression. In his view, transactions in a market economy are voluntary, and the wide diversity that voluntary activity permits is a fundamental threat to repressive political leaders and greatly diminish power to coerce. Friedman's view was also shared by Friedrich Hayek and John Maynard Keynes, both of whom believed that capitalism is vital for freedom to survive and thrive.

Austrian School economists have argued that capitalism can organize itself into a complex system without an external guidance or planning mechanism. Friedrich Hayek coined the term "catallaxy" to describe what he considered the phenomenon of self-organization underpinning capitalism. From this perspective, in process of self-organization, the profit motive has an important role. From transactions between buyers and sellers price systems emerge, and prices serve as a signal as to the urgent and unfilled wants of people. The promise of profits gives entrepreneurs incentive to use their knowledge and resources to satisfy those wants. Thus the activities of millions of people, each seeking his own interest, are coordinated.

This decentralized system of coordination is viewed by some supporters of capitalism as one of its greatest strengths. They argue that it permits many solutions to be tried, and that real-world competition generally finds a good solution to emerging challenges. In contrast, they argue, central planning often selects inappropriate solutions as a result of faulty forecasting. However, in all existing modern economies, the state conducts some degree of centralized economic planning (using such tools as allowing the country's central bank to set base interest rates), ostensibly as an attempt to improve efficiency, attenuate cyclical volatility, and further particular social goals. Proponents who follow the Austrian School argue that even this limited control creates inefficiencies because we cannot predict the long-term activity of the economy. Milton Friedman, for example, has argued that the Great Depression was caused by the erroneous policy of the Federal Reserve.

Ayn Rand was a prominent philosophical supporter of *laissez-faire* capitalism; her novel Atlas Shrugged was one of the most influential publications ever written on the subject of business and continues to be a best-seller. The first person to endow capitalism with a new code of morality (Rational Selfishness), she did not justify capitalism on the grounds of pure "practicality" (that it is the best wealth-creating system), or the supernatural (that God or religion supports capitalism), or because it benefits the most people, but maintained that it is the only morally valid socio-political system because it allows people to be free to act in their rational self-interest. These thinkers have had a substantial influence on the Libertarian Party. The Libertarian Party strongly advocates the elimination of most, if not all, state involvement in the marketplace. The Republican Liberty Caucus is the libertarian branch of the Republican Party.

Criticism

Prominent leftist critics have included socialists (like Karl Marx, Friedrich Engels, Vladimir Lenin, Mao Zedong, Leon Trotsky, Antonio Gramsci, Rosa Luxemburg, Slavoj Zizek, Che Guevara, Fidel Castro) and anarchists (including Benjamin Tucker, Lysander Spooner, Pierre-Joseph Proudhon, Mikhail Bakunin, Peter Kropotkin, Emma Goldman, Murray Bookchin, Rudolf Rocker, Noam Chomsky, and many others). Movements like the Luddites, Narodniks, Shakers, Utopian Socialists and others have opposed capitalism for various reasons. Marxism advocated a revolutionary overthrow of capitalism that would lead eventually to communism. Marxism also influenced social democratic and labour parties, which seek change through existing democratic channels instead of revolution, and believe that capitalism should be heavily regulated rather than abolished. Many aspects of capitalism have come under attack from the relatively recent anti-globalization movement.

Some religions criticize or outright oppose specific elements of capitalism. Some traditions of Judaism, Christianity, and Islam forbid lending money at interest, although methods of Islamic banking have been developed.

Christianity has been a source of both praise and criticism for capitalism, particularly its materialist aspects. The first socialists drew many of their principles from Christian values (see Christian socialism), against "bourgeois values of profiteering, greed, selfishness, and hoarding". Christian critics of capitalism may not oppose capitalism entirely, but support a mixed economy in order to ensure adequate labour standards and relations, as well as economic justice. In addition, there are many prominent Protestant denominations (particularly in the United States) who have reconciled with — or are ardently in favour of — capitalism, particularly in opposition to secular socialism. However, in the U.S. and around the world there are many Protestant Christian traditions which are critical of, or even oppose, capitalism. Another critic is the Indian philosopher P.R. Sarkar, founder of the Ananda Marga movement, who developed the Social Cycle Theory as a solution to the problems of capitalism called the Progressive Utilization Theory (PROUT).

Some problems said to be associated with capitalism include :

- unfair and inefficient distribution of wealth and power; a tendency towards market monopoly or oligopoly (and government by oligarchy);
- imperialism and various forms of economic and cultural exploitation; and
- phenomena such as social alienation, inequality, unemployment, and economic instability.

Critics have maintained that there is an inherent tendency towards oligopolistic structures when *laissez-faire* is combined with capitalist private property. Because of this tendency either *laissez-faire*, or private property, or both, have drawn fire from critics who believe an essential aspect of economic freedom is the extension of the freedom to have meaningful decision-making control over productive resources to everyone. Economist Branko Horvat asserts, "It is now well known that capitalist development leads to the concentration of capital, employment and power. It is somewhat less known that it leads to the almost complete destruction of economic freedom". Economics Professor and *New York Times* best-selling author, Ravi Batra, has maintained that excessive income and wealth inequalities are a fundamental cause of financial crisis and economic depression in the capitalist economy.

Near the start of the twentieth century, Vladimir Lenin argued that that state use of military power to defend capitalist interests abroad was an inevitable corollary of monopoly capitalism. This concept of political economy concerning the relationship between economic and political power among and within states includes critics of capitalism who assign to it responsibility for not only economic exploitation, but imperialist, colonialist and counter-revolutionary wars, repressions of workers and trade unionists, genocides, massacres, and so on.

Some environmentalists argue that capitalism requires continual economic growth, and will inevitably deplete the finite natural resources of the earth, and other broadly utilized resources. Such thinkers, including Murray Bookchin, have argued that capitalist production externalizes environmental costs to all of society, and is unable to adequately mitigate its impact upon ecosystems and the biosphere at large. Supporters maintain, however, that it would be imprudent for capitalist societies to deplete resources to such an extent.

Some labour historians and scholars, such as Immanuel Wallerstein, Tom Brass and, latterly Marcel van der Linden, have also argued that unfree labour — the use of a labour force of slaves, indentured servants, criminal convicts, political prisoners, and/or other coerced persons — is compatible with capitalist relations.

Democracy, the State, and Legal Frameworks

The relationship between the state, its formal mechanisms, and capitalist societies has been debated in many fields of social and political theory, with active discussion since the nineteenth century. Hernando de Soto is a contemporary economist who has argued that an important characteristic of capitalism is the functioning state protection of property rights in a formal property system where ownership and transactions are clearly recorded. According to de Soto, this is the process by which physical assets are transformed into capital, which in turn may be used in many more ways and much more efficiently in the market economy. A number of Marxian economists have argued that the Enclosure Acts in England, and similar legislation elsewhere, were an integral part of capitalist primitive accumulation and that specific legal frameworks of private land ownership have been integral to the development of capitalism.

New institutional economics, a field pioneered by Douglass North, stresses the need of capitalism for a legal framework to function optimally, and focuses on the relationship between the historical development of capitalism and the creation and maintenance of political and economic institutions. In new institutional economics and other fields focusing on public policy, economists seek to judge when and whether governmental intervention (such as taxes, welfare, and government regulation) can result in potential gains in efficiency. According to Gregory Mankiw, a New Keynesian economist, governmental intervention can improve on market outcomes under conditions of "market failure", or situations in which the market on its own does not allocate resources efficiently. The idea of market failure is that markets fail to realize all potential gains from trade. This means that markets fail to deliver perfect economic results. Critics of market failure theory, like Ronald Coase, Harold Demsetz, and James M. Buchanan argue that government programmes and policies also fall short of absolute perfection. Market failures are often small, and government failures are sometimes large. It is, therefore, the case that imperfect markets are often better than imperfect governmental alternatives. While all nations currently have some kind of market regulations, the desirable degree of regulation is disputed.

The relationship between democracy and capitalism is a contentious area in theory and popular political movements. The extension of universal adult male suffrage in nineteenth century Britain occurred along with the development of industrial capitalism, and democracy became widespread at the same time as capitalism, leading many theorists to posit a causal relationship between them, or that each affects the other. However, in the twentieth century, according to some authors, capitalism also accompanied a variety of political formations quite distinct from liberal democracies, including fascist regimes, monarchies, and single-party states, while it has been observed[who?] that many democratic societies such as the Bolivarian Republic of Venezuela and Anarchist Catalonia have been expressly anti-capitalist. While some thinkers argue that capitalist development more or less inevitably eventually leads to the emergence of democracy, others dispute this claim. Research on the democratic peace theory further indicates that capitalist democracies rarely make war with one another and have little internal violence. However critics of the democratic peace theory note that democratic capitalist states may fight infrequently or never with other democratic capitalist states because of Political similarity or political stability rather than because they are democratic (or capitalist).

Some commentators argue that though economic growth under capitalism has led to democratization in the past, it may not do so in the future. Under this line of thinking, authoritarian regimes have been able to manage economic growth without making concessions to greater political freedom.

In response to criticism of the system, some proponents of capitalism have argued that its advantages are supported by empirical research. For example, advocates of different Index of Economic Freedom point to a statistical correlation between nations with more economic freedom (as defined by the Indices) and higher scores on variables such as income and life expectancy, including the poor in these nations.

Constitution of India

Constitution of India promises not only political but social and economy democracy also. In fact, social democracy and economic democracy is the foundation on which alone political democracy can rest. To bring about economic justice Chapter IV of the Constitution of India, namely *Directive Principles of State Policy* was instituted not to banish poverty alone but to multiply the national wealth resource and foster and equitable distribution of them.

The Directive Principles of State Policy enshrined in Part IV of the Constitution (Articles 36–51) are a 'complex of values' "which aim at the establishment of a 'welfare state' as distinguished from a 'police state' ". These principles have been described as the 'life giving provisions' of the Constitution. The insertion of these principles of social policy in the constitutional text was a deliberate attempt on the part of the framers of the Constitution who felt the pulse of the time that the rights and interests of the individual must be engineered and balanced with the interests of the society at large. Further, the framers of the Constitution who were influenced by the American Bill of Rights : were mindful of the difficulties that the American Government had to face in the 'New Deal' Era to bring socio-economic legislation. The Supreme Court of America tried to frustrate the attempts of the government to bring socio-economic legislation by striking it down on one pretext or the other. P. K. Tripathi observes in the context that in the beginning the Supreme Court of the United States "would not appreciate the significance of the transformation of the entire structure of political economy and would stick to notion as to province of the fundamental rights with such tragic faith as to force the very drugs of those rights down the throat of sprawling fainting community". It, however, soon took an enlightened view of the new balance between the fundamental rights and social needs and permitted the government authority a convenient scope for efficient action. They would thus, not leave it entirely to the courts to take cognizance of the need for social change and to interpret the Constitution to that effect. They followed the Irish practice and incorporated certain principles instituted as the Directive Principles of State Policy (Part IV) of the Constitution.

The Nature of Directive Principles

The Fundamental Rights embodied in Part III of the Constitution secure an egalitarian society and the Directive Principles enumerated in Part IV are aimed at securing a social order. Article 38 clearly states: "the state shall strive to promote the welfare of the people by securing and protecting as effectively as it may, a social order in which justice—social, economic and political—shall inform all the institutions of national life".

The principles enlisted in Part IV are to provide adequate means of livelihood, equitable distribution of material resources to subserve common good, no concentration of wealth, equal wages, humane conditions of work protection of children and youth against exploitation right to work, living wages, education, public assistance in case of unemployment, old age etc., free and compulsory education for children; organization of Panchayati Raj, organization of agriculture and animal husbandry, separation of judiciary from the executive, promotion of international peace and security, etc.

The Forty-second Amendment introduces a few more directives, namely, equal justice and free legal aid, (Article 39-A), participation of workers in the management of industries (Article 43-A) and protection and improvement of environment and safeguarding of forests and wild life (Article 48-A).

The 44th Amendment has also introduces one directive [38(2)], namely to minimize the inequities income and endeavour to eliminate inequalities in status, facilities and opportunities, not only amongst individuals but amongst groups of people.

These principles which are in the nature of positive directions to the state though fundamental in the governance of the country, are not enforceable by any court of taw. Article 37 clearly says: "The provisions in the Part (Part IV) shall not be enforceable by any court but the principles therein laid down are nevertheless fundamental in governance of the country and it shall be the duty of the state to apply these principle in making the laws".

Gandhian Approach, Globalization and Indian Economy

A critique of some parameters of the evolved economic situation in India—ranges from politics of macroeconomic policy in general to failing agriculture and marginalization of peasantry at the regional level. The important point to notice is that economic policy is not free from political calculations and in that sense it departs from Gandhian alternative.

Globalization in the Historical Perspective

At the end of twentieth century, as the sense of transformation grew, three kinds of narratives achieved wide currency.

The accounts of these three narratives overlapped and they are partially related to each other:

(1) First idea was that of *post modernity.*
(2) Second idea was that of post *Cold-War World.*
(3) Third idea was that of *globalization.*

(1) ***Post-modernity***—At the core was the denial of the certainties of the modern world. Post-modernism challenged all traditional models of understanding. As a result, intimate links of post-modernity to modernity were proposed.

We will not go into details because that is not the main focus of this presentation.

2. ***Second idea was that of a post-Cold War World***—This reflected the apparently dramatic significance of changes in international politics. At the centre of post-Cold War narratives was the idea that winding down political and military conflict between blocs world involve fundamental transformations of political—and hence perhaps social and cultural—relations in general.

3. ***The third idea, of course, was globalization***—This emphasized technical, economic and cultural transformations that were having impact on even boundaries of nation-states. This narrative was often presented as a new certainty. Its proponents suggested that, indeed, it reflected unstoppable forces, Jaques

> Derrida (1997) as a result of questioning, agreed that the political phenomena to which he was referring was what is conventionally called globalization.

Post-modernity and globalization both began to emerge as serious concepts of change in the 1970s. This was the decade of the détente, the period in which Cold War rivalries appeared to have relaxed, yet the crisis of post-war boom produced great global economic instability and there was a widespread sense of dissolution of traditional cultural and social relations.

In the 1970s, however, although there was widespread sense of crisis and dissolution after the relative stability of earlier post-war decades, there was not yet a strong feeling of transition. Indeed the Second Cold War of the early 1980s reinforced awareness of a definite world structure, after the loosening of the previous decade. It was only when this faded, in the middle of 1980s that the sense of transition came into its own. It is from the point onwards that we can trace the definite influence of narrative of change. Today we are living at the threshold of new global civilization. As the whole world is an indivisible whole, its parts are interrelated and interdependent so that what happens to one part ultimately affects the whole. Progress in one cannot succeed unless it ultimately spells progress for the whole.

Globalization is essentially a process of unification, unity, convergence and uniformity. This, indeed, is a new phenomenon, but the process of unification of people coming together, of ideas merging with one another, has been going on from time immemorial. Evolution from a diversified world to a global village was made possible with help of technological breakthrough, dramatic and drastic reduction of distances, universalisation of electronic media and other powerful means of communication. As a global village or as a network system, everyone in the four corners of the world is expected to follow the global stereotypes, which for the most one dictated or circulated by the developed countries.

The current trend towards globalization is estimated to create the necessary infrastructure for individual and nations to interact with each other and mutually benefit from such a process. A globalised world is one in which political, economic, cultural and social events become more and more multidirectional yet interconnected, and also one in which they have more impact.

Globalization is taking place at all levels—it is integrating economies, changing the face of families universalizing the nation of human rights, environment, and education and changing the role of governments. It is about restructuring the society in a fundamental manner.

But in this restructuring game there are some winners and some losers. For the winners, there is much that is attractive about the prospect of world of constant travel and multimedia communication in a networked global village and global marketplace.

But for the losers it is a whole of global pillage in which the gap between the powerful and powerless, rich and poor, privileged and underprivileged continues to widen.

II

Gandhian Approach

Gandhi was a many-sided personality. He was at once a saint and politician, an educationist and a journalist, a humanist and a social reformer.

This little man, so frail in appearance was a giant among men, measured by the greatness of his soul. His profound sincerity and spirit, his freedom from hatred and his mastery over himself, his human friendly, all-embracing charity, his strong conviction which he shared with great ones of history—and which he successfully put to test in many dramatic situations—show the impact of religion or life. The impact of eternal values on the shifting problems of the world of time.

Gandhi looked at politics not as a struggle for power and wealth, but a persistent and continuous effort to enable the submerged millions to attain good life, to raise the quality of human beings, to train them for freedom and fellowship for spiritual depth and social harmony. In fact, Gandhi saw a very close relationship between religion and politics. He condemned politics which was bereft of religion on the ground that it makes a man corrupt.

For our relevance, in this presentation, let us visualize Gandhi's views on ends and means. He rejected Machiavelli, Hitler, etc., who celebrated power by saying that 'ends justify the means'. Gandhi was against this concept and he held diametrically opposite views and that is, that it was neither possible nor desirable to detach ends from means. If means are wrong, how can ends be good he logically argued? If you sow *neem* you can't expect mangoes from.

Referring to Gandhi's views on Trusteeship we can see that he had an alternative even in the times in which he lived. The relevance of his alternative methods has become a subject of study at the famous American University, Harvard.

Gandhi emphasized the ideal of a simple life and insisted that a person should only possess what is absolutely essential for his day-to-day life and attainment of self-realization. He was against the unnecessary accumulation of wealth and goods. Gandhi's trusteeship theory was designed to point a way towards the painless extinct of capital and property that were a source of inequality and consequent violence and exploitation in social relations. Gandhi recognized that acquisitions and ownership property in any form go with the excessive of certain functions and qualities which must not be used for selfish ends, but for the good of community. He thought that it was possible to inspire capitalist (or the man of property) to use, for the good of the society, his intelligence and talents that are responsible for the acquisition and ownership of capital and property. Capital is the result of the labour and cooperative efforts of the society.

Therefore, Gandhi argued, the wealth producing power embodied in capital must be held in trust for the good of community, nor for acquiring power over often men, and using it for anti-social ends or misusing it in other ways.

'Let the society benefit by the power that capital creates and by the intelligence that the capitalists possess and the workers lack.'

Trusteeship is desired from the basic Gandhian concepts of non-violence, *swaraj* and equality which are all interlinked with one another. He wrote:

> 'A society based on non-violence cannot mature any other ideal.' Further, 'the more we are committed to achieve the goals of equal distribution the more we will lay the foundation of a non-violent society'.

Gandhi said rich should be made a feel that they have no justification for keeping surplus wealth with them. He summed up his concept of trusteeship this in six principles:

1. Trusteeship provides a means of transforming the present capitalist order of society into equalitarian one;—it gives the present owning class a chance of reforming itself. It is based on the faith that human nature is not beyond redemption.
2. It does not recognize any right of private ownership of property except as it may be permitted by society for its own welfare.
3. It does not exclude legislative regulation of ownership and use of wealth.
4. Thus, under state regulated trusteeship, on individual will not be free to hold wealth in disregard of the interest of society.
5. Just as it is proposed to fix a decent minimum living wage, even to a limit should be fixed for the maximum income that could be allowed to any person in society.

The difference between minimum and maximum must be reasonable and equitable and variable from time to time.

The present globalization does not allow this and this is the crux of the problem.

6. Under Gandhian economic order the character of production will be determined by social necessity and not by present greed.

Though trusteeship does not prelude state action and legislative steps to bring it into existence the method or approach will largely remain one of persuasion, non-violence and mass *satyagraha.*

This is a powerful alternative based on logic and appeals to the spiritual aspect of human life. This alternative is important and assumes special significance in present times that are driven by corporate governance and where stress levels are indeed very high.

III

The present Indian economy in the context of globalization and makes a presentation of Gandhian alternative as assimilated in the land where he was born.

Indian economy is viewed from various points of view and is considered: Underdeveloped, developing, dualistic and mixed.

Contributing to underdeveloped economy is the factor of 64 per cent of population being dependent on agriculture. And which there is nothing wrong with being agricultural the problem lies with the techniques of production that are not advanced in the agricultural sector although they sustain two-thirds of the population.

On the other hand the industry sector has become pervaded by modern techniques of production, but they are less advanced than those in use in the developed economies.

- 38 per cent of population lives below poverty line. The problem of mass poverty is complementary to income inequalities. Surge in number of Working Age Indians will provide crucial edge in an ageing world. Thank God we failed in population control (*Times of India,* 24 April, 2005, p. 1).
- Private enterprise in India has failed to play a prominent role in development and there is one of the single major factors behind India's underdeveloped status.

- Scarce availability of capital is another major setback to the country's development plans. Less than 40 per cent of total resources are with the government channels while roughly 60 per cent lies in private sector. This is an alarming statistic and gives one crude jolt. Referring to the Structural Aspect of Indian economy.
- A glance at statistics will reveal that the share of agriculture and allied sectors in India's economy has come down over the years. The industry sectors' share of GDP (including mining, manufacturing, electricity supply and construction) has witnessed a rise since 1960s. It stood at 31 per cent in 1996-97.

The service sector (including trade, hotel, transport, communication, finance, real estate, personal services contributed about 48 per cent to the GDP (2000-01).

Referring to the Quantitative Aspect of Indian economy—a study of national income trend over past years from 1950-57 to 1993-94 it has grown 10 times. Though national income has not been rising at a steady pace, its rate of increase has been higher than the rate of population growth. So per capita consumption has seen some improvement and capital accumulation has been possible to some extent. Per capita income has shown a growing trend from Rs. 3,687 in 1950-51 to Rs. 10,254 in 2000-01.

Progress in financial sector has been in terms of better money organization, capital markets and establishment of specialized industrial set-ups related to finance. The banking sector has witnessed growth in banking service mainly through commercial banks and cooperative credit societies.

Dualistic Nature

Indian economy reveal dualistic nature—it exhibits features of a modern economy as well as a traditional one.

While traditional sector is associated with agriculture or small industries, and has variable technical production co-efficient and labour-intensive methods of production, the advanced sector has large industries fixed technical coefficient production and capital-intensive methods of production.

In agricultural and handicrafts sectors, there has been slow technological progress but in the industrial sector, technological development is noticeable.

Mixed Economy

Another feature of Indian economy has been 'mixed economy'—a special kind of planned economic that was adopted by India at the behest of Nehru, soon after independence. Planning means a systematic utilization of the available resources at a progressive rate so as to secure and increase in output, national dividend, employment and social welfare of people. The essence of planning is that economic activity is regulated by the state with a view to achieving, well-defined goals within a specified period of time.

Nobel laureate, Amartya Sen has propounded a new concept for the estimation of poverty. This is called Sen Index. This method combines the best of both—the head count method and income gap method. In his Presidential address of **Development Studies Association** in 1982, Sen pointed out that traditional development economies suffer from a serious shortcoming, in that it focuses only on the qualitative parameters of growth such as national income, per capita income, capital formation, notwithstanding the qualitative parameters of growth. Sen argues that unlike the concept of economic growth, the concept of economic development focuses on changes in economic welfare, particularly for the low income population. Economic welfare measures aim at eradication of illiteracy, epidemics and infant mortality.

"Ultimately the process of economic development has to be concerned with what people can do or cannot do, for example, whether they can live long, escape avoidable morbidity, be well nourished, be able to read and write and communicate, take part in literary and scientific pursuits, and so forth."

Amartya Sen is of the view that economic development should not merely focus on greater production of goods and services or generation of utility with minimum possible cost of production. Instead, economic development is the process of enhancing capabilities to maximize entitlement of the people's well-being. Here, the concept of well-being points to qualitative aspects of human life.

Thus, writes Amartya Sen, "Ultimately the process of economic development has to be concerned with what people can or cannot do, e.g., whether they can live long, escape avoidable morbidity, be well nourished, be able to read and write and communicate, take part in literary and scientific pursuits and so forth". Sen's views thus, are the hypothesis of capability and entitlement.

Foundations of the Theory of Development

Sen's theory of development is founded on three basic parameters as under:

(i) ***Endowments*****:** Endowment is defined as the combination of all tangible and intangible resources legally owned by a person.

In the above definition, tangible resources include land, tools and implements as well as all cattle power. Intangible resources include knowledge, skill and labour power. The term legal in the above definition includes not only the laws or legislation of the government but also the laws framed by the communities or the societies.

(ii) ***Capability*****:** Sen defines capability as the ability to transform Rawlsian primary goods to the achievement potential of well-being. Rawlsian Primary goods are things that every rational man is presumed to want and include income and wealth, the basic liberties, choice of occupations, responsibilities and self-respect. Capability of a human being is his ability of functioning in different capacities in society, such as to enable him to achieve the components of his well-being. Here, well-being includes nutritious food, health services, education and social security. Sen includes all these parameters in his Capability Index. This also constitutes the basis for Human Development Index which is often used by the World Bank for international economic comparisons.

(iii) *Economic Entitlement*: The entitlement is defined as the set of all possible combinations of goods and services that a person can legally and socially obtain by using the resources of his endowment. Following are the notable features of the term 'entitlement':

(a) Given his endowment, a person can obtain a set of different combinations of goods and services.

(b) To obtain different goods and services, resource endowment can be used in different ways. For example, a farmer, by using his land, labour and other resources, can grow foodgrains. A worker can earn food for his family as a compensation for his work. A weaver, by using his labour and handloom, can produce cloth, which he can exchange for food for his family.

(c) The use of resource endowment by a person must have a legal sanction from the society as well as the government.

According to Sen, the concept of economic entitlement is applicable not only in market economies but social economies as well. In socialist economies, economic entitlements imply the transfer of goods and services from the state to the citizens, on the basis of social norms or state regulations—In non-socialist economies also, the concept of social security further strengthens the concept of economic welfare and economic entitlements.

Sen is of the view that the conventional concept of development lays a greater stress on the supply of goods and services rather than the fundamental parameters of economic entitlement and capabilities. It must be kept in mind that economic entitlement does not depend exclusively on economic parameters. It also depends on the nature of political system of a country. Political system of a country is an important factor in the context of the supply of goods and services and in the context of capabilities of the individuals to secure goods and services.

In short, the concept of economic development as propounded by Sen is founded on the parameters of capabilities and economic entitlements of the individuals to secure goods and services for their well-being. Capability to work is related to the freedom to secure economic well-being. In other words, "Economic Development is that state in which the capabilities to use economic entitlements are enhanced to raise the people from the level of poverty, to satisfy their basic needs, to maintain their self-respect and to give them freedom from ignorance, disease and squalor".

Recent Changes

Since 1991, the Government of India has introduced new policies arrived at by bringing about a qualitative change in the economy by effecting structural adjustments in the economy. Some of the features are:

- A market-oriented economy is emerging with increase in competition as a result of doing away with regulations, contracts and government restriction that had checked the growth of private sector in the past. Liberalization of economy has largely released imports and exports from government imposed restrictions.
- Reductions in custom duty rates and encouragement to foreign investment have placed Indian economy inline with those of other countries.
- While planning has not been discarded, it has become more indicative than before setting directions for economy rather than rigid targets forms the basic root of planning now. State intervention is more market oriented.

Having said this, let us now go back to what we said in earlier part, Part I of this presentation. The rules are set by developed states and globalization and liberalization has not succeeded in alienating poverty. Instead it has resulted in producing a small thin layer of ultra-rich elites—thereby increasing the gap between rich and poor. This gap is at two levels—one within the nation and second among nations.

To conclude if on the one hand, India has crossed billion dollars economy mark, we yet face the painful reality of farmer suicides throughout the country. The statistics of the State of Punjab are the eye opener. The Voluntary Health Association of Punjab in collaboration with Human Rights Law Network with the help of eight major farmer organizations in seven districts of Punjab (2006) reveals that the average number of suicides per village is 11 and the range extends from 5 to 74 (Kalka village in Sangrur district has the highest number of suicide cases).

Of the analyzed cases 21.48 per cent were committed in 1990-95, 33.14 in 1996-2000 and 45.38 per cent in 2001-2006 showing a consistently rising trend, which is alarming.

Largest number of suicides were reported in :

Sangrur	1010, followed by
Bhatinda	540
Moga	434
Ferozepur	68
Muktsar	58 and
Faridkot	25.

END NOTES

Bacher, Christian (2007). *Capitalism, Ethics and the Paradox of Self Exploitation*, Grin Verlag, p. 2.

De George, Richard T. (1986). *Business Ethics*, p. 104.

Freidman, Milton (1962). *Capitalism and Freedom*, University of Chicago Press.

Fulcher, Fames (2004). *Capitalism*, Oxford University Press, 45.

Galbraith (1993). *American Capitalism* : Concept of Countervailing Power, Transaction Publishing, New Brunswick, New Jersey (Originally Published by Houghton Miffin Co, Boston, 1952.

Growth pegged at 8.1 per cent as a result of big push from manufacturing sector and borrowing services sector. *The Hindu*, 8 February, 2006, p. 1.

Harvey, David (1990). *The Political Economic Transformation of Late Twentieth Century Capitalism*, Cambridge.

Hayek, Freidrich A. (1963). *Capitalism and the Historians*, Chicago.

Heibroner, Robert L. (1966). *The Limits of American Capitalism*, Academy Library.

Lash, Scott and Urry, John (2000). Capitalism, In Nicholas Abercrornbie, S. Hill & BS Turner (Eds.). *The Penguin Dictionary of Sociology* (4th ed.), pp. 36-40.

Mehta, Ved (1961). *Gandhism is not Easily Copied*, The New York Times Company.

Obrinsky, Mark (1983). *Profit Theory and Capitalism*. University of Pennsylvania Press.

Parthasarthy, Dr. Swami, (2007). 'Corporate Governance' talk delivered at ICSSR complex, Panjab University, 10th August.

Whalen Charles J. (ed) (1996). *Political Economy for the 21st Century: Contemporary Views on the Trend of Economics*, ME Sharpe, INC, USA.

Wolf, Eric, University of California Press (1982),. *Europe and the People without History*.

Wood, Ellen Meiksins (2002). *The Origins of Capitalism: A Longer View*, London: Verso.

5

Right to Information Act 2005 and Rule of Law

In a democratic set-up, the people have a right to know every public act and conduct discharged by their public functionaries. The right to know is necessary outcome of the concept of freedom of speech and expression. At the same time open government does not mean that the whole government transactions are to be carried out in the market place. To cover with veil of secrecy the matters relating to national safety and security is not in the general public interest. In this sense, the right to know has to be counterbalanced in just and reasonable constitutional norms. Information and communication are powerful tools and have a potential to shape and shake social and political development of the society. 'Men make their history but not as they please', said Karl Marx. It depends on the quality and quantity of information supplied to them. Accordingly, in this chapter an attempt has been made to examine the parameters of freedom of information and its pitfalls in constitutional dynamics.

Significance of the Right to Information

Savoir est pouvoir (knowledge is power) is a French saying. Today information is power. *Asato mam sat gamaya* and *tamaso mam jyotir gamaya,* were not merely empty words of prayer but were demands for an open mind and open world. "I regard legislation on the right to information as vital weapon of the citizen against abuse of power' , said *V.R. Krishna Iyer.* There is a wide information gap in our legal system in the matrix of various rights and freedoms enshrined in our Constitution. Article 19[1] confers upon every citizen a fundamental right called freedom of speech and expression. In order to meaningfully enjoy this freedom, a citizen must also have an ancillary right to secure all necessary information on matters of public interest from public authorities.[2] Such a right is a *sine qua non* of an open, democratic, responsive and responsible polity. Such polity can throb and survive if its citizens are sufficiently informed and kept informed. The right to information will enable the citizens to criticise, comment and approve policies and programmes of the rulers. Thus in the words of V.R. Krishna Iyer: "Informational justice has a constitutional basis." Bhagwati J. in **S.P. Gupta** v. **Union of India**[3] described democracy as a continuous process of government, an attitude and habit of mind, in which people have to play important role only "if it is open government where there is full access to information in regard to the functioning of the government". There is hardly any need to emphasise the fact that secrecy in the working of the government would tend to promote and encourage oppression, corruption and abuse of authority. Public scrutiny and public exposure of governmental processes help achieve a clean and healthy government. Such a government has to justify its trusts of policies by giving facts for and against a selected course of action. The Court pronounced: "The concept of an open government is the direct emanation from the right to know which seems to be implicit in the right of free speech and expression guaranteed under Article 19(1)(a)". In the eloquent words of Mathew J. in **State of Uttar Pradesh** v. **Raj Narain.**[4]

> In a government of responsibility like ours, where all the agents of the public must be responsible for their conduct, there can be but few secrets. The people of this country have a right to know every public act, everything that is done in a public way, by their public functionaries. They are entitled to know the particulars of every transaction in its bearing. The right to know, which is derived from

the concept of freedom of speech, though not absolute, is a factor which should make one vary, when secrecy is claimed, for transactions which can, at any rate, have no repercussion on public security. To cover with veil of secrecy the common routine business is not in the interest of the public.[5]

The very rationale of democratic government is that it is founded on the consent of the governed. This consent of necessity has to be both free and informed, it has to be shaped by the widest possible dissemination of information from all quarters and sources. Informed citizens help in informed and intelligent decision-making. At the same time open government does not mean that the whole government processes are to be carried out in the market place. The right to know has to be counterbalanced by the privacy of government decision-making. This right is meant to unfold the needless and excessive secrecy in decision-making processes. To focus public attention on the importance of this right in our democratic policy the public Relations Society of India every year celebrates April 21 as a right to information day.[6]

Comparative Overview of Right to Information

Cautious Approach in England

English law seems to have adopted quite a cautious approach in this regard. Professor Campbell explained the position in England in these words: "Governmental reluctance to disclose documents is a legacy from the time public administration was simply an extension of the Crown's administration of its properties, when the distinction between private and public administrations was by no means clear cut." Yet we find a small and limited area of this right in the Crown Proceedings Act 1974 under which legal action against the Crown and Government departments can be initiated. Section 28(1)(i) of this Act provides that "in any civil proceedings . . . to which Crown is a party, the Crown may be required by the court to make discovery of documents and produced those documents for inspection". It is also provided that "the Crown may be required by the court to answer interrogatories...". However, the common law did not favour this right of disclosure. **Smith** v. **East India Co.**[7] and **Beatson** v. **Skene**[8] are noteworthy illustrations of early setbacks. In the former the court disallowed the request of disclosure of certain documents in court as it amounted to restrain the freedom of communication between the East India Company and its Board of Control. In the other case the court refused the compulsion of production of certain documents regarding a court of inquiry conducted by the secretary of state. Lord Chancellor Kilmuier in a later case[9] stated two grounds when such a crown privilege for documents can be claimed: (a) the disclosure of the contents of the particular document would injure the public interest, e.g., by endangering public security, or prejudicing diplomatic relations; and (b) the document is of such a class which the public interest requires to be withheld from production. This rigid position, however, was a little liberalised in a later case[10] in which it was held that inspection by the court of documents could not cause harm. The only requirement, in the words of Lord Wilberforce, was that "there must be a likelihood that the documents would support the case or the party seeking discovery".

Prompt and Cheap Disclosure Approach in Australia

In Australia before the enactment of Freedom of Information Act 1982 the courts did not favour production of documents possessed by state authorities. It was held that "counsels of the Crown are secret and an inquiry into the grounds upon which the advice was tendered" was not allowed,[11] however, later on courts refused to accept the conclusiveness of the executive certificate of privilege. Thereafter the aforesaid Act was made. Its salient features were: (i) the general right to access for the public to official documents in the possession of ministers and agencies except the one that were specifically exempted; (ii) the right to correct inaccuracies; (iii) the internal law of the Commonwealth agencies to be published every year;

and (iv) a proper procedure for the disposal of requests for access to documents. Thus this Act enabled prompt and cheap disclosure of information.

Transparent and Crucial Approach in U.S.A.

The founders of the American democracy did recognize fully of crucial importance of information.[12] Perhaps the strongest statement in support of access to information was made by James Madison: "Knowledge will forever govern ignorance. And a people who mean to be their own governors, must arm themselves with the power knowledge gives. A popular government without popular information of the means of acquiring it, is but a prologue to a farce, or a tragedy, or perhaps both." Thomas Jefferson was emphatic to give the people "full information of their affairs through the channels of the public papers, and to contrive that these papers penetrate the whole mass of the people. The basis of our government being the opinion of the people the very first object should be to keep that right; and were it left to me to decide whether we should have a government without newspapers or newspapers without a government, I should not hesitate a moment to prefer the latter". "Patrick Henry, who was often in disagreement with other leaders on other matters, shared their views on the necessity for an informed public opinion; said :

> The liberties of the people never were, or never will be, secure, when the transactions of their rulers may be concealed from them . . . I am not an advocate for divulging indiscriminately all the operations of government, though the practices of our ancestors, in some degree justify it. Such transactions as relate to military operations of affairs of great consequence, the immediate promulgation of which might defeat the interests of the community, I would not wish to be published, till the end which required their secrecy should have been effected. But to cover with the veil of secrecy the common routine of business, is an abomination in the eyes of every intelligent man.[13]

In the United States of America, the Original Freedom of Information Act (FOIA) was enacted in 1966 as an amendment to the Administrative Procedures Act. Its purpose was: "To establish a general Philosophy of full agency disclosure unless information is exempted under clearly delineated statutory language "The Act exempted classified material, business proprietary material, information whose release would invade personal privacy and other material whose disclosure would compromise the public interest. This Act had little effect even after several years or its enactment. So in 1974, the Act was amended and time limits were provided to respond to requests. Internal appellate machinery was provided. It also empowered courts to intervene to enforce deadlines and review agency decisions. Arbitrary and capricious withholding of information by officials was made punishable. Only information relating to foreign policy, defence, national security, trade secrets, personal and medical files are not allowed under the Act. At that time it was estimated that its costs will not exceed $50,000 in 1974 and $100,000 for each of the succeeding five fiscal years. But thereafter the costs have exceeded these estimates. The FOIA costs of the FBI alone have exceeded $55 million between 1974 and 1983.[14]

By 1987 federal agencies received more than 3,75,000 FOIA requests annually and spent about $60 million a year to answer them. FOIA fees covered only about five per cent of the costs. The Department of Defence, for example received 87,179 requests and it spent $30 million in responding to them but recovered less than $1 million as fees. Sometimes a "segregability review" of hundreds of documents had to be undertaken to determine what material should be released and what not. This sometimes required the services of highly qualified technical and security experts. It must, however, be highlighted that if there were uses of FOIA there were its abuses too to render it "much a burden as a benefit". The New York Bar Association in 1979 warned that it was not Congress' intent that the FOIA be used as a *carte blanche* for unrestricted access to otherwise non-public information submitted by private citizens and businesses. And yet businessmen sought information on their competitors. In one such mistaken disclosure case a corporation lost its domination of a $ 450 million per year market. Besides businessmen this law has been widely exploited by lawyers for clients who used government data to fight federal investigations, spying on the competitors and discovering how strictly regulations were really enforced.[15]

All these led to its further amendment in 1986. The criminals also have not lagged behind in abusing FOIA. Prisoners used it to know who incriminated them. Others used it to avoid prosecution. The organised criminals in Detroit had been instructed to submit FOIA requests to identify FBI sources. They were supplied over 12,000 pages of FBI documents. From 1975 to 1981, FBI was forced to release over 60,000 pages of documents concerning an underground crime gang. Powerful persons have sought information about investigation of allegations of political corruption against them and have thereafter subtly changed their mode of operation.

The law has been used to get technical information about intelligence. The CIA was approached for information about its agents and informants. Ultimately, the Congress made "operational files" of the CIA automatically inaccessible to FOIA requests. Also "technical data having a space or military application" were protected.

The use of FOIA by news media and public interest groups has been uneven and scattered. Some have used it extensively while others have rarely done so. But the FOIA has been extensively used by litigants against federal government. It is used to supplement the legal discovery process. It is resorted to for three reasons: it is inexpensive; it has rigid time frames enforceable by law, and makes available that material which is otherwise not available.[16]

Another adverse effect of the FOIA must not be lost sight of government officials have now started to avoid to fully document the process by which they arrived at a given policy decision. Though "pre-decisional" material is exempted from the FOIA the factual information leading to a decision has to be released. Consequently, senior executives have avoided memorialising useful background information. Officials are warned to be cautious about what they write. They, are ordered to destroy all draft copies after the final document is issued.[17]

But in spite of its above pitfalls the FOIA has to stay. It provides a useful window to peep into otherwise dark governmental processes. Richard A. Guida has suggested the following amendments to the FOIA to build that window better. He warned that unless these reforms were enacted the costs of free information will counterbalance its benefits.

1. Requests for information should be limited to U.S. citizens, and to those who are not in prison or acting on behalf of prisoners.
2. All material from criminal investigations should be exempted FOIA requests.
3. The FOIA should be changed to prohibit its use in the legal discovery process.
4. Time limits for responding to requests, particularly those seeking many documents or old material, should be substantially increased. The responding agency should be able to establish a schedule for responses which takes into account volume, age, complexity of material, necessary review time, and so on. A request for fity documents comprising three thousand pages of classified material might face a standard response time of several months, while the current two-week deadline could continue to apply to simple requests.
5. The full cost of administering the FOIA should be borne by the users. Though the news media are now specifically exempted from FOIA fees, this exemption should be abolished. The fees should cover search time, segregability review time, the effort required to decide whether to release material, and the cost of copying documents and mailing them to the requester.
6. The FOIA should be extended to cover congressional committees and agencies.

Parallel to the Freedom of Information Act at the federal level there is a more recent "open meetings" statute, called the

Government in Sunshine Act 1976. There has been relatively little litigation under this statute. In general, the Act requires about fifty federal agencies, including major regulatory such as the Federal Communications Commission, the National Labour Relations Board, and the Securities and Exchange Commission, to hold their meetings in public. However, the Act allows closed sessions if the subject matter falls within FOIA, though there are some important differences. The Act also prescribes in detail the procedures that must follow to hold a closed meeting. In addition to this federal Act, all fifty states and the District of Columbia have also enacted open meetings statutes. Though these statutes vary tremendously in scope, they have much in common with each other and the federal Sunshine Act.

Parameters of Freedom of Information in India

The need for giving a statutory shape to a judicially recognised and pronounced right to know needs not to be justified. The Central Government has acknowledged that, "free flow of information is a prerequisite for democracy" and assured the electorate that "the right to information will be enshrined in our Constitution".[18] But one need, not wait for a constitutional amendment, which would require suitable political balancing to ensure adequate support in the Parliament for its passage. Even if such an amendment is contemplated it can be safely passed, it is submitted that it is not necessary. After all its incorporation in the Part III of the Constitution will be in general, broad and wide terms with attendant reasonable restrictions. Instead, it is submitted that an appropriate statute, say, Freedom of Information, may be enacted which could be passed with simple majority, unlike a constitutional amendment requiring special majority. Such a statute must provide the parameters of this freedom and make adequate provisions to avoid the pitfalls of the U.S. FOIA.

The policy underlying the U.S. FOIA, has been articulated as: (i) disclosure to be the general rule, and not the exception; (ii) all individuals have equal rights of access; (iii) the burden is on the government to justify the withholding of a document and not on the person who requests it; (iv) individuals improperly denied access to documents have a right to seek injective relief in the courts; and (v) there should be a change in government policy and attitude.

Soli Sorabjee articulated the objectives of any legislation giving statutory shape to freedom of information as follows: (i) protection of the rights or individuals by giving citizens right to access to information about themselves held in government or other official files; (ii) the right to correct that information if it is misleading or untrue; (iii) it should ensure wider dissemination of information gathered at the public expenses on topics such as product safety, land records, health and environmental hazards, ecological data, etc., and (iv) it should throw the spot light of public scrutiny on policy formulation and administration and thereby improve the quality of decision making; (v) access to information should be within easy reach and at affordable cost.[19]

Within the above objectives framework a comprehensive statute delineating the parameters and defining the various components of the freedom of information should be enacted. At the same time such a contemplated statute must have adequate provisions to avoid the pitfalls and drawbacks experienced in the working of the U.S. FOIA. This will necessitate conceptual clarity on the part of the law makers. In addition to these there are complex issues of social engineering in regard to balancing and counterbalancing freedom of information *vis-à-vis* various interests, concepts and issues.[20] Such as: freedom of speech and expression of mass media and individual's defamation, contempt of courts, privacy, human rights, copyright, patents/trade marks, news gathering and confidentiality of source of news, national security, public law and order, internal secrecy rules of autonomous institutions corporations, protection against catch-all provision, trade secrets, official secrets, law enforcement, coverage of court proceedings, social interest litigation, activists movements, morality and public safety, communal, election, religious and violent crime and correctional matters advertising commissions of inquiry, atomic and nuclear energy defence industry and strategies, etc. Each of these areas will need re-examination and re-evaluation in the context of freedom of information.[21]

In addition to these some very important issues will need policy decisions. For example, who should have and not have this freedom; when to have it and when not; against whom and under what circumstances; and to what extent at what costs and within how much time, machinery regarding appeals and other relief; whether we should have our own version of "Sunshine Act"[22] what could be the reasonable restrictions and exemptions of this freedom, and so on. Soli Sorabjee suggested exemptions permitting government to withhold access to information in respect of the following matters:

(i) International relations and national security;
(ii) Law enforcement and prevention of crime;
(iii) Information deliberations of the government;
(iv) Information obtained in confidence from some source outside the government;
(v) Information, which, if disclosed, would violate privacy of an individual;
(vi) Information, particularly of an economic nature, which if disclosed, would confer an unfair advantage on some person or subject some person or government to an unfair disadvantage; and
(vii) Information about scientific discoveries and inventions and improvements, essentially in the field of weaponry.

The Concept of Open Government

Article 74 (2) of the Constitution says that the question whether any, and if so what, advice was tendered by Ministers to the President shall not be inquired into in any Court. Accordingly, the Supreme Court has held in **Davpack Systems Pvt. Ltd.** v. **India**[23] that it is the duty of the Court to prevent disclosure where Article 74(2) is applicable. The cabinet papers are protected from disclosure not by reason of their content but because of the class to which they belong. The expression

"Cabinet papers—would also include papers brought into existence for the purpose of preparing submission to the Cabinet.[24] The notings of the officials which lead to the Cabinet note leading to the Cabinet decision also form part of the advice tendered to the President. The Court got support for this view from certain observations in *S.P. Gupta* v. *India*.[25]

In **Bihar** v. **Kripalu Shankar,**[26] the Supreme Court has laid down an important proposition designed to facilitate the internal working of the government. The Court has stated that notings made by government officials in the departmental files cannot be made a ground for a proceeding for contempt of Court. The Court has advanced several sound reasons for taking such a view. A government functions by taking decisions on the strength of views and suggestions expressed by various officers at different levels, ultimately resulting in a final decision by the Minister concerned. There should be no fetter on fearless and independent expression of views by officers on files coming before them, even including Court orders. The expression of opinion by the officers in the internal files are for the use of the department and not for outside exposure or publicity. These internal notings are in fact privileged documents. To find officers guilty of expressing their independent opinion, even against Court orders in deserving cases, would cause impediments in the smooth functioning of government to find notes in the files would impair the independent functioning of the civil service essential to democracy as it would hamper a fearless expression of views by government officers. While a Court can direct production of even confidential papers for it to see, there is an implied understanding that these will not be used for any other purpose.[27]

The Court has emphasized in this connection. In democratic countries, at the present moment, the accent is on open government. Of course, there are quite a few things, which must be kept confidential in the interest of public security or national interest. Sometimes the law may impose secrecy in the interest of the individual.[28] But then the secrecy ought not to be more than what is absolutely necessary. In this area, what is necessary is to draw a balance between 'secrecy' and 'openness' with an accent on the latter. There are many reasons suggesting an open government. Participation in government by the people is regarded as an important aspect of democracy and people cannot participate unless they have information as to what is going on in the country. A modern democratic state being answerable to the people, the people are entitled to know what policies and programmes, how and why, are being followed by the government.[29] People have to pass verdict every five years on the performance of the government, and decide whether it should stay in office or not. People cannot exercise their choice intelligently unless they are given adequate information about the functioning of the government.[30] Another factor justifying openness by the government is that being an activist entity, government gathers a vast arsenal of powers in a welfare state as has been described in the previous pages. These powers are used to affect economic interests and personal liberty of the individual. It is important that these powers are exercised for public good, not improperly, and for the purposes for which the powers are conferred. This objective is best ensured by giving access to the individual to governmental information and not shroud in secrecy as to how the government exercises its powers in individual cases. Since power tends to corrupt, and absolute power tends to corrupt absolutely, there is an inherent danger that the vast powers available to the executive may be used not for public good but for private gain, or for corrupt motive. It is, therefore, essential that the people have as much information about government operations as possible.[31]

Openness in government is bound to act as a powerful check on the abuse or misuse of power by the government. It has already been emphasized earlier that there should be public consultation in the exercise of legislative powers by the government. This idea has to be made applicable to the whole gamut of governmental functioning. As Schwartz emphasizes: "Americans firmly believe in the healthy effects of publicity and have a strong antipathy to the inherent secretiveness of government agencies". In India, so far, the progress towards open government has been rather tardy. But the consciousness is there. As Bhagwati J. advised in **S.P. Gupta** v. **President of India:**

Open government is the new democratic culture of an open society towards which every liberal democracy is moving and our country should be no exception.[32]

This approach is depicted by a British case **Attorney General** v. **Jonathan Cape Ltd.**[33] An action was brought for injunction to restrain the publication of the political diaries of the late Richards Crossman who was a cabinet minister in the Labour Government of 1964 to 1970. The plea was that the publication of the diaries would reveal the cabinet secrets and infringe the principle of collective responsibility of the government. Lord Widgery C.J. accepted the proposition that when a cabinet minister receives information in confidence the improper publication of such information can be restrained by the Court. Collective responsibility was held to be "an established feature of the English form of government" and that "some matters leading up to a cabinet decision may be regarded as confidential". But, in the instant case, injunction was refused against publication of the materials in question as they were about ten years old and no longer required protection in public interest. The Court emphasized that it should intervene "only in the clearest of cases where the continuing confidentiality of the material can be demonstrated".

Reference may also be made in this connection to an Australian case **Commonwealth of Australia** v. **John Fairfax & Sons Ltd.**[34] Two journalists had obtained a number of foreign office cables and memoranda covering several matters like Indonesia, East Timor, Anzus defence treaty. The government applied for an injunction to prohibit publication of the materials on the ground of breach of confidentiality. Mason J. said in this connection: "But it can scarcely be a relevant detriment to the government that publication of material concerning its actions will merely expose it to public discussion and criticism. It is unacceptable in our democratic society that there should be a restraint on the publication of information relating to the government where the only vice of that information is that it enables the public to discuss and criticise government action".

Mason J. also said: "The court will determine the governments claim to confidentiality by reference to the public interest. Unless disclosure is likely to injure the public interest it will not be protected. The court will not prevent the publication of information which merely throws light on the past workings of government, even if it be not public property, so long as it does not prejudice the community in other respects. Then disclosure will itself serve the public interest in keeping the community informed and in promoting the discussion of public affairs. It, however, appears that disclosure will be inimical to the public interest because national security, relations with foreign countries or the ordinary business of government will be prejudiced. T disclosure will be restrained".

There are several aspects of open government, e.g. (1) Presentation of documents by the government in the Court in the course of some litigation; (2) Official Secrecy; and (3) Access to Information. People's right to know has two aspects: (1) How far government should use criminal sanction to deter free flow of information? (2) How far government is under a positive obligation to make available, on demand, information to the people not in the prohibited category.

Presentation of Documents in the Court

This matter has already been considered earlier. It has been seen that, in course of time, the courts have loosened the government privilege not to produce unpublished documents in the Court in the course of a Court proceeding against it. Since the writing of the aforesaid piece, one or two aspects of the government reluctance from making public certain secret documents have come to light.[35] These may be mentioned here.

One significant judicial pronouncement to be noted here is Khatri. A writ petition was brought in the Supreme Court under Article 32 by certain under-trials for enforcement of their fundamental right under Article 21 on the allegation that they were blinded by the police officer whilst in police custody.

The Court called for production or certain documents by the state. The state objected to the production of these documents on the ground that they were protected by Sections 162 and 172 of the Criminal Procedure Code and that the petitions were not entitled to see them or to make any use or them in these proceedings. The Court considered the point in **Khatri** v. **Bihar.**[36]

The Court held that Section 162 has no application in a proceeding under Article 32 or 226. Section 162 has been enacted for the benefit of the accused.[37] A writ petition for enforcement of fundamental rights under Article 21 is nether an "inquiry" nor a "trial" in respect of any offence and so Section 162 cannot be invoked by the state. Even a statement made before a police officer during investigation can be produced and used in evidence in a writ petition under Article 32 provided it is relevant under the Indian Evidence Act and Section 162 cannot be urged as a bar against its production or use. Similarly, the bar placed by Section 172 operates only in an inquiry or trial for an offence and can have no application in proceedings under Article 32 or 226. Accordingly, the Court directed the production of the Documents in Question.

The Official Secrets Act 1923

The Official Secrets Act 1923 deals with two aspects—(i) espionage or spying activity; and (ii) disclosure of other secret official information. The former is dealt with by Section 3 and the latter by Section 5. Section 3 is not relevant for our discussion here. Section 5 is more relevant and important for our purposes. The provisions of Section 5 may be analysed under the following heads:

(a) Persons in Possession of Official Information

The coverage of persons having possession of official information who are liable under the section is extremely wide. It includes the following:

(a) Any person in possession or control of secret official information.
(b) Any person obtaining information in contravention of this Act.
(c) Any person to whom official information has been entrusted in confidence by any person holding office under the government.
(d) Any person obtaining or having access to information owing to his holding any office (present or past), or holding any government contract, or any person holding office under any of these persons.

(b) Persons Receiving the Information

Not only is the person communicating the information guilty of an offence under Section 5, but also the person receiving it. It applies not only to government servants but also to all persons who have obtained the secret information in contravention of the Act. Under Section 5(2), any person to whom secret official information has been communicated in contravention of the Act, in other words, a person who is not a person being in lawful possession of the secret information commits an offence by the mere fact of receipt of the same. An offence is also committed if the person receiving secret information from a public officer further communicates it to another person.[38]

(c) The Secret Information

The official information covered by the section is also extremely broad. Any kind of information is covered provided it is "secret". This includes any official code, pass word, sketch, plan, model, article, note, document or information. The only qualification is that it should be "secret". Nowhere the word "secret" or words "official secrets" are defined in the Act. However, one thing is clear: the Act extends only to official secrets and not to secrets of a private nature.[39] Thus, the Act extends to secrets of a ministry or department of the government, but not to an incorporated body like a university, government company, or public corporation.

In the absence of any definition in the Act, it is for the government to decide what it should treat as secret and what not. But does the government have an unquestioned right to decide what information it would classify as secret and so keep it away from the public? Will any information classified as secret be "official secrets" and would be caught by the Act? It appears from the cases mentioned below that the government does not seem to be the sole judge of the matter and that the Courts can review the decision of the government. The practice of the government is to treat an information secret, even though there may be no danger to national security or public safety or any other public interest, merely because it may embarrass the government, that is, the political party in power.

The newspaper *Blitz* published an article inviting the public to send in official secrets to the editor for which a lavish payment was promised. The question was whether such an article would fall under Section 5 (1) of the Official Secrets Act. The Bombay High Court ruled in **R.K. Karanjia** v. **Emperor**[40] that the said article would fall under Section 5 (1) of the Official Secrets Act. The Court said that the expression "official secrets" was nowhere defined, "but looking to the purpose and scheme of the Official Secrets Act, especially Sections 3 to 10, which create offences against the government for publication of official secrets, they have all reference to secrets of one or the other department of the Government or the State and not to any secret of a private office". A secret pertaining to any private office, e.g., university or a corporation would not be called an official secret. The Court refused to accept the contention that the term "official secret" used in the said article included secrets of any private institution. Referring to Section 5 (I) of the Official Secrets Act, the Court characterised the provision as "very comprehensive in its nature" and "it applies not merely to Government servants but also to all persons who have obtained that secret in contravention of this Act". The invitation to the public to send official secrets would fall under Section 5 (J) as "it is really an invitation encouraging or inciting any person to commit an offence". The Court said that it was not concerned with the intention or the motive underlying the article in question "but only with the direct or indirect tendency of the words used in the article itself", and in the Court's opinion that tendency was "to encourage or incite any person to omit an offence", concerned will be liable to an action under the Act. Section 5 (I) (a) uses blanket language by making punishable "wilful communication" of any official secret to any person, other than a person to whom he is authorised to communicate it, or a Court of Justice or a person to whom it is in the interests of the State, his duty to communicate it. There are no exceptions like communication in public interest, etc. Everything is punishable whether national security or any other interest worth protecting is endangered or not. The section gives carte blanche to the executive to prosecute anyone disclosing official information or, as per Section 5(2), any person voluntarily receiving such information knowing or having reasonable ground to believe that such information is being given in contravention of the Act.

In **State** v. **K. Balakrishna**[41] certain parts of the budget were published in a newspaper before the presentation of the budget. It was held that the budget being a secret document of the government, the reception and publication thereof fell within the mischief of Section 5(2) and Section 5(1)(b) of the Official Secrets Act. Although there is no written rule declaring budget papers before being presented in the legislature as secret documents, on a consideration of the views expressed in constitutional law books and the statements made by several witnesses, there can be no doubt that the budget papers are usually treated as highly confidential before these are presented to the legislature. The budget papers are "official secrets" and that it would amount to an offence under Sections 5(2) and Section 5(1)(b) of the Official Secrets Act to publish them before they are actually presented to the Legislature. The Court also said that it was not a mere 'technical offence' but a "serious offence which might have far reaching consequences and repercussions on the economy of the State." **In Nandlal More** v. **The State,**[42] the Punjab High Court again considered the question of the premature leakage of budget information. This was held to be an offence under the Official Secrets Act. The Court rejected the argument that the Budget proposals cannot be regarded as "official secrets" as they have to be made public after some time. According to the Court, "the fact that on a subsequent date the budget proposals have to be made public would not detract from the secrecy of those proposals till such time as they are announced in Parliament."

(d) The Disclosure of Secret Government Information

A literal reading of Section 5 indicated that disclosure of any kind of secret information will attract prosecution under the Act whatever be the purpose or its impact. Even if disclosure is justified in public interest the person or persons concerned will be liable to an action under the Act. Section 5 (1) (a) uses blanket language by making punishable "wilful communication" of any official secret to any person, other than a person to whom he is authorised to communicate it, or a Court of Justice or a person to whom it is in the interest of the State, his duty to communicate it. There are no exceptions like communication in public interest, etc. Everything is punishable whether national security or any other interest worth protecting is endangered or not.[43] The section gives carte blanche to the executive to prosecute anyone disclosing official information or, as per Section 5(2), any person voluntarily receiving such information knowing or having reasonable ground to believe that such information is being given to him in contravention of the Act.

These provisions are harsh and the only redeeming feature is that *mens rea*, or the mental element, is the necessary ingredient of an offence under the provisions, for the words used are "wilfully", "voluntarily", "knowing" or "having reasonable ground to believe". Thus a mere "leak", unless it was intentional or wilful, will not be covered by the Act. The burden is on the government to prove *mens rea* as in the case of any other offence.[44] In a department where a matter or an information is handled by different persons it may be difficult to prove *mens rea* or fix responsibility on anyone for the leakage.

This does provide some kind of safeguard to an individual against the hardships of the law.

(e) Punishment under Section 5

The Act by itself does not classify punishments according to the degree or the nature of harm caused by the disclosure of secret information. There is a blanket provision which says that a person guilty of an offence under the section shall be punishable with imprisonment which may extend to three years, or with fine, or with both. Thus, it is a matter of judicial discretion to fix punishment in an individual case, subject to the maximum, laid down in the section, keeping in view the circumstances of the case and the degree of harm caused to the nation.[45]

According to Section 13(3) of the Official Secrets Act, no court can take cognizance of any offence under the Act unless upon complaint made by order of, or under authority from, the appropriate government or some officer empowered by the appropriate government in this behalf. This executive control over prosecutions under the Act makes such a drastic law tolerable in practice.[46]

It can be seen that the provisions of Section 5 are so general, wide and obscure that everything connected with the government could be brought within its fold. This omnibus and "catch-all" provision is neither fair nor purposeful. In a democracy some information must be revealed to the public to ensure good and proper government. Section 5 makes a criminal offence of all unauthorised disclosure of information from official sources, regardless of the consideration whether the public interest really demands secrecy. Literally read, it is the "disclosure" which is punishable and not the purpose or disclosure or prejudicial effect on certain interest deserving of protection in the national interest. Both the person communicating, and the person receiving official information, are guilty of an offence under the Act. If literally read and strictly applied, there will be daily innumerable prosecutions of the press, completely hampering its work. Fortunately, however, this does not happen. What makes the statute bearable is its extremely rare use by the government.

But the threat for its use is always there. The Franks Committee has stated that Section 2 of the English Act is rarely activated in the Court room, but is seen by many as having a pervasive influence on the work and the behaviour of hundreds of thousands of people.

Government of India's Practice regarding Official Secrecy

The normal rule in the Government of India is secrecy, and openness is an exception. Government papers and documents are divided into two categories, namely, "non-classified" and "classified". Greater secrecy is to be observed in the case of the latter. The classified documents divided into four categories, namely, "top secret", "secret", "confidential" and "personal—not for publication". The "top secret" grading is given to information of a vital nature affecting national security such as military secrets, matters of high international policy, intelligence reports, etc.[47] The "secret" marking is given to papers of information which is likely to endanger national security or cause injury to the interests or prestige of the nation or would cause serious embarrassment to the government either within the country or in its relations with foreign nations.[48] The word "confidential" pertains to information whose disclosure would be prejudicial to the interest of the nation or given advantage to a foreign nation or even cause administrative embarrassment. "Personal—not for publication" is meant for cases where the information is fit for communication to the individual members of the public, but it is desired that the information given to an individual is not meant for publication. These are arbitrary divisions without having any legal sanction. What is marked, and how it is marked, are matters within the prerogative of the government. It is also not clear whether there is any procedure to reconsider the classification of documents. So, the initial classification lingers on long after the document has ceased to be important.

As regards "non-classified" papers, the rule is that no official is to communicate any information to anyone, which has come into his possession in the course of his official duties, unless so authorised by general or special orders. Similarly, note portions of a file referred by one department to another are to be treated as confidential.[49] A government servant under the civil service rules is under an obligation not to disclose to anyone including a fellow government servant any information acquired by him during the course of his official duties. This is provided by Rule 8 of the Central Civil Service (Conduct) Rules 1955. A violation of this rule will subject the civil servant to disciplinary action, apart from punishment under any other law, e.g., the Official Secrets Act 1923.

The extent of the secrecy in government will be clear from one instance. Under Article 77 of the Constitution, the President has to make rules for the more convenient transaction of the business of the Government of India and for the allocation amongst ministers of the said business. Under this article the President has framed the Transaction of Business Rules and the Government or India (Allocation of Business) Rules 1961 which are also known as the Rules of Business. The allocation rules were published till 1973 and were available to the public but these are now treated as confidential. These rules mention the items of business allotted to each ministry or department of the Government of India. The Rules of Business which provide for the exercise of powers vested in the Government of India have always been treated as confidential by the government, and are not accessible to the public.[50] However, these rules have been supplied by the government to the courts as and when the question has arisen whether or not the power was discharged by an authorised officer.[51] It is somewhat illogical that though the President makes these rules under the Constitution, yet they are treated as confidential without the Constitution explicitly giving any confidentiality to them. In treating these rules as confidential the government intends to cover up its own irregularities and deficiencies rather than protect, even remotely, any public interest.[52]

There are innumerable instances when the most trivial matters are treated as secret which do not serve any interest of the nation except perhaps saving the government from embarrassment. The reports of various enquiry committees and commissions (like plane crashes or accidents) are treated as secret. Even the recommendations made by the Interdepartmental study group, set up by the Government of India in 1977, to look into the Official Secrets Act, 1923, have been treated as confidential. Printed Office manuals are kept secret. This Act uses criminal sanctions to suppress communication of official secrets. There is no law as yet imposing a positive obligation on the government to supply information to an individual when he asks for it. Such laws have been passed in the U.S.A., Australia and New Zealand and imposing a duty on the government to permit access to information in possession of the government within certain exceptions.

On the U.S. Freedom of Information Act 1966, Schwartz says: "Before then, the people's 'right to know' was a journalistic slogan rather than a legal right. The 1966 statute changed all this, since it gave the citizen, for the first time, a legally enforceable right of access to government files and documents. The FOIA effects a profound alteration in the position of the citizen *vis-á-vis* government. No longer is the individual seeking information from an administrative agency a mere suppliant".

General Observations

Importance of freedom of information in a democratic polity needs no justification. It is a *sine qua non* of an open government. To achieve its embodiment, a statute on the lines of reformed Freedom of Information Act of the U.S. would be a proper strategy rather than a constitutional amendment. However, its enactment is not easy. Even advanced democratic countries had such statute only recently after a prolonged experience of running an open liberal democratic polity. India must be very cautious in rushing to legislate on this freedom. There should be full and total conceptual clarity. The parameters of this freedom should be clearly defined.

The reasonable restrictions on it, and exceptions to it need careful consideration and elaborate articulation. The Indian

Statute shall endeavour to keep the pitfalls and drawbacks of the U.S. FOIA at bay. A half baked enactment may kill otherwise laudable object. Let it not be a fertile ground for legal profession to litigate eternally. Besides, the costs of free information are bound to be heavy. It should be available at an affordable cost within specified certain, definite and reasonable time limits. There should be adequate remedies against undue delay in its supply. This freedom will be meaningless if there is no adequate infrastructure of modem information technology in the form of storage and retrieval systems. At the same time care must be taken to see that freedom meant to expose government corruption itself does not become a tool to enhance governmental corruption in matters relating to supply and suppression of information. Also bureaucratic initiative and freedom in decision making processes need not be unduly curbed.[53] Really, the task is not so easy as it appears to be. After all information in the present age of information explosion is a very explosive matter. It needs to be handled with utmost care.

END NOTES

1. Constitution of India, Part III, Article 19, Fundamental Rights.
2. Singh, M.P. (2001), Constitution of India, 10th ed., Eastern Book Co., Lucknow.
3. S.P. Gupta *v.* Union of India, (1982).
4. State of Uttar Pradesh *v.* Raj Narain (24 January, 1975).
5. *Ibid.*
6. *Ibid.*
7. Smith *v.* East India Co., 1845, Ph. 50.
8. Beatson *v.* Skene, 1860, SH & M 838.
9. 1942, AC 624.
10. 1968, AC 910.
11. 1951 (83), CCRI.
12. John Agresto, The Supreme Court and Constitutional Democracy (1986), p. 112.
13. Alexander M. Bickel, The Supreme Court and the Idea of Progress (1970), p. 191.
14. For this and other information see Richard A. Guida, The Costs of Free Information, Published in public interest, fall 1989, 87-95.

15. Wattern Berns, Taking the Constitution Seriously (1987), p. 19, 144.
16. Karl Barth, Current Legal Problems, (1988).
17. L. Morrit, Making of Document (1999), 133, 144, 168.
18. Ashish Mullick, Cross Media Curbs—Unrealistic Against Public Sentiment (1997).
19. Soli J. Sorabjee, 'Information Bill in Winter Session', *The Telegraph*, October 13, 1997.
20. Jasjit Singh, National Security—International and External.
21. Challenges, *The Times of India*, 12 August, 1998.
22. Qulae Niranjan, 'Right to Information and Road to Heaven', *Economic and Political Weekly*, Vol. 40, No. 47, 19 November, 2005, 70-72.
23. Daypack Systems P. Ltd. *v.* India AIR 1986, SC 786.
24. Morritt, Making of Document (1999), 212-228.
25. S.P. Gupta *v.* India AIR (1982), SC 149, 238.
26. Bihar *v.* Kripalu Shankar AIR (1987), SC 1554.
27. In this connection the Supreme Court has referred to House of Lords in Harman *v.* Secretary of State, 1983, AC 280.
28. Jasjit Singh, *op. cit.*
29. B.P. Sanjay, Emerging Concerns (1993), 22.
30. Editorial, People Must Know, *Tribune*, 17 December, 2004.
31. Sidharth Vardrajan 'Broadcast' Bill—Restricting the Right to Information'.
32. S.P. Gupta *v.* President of India, AIR (1982), SC 149, 234.
33. Attorney General *v.* Jonathan Cape Ltd. (1975), 3 AIIER, 485.
34. Commonwealth of Australia *v.* John Fairfax & Sons (1981), 147, CLR 39, 52.
35. Bharat Dogra, Case for Enforcing Right to Know, *The Times of India*, 20 August, 1997.
36. Khatri *v.* Bihar, AIR 1981, SC 1068.
37. Tehsildar Singh *v.* UP, AIR 1959, SC 1912.
38. Yogesh Mehta, Autonomy to Electronic Media, The Promise and Prospects, 1991, Vol. XI.
39. R.R. Vadodaria, Keeping Secret for Fifty Years, AIR 1998, *Journal* 161-164.
40. R.K. Karanjia *v.* Emperor, AIR (1946), Bombay, 322.
41. State *v.* K. Balakrishna, AIR (1961), Ker. 25.
42. Nandlal More *v.* the State (1965), Cr. L.J., 392 (Pb.)
43. Yogesh Mehta, Autonomy to Electronic Media, The Promise and Prospects 1991 Vol. XI.
44. Pica to Security outfits from preview of Act (Views of Counter Views) TI 12 December, 2005, 16: 3-6.
45. Bharat Dogra, Where Ignorance is Not Bliss, *The Times of India*, 16 October, 1999.

46. Franklin S. Heimmen, *Speech and Law in Free Society* (1990), p. 130.
47. Dunu Roy, Wrong Information, Right Choice? *Seminar*, Vol. 55, July 2005, 55-58.
48. R.K. Vadodaria, *op. cit.*
49. S.K. Gaur, Status of Right to Information in India, 1998, 130.
50. P.B. Sawant, Dynamic Shifts Towards the Recognition of Right to Information, (1997), 111.
51. Sanwal Ram *v.* Addl. Dist. Magistrate, AIR 1982, Raj. 139.
52. H.D. Shourie, Private Organisation under the Purview for Right to Information, *Galaxy*, 1996.
53. See Editorial, "Bending Before Babus", *The Times of India*, 25 July, 2006.

6

Development of Right to Information Act

A chronological legal account from the early nineties till date, which details the efforts to institute right to information as a statutory right, is amply documented in the commentaries of the MKSS (Mazdoor Kisan Shakti Sangathan), the National Campaign for the People's Right to Information (NCPRI) which was formed in 1996, Commonwealth Human Rights Initiative (CHRI) and state specific movements and organizations involved in the struggle for RTI. The process of law making itself generated substantial writings. The makings of a national right to information law, took seed in a meeting of civil servants, lawyers and social activists at the Lal Bahadur Shastri National Academy of Administration, Mussoorie in October 1995 initiated by some serving officials of this institute and heralded a watershed in the national movement on the right to information.

The workshop proceedings of the Press Council of India in 1996, deriving from this earlier meeting, gave rise to the first draft bill on RTI. Careful thought was given not only to what information could be sought under the law but also what could not. At the time, the bill envisaged the applicability of the RTI not only to the state but the corporate and NGO sectors as well. A draft by the Consumer Education Research Council (CERC) followed, proposing an outright repeal of the Official Secret Act 1923. In 1997, the Government of India constituted a committee under the chairmanship of consumer activist H.D. Shourie to draft a legislation. In its report, the committee improved on the Press Council draft by explicitly bringing the judiciary and legislatures under the purview of the proposed legislation, but diluted its provisions in most other crucial aspects.

Put on the backburner with a change of guard at the Centre in quick succession, the Shourie draft reincarnated in an even weaker form as the Freedom of Information (FOI) Bill in 2000. It was finally passed in 2002 during the NDA government's tenure but never notified. The struggle for a strong national RTI law received a shot in the arm with the new UPA government committing to it in its Common Minimum Programme. Upon the NCPRI's recommendations, the National Advisory Council submitted its draft to the government in August 2004, which was worked on by the Department of Personnel and Training and the invisible hand of nameless bureaucrats to be finally tabled in Parliament in December 2004 as the Right to Information Bill.

Both the FOI Bill 2002 and the draft RTI Bill 2004 evoked criticisms in their own right, in so far as they violated the basic tenets of a strong and tenable right to information law (of maximum disclosures, independent appeal, penalties and effective mechanisms for access to information). Although the latter represented step forward from the FOI in various aspects, it crucially restricted the applicability of the proposed law to Central Government offices only. Predictably, both times, the handiwork of uncomfortable bureaucrats ensured that the bills went through similar processes of dilution. But as mentioned earlier, none of the opposition to the right to information was penned down openly.

In the meanwhile, some State governments took the initiative to pass RTI laws or orders incorporating certain provisions for disclosures. Wherever the demand for it sprung from the people, the laws too were stronger or more effectively enforced.

The RTI Bill 2004 was referred to a Parliamentary Standing Committee which came out with its report in April 2005. Its recommendations, commendably, attempted to bring the derailed bill tight back on track. When the bill finally came up for discussion in Parliament on 11 May, 2005, it looked fairly close to the original NAC draft, and was passed in this form. A reading into these different versions of the bill clearly reveals a bargaining process what dilutions were attempted, and how they were checked.

RIGHT TO INFORMATION ACT

Main Characteristics of Right to Information Act 2005

The Right to Information Act 2005 (Act No. 22/2005) is a law enacted by the Parliament of India giving citizens of India (except those in the State of Jammu and Kashmir who have their own special law) access to Government records. Under the terms of the Act, any person may request information from a "public authority" (a body of Government or instrumentality of State) which is required to reply expeditiously or within thirty days. The Act also requires every public authority to computerize their records for wide dissemination and to proactively publish certain categories of information so that the citizens need minimum recourse to request for information formally.

This law was passed by Parliament on 15 June, 2005 and came into force on 13 October, 2005. Information disclosure in India was hitherto restricted by the Official Secrets Act 1923 and various other special laws, which the new RTI Act now overrides.

Background

Disclosure of Government Information in India is governed by a law enacted during the British Rule, the Official Secrets Act of 1889, which was amended in 1923. This law secures information related to security of the State, sovereignty of the country and friendly relations with foreign states, and contains provisions which prohibit disclosure of non-classified information. Civil Service conduct rules and the Indian Evidence Act put further restrictions on govermnent officials' powers to disclose information to the public.

In 1975, the Supreme Court delivered a judgement that has been described as a "landmark", which held that "the people . . . have a right to know every public act, everything that is done in a public way, by their public functionaries".

State-Level Laws

The RTI Laws were first successfully enacted by the State governments—Tamil Nadu (1997), Goa (1997), Rajasthan (2000), Karnataka (2000), Delhi (2001), Maharashtra (2002), Madhya Pradesh (2003), Assam (2002) and Jammu & Kashmir (2004).

The Maharashtra and Delhi State level enactments are considered to have been the most widely used. The Delhi and Jammu & Kashmir RTI Acts are still in force.

Freedom of Information Act

Passage of a national level law, however, proved to be a difficult task. Given the experience of State governments in passing practicable legislation, the Central Government appointed a working group under H. D. Shourie and assigned it the task of drafting legislation. The Shourie draft, in an extremely diluted form, was the basis for the Freedom of Information Bill 2000 which eventually became law under the Freedom of Information Act 2002. This Act was severely criticized for permitting too many exemptions, not only under the standard grounds of national security and sovereignty, but also for requests that would involve "disproportionate diversion of the resources of a public authority". There was no upper limit on the charges that could be levied. There were no penalties for not complying with a request for information. The FOI Act, consequently, never came into effective force.

Enactment

The doomed FOI Act led to sustained pressure for a better National RTI enactment. The first draft of the Right to

Information Bill was presented to Parliament on 22 December, 2004. After intense debate, more than a hundred amendments to the draft Bill were made between December 2004 and 15 June, 2005, when the bill finally passed. The Act came into effect on 13 October, 2005.

Scope

The Act covers the whole of India except Jammu and Kashmir. It is applicable to all constitutional authorities, including the executive, legislature and judiciary; any institution or body established or constituted by an Act of Parliament or a State Legislature or by order or notification of appropriate government. In special circumstances bodies "owned, controlled or substantially financed" by government, or non-Governmental organizations "substantially financed, directly or indirectly by funds" provided by the government are also covered.

Private bodies are not within the Act's ambit directly. However, information that can be accessed under any other law in force by a public authority can also be requested for. In a landmark decision of 30 November, 2006 (**Sarbajit Roy** *v.* **DERC**) the Central Information Connection also reaffirmed that privatized public utility companies continue to be within the RTI Act—their privatization notwithstanding. The Act also explicitly overrides the Official Secrets Act and other laws in force on 13 October, 2005 in the event of any inconsistency.

Information

The Act specifies that citizens have a right to:

- request any information (as defined);
- take copies of documents;
- inspect documents, works and records;
- take certified samples of materials of work; and
- obtain information in form of printouts, diskettes, floppies, tapes, video cassettes or in any other electronic mode or through printouts.

Process

Under the Act, all complying departments have to designate an official as the Public Information Officer (PIO). Any citizen of India may submit a request to the PIO for information in any format, paper or electronic. It is the PIO's responsibility to ensure that the information is obtained from the appropriate department or section. If the request pertains to another public authority (in whole or part) it is the PIO's responsibility to transfer/forward the concerned portions of the request to a PIO of the other within 5 days. In addition, the Central Government has designated certain officials as Assistant Public Information Officers (APIOs). Their charge is not confirmed to any specific department, but they have the responsibility of receiving all RTI requests and forwarding it to the PIOs of the appropriate departments.

The person making the request is not obliged to explain why the information is needed. The Act specifies timeframes for complying with the request :

- If the request has been made to the PIO, compliance is expected within 30 days.
- If the request has been made to an APIO, compliance is expected within 35 days.
- If the PIO transfers the request to some other department (better concerned with the information requested), the time allowed is 35 days.
- Information about Human Rights violations by Security agencies have to be provided within 45 days.
- However, in any of the above cases, if life or liberty is involved, the PIO has to comply within 48 hours.

Since the information is to be paid for, the time between the reply of the PIO and the time taken to deposit the further fees for information is excluded from the time allowed.

If information is not provided within this period, it is treated as a refusal. Refusal with or without reasons may be ground for appeal.

For Central departments as of 2006, there is a fee of Rs. 10 for filing the request, Rs. 2 per page of information and Rs. 5 for each hour of inspection after the first hour. States fix their own rules.

Provisions

- Obligations of public authorities [S. 4(l)].
- Designation of Public Information Officers and Assistant Public Information Officers [Ss. 5(1) and 5(2)].
- Constitution of Central Information Commission (Ss. 12 and 13).
- Constitution of State Information Commission (Ss. 15 and 16).
- Non-applicability of the Act to Intelligence and Security Organizations (S. 24).
- Power to make rules to carry out the provisions of the Act (Ss. 27 and 28).

Information Defined

In terms of the Section 2(f) of the Act, information has been defined as any material in any form including records, documents, memos, e-mails, opinions, advices, press releases, circulars, orders, log books, contracts, reports, papers, samples, models, data material held in any electronic form and information relating to any private body which can be accessed by a public authority under any other law for the time being in force.

Right to Information

Under the Act [Section 2 (j)], right to information includes the right to—

- Inspect works, documents, records.
- Take notes, extracts or certified copies of documents or records.

- Take certified samples of material.
- Obtain information in form of printouts, diskettes, floppies, tapes, video cassettes or in any other electronic mode or through printouts.

What is Not Open to Disclosure?

The following is exempt from disclosure [S 8]

- Information, disclosure of which would prejudicially affect the sovereignty and integrity of India, the security, strategic, scientific or economic interests of the State, relation with foreign State or lead to incitement of an offence;
- Information which has been expressly forbidden to be published by any court of law or tribunal or the disclosure of which may constitute contempt of court;
- Information, the disclosure of which would cause a breach of privilege of Parliament or the State Legislature;
- Information including commercial confidence, trade secrets or intellectual property, the disclosure of which would harm the competitive position of a third party, unless the competent authority is satisfied that larger public interest warrants the disclosure of such information;
- Information available to a person in his judiciary relationship, unless the competent authority is satisfied that the larger public interest warrants the disclosure of such information;
- Information received in confidence from foreign government;
- Information, the disclosure of which would endanger the life or physical safety of any person or identify the source of information or assistance given in confidence for law enforcement or security purposes;
- Information which would impede the process of investigation or apprehension or prosecution of offenders;

- Cabinet papers including records of deliberations of the Council of Ministers, Secretaries and other officers;
- Information which relates to personal information the disclosure of which has no relationship to any public activity or interest, or which would cause unwarranted invasion of the privacy of the individual;
- Notwithstanding any of the exemptions listed above, a public authority may allow access to information, if public interest in disclosure outweighs the harm to the protected interests. [**NB**: This provision is qualified by the proviso to sub-section (1) of Section 11 of the Act which exempts disclosure of "trade or commercial secrets protected by law" under this clause when read along with 8(l)(d)].

Partial Disclosure

In terms of the Section 10 of the Act, only that part of the record which does not contain any information which is exempt from disclosure and which can reasonably be severed from any part that contains exempt information, may be provided.

Exclusions

Central Intelligence and Security agencies specified in the Second Schedule like IB, RAW, Directorate of Revenue Intelligence, Central Economic Intelligence Bureau, Aviation of Enforcement, Narcotics Control Bureau, Aviation Research Centre, Special Frontier Force, BSF, CRPF, ITBP, CISF, NSG, Assam Rifles, Special Service Bureau, Special Branch (CID), Andaman and Nicobar, The Crime Branch (CID-CB), Dadra and Nagar Haveli and Special Branch, Lakshadweep Police. Agencies specified by the State Governments through a Notification will also be excluded. The exclusion, however, is not absolute and these organizations have an obligation to provide information pertaining to allegations of corruption and human rights violations. Further, information relating to allegations of human rights valuations could be given but only with the approval of the Central or State Information Commission.

Role of the Government

As stated in the Section 26 of the Act,—the Act enjoins upon the Federal Government, as also the State governments of the Republic of India to initiate necessary steps to:

- Develop educational programmes for the public especially disadvantaged communities on RTI.
- Encourage Public Authorities to participate in the development and organization of such programmes.
- Promote timely dissemination of accurate information to the public.
- Train officers and develop training materials.
- Compile and disseminate a User Guide for the public in the respective official language.
- Publish names, designation postal addresses and contact details of PIOs and other information such as notices regarding fees to be paid, remedies available in law if request is rejected, etc.

Power to Make Rules

- Central Government, State Governments and the Competent Authority as defined in Section 2(e) are vested with powers to make rules to carry out the provisions of the Right to Information Act 2005. (S. 27 and S. 28)
  Who has the power to deal with the difficulties while implementing this Act?
- If any difficulty arises in giving effect to the provisions in the Act, the Central Government may, by Order published in the Official Gazette, make provisions necessary/expedient for removing the difficulty. (S. 30)

Effects

In the first year of National RTI, 42,876 (not yet official) applications for information were filed to Central (i.e. Federal) public authorities. Of these 878 were disputed at the final appellate stage—the Central Information Commission at New Delhi. A few of these decisions have thereafter been mired in further legal controversy in the various High Courts of India. The first stay order against a final appellate decision of the Central Information Commission was granted on 3 May, 2006 by the High Court of Delhi in WP(C)6833-35/2006 cited as **"NDPL & Ors.** *versus* **Central Information Commission & Ors".** The Government of India planned to amend the RTI in 2006 but was compelled to abandon the changes due to public outcry.

RTI IMPLEMENTATION CONFERENCE

After nearly a decade of hectic lobbying, the efforts of civil society for entrenching the right to information in India were finally rewarded on 15 June, 2005 with the President's assent to the Right to Information Act 2005. By 12 October, 2005, the Right to Information Act must be 'fully functional' in every city, township and village. At a national conference held soon after the law was passed, government officials, civil society groups and national and international experts had met to chalk out an agenda to make this happen. The greater challenge now is the actual implementation of the Act. The clock has already started ticking—Central and State governments have only 120 days from the date of Presidential assent to implement the Act in its entirety. By 12 October, 2005, the Right to Information Act must be fully functional in every city, township and village across the country without exception.

In real terms, implementation poses a huge challenge to government—the new law covers all Central, State, local and panchayat government agencies; with the exception of those in the State of Jammu and Kashmir. These authorities need to be already working swiftly to satisfy the key provisions of the Act and be ready to process applications from the public as soon as possible.

Barely two weeks after the Lok Sabha gave its stamp, and to assist governments to manage the many implementation issues that will need to be tackled, the Commonwealth Human

Rights Initiative (CHRI) organised a Conference on "Effective Implementation: Preparing to Operationalise the New Right to Information Act 2005" in New Delhi, on 24-26 May, 2005. The conference was funded by the British High Commission and brought together government officials from the Centre and the States and civil society representatives. The significance of the conference was that it was a major consultation that saw public officials and citizen groups come together and talk about the new law.

The focus was on some of the major implementation issues and challenges that come with the new law. There was broad representation from the States.

Issues, Discussion, Questions and Consensus

There were overarching questions that were consistently raised, debated and discussed. While the conference was able to answer some of these, more broadly the questions were recorded for consideration by the Central Government. There was also a broad consensus on a number of areas and implementation of the new law. These were in the way of suggestions for action rather than actual commitments.

Will the Central Act Override Existing State Acts?

How the new national law and existing State laws would interact was a major point of discussion. One participant noted that Minister Shri Suresh Pachouri (the Minister who introduced the Bill in Parliament) indicated in the Lok Sabha that the Central Government envisaged the Central and State Acts coexisting. Citizens would have an option to apply for information under either Act and where there was a conflict the Central Act would prevail.

However, others felt that this approach could lead to complications, particularly in terms of practical processing of applications and complaints by public officials in the States. Some felt that any conflict at the edges would simply have to be decided by the Courts. Participants agreed that it would be very helpful for the Central Government to clarify the position on how to implement the new law in the States, in particular in those States that already have an RTI Act. It was also felt that if the Central Act was well implemented, State Acts might eventually simply fade away.

Information Commissions

The new law provides for the establishment of Central Information Commissions as well as State Information Commissions throughout the country. The commissions will act as independent bodies to handle appeals and monitor implementation. Problematically, however, the Act contains a number of ambiguities in relation to the practical functioning of the new Information Commissions, which remain in need of urgent clarification.

For example, it is important to clarify how the Central and State Commissions will interact in practice, an issue that goes again to the question of Centre *versus* State. The information commissions must have operational, budget and rule making autonomy. The structure of the commission needs clarification—will it operate as a collegiate body making decisions by majority or with individual commissioners and commission staff making decisions.

Participants also raised concerns about the criteria and procedures for appointment of the information commissioners. The RTI Act allows ex-government officials to be eligible for appointment. And in giving the new Chief Information Commissioners the same rank as an Election Commissioners, the law has now potentially created around 30 posts at the level of the Chief Election Commissioner and upto another 300 posts at the level of the Election Commissioner, which could come to be seen as easy options for senior bureaucrats. The first information commissioners who will be appointed for 5 years will set the standards for openness *via* his/her early decisions, so it is critical to ensure that they are chosen well, participants felt. Given this, the need for openness between government and civil society during the selection process was deemed essential.

A number of other points were discussed. Each public authority must clarify who would be responsible for managing, monitoring and interfacing with the Information Commission and the State's agency for the Right to Information law. Governments must also put in place application and appeals monitoring systems, to ensure that proper information can be collected for the annual reports required to be produced by the Information Commissions.

Information Commissions must have the power to initiate their own complaints so that they can monitor and, where necessary, investigate patterns of non-compliance and not just individual cases.

Since the conference though, there have been no reports on the appointment of the Central Chief Information Commissioner or for that matter about the committee supposed to make this appointment—consisting of the PM, Leader of the Opposition and a Union Minister nominated by the PM. DOPT in its circular to State Governments has alerted them on the need to set up State Information Commissions. In Karnataka, the former Chief Secretary, K.K. Mishra was recently appointed as the State's Chief Information Commissioner. The State Governments of Uttarakhand, Orissa, and Maharashtra have already set up their selection committees. The debate on criteria for appointment — whether the commissioner should be a retired civil servant or chief justice — is on going within civil society.

There have been no reports on the appointment of the Central Chief Information Commissioner or for that matter about the committee supposed to make this appointment—consisting of the PM, Leader of the Opposition and a Union Minister nominated by the PM.

There has been more progress in some States. The State Governments of Uttarakhand, Orissa, and Maharashtra have already set up their selection committees. In Karnataka, the former Chief Secretary, K.K. Mishra was recently appointed as the State's Chief Information Commissioner.

Framing Rules under the Law

It was felt that the rules should be developed participatorily and should be open for public comment. The rules should be consistent across the country to minimise confusion in implementation.

CHRI has learnt that the DOPT has apparently framed rules, but these have not been made available for public comment. The National Campaign for the People's Right to Information (NCPRI) and CHRI have both framed draft rules for consideration by the Central Government. Interestingly, in his contents as he signed the RTI bill into law, one of the suggestions President A.P.J. Abdul Kalam gave to the PM was that rules be framed by the Centre uniformly to avoid any confusion in implementation. Under the Act, State governments have the power to frame rules in furtherance of their obligations and duties under the Act.

Preparing for Implementation

Senior government officials from Delhi and Maharashtra both stressed the need for sufficient lead-time to set in place systems for effective implementation. The Delhi and Maharashtra experiences in implementing State RTI laws were recalled. The Delhi State Government had no plan for implementation until after its RTI Act came into force. This was clearly not ideal. When the government finally took action, it suggested training of both Competent Authorities (the equivalent to Public Information Officers or PIOs) and other support personnel. NGOs actually provided some of the impetus for this training. The Delhi government also worked with Resident Welfare Associations on an information dissemination campaign.

Similarly, it was pointed out that the Maharashtra Government was not prepared at all when the Maharashtra Right to Information Act (MRIA) was brought into force, and this weakened the Act from the outset. Much of their implementation work came in response to problems identified by the Office of the Lokayukta and the MRTI Council, which includes civil society representatives. Consequently, YASHADA (Yashwantrao Academy of Development Administration), the State Government's training institution, was given the task to undertake training activities across the State.

With a tight implementation schedule included in the new national law, governments will need to learn from these previous experiences with the State laws and focus on setting in place the infrastructure upon which the entire information access system will rest. Governments will need to ensure that the superstructure is not left to wobble on shaky foundations.

It was also suggested that the DOPT which is the national nodal agency responsible for implementation must develop an action plan identifying what systems and tools, i.e., guidance notes, procedures manuals, information technology based monitoring systems, etc., will need to be developed to support implementation. This should be in collaboration with the State nodal agencies, other key departments (e.g., Panchayati Raj, Finance, Law, Social Development), Administrative Training Institutes, civil society, the media, academics and international RTI officials. Central and State governments must develop guidelines to ensure consistent decisions by PIOs and AAs and ensure that all officials with duties under the law properly know how to discharge their functions.

Guidelines on making proactive disclosure obligations and the methods of their publication should be developed, recommended the participants. Leadership for ensuring effective proactive disclosure should come from Chief Ministers, Chief Secretaries—with the Heads of Department directly responsible for implementation and the Information Commissions responsible for monitoring.

Since the conference, the DOPT has sent letters to the Chief Secretaries of all States requesting them to start the process of implementing the national RTI law including such key measures as preparing manuals under the proactive disclosure provisions of the law, appointing public information officers (PIOs) and first level appellate authorities (AAs) setting up the State Information Commission, etc. While the letter is silent on the fate of those States which already have RTI laws, Karnataka, Maharashtra and Goa have volunteered to phase out their laws in favour of the national law.

For example, it is important to clarify how the Central and State Commissions will interact in practice, an issue that goes again to the question of Centre *versus* State. The information commissions must have operational, budget and rule making autonomy. The structure of the commission needs clarification—will it operate as a collegiate body making decisions by majority or with individual commissioners and commission staff making decisions?

Several questions remain in need of clarification—how receipts for RTI applications will be given, and how fees will be paid, how Assistant PIOs and their superiors, the PIOs, will interact, to name some. Governments must clarify how AAs will be appointed and supported in their duties. Clarify how AAs and information commissions are expected to function, in terms of their hearing processes, their outreach, the interaction between the various commissioners, etc.

Since the conference, the Central Government has sent letters to the Chief Secretaries of all States requesting them to prepare manuals covering the proactive disclosure provisions of the law, appoint public information officers and first level appellate authorities, set up the State Information Commission, etc.

Meanwhile, Karnataka, Maharashtra and Goa have volunteered to phase out their laws in favour of the national law.

Training for Government Officials and Staff

It was felt that the Training Division of the DOPT should be the lead agency for coordinating the training programme for government officials nationwide. The DOPT needs to develop a training strategy as a matter of immediate priority. Its strategy should identify who will have responsibility both for undertaking training, monitoring the implementation of the training programme, and preparing training modules and materials. It should be time-bound. Participants noted that PIOs and AAs needed to be identified and trained as a matter of priority. Records management and archiving need to reviewed and improved as necessary.

CHRI has also learnt that that DOPT will likely be working with YASHADA—the Maharashtra Training Institute which undertook RTI training for 3,000 officials in relation to the MRTI Act—on devising and implementing a National Training strategy.

Since the conference, most States will have begun the process of identifying and appointing PIOs and appellate officials in their departments. However, it is apparent from the requests for assistance from government that CHRI has been receiving that some state governments are genuinely nonplussed how to go about this task.

Public Awareness

The new RTI law places obligations on all public authorities to raise awareness about the law, its key provisions and how to access it as a right amongst the public. The obligations involve developing, organising and producing educational materials and programmes.

The conference recommended that a directory of PIOs and other key officials responsible for implementing the law should be collated and published as a matter of absolute priority by each department at the level of the Centre and the States. Additionally, government departments must produce a users guide or manual for the public, and it must regularly be updated and published. Individual departments at the Centre and in the States should be responsible for implementing outreach strategies through their publicity/ information departments. At the district level, District Magistrates, revenue officers and panchayat representatives should be made responsibie for outreach. Partnerships with civil society are also crucial when undertaking public outreach activities.

Meeting of the States

Participants agreed that a national conference of Chief Ministers and/or Chief Secretaries to set up an empowered Committee looking into implementation of the law must be organised as an immediate and urgent priority.

Currently, there has been no indication from government on this issue. CHRI has written to Prime Minister, Manmohan Singh, urging him to call for such a national conference of all Chief Ministers and/or Chief Secretaries.

Going Forward

Since the conference, the Central Government has in particular welcomed information on implementation in terms of best practice from other jurisdictions, assistance in records management strategies and a concept note on raising public awareness. CHRI has also been receiving similar requests from several States, in particular Karnataka, Uttarakhand, Meghalaya, Haryana, Madhya Pradesh and Delhi for assistance in capacity building of officials, developing internal guidelines and procedures, implementing proactive disclosure, etc.

Civil society organisations have expressed a genuine interest in liaising and working towards building strategic partnerships with government where possible to assist in the implementation process. Civil society is also likely to take a lead in raising public awareness about the new law.

The Right to Information Act 2005 is a landmark piece of legislation. If implemented well, it could be a major step towards more accountable and transparent government. However, it is imperative to recognise that the road to implementation is a long one and there will be many hurdles and roadblocks yet. With proper governmental support and a willingness to adapt, it is a golden opportunity for India to end the culture of governmental secrecy and fulfil its potential as a truly great democracy.

HOW TO USE RIGHT TO INFORMATION

In the form of Question and Answer an attempt has been made in this subheading to explain the RTI Act and also elaborate how to use Right to Information Act.

What is Right to Information?

What is RTI?

RTI stands for Right to Information. Right to Information is a part of fundamental rights under Article 19(1) of the Constitution. Article 19(1) says that every citizen has freedom of speech and expression. As early as in 1976, the Supreme Court said in the case of **Raj Narain v. State of UP,** that people cannot speak or express themselves unless they know. Therefore, right to information is embedded in Article 19. In the same case, Supreme Court further said that India is a democracy. People are the masters. Therefore, the masters have a right to know how the governments, meant to serve them, are functioning. Further, every citizen pays taxes. Even a beggar on the street pays tax (in the form of sales tax, excise duty, etc.) when he buys a piece of soap from the market. The citizens, therefore, have a right to know how their money was being spent. These three principles were laid down by the Supreme Court while saying that RTI is a part of our fundamental rights.

If RH is a Fundamental Right, then why do we need an Act to give us this right?

This is because if you went to any Government Department and told the officer there, "RTI is my fundamental right, and that I am the master of this country. Therefore, please show me all your files, he would not do that. In all probability, he would throw you out of his room. Therefore, we need a machinery or a process through which we can exercise this fundamental right. Right to Information Act 2005, which became effective on 13th October, 2005, provides that machinery. Therefore, Right to Information Act does not give us any new right. It simply lays down the process—how to apply for information, where to apply, how much fees, etc.

When did RTI Act come into force?

The Central Right to Information Act came into force on the 12th October, 2005. However, before that nine State Governments had passed State Acts. These were J & K, Delhi, Rajasthan, Madhya Pradesh, Maharashtra, Karnataka, Tamil Nadu, Assam, and Goa.

What Rights are available under RTI Act 2005?

Right to Information Act 2005 empowers every citizen to ask any question from the Government or seek any information:

- Take copies of any government documents.
- Inspect any government documents.
- Inspect any Government works.
- Take samples of materials of any Government work.

Who is covered under RTI?

The Central RTI Act extends to the whole of India except the State of Jammu and Kashmir. All bodies, which are constituted under the Constitution or under any law or under any Government notification or all bodies, including NGOs, which are owned, controlled or substantially financed by the Government are covered.

What is "substantially financed"?

This is neither defined under RTI Act nor under any other Act. So, this issue will evolve with time, may be through some Court orders etc.

Are Private bodies covered under the RTI Act?

All private bodies, which are owned, controlled or substantially financed by the Government, are directly covered. Others are indirectly covered. That is, if a government department can access information from any private body under any other Act, the same can be accessed by the citizen under the RTI Act through that government department.

Isn't Official Secrets Act 1923 an obstacle to the implementation of RTI Act?

No. Section 22 of the RTI Act 2005 clearly says that RTI Act would override all existing Acts including Official Secrets Act.

Can the PIO refuse to give me information?

A PIO can refuse information on 11 subjects that are listed in Section 8 of the RTI Act. These include information received in confidence from foreign governments, information prejudicial to security, strategic, scientific or economic interests of the country, breach of privilege of legislatures, etc.

There is a list of 18 agencies given in second schedule of the Act to which RTI Act does not apply. However, they also have to give information if it relates to matters pertaining to allegations of corruption or human rights violations.

Does the Act provide for partial disclosure?

Yes. Under Section 10 of the RTI Act, access may be provided to that part of the record which does not contain information which is exempt from disclosure under this Act.

Can access be denied to file notings?

No. File notings are an integral part of the government file and are subject to disclosure under the Act. This has been clarified by the Central Information Commission in one of its orders on 31st January, 2006.

How do I locate the full Act?

The full Act in Hindi and English is available on the website of Department of Personnel and Training www.persmin.nic.in

Who will give me information?

One or more existing officers in every Government Department have been designated as Public Information Officers (PIO). These PIOs act like nodal officers. You have to file your applications with them. They are responsible for collecting information sought by you from various wings of that Department and providing that information to you. In addition, several officers have been appointed as Assistant Public Information Officers (APIOs). Their job is only to accept applications from the public and forward it to the right PIO.

Where do I submit application?

You can do that with the PIO or with APIO. In the case of all Central Government Departments, 629 post offices have been designated as APIOs. This means that you can go to any of these post offices and submit your fee and application at the RTI counter in these post offices. They will issue you a receipt and acknowledgement and it is the responsibility of that post office to deliver it to the right PIO. The list of these post offices is given at http://www.indiapost.gov

Is there any fee? How do I deposit that?

Yes, there is an application fee. For Central Government Departments, it is Rs. 10. However, different States have prescribed different fee. For details see rules framed by the States on this website. For getting information, you have to pay Rs. 2 per page of information provided for Central Government Departments. It is different for different States. Similarly, there is a fee for inspection of documents. There is no fee for first hour of inspection, but after that, you have to pay Rs. 5 for every subsequent hour or fraction thereof. This is according to Central Rules. For each State, see respective State rules. You can deposit fee either in cash or through a DD or bankers cheque or postal order drawn in favour of that public authority. In some States, you can buy Court fee stamps and affix it on your application. This would be treated as if you have deposited the fee. You can then deposit your application either by post or by hand.

What should I do if the PIO or the concerned Department does not accept my application?

You can send it by post. You should also make a formal complaint to the respective Information Commission under Section 18. The Information Commissioner has the power to impose a penalty of Rs. 25,000 on the concerned officer who refused to accept your application.

Is there an application form for seeking information?

For Central Government Departments, there is no form. You should apply on a plain sheet of paper like an ordinary application. However, many States and some ministries and departments have prescribed formats. You should apply in these formats. Please read rules of respective States to know.

How can I apply for information?

Draft your application on a normal sheet of paper and submit it by post or in person to the Public Information Officer (PIO). [Remember to keep a copy of the application for your personal reference].

How can I deposit my application fee?

Every State has a different mode of payment for application fee. Generally, you can deposit your application fee via:

- In person by paying cash [remember to take your receipt].
- By Post through:
  - ◆ Demand Draft
  - ◆ Indian Postal Order
  - ◆ Money Orders (only in some States)
  - ◆ Affixing Court Fee Stamp (only in some States)
  - ◆ Banker's cheque
- Some State governments have prescribed some head of account. You are required to deposit fee in that account. For that, you can either go to any branch of SBI and deposit cash in that account and attach deposit receipt with your RTI application. Or you can also send a postal order or a DD drawn in favour of that account along with your RTI application.

Please see respective State rules for complete details.

Can I submit my application only with the PIO?

No, in case the PIO is not available you can submit your application with the Assistant PIO or any other officer designated to accept the RTI applications.

Where can I locate the concerned PIO?

A list of PIOs/APIOs and Appellate Authorities for all Central and State departments/Ministries is available online at www.rti.gov.in

What if I cannot locate my PIO or APIO?

In case you have problems locating your PIO/APIO you can address your RTI application to the PIO C/o Head of Department and send it to the concerned public authority with the requisite application fee. The Head of Department will have to forward your application to the concerned PIO.

Do I have to personally go to deposit my application?

Depending on your State rules for mode of payment you can deposit your application for information from the concerned departments of your State government *via* post by attaching a DD, Money Order, Postal Order or affixing Court Fee Stamp.

For all Central Government departments the Department of Posts has designated 629 post offices at the national level. The designated officers in these post offices work as Assistant PIOs and collect the application to forward to the concerned PIO. A list is available on http://www.indiapost.gov.in/rticontents.htnil

Is there a time limit to receiving information?

Yes. If you file your application with the PIO, you must receive information within 30 days.

In case you have filed your application with Assistant PIO then information has to be made available within 35 days.

In case the matter to which the information pertains affects the life and liberty of an individual, information has to be made available in 48 hours.

Do I have to give reasons why I want a particular information?

Absolutely not ! You are not required to give any reasons or additional information other than your contact details (i.e., Name, Address, and Phone No.). Section 6(2) clearly says that no information other than contact details of the applicant shall be asked.

Can the PIO refuse to accept my RTI application?

No. The PIO cannot refuse to accept your application for information under any circumstances. Even if the information does not pertain to his/her department/jurisdiction, he/she has to accept it. If the application does not pertain to that PIO, he would have to transfer it to the right PIO within 5 days under Section 6(2).

Why is it that RTI works when no other law has worked

There have been many good laws in this country but none of those laws worked. Why do you think this law would work?

This law is already working. This is because for the first time in the history of independent India, there is a law which casts a direct accountability on the officer for non-performance. If concerned officer does not provide information in time, a penalty of Rs. 250 per day of delay can be imposed by the Information Commissioner. If the information provided is false, a penalty of a maximum of Rs. 25,000 can be imposed. A penalty can also be imposed for providing incomplete or for rejecting your application for *mala fide* reasons. This fine is deducted from the officer's personal salary.

Has any penalty been imposed so far?

Yes, some officers have been penalized by the Central as well as State Information Commissioners.

Does the Applicant get the amount fined to the PIO?

No. The amount fined is deposited in the government treasury. However, under Section 19, the applicant can seek compensation.

What should I do if I do not receive Satisfactory Information?

What can I do if I do not receive information?

If you do not receive information or are dissatisfied with the information received, you can file an appeal with the first appellate authority under Section 19(1) of the Right to Information Act.

Who is a First Appellate Authority?

Every public authority must designate a First Appellate Authority. This officer designated is the officer senior in rank to your PIO.

Is there a form for the first appeal?

No, there is no form for filing a first appeal (but some State governments have prescribed a form). Draft your appeal application on a blank sheet of paper addressed to the First Appellate Authority. Remember to attach a copy of your original application and a copy of the reply in whatever form (if received) from the PIO.

Do I have to pay a fee for the First Appeal?

No. You are not required to pay any fee for the first appeal. However, some State governments have prescribed a fee.

In how many days can I file my first appeal?

You can file your first appeal within 30 days of receipt of information or within 60 days of filing RTI application (if no information received).

What if I do not receive the Information after the First Appeal process?

If you do not receive information even after the First Appeal then you can take the matter forward to the Second Appeal stage.

What is a Second Appeal?

A Second Appeal is the last option under the RTI Act to get the information requested. You can file second appeal with the Information Commission. For appeals against Central Government Departments, you have Central Information Commission (CIC). For evenly State Government, there is a State Information Commission.

Is there a Form for the Second Appeal?

No, there is no Form for filing a Second Appeal (but some State governments have prescribed a form for second appeal too). Draft your appeal application on a normal sheet of paper addressed to the Central or State Information Commission. Carefully read the appeal rules before drafting your Second Appeal. Your Second Appeal application can be rejected if it does not comply with the appeal rules.

Do I have to pay a fee for the Second Appeal?

No. You are not required to pay any fee for the second appeal. However, some States have prescribed a fee for that.

In how many days can I file my Second Appeal?

You can file your second appeal within 90 days of disposal of first appeal or within 90 days of the date, by when first appeal was to be decided.

How does this law help me in getting my work done?

How does this law work so effectively for pending works, i.e., why is it that the government officials end up doing your work which they were not doing earlier?

Let us take the case of Nannu. He was not being given his ration card. But when he applied under RTI, he was given a card within a week. What did Nannu ask? He asked the following questions:

1. I filed an application for a duplicate ration card on 27th January, 2004. Please tell me the daily progress made on my application so far, i.e., when did my application reach which officer, for how long did it stay with that officer and what did he/she do during that period?
2. According to the rules, my card should have been made in 10 days. However, it is more than three months now. Please give the names and designations of the officials who were supposed to take action on my application and who have not done so?
3. What action would be taken against these officials for not doing their work and for causing harassment to the public? By when would that action be taken?
4. By when would I get my card now?

In normal circumstances, such an application would be thrown in a dustbin. But this law says that the Government has to reply in 30 days. If they don't do that, their salary could be deducted. Now, it is not easy to answer these questions.

The first question is—please provide the daily progress made on my application

There is no progress made. But the government officials cannot write in these many words that they have not acted for so many months. Else that would be admission of guilt on paper.

The next question is—please provide the names and designations of the officers who were supposed to take action on my application and who had not done so.

If the government provides names and designations of the officials, their responsibility gets fixed. Any officer is most scared of fixing of responsibility against him in this manner. So, the moment one files such an application, his/her pending work is done.

What should you do after getting information?

There cannot be one answer for that. It depends on why you asked for that information and what type of information is it. Often a lot of things start falling in place just by asking for information. For instance, you would get your passport or a ration card just by your asking for the status of your application. In many cases, roads got repaired as soon as the money spent on its repairs in the last few repairs was asked. So, seeking information and questioning the government is an important step, which in itself is complete in many cases.

But suppose you expose some corruption or wrongdoing using RTI. Then, you can complain to vigilance agencies, CBI or even file an FIR. But it is seen that the Government does not take any action against the guilty even after repeated complaints. Though one can keep up the pressure on vigilance agencies by seeking to know the status of complaints under RTI, however, the wrongdoings can also be exposed through media. However, experience has not been very encouraging at getting guilty punished. But one thing is certain. Seeking information like this and exposing wrongdoings does improve the future. The officials get a clear message that the people of that area have become alert and any wrongdoings in future would not remain hidden as they were in the past. So, their risks of getting caught increase.

Won't You Be Victimized If You Used TRI

Have people been victimized who used RTI and exposed corruption?

Yes, there have been some instances where people were physically harmed when they sought information which exposed large scale corruption. But this does not mean that every applicant faces such a threat. Filing application to seek status of your grievance or for knowing other similar routine matters does not invite any retaliation. It is only when information is likely to expose bureaucratic-contractor nexus or any kind of mafia that there could be a possibility of retaliation.

Then why should you use RTI?

The entire system has become so rotten that if all of us individually and together do not do our bit, it will never improve. If we don't do it, who will? Therefore, we have to act. But we should do that with a strategy and minimize risks. And with experience, there are some safeguards and strategies available.

What are these strategies?

Please go ahead and file RTI application for any issue in the first instance. Normally, anyone would not attack you immediately. They would first try to cajole you or win you over. So, the moment you file any inconvenient application, someone would approach you very politely to request you to withdraw that application. You should gauge the seriousness or the potential of the person approaching you. If you consider it to be serious enough, ask 15 of your friends to immediately apply to the same public authority asking for same information. It would be better if these 15 friends were from different parts of India. Now, it would be most difficult for anyone to target all of your 15 friends all across the country. And if they threaten anyone from amongst the 15, let more people file similar applications. Your friends from other parts of India can file their applications by post. Try and give it wide media publicity. This will ensure that you will get the requisite information, and you would have sufficiently minimized risks.

Bureaucracy's Fears

Can't people blackmail government servants by obtaining information?

Let us ask ourselves—what does RTI do? It just brings truth in public domain. It does not create any information. It just removes curtains and brings truth in public domain. Is that bad? When can it be misused? Only if an officer has done something wrong and if that information comes out in public. Is it bad that wrongdoings within the Government should become public and be exposed rather than keeping it under wraps. Yes, once such information is obtained by someone, he could go and blackmail that officer. But why do we wish to protect wrong officers. If any officer is blackmailed, he/she has options available under Indian Penal Code to go register an FIR against a blackmailer. Let that officer do that. However, we can even avoid the possibility of any individual officer from being blackmailed by any individual complainant by putting all information, sought by any applicant, on the website. An applicant is able to blackmail an officer only when that applicant is the only person who obtained that information and threatens to make that public. But if all informations sought by him were to be put on website, the possibility of blackmail would be substantially reduced. Chief Information

Commission, Shri Ramesh Inder Singh of Punjab Information Commission has recorded this: 'We are pro-law. As a quasi-judicial court we take decisions on facts of the case, as presented......If you speak to government officials, they will tell you the commission is hounding them.

Won't Government get flooded with RTI applications and won't it jam government machinery?

These fears are hypothetical. There are more than 65 countries in the world, which have RTI laws. There are nine States in India, who had RTI laws, before this law was passed by the Parliament. None of these Governments were flooded with applications. Such fear emanates from an assumption that the people do not have anything to do and are totally free. Filing an RTI application and pursuing it takes time, energies and resources. Unless a person really wants any information, he/she does not file it.

Let us consider some statistics. In Delhi, 14,000 applications have been filed in 120 departments in more than 60 months. This means less than two applications per Department per month. Can we say that Delhi Government got flooded with RTI applications? In sharp contrast, US Government received 3.2 million applications under their RTI Act during 2003-04. This is despite the fact that unlike India, most of the Government information is already available on the net and there should be much less need for the people to file applications. But US Government is not contemplating scrapping the RTI Act. On the contrary they are setting aside more and more resources to implement it. During the same year, they spent $ 32 million to implement it.

Won't it require huge amount of resources to implement RTI Act?

Any amount of resources required to implement RTI Act would be well spent. Most countries like the US have realized it and are already spending huge resources to make their governments transparent. Firstly, all the cost spent on RTI gets more than recovered the same year by the amounts of money that the Government saves due to reduction in corruption and malpractices. For instance, there is strong evidence to show how leakages in drought relief programme in Rajasthan and Public Distribution System in Delhi substantially reduced due to extensive use of RTI.

Secondly, RTI is very essential for democracy. It is a part of our fundamental right. For people to participate in governance, the prerequisite is that they first know what is going on. So, just the way we treat all expenses made on the running of our Parliament as essential, we have to treat all expenses made in the implementation of RTI as essential.

But often people file applications to settle personal scores, etc.

As written above, RTI simply brings truth in public domain. It does not create information. Any attempt at hiding truth or putting a cover over it is not in the best interests of society. Rather than serving any useful purpose, any attempt at promoting secrecy would only increase the scope for corruption and wrongdoing. Therefore, our entire efforts should be to make governance completely transparent. However, if anyone blackmails someone subsequently, there are ample provisions under law to address that. Secondly, there are sufficient safeguards under Section 8 of RTI Act. It states that any information, which relates to private affairs of any individual and has no public interest would not be disclosed. Therefore, the existing laws have sufficient provisions available to address genuine concerns of the people.

How to Avoid People from Filing Frivolous Applications?

There is no frivolous application

What is frivolous? My pending water connection could be the most critical issue for me, but it could be treated as frivolous by a bureaucrat. Some vested interests within the bureaucracy have raised this bogey of frivolous applications. Right now, RTI Act does not permit any application to be rejected on the ground that it was frivolous. But some sections of bureaucracy want the PIO to be empowered, to reject any application if he feels that it was frivolous. If that happens, every PIO will declare every other application to be frivolous and reject it. It would mean a death knell to RTI.

File nothings should not be made public as that would prevent honest officers from rendering honest advice?

This is wrong. On the contrary, every officer would now know that whatever he writes on the file would be subject to public scrutiny. This would force him to write things which are in best public interest. Some honest bureaucrats have admitted in private that RTI has helped them immensely in warding off political and other undue influences. Now, the officers simply say that if they did the wrong thing, they might get exposed if someone asked for that information. Therefore, officers have started insisting that the seniors gave directions in writing. The Government is learnt to be contemplating removing file notings from the purview of RTI Act. For the above reasons, it is absolutely essential that file notings should be allowed to be covered under RTI Act.

Civil servant has to make decisions under many pressures and the public will not understand this?

As discussed above, on the contrary, possibility of exposures to illegitimate pressures would reduce.

Government records are not in proper shape. How could RTI be implemented?

RTI would force the system to start maintaining records properly now. Else the officials would face a penalty under the Act.

Applications seeking voluminous information should be rejected?

If I seek for some 'information, which runs into a lakh of pages, I would do that only if I need it because I will have to pay

Rs. 2 lakh for that. This is an automatic deterrent, if application were rejected only on this account, the applicant could break his application and file 1,000 applications seeking 100 pages through each application, which would not benefit anyone. Therefore, applications should not be rejected only on this pretext.

People should be allowed to seek information only about themselves. They should not be allowed to ask questions about other spheres of governance, totally unrelated to the Section 6(2) of RTI Act clearly says an applicant cannot be questioned why he/she were asking for any information. In any case, RTI flows from the fact that people pay taxes. This money belongs to them and, therefore, they have a right to know how their money were being spent and how they were being governed. So, people have a right to know everything about every sphere of governance. They may or may not be directly related to the matter. So, even a person living in Delhi can ask for any information from say, Tamil Nadu.

The Right to Information Act, 2005 (RTI) is facing turbulence from the bureaucracy even before it celebrates its first birthday. A powerful lobby of the bureaucracy has apparently been successful in prevailing over the coalition government at the Centre and convinced it to amend the law. Termed by many as a retrograde step, the proposed amendment is far reaching because it envisages banning 'file notings' from access by citizens. But file notings are everything in the process of decision making, and if they are blocked, it drops an iron curtain on public records, which is against the very aim of the RTI law.

The proposed amendments to this Act are:

1. All file notings to be exempted except for social and development projects.
2. No cabinet paper to be disclosed even after a decision has been taken.

Both of these amendments are fatal to the letter and spirit of the main Right to Information Act of 2005. File notings were not exempted from disclosure even under Section 8 of the law (which covers exemptions) or anywhere else. The government's intent in confining it only to social and development projects is a very worrisome limitation. Any file note may end up being considered as not pertaining to social or development project, just to deny access.

Further, in the current law, cabinet papers are allowed to be disclosed for a decision that had been taken. This includes file notings, deliberations in the cabinet and the material papers over which the decision had depended. The Manmohan Singh government now wants to deviate from the earlier commitment by excluding every cabinet paper through the proposed amendment.

What are Files and File Notings?

A file in public office is nobody's private affair. Any such file contains various documents including file notings which indicate the process and steps involved in making a decision. File notings are the life of the file and the source of decisions taken. They are that part of the file on which officers of different ranks write their comments. File notings are not an individual officer's opinion note, but a compilation of different opinions and analysis of all the positions and application of rules to a particular situation so that the final authority—like the Chief Secretary or Chief Minister or a Council of Ministers—takes an appropriate decision, in public interest. File notings, thus, offer the reasons for the decision.

Though it is the government that takes a decision, it is taken for the purpose of people and their welfare. The claim of the government that it will reveal the decision but not the reason for it, is anti-democratic and against the norms of administrative law. If the file note is not accessible, the reasons for the decisions become 'classified'. In democracy, people need the reasoned decisions, reasons for decisions and not just decisions without reasons. To propose that the government will now deny the reasons for decisions is itself an unreasonable decision of the UPA executive.

Parivartan, a voluntary organisation, obtained file notings regarding the privatisation of water management in Delhi, in 2005. The notings revealed that Price Waterhouse Coopers did not even qualify in the preliminary round, but the World Bank twisted the arm of the Delhi Government to cancel bids, force rebidding and ultimately changed the selection criteria. File notings also revealed that some honest officers had protested. If Parivartan had not exposed this using the RTI Act, the deal could have made the Delhi citizens shell out more than 10 times than the present rates of water. The file notings also revealed that how the son of a VVIP was appointed as consultant by Delhi Jal Board without any advertisement or interview.

File notings can save thousands of crores of rupees for a nation like ours. Enron is the example of a disastrous deal for a high cost electricity between Dhabol Power Company (of Enron) and Maharashtra Electricity Board, guaranteed by Government of Maharashtra and Government of India, which ran into trouble and ultimately closed down. All this could happen because the terms of agreement were kept secret and not revealed in spite of the demand from NGOs in Maharashtra. The people need right to such information which will be hidden in invisible folds of file notings.

Despite all this, the steel frame of the country, the bureaucracy, loves their file notings and prefers to keep them close to their chest, because the file notings reveal them totally. So, they do not want it to be known on request. According to the RTI law, file notings are not exempted from disclosure unless they fall under general clauses of exceptions and exemptions, defined in Section 8 of the law, which we will come to later in this article. Still, the State machinery had wanted to secure file notings and was perhaps never comfortable with their access by citizens.

Attacking the Definition of 'Information'

If this amendment is passed, the definition of 'information' under the access law suffers a dent. Section 2(f) of the RTI law says: "Information means any material in any form including records, documents, memos, e-mails, opinions, advices, press releases, circulars, orders, logbooks, contracts, reports, papers, samples, models, data material held in any electronic form and information relating to any private body which can be accessed by a public authority under any other law for the time being in force". File notings are covered under the expressions 'any material in any form' and 'opinions, advices'. The nature of file notings is inevitably that of advice, opinions, recommendations or suggestions, etc., which are specifically covered by the above definition of 'information'.

Exempting file notings will limit the expressions such as 'file', 'information', 'opinions' and 'advice' in Section 2(f) in the Act. Similarly exclusion of notings would completely nullify the operation and the import of Section 4(l)(c) and (d) which requires every public authority to proactively "publish all relevant facts while formulating policies or announcing the decisions to affected persons" and "provide reasons for its administrative or quasi-judicial decisions to affected persons".

Section 4(l)(b) of the Act makes it mandatory for every public authority to publish amongst other things—"the procedure followed in the decision making process, including channels of supervision and accountability" and "the norms set by it for the discharge of its functions".

Do exemptions currently in force through Section 8 already apply to file notings and cabinet papers?

The category of 'file notings' does not figure under Section 8(1) of the RTI Act, which lists out the types of information that the government is under "no obligation to give any citizen". Thus, the file notings come firmly within the access as per the RTI Act and must be made public on request. Even where notings may fall within the Section 8 criteria, they can still be made public where the public interest is served in disclosing the information.

As regards cabinet papers, Section 8 mentions cabinet papers including records of deliberations of councils of ministers, and provides that "decisions and the material on the basis of which decisions were taken shall be made public after the decision has been taken". Clearly, the Act requires that not only must decisions be made public, but the reasons and the material on the basis of the decisions be made public after the matter is complete and over. Even cabinet papers which may otherwise be exempt from disclosure, under Section 8(l)(i) of the Act are still ultimately subject to disclosure.

The Manmohan Singh government now proposes to amend the law so that the "material on the basis of which decisions were taken" is deleted from clause 'F' of Section 8. The proposed provision says: "No cabinet paper would be disclosed even after a decision has been taken". This would put cabinet notes, records and other documents based on which the decisions are taken, also out of the reach of access and out of the Central Information Commission.

The Central Government has every authority to amend this access legislation. Apart from this general power, Section 30 of the Act empowers to remove difficulties, hindrances and obstacles to give full effect to the goals and objectives of the law. Under Section 25(3)(g) of the Act, Ministries can also recommend amendments for enforcing the right to access information.

But the proposed amendments are neither initiated by ministries nor intended for removing any difficulties. Instead they propose to destroy the accessibility to a maximum extent. If the amendment is really needed, it should have been based on the practical experience. The RTI law also needs to be made difficult to amend as any political party at the office might be interested in hiding any sort of information from the people. Finally, it is for the people to secure the hard-earned right to information.

In January this year, ruling in a case concerning the refusal of the public sector Telecommunications Consultants India Ltd. (TCIL) to provide a file noting, the Central Information Commission ruled that unless the public authority clearly specified that the file notings relate to commercial confidence or trade secret or intellectual property or available to TCIL in its fiduciary relationship, the appellant should be given file noting on the document specified.

On 1 December, 2005, Prime Minister Manmohan Singh had instructed the Department of Personnel and Training (DoPT) to exempt file notings on identifiable individuals, organisations, appointments, and matters relating to inquiries and departmental proceedings from the purview of the RTI Act. However, the government had said that "substantive file notings" relating to plans, schemes, programmes and projects of the Government related to development and social issues could be disclosed. Reacting to this, Dr. O.P. Kejariwal, one of the Central Information Commissioners, wrote a letter to the Central Government opposing the order. He described it as the first blow to the Act widely seen to be one of the most important pieces of legislation to have been enacted in independent India.

As the backdoor methods did not work, and rulings from Information Commission are apparently opposing these attempts, the Union Cabinet on 20 July, 2006 announced its decision to amend the law to exclude notings on files by officials from the ambit of this law so that the CIC's decisions on notings would become ineffective.

The Union Information and Broadcasting Minister, Priyaranjan Das Munshi said: "Decisions can be conveyed, not in terms of details about what the Under Secretary or Joint Secretary wrote or what the Secretary disapproved". He thus made it clear that details of the notings—"who said what" at various stages of the decision-making—would be out-of-bounds for the public. The proposed amendment also accedes to the UPSC's request that the sensitive area of its selection process be put out of the RTI law's purview.

Unfortunately the UPA Government is not hesitating to sacrifice the 'life' of the access law to secure 'file' of decisions. There is a satiric remark on files in Secretariat, where the 'not approved' becomes 'note approved' at a later point of time, without any substantive reasoning. To add that letter 'e', what transpires—under the table or behind the curtain is left to anybody's imagination. If the file notings are kept 'covered', the reasons for changes and reversals of decisions will never be 'discovered' and discussed. Hiding files and file notes amount to encouraging or hiding corruption, and allowing the official and non-official public servants not to be accountable.

It is a principle of administrative law that the cabinet decisions and debates should be revealed to the people, unless they disclose any sensitive and security information. Government should understand that the secrecy or classification of information must be confined to security interests, privacy issues, and trade related rights, and no more than that. In fact, the information is generated for the people as those files pile up on the initiative of a representation or complaint or requirement. A file in public authority is not compilation of documents containing trade secret or pieces of poetry copyrightable to the writer. It is the data generated, opinions sought, precedents analysed, pros and cons discussed and impact on public exchequer examined, for advancing the public interest or answering a vociferous public demand, etc.

Furthermore, in any democracy the discussion should precede the decision. The information on the file and its notings is neither the property of the officers who express opinion based on their experience and performance of a legal obligation, nor the property of the government. If the cabinet has preferred not to decide on a particular item of agenda, why should it not reveal the reasons for deferring the decision? Why not let the people know who said what on that vital issue connected to the welfare and development of the people?

Neither the UK nor USA or Australia have exempted file notes from the access to public. In India also, both the Judiciary and Parliament are long used to functioning openly without any adverse effects and it is only the bureaucracy that presently functions under this unnecessary veil of secrecy. Amending the law to take away file notings from the public domain is a retrograde measure that will appease only that miniscule part of officialdom that stands to unduly benefit from such secrecy and denies the people the benefit of their own information, their empowerment and active participation in democratic decision making process.

The character of state and sovereignty is manifest in three important wings—Executive, Legislature and Judiciary. As the open trial is the basic norm of judicial enquiry, the courts always function in public, while every aspect of proceedings in legislature is reported in media or recorded and made available to all. Most of the legislative proceedings are now being telecast live.

The only wing that runs in secrecy is the Executive. The decisions at the Council of Ministers level or secretary level are not easily available to common people, which leads to absence of accountability of decision makers. Even if the decisions are made available by spokesperson of the cabinet, the reasons for decision, and different opinions expressed before they arrived at that particular decision are usually beyond access. This has been our Executive's culture, and seen from this vantage point, the RTI law of 2005 was a path-breaking legislation that gave people the power to demand information that is rightfully theirs.

In sum, the promotion of "transparency and accountability" in the working of public authorities—the stated object of the landmark RTI legislation—does not stop merely with making the decisions of government public. It also lies—and critically—in making it possible for people to know on what grounds these decisions were taken. Access to file notings by officials is necessary to evaluate the process of decision-making, to understand such things as which options were considered, which were not, and why some were rejected. It is not proper to close the doors before they are fully opened and the 'enlightenment' transformed into empowerment.

END NOTES

- On September 4, 2007 for the first time, Punjab and Haryana High Court got its public information officers Mr. M.M. Dhoncha who has been appointed as the first PIO of the High Court rules of which have been notified. A committee for the purpose was formed in early 2007.
- Public Information officers for the District Courts have also been finalized.
- Interview with Chief Information Commissioner, Ramesh Inder Singh (The Punjab Information Commission) "can't be held to ransom by Street Protests" in *The Hindustan Times*, 30 December, 2010.

7

Right to Information and Public Accountability

The National Commission to Review the Working of the Constitution while recommending that Article 19(1)(a) should be amended *inter alia* said:

Further the Commission said, "They (citizens) shy away from questioning officers handing their cases because of the latter's snobbish attitude and bow-wow style. Right to Information should be guaranteed and needs to be given real substance. In this regard, government must assume a major responsibility and mobilize skills to ensure flow of information to citizens. The traditional insistence on secrecy should be discarded. In fact we should have an oath of transparency in place of an oath of secrecy. Administration should become transparent and participatory".

The need for this deliberation on Public Accountability and Right to Information Act is perhaps because an attempt is increasingly needed to redefine the relationship between state and individual.

The state and whose functionaries are accountable to public on the one hand and the individual citizen who has right to information on the other.

The Right to Information is not Fundamental Right although it can be traced to Article 19 of Fundamental Rights. But this right is pre-constitutional — the right to know, speech, discuss are as old as human life existed.

All are stakeholders in Right to Information Act and the issue of Public Accountability of government bureaucracy, citizens, media, corporate sector and there are even some unexpected areas like World Bank is depending on Information Commission to public cross-check information about funds, their utilization and transparency in that regard. The Chief Information Commission, Rajan Kashyap, referred to this in his key note (National Seminar on Right to Information Act, ICSSR Complex, Panjab University, 13 September, 2007).

That nearly all political regimes throughout the world style themselves as democracies and claim adherence to democracy. Democracy seems to bestow an aura of legitimacy on modern life laws, policies seem more justified if they are based on democratic principles. It has a universal appeal to mankind as democratic life offers respect and dignity to human being. Democracy has the dimension of an inner ocean offering any number of opportunities to individual to realize his aims — personal, social, political. Adoption of Democracy as a way of life in India seems to be a feasible path through which it can reach its goals.

The Right to Information Act (2005) is a law enacted by the Parliament of India giving Indians (except in the State of Jammu and Kashmir who have their own special law) access to government records. Under the act, any person may request information from a 'public authority' (i.e., a body of government or instrumentality of State) which is expected to reply within thirty days.

The Act also requires every public authority to computerize their records for wide dissertation and to proactively publish certain categories of information so that the citizens need minimum recourse to request for information formally. This law was passed by Parliament on 15 June, 2005 and came into force on 13 October, 2005.

State Level Laws

The RTI Laws were first successfully enacted by the State governments—Tamil Nadu (1997), Goa (1997), Rajasthan (2000), Karnataka (2000), Delhi (2001), Maharashtra (2002), Madhya Pradesh (2003), Assam (2002) and Jammu and Kashmir (2004).

The Maharashtra and Delhi State level enactments are considered to have been most widely used.

Reach of the RTI Act

For the first time there is a law which casts a direct accountability on the office for non-performance. If the concerned officer does not provide information in time, a penalty of Rs. 250 per day of delay can be imposed by the Information Commission. If the information provided is false, a penalty of a maximum of Rs. 25,000 can be imposed. A penalty can also be imposed for providing incomplete information or for rejecting the application for *mala fide* reasons. This fine is deducted from the officers' personal salary.

This Law has given teeth to the process of accountability in Indian democracy. Some offices have been penalized by the Central as well as State Information Commissions. The amount collected as fine is deposited in the government treasury.

This Act empowers the people *vis-à-vis* the State apparatus. A person making a request for information is not obliged to explain why the information is needed. The Act has specified time frame for complying with the request for information, i.e., PIO must comply within 30 days and APIO within 35 days. If the PIO transfers the request to some other department which is better concerned with the requested information, the time allowed is 35 days. Information about Human Rights violations by security agencies has to be provided in 45 days. However, in case of life or liberty of the individual is concerned, the PIO is required to comply within 48 hours.

Since the information is paid for, the time elapsing between the reply of PIO and time taken to deposit the further fees for information is excluded from the time allowed. In case information is not provided within this period, it is treated as refusal. Refusal with or without reasons may be ground for appeal by the individual.

For the Central Government departments, there is a fee of Rs. 10 for filing the request, Rs. 2 per page of information and Rs. 5 for each hour of inspection after the first hour. States fix their own rules in this connection.

Role of the Government

The Act under Section 26 enjoins upon the Central Government and State governments to initiate necessary steps leading to the following developments:

(i) Develop educational programmes for the public especially disadvantages section on RTI.
(ii) Encourage public authorities to participate in the development and organization of such programmes.
(iii) Promote timely dissemination of accurate information to the public.
(iv) Give training to offices and develop training materials.
(v) Compile and disseminate a User Guide for the public in respective official language.
(vi) Publish names, designations and postal addresses and contact numbers of PIOs and other information, such as notices regarding fees to be paid, remedies available in law if the request is requested, etc.

Right to Information Act

In a democratic set-up people have a right to know every public Act and conduct discharged by their public functionaries. The right to know is necessary outcome of the concept of freedom of speech and expression.

At the same time open Government does not mean that whole government transactions are to be carried out in the open. To cover with veil of secrecy, the matters relating to national security and safety is in the general public interest. In this sense, right to know has to be counterbalanced in just and reasonable constitutional norms. Information and communication are powerful tools and have a potential to shape and shake social and political development of the society. Man make their place in history, when quality and quantity of information supplied to them.

The significance of Right to Information Act lies in the fact that knowledge is power. Justice Bhagwati in **S.P. Gupta** v. **Union of India** (1982) described democracy as a continuous process of government, an attitude and habit of mind, in which people have to play important role only if "it is open government (and) there is full access to information in regard to functioning of the Government". In short, secrecy in working of the Government would promote and encourage oppression corruption and abuse of authority. The last forty years or so have seen the passage of freedom of information legislation in several countries beginning with the United States in 1966, Denmark and Norway in 1970, Australia and New Zealand in 1982, Canada in 1983, Ireland in 1988 and India in 2005. There are several reasons why development of freedom of information, legislation is a welcome trend.

First, RTI legislation breaks with the entrenched tradition of secrecy in several countries, and in doing so, help empower the citizen *vis-à-vis* the state, thus deepening democracy and enhancing citizen control of political process.

Second, more information helps citizens make better and more reasoned choices about important public policy and electoral issues, and participate in the political process more fully.

Thirdly, the capacity to demand information from government is a powerful deterrent against governmental corruption and graft or plain inefficiency.

The RTI Act or Right to Information Act was passed by the Parliament of India in 2005. Under this empowering piece of legislation, the citizens have access to more information and this act ushers in the new era of transparency and accountability in Government.

The RTI Act was passed with an intent of creating accountability and putting power where it belongs—in the hands of people. It was designed to reduce the discretions and biases that plague government decision-making. The Right to Information is a powerful tool. It enables citizens to get most information held by the government. The Act makes real the fundamental right to know. It recognizes the difficulties associated with getting information out of bureaucracy so it lays down:

(i) a large category of information which the government must put out without being asked,

(ii) another category which the government must give if requested by a citizen, and

(iii) finally a residuary category which won't be given unless it can be shown; that is, it is in the public interest to give it.

More importantly, the Act lays down penalties for unjustifiably withholding information. There have been plenty of cases where too little information has resulted in people being left in the dark and thereafter being taken for an unending side. The RTI Act acknowledges this fact. The old cliché about knowledge being power had never really been 'experienced' in this country until the right to information became law. Going against the bureaucratic prudery, the Prime Minister Manmohan Singh in December 2005, intervened to make 'file notings' in official documents accessible.

Noting in some ways are heart of official decision-making. They include a list of records, documentations, memos, e-mails, opinions, advises, press releases, circulars, order, etc.

To have access to file notings—the various opinions made on the margins of files by bureaucrats—is not only to know how the process works, but also why the process is at times delayed or stalled.

Certain 'sensitive' issues have been kept out of public purview, at least for specified time. Military and paramilitary information has been excluded from purview of the RTI Act.

In a nutshell RTI Act makes the government fully accountable to every citizen. It is much greater sense of responsibility. It is a power that is given to every citizen in recognition of the fact that it is a government of the people, for the people and by the people—the essence of democracy.

Section 3 of the RTI Act makes it incumbent on public authorities to maintain all records duly categorized and indexed and to provide as much information *suo moto* to the public at regular intervals.

Challenges are:

1. Bureaucratic initiative and freedom in decision making process need not be unduly curbed;

2. All information in the present age of information is explosive. It needs to be handled with utmost care.
3. In the light of RTI Act, there is a need to repeal the Official Secrets Act and bring about reform in the Conduct of Rules of Government of India;
4. RTI Act can be made effective and economical the emerging concept of Cyber Technology.

Unique Features of Information Commission

It is a feedback system. It is extremely useful for bringing about accountability in the system and reusing the recovering of veil of secrecy in which bureaucracy has reserved enlisted in the past independence era.

Commission keeps on cajoling the government to take action. In Punjab since 2005 to 2007, 3,003 cases were filed under RTI Act (Information by the head of the Commission, Shri Rajan Kashyap at ICSSR Complex, Punjab University, Chandigarh during National Seminar on RTI Act, 13-14 September, 2007).

Out of 3,003 cases filed, 1,885 have been settled and 1,200 are pending, he revealed penalties are imposed in rare cases. In case of Punjab, in 43 cases fine was imposed in case of wilful default and negligence. The areas where maximum complaints were raised include Municipal Corporation, Police and Education.

The great Upnishadic verses describe man as 'child of mortality' and his mission in life is to realize the ultimate truth. Ignorance is darkness and must be dispelled. Information is light and must be processed through consciousness. Knowledge and wisdom spring from the base of facts sensitively structured and finished. Mere jumble of information may be bewildering or misleading mess. Knowledge is power but information is fuel of knowledge. Obviously a citizen cannot achieve knowledge unless he has certain basic freedoms such as freedom of thought, freedom of information, freedom of conscience, freedom of speech and expression, freedom of locomotion and so on so forth. These freedoms represent the basic values of life in a civilized society and have been given a place of pride in our Constitution, i.e., Fundamental Right which are inviolable tough subject to some reasonable restrictions. These restrictions are meant to protect the national interest and to safeguard the fundamental rights of the other persons. Freedom of information has been gradually receiving acceptance and recognition the globe over.

Implication of the Term Right to Information in a Democratic Set-Up

Transparency in administration is a sure technique to minimize the abuse and misuse of administrative discretion. As knowledge is a guarantee against ignorance so is government openness a guarantee against misconduct. Openness negatives the ideas of fantastic, arbitrary and oppressive form of government action. Justice V. R. Krishna lyer rightly said:

> "A government which reveals in secrecy in the field of people's liberty not only acts against democratic decency but burying itself with its own burial. That is writing on the wall if history was our teacher, memory our mentor and decline of liberty not our unwitting endeavour. Public power must rarely hide its heart in an open society and system."

Into that, heaven of freedom, my Father, let my country awake

Truth does not dawn but is born of discussion of public affairs, which is preceded by expression of views of individuals. The raw material for formation of opinion is information. Thus the free availability of facts is essential for sound judgement of citizens and sensible participation in government. Infallibility of authority and immunity from criticism pave the way to dictatorial form of government. This unwanted end is promoted by closing the doors of information on public matters although the only way to responsible and responsive government is to clothe every person with a legal right to seek information whenever he desires, however uncomfortable the disclosure of facts may be to the administrators.

To say in the spirit of a democratic world order, it is necessary that each one of us everywhere on this earth under the Sun has a right to know and a duty to shape the course of things, on a national as well as on international level. The philosophy of freedom of information and open government has been well described by the U.S. House Committee on Government Operations, which approved the Freedom of Information Act, in 1966:

"A democratic society requires an informed, intelligent electorate, and the intelligence of the electorate varies as the 'quantity and quality', of its information varies. A danger signal to our democratic society in the United States is the fact that such a truism needs repeating."

The root truth is that freedom without information is meaningless and liberty without light will perish because all governments are obscure and invisible.

There is a burden on the government to justify secrecy. Failure on this front is bound to spell dangerous consequences. In a democracy citizens' right to know is assumed rather than guaranteed. This right is derived from the accountability and answerability of the government to the people.

'Right to know' has been given status of fundamental right by the highest Court of the land in *Judges Transfer Case.* The Apex Court held that the right to know is implicit in the right of free speech and expression guaranteed under our Constitution in Article 19(1)(a).

Right to know is also implicit in Article 19(1)(a) as natural concomitant to free press which right is deducible from fundamental right of freedom of speech and expression. In S.P. Gupta's case, the Apex Court also recommended change in century-old provisions of Section 123 of the Indian Evidence Act 1872 so as to be conducive to the republican form of government and the open society, which, we the people of India have established. Section 123 relates to immunity from production of documents and was enacted to suit the needs of the empire builders.

The Supreme Court has reaffirmed this legal position in its subsequent decisions in **Reliance Petro Ltd. Case** and **Secretary, Ministry of Information and Broadcasting** v.

Cricket Association, Bengal. In Reliance Petro's case, the Supreme Court has observed that the right to know has reached new dimensions and urgency and is basic right which citizens of a free country aspire in the broaden horizons of the right to live in this age on our land under Article 21 of the Constitution. The people at large have a right to know in order to be able to take part in a participatory development in the industrial life. In **Secretary, Ministry of Information and Broadcasting's case,** the Apex Court has given a very broad definition to the right to receive and disseminate information through any media including air waves and electronic media. Right to information is inherent in right to live as enshrined in Article 21 and freedom of speech and expression as guaranteed under Article 19(1)(a) of our Constitution. Right to information thus emanates from the fundamental right to life and fundamental freedom of speech and expression.

These freedoms guaranteed by the Constitution have to be enjoyed subject to some reasonable restrictions. But these restrictions can never outweigh and dominate the freedoms. After all what is fundamental are the freedom and not the restriction.

Under the mantle of Welfare State, the Government today is engaged in variety of activities which cannot be termed as sovereign functions of the Government. These activities do not constitute 'Affairs of the State' in strict sense. The Government, especially of a welfare state, is responsible for socio-economic development and uplift of the people, besides maintaining routine law and order. One of the Directive Principles of the State Policy says: "the State shall strive to promote the welfare of the people by securing and protecting as effectively as it may, a social order in which justice, social economic and political, shall inform all institutions of the national life. The State shall in particular strive to minimize the inequalities in income and endeavour to eliminate inequalities in facilities and opportunities not only amongst individuals but also amongst groups of people residing in different areas or engaged in different vocations". In an independent, democratic and welfare state, the citizens occupy quite an important position. They are the ones who are not only being governed but also govern by way of exercising their right of franchise and electing their representatives, who in turn formulate policies in accordance with which the administrators are supposed to govern—for the benefit of the society. The benefits are to be accorded to or conferred on the citizens by the administration in a manner whereby most optimum position is attained and no one is favoured or deprived of at the cost of or for favouring the other one. In such a system, it is expected of the administration to provide to all the members of the society a reasonable dignified standard of life in which there is no risk of insecurity or stagnation on the economic front. No individual should have any fear of suspicion and mistrust towards the system in his mind. This is possible only by disseminating proper information, of course, without leaking out the vital secrets. More than fifty per cent of the citizens' problems could be sorted out promptly through a proper communication between different channels in the administration.

The Government, today, is called upon to make policies on an ever increasing range of subjects, and many of these policies must necessarily impinge on the lives of the citizens. It may sometimes happen that the data made available to the policy makers is of a selective nature and even the policy-makers and their advisers may deliberately suppress certain viewpoints and favour others. Such bureaucratic habits get encouragement in an environment of secrecy; and openness in governmental work is possibly the only effective corrective to it, also raising, in the process, the quality of decision-making. Besides, openness has an educational role inasmuch as citizens are enabled to acquire a fuller view of the pros and cons of matters of major importance, which naturally helps in building informed public opinion, no less than goodwill for the Government.

Justice Krishna Iyer while commenting on the public functionaries remarked, "Be you ever so high, the law is above you". The public power must not hide its heart in a welfare state and open system. The normal rule in the Government of India is secrecy and openness the exception. There is the Official Secrets Act 1923 which makes unauthorized communication of information including documents, an offence punishable with imprisonment which may extend up to three years. This Act covers all documents and information and makes no distinction of kind or of degree. A blanket is thrown over everything. Nothing escapes. By secrecy system the government safeguards its reputation, buries its mistakes, manipulates its citizens, maximizes its powers and corrupts itself. In the backdrop of judgement of the Supreme Court in the *Judges' Transfer case,* the provisions of the Official Secrets Act 1923 and of Section 123 of the Evidence Act 1872 suffer from the stigma of unconstitutionality. These colonial provisions need to be "pensioned off". In Sweden the Constitution itself contains a provision guaranteeing access to information. Even the Russian people have been voicing their concern for 'Glasnost and Perestroika System' (transparency and freedom of expression). In England, thrust of legislation is on 'secrecy' notwithstanding enactment of Access to Personal Files Act, the Official Secrets Act and enforcement in 1994 of Code of Practice on Access to Government Information. Australia and Canada have their own Freedom of Information Acts enacted in 1982 and 1986 respectively. Freedom of Information Ordinance was promulgated in Australia in 1989. The USA has enacted Freedom of Information Act 1966 and Electronic Freedom of Information Act Denmark, the Netherlands, Germany, Norway and France have also their legislation, which provides for access to information.

Non-Aligned Movement meeting in Zimbabwe reviewed the progress of new information order and pressed for an enduring foundation for Freedom of Information without Western pressure and distortions.

Referring to the right to obtain information and to publish it in U.S.A. and England, Mr. Howard Simpson, Managing Editor of the *Washington Post,* observed:

> "In U.S.A. the publishers have a right to print anything. If we get hold of a State secret, it is the editor who has the determining authority whether to hold it or print it. The government has the right to keep secrets, but if we come by it, nobody can stop us. Whereas in Britain, the press

> believes in national security, which means they can be told to hold a story back. They have Official Secrets Act, etc."

The judiciary in U.S.A. shares the same concern of the Congress, which is reflected in the Freedom of Information Act 1966.

Secrecy in government is fundamentally anti-democratic, perpetuating bureaucratic errors. Open discussion based on full information and debate on public issues are vital to our health.

Woodrow Wilson has rightly said, "A democratic Government ought to be an outside and not inside". Unbridled freedom is not possible in our world of perils and evil designs. Truth may have to be withheld in moments when a nation's survival is in imminent danger. In Churchill's words: "In time of war, the truth is so precious that it must be escorted by a bodyguard of lies". No State should adopt the mendacious methodology of Goebbels and mislead its subjects, whatever the crisis. However, quite often the right to information is denied and a seemingly authentic diet of official lies is served with a view to condition the minds of men and they are expected to consume government's version. Free speech is sabotaged from within by fouling the fountains of information. The bureaucracy itself is banned from telling the truth by forced statutory secrecy. Administrative secrecy relating to classified documents concerning national security and foreign policy is justified. But routine claim to secrecy or privilege by the government and public bodies may jeopardize the very survival of democracy in India because this immunity is anti-democratic. Therefore, no government should think that people must be told only that much which it thinks to be good for the people and safe for itself.

Dangers of burying the truth have been very powerfully put by Emile Zola:

> "When truth is buried underground it grows, it chokes, it gathers such an explosive force that on the day it bursts out, it blows up everything with it."

Equally forceful are the views of Kurt Eisner, who says that the truthful information must not be withheld because:

"Truth is the greatest of all national possessions. A state, a people, a system which suppresses the truth or fears to publish it, deserves to collapse."

Right to Information and Human Rights Jurisprudence

The right to information is embedded in Article 19(l)(a) of the Constitution of India and even the Universal Declaration of Human Rights recognised this right as a *sine qua non* for democracy. When journalists purvey news and information, it sometimes results in violation of another fundamental human right—the right to privacy contained in Article 21. In a large number of cases, exercise of the right to information by the majority (represented by journalists, who are supposedly the eyes and ears of the populace) infringes the right to privacy of the minority. It will become obvious from the above discussion that the Right to Information which is included in Article 19(1)(a) comes into conflict with the Right to Privacy which the Supreme Court has interpreted as coming under the number umbrella or Article 21. Hence both these rights are mutually antagonistic. Exercise of the Right to Information or the Right to Know results in invasion of privacy of citizens. We shall briefly recapitulate the international provisions made on the Right to Information and the Right to Privacy. The United Nation's declaration in 1948 declared that: "Freedom of opinion and expression, including the freedom to seek and receive and impart information and ideas through any media, regardless of frontiers" is one of the most basic human rights. It was in 1948 again that Article 12 of the Universal Declaration of Human Rights enunciated: "No one shall be subjected to arbitrary interference with his privacy, family, home or correspondence nor to attacks upon his honour and reputation. Every one has the right to the protection of the law against such interference or attacks".

The U.N. declarations stresses on the freedom of opinion and expression. In the words reproduced above, there are no limitations placed on the right to information. Similarly, the right to privacy does not make any exception or limitation. However, the protection extended by Article 12 has to be circumscribed. It is humbly submitted that no right can be absolute. If that were so, it would degenerate into licence. The U.S. Supreme Court has laid down in **Roth** v. **United States** that the First Amendment protection which in its phraseology appears absolute, does not protect obscenity. Hence, no right is ever absolute. Similarly, Article 19(1)(a) which guarantees freedom of speech and expression also guarantees the right to information only in limited areas.

In a conflict between the right to information or the right to know *versus* the right to privacy of individuals, which right will prevail over which is to be analysed in this thesis. At the outset, it can be postulated that when an individual is a public figure, a certain amount of invasion of privacy should be tolerated. This would subject the public figure to mental torture and expose his family and friends to unsought for publicity. To what extent the Bentamite dictum that the good of the majority should override the interests of the few will be examined. At the centre of the problem lies the issue of a public figure. The U.S. Supreme Court has defined a public figure in very wide terms. This researcher has attempted to redefine as to who constitutes a public figure. The basic concept of privacy did not evolve in the twentieth century. It goes back to 1890 when an American legal scholar, Thomas Cooley, first defined privacy as a basic right. Towards the end of the nineteenth century, two Harvard researchers, Samuel Warren and Louis Brandeis, published an article in the *Harvard Law Review*. This article first brought the concept of privacy to the notice of legal scholars, lawyers and judges. In the article, the authors argued that the right to privacy was necessary to facilitate the development of the individual. It is the individual's right to be let alone, free from unwanted publicity, where his "home was his castle". The concept of the *purdah* system in India too can be viewed as a variation of the right to privacy. Here, women were segregated and strangers were not allowed to enter a part of the homestead which was used exclusively by women. Even while leaving their homes, these women kept their faces covered by veils. These practices and customs have devolved from ancient usage and custom in India.

In **Curtis Publishing Co.** v. **Butts,** the U.S. Supreme Court held that "public figures" are persons who "often play an influential role in ordering society. As a class, these public figures have as ready access as public officials to mass media of communication, both to influence policy and to counter criticism of their views and activities". Justice Black, Douglas, Brennan and White jointed Chief Justice Warren's separate opinion in *Curtis Publishing Co.* to the extent that they held that "public figures" suing for libel must prove there was "actual malice" on the part of a journalist or media-defendants. Hence, it was not sufficient to prove that what was published was inaccurate. The court further defined who constituted a "public figure: in two other cases, viz. **Wolston** v. **Readers Digest Association** and **Hutchinson** v. **Proxmire**". The definition of public figure as those who often play an influential role in ordering society is acceptable but not accurate in all circumstances. Furthermore, it is submitted that the opinion of the judges that public figures have as ready access as public officials to mass media of communication, both to influence policy and counter criticism of their views is not accurate in all cases. To buttress this argument, one can consider the case of notorious criminal, Charles Sobhraj. Two books have already been written on his life history. Although he has figured several times in the news columns of the national press the major national newspaper may not unstintingly permit this criminal to use their space to propagate his philosophy of life. Hence, Charles Sobhraj is an individual who interests the reading public. He "makes" news in journalistic parlance but it is submitted that he does not and should not be allowed access to the mass media to influence policy and counter criticism.

Now, the U.S. Supreme Court does not consider those convicted of crimes to constitute public figures. This dictum has been reaffirmed in several decisions. This, it is humbly submitted, is erroneous. A criminal of the stature of Charles Sobhraj evokes interest among the reading public and could indirectly influence the lives of those impressionable enough. A public figure is any individual (including a class of persons), who has the potential to influence the lives, either directly or indirectly of at least a hundred other people. By this redefinition, judges, cricketers, film-stars, cabinet ministers, university vice chancellors and others in such categories fall within the definition of "public figures". All these classes of persons have the potential to influence the lives of at least one hundred other people, directly or indirectly.

The Supreme Court laid down in fast judges task case that:

> "The demand for openness is based principally on two reasons. It is now widely accepted that democracy does not consist merely of people exercising their franchise, once in five years to choose their rulers and once the vote is cast, then retiring in passivity and not taking any interest in the government. Today, it is common knowledge that democracy has more positive intent and its orchestration has to be continuous and pervasive. This means *inter alia* that people should not only cast intelligent and rational votes but should also exercise judgement in the conduct of the government and the merits of public policies, or that democracy does not remain merely a sporadic exercise in voting but becomes a continuous process of government — an attitude and habit of mind. But this important role people can fulfil in a democracy only if it is an open government where there is full access to information in regard to the functioning of the government.

The Apex Court laid down that the Right to Information formed part of Article 19(1) (a). In **Indian Express** v. **Union of India,** Justice Venkatramiah speaking on behalf of a bench consisting of himself, O. Chimanappa Reddy and A.P. Sen JJ observed:

> Public interest in freedom of discussion (of which freedom of the press is one aspect) stems from the requirement that members of a democratic society should be sufficiently informed that they may influence intelligently the decisions which may affect themselves.

Similarly, in **L.K. Koolwal** v. **State the Rajasthan,** the High Court while considering a public interest petition by a citizen seeking protection against the neglect of sanitation by the state, which led to pollution hazards, said:

> "The citizen has a right to know about the activities of the State, the instrumentalities, the departments and the agencies of the State. The privilege of secrecy which existed in old times that the State is not bound to disclose certain facts to its citizens does not survive to a great extent now."

From the three decisions cited above, one can safely conclude that the right to information is a fundamental right under the umbrella of Article 19(1)(a), the right to privacy or the right to be let alone is also a fundamental right. Though it is not expressly mentioned in the Constitution, the Supreme Court has laid down in **Kharak Singh** v. **State of U.P.** that it comes under the umbrella of Article 21 which guarantees all citizens the right to life and liberty.

The few examples that have been recorded are encouraging. These — the MKSS in Rajasthan, Chetna in U.P., Parivartan in Delhi and a few other places emphasize two aspects that are crucial for the right to information: a deliberate will to take up a cause and, procuring information that enables the masses to rally against any form of oppression by the Government and other agencies.

The fight against oppression has been made possible by accessing documents that reveal the extent and nature of irregularity and consequent oppression. It also emphasises the role of committed intermediaries who can decipher the information to reveal the nature of oppression.

The debates and background related to the right of information revolved essentially around the governments and their inclination to legislate and implement access to information. This is also based on the fact that governments in fact are vast repositories of information. In the earlier context it was felt that the state had the right to protect its information base in the areas of security, public safety, prevention of crime and commercial confidentiality. However, when the state moved into areas beyond these sacrosanct domains it is now felt that they cannot deny information. Information management by the government includes a balancing proposition where it has to weigh the privacy of its citizens against the public interest or sphere. Further, the amount of information that is being demanded is quite large and an institutional mechanism will have to emerge to cater to this demand.

RTI Act—A Role Reversal

The Right to Information Act is a reflection of the role reversal between government and citizen, i.e., it has led to a change in clientelism. In the immediate post-independent era, Indian politics reflected a portion—client behaviour in which the client (or citizen) was full of gratitude towards the patron for giving independence from the British yoke. Three aspects are embedded in the RTI Act. They are as follows:

(1) Transparency of government;
(2) Accountability of bureaucracy; and
(3) Empowerment of public.

Accordingly there are several stakeholders in the functioning of the RTI Act as it affects everyone. Bureaucracy has a new role. From the position of custodian of information, the bureaucracy in India has moved to the position of being a trustee. This is just as well because bureaucracy in India was still carrying on its original stance which was made by the British to ensure the substance of the local population. This stance has long become redundant but it took Indian governance long six decades to bring about the change.

Bureaucracy was defending its *status quo* long after quo had lost its status effectively. The RTI Act will in this sense ensure the longevity of the bureaucratic system along with its transparency.

Common man or citizen is the greatest beneficiary. He is the master and RTI Act is a step towards the curbing of corruption.

The unique feature of RTI Act is the formation of Information Commission. These are the feedback system which are extremely useful for bringing about accountability in the system.

In conclusion one can say that RTI Act is undoubtedly a mirror in regard to transparency and efficiency. The method of filing a complaint under RTI Act, however, needs to be simplified even more, to save the common man from harassment of running from pillar to post.

As far as the official machinery goes, there is no need for it to be afraid if there are no skeletons. 68 countries access the world and 9 States of India have utilized the RTI Acts without any hackings. To make the Act more effective we need to focus on record — management. We have volumes of records which need to be weeded. RTI Act is a landmark difference already and has a potential for further empowerment of people thereby deepening the reach of democracy in India. From culture of secrecy to culture of openness this transition is not easy.

END NOTES

A Fight For 'Right To Know'. Aruna Roy and Others. *Yojana,* Vol. 50, January 2006; 2-8.

A New Era. Prakash Kardaley. *Seminar,* Vol. 551, July 2005; 17-23.

Access, Diversity and Representation. Kalpana Kannabiran. *Yojana,* Vol. 50, January 2006; 17-20.

Addressing The Digital Underside. Sucheta Dalal. *Financial Express* 14 August, 2006; 3-6.

Administrative Stagnancy and Public Indifference. V.R. Shenoy. *Janata,* Vol. 60, No. 27, 31 July, 2005; 7-8

Amit Bhaduri. *Economic and Political Weekly,* Vol. 40, No. 4, 22 January, 2005; 267-69.

Bending Before Babus (Editorial) *The Times of India,* 25 July 2006, 14; 1-2.

Boundaries of Disclosure (Editorial). *Financial Express* 20 April, 2006; 6; 1-2.

Breaking the Bureaucratic Mould. Indra J. Mistry. *Yojana,* Vol. 50., January 2006; 9-11.

Changing Discourse. Sowmya Sivakumar and Eric Kerbart. *Seminar,* Vol. 551, July 2005; 50-54.

Changing Governance Forever. Shekhar Singh & Misha Singh. *Yojana,* Vol. 50, January 2006; 33-35.

Dirty Harrys (Editorial). *The Times of India,* 30 August, 2005; 8: 1-2.
Disclosure Norms. Trilochan Sastry. *Seminar,* Vol. 551, July 2005; 24-26.
Don't Dilute RTI Act, Please. Virendra Kumar. *The Tribune,* 6 August, 2006; 13: 13-6.
Exempt File Noting From RTI Ambit: Aruna Roy & S. Mahawal. *Economic Times,* 28 July, 2006; 12: 4-5.
Exercising the Right to Seek Information. Kathyayini Chamaraj. *Yojana,* Vol. 50, January 2006; 21.
Expanding the Public Domain. Kalpana Kannabiran. *Seminar,* Vol. 551, July 2005; 37-40.
File Noting Must be Shown to Public. Aruna Roy & R. Suramurthy. *The Tribune,* 30 July, 2006; 8: 3-6.
From Freedom to Right. Ajit Bhattacharjee. *Seminar,* Vol. 551, July 2005; 15-17. Guarantee Employment and the Right to Information.
Amit Bhaduri. *Economic and Political Weekly,* Vol. 40, No. 4, 22 January, 2005; 267-69.
Hide and Seek. Ajit Bhattacharjea. *Hindustan Times,* 7 August, 2006; 8: 3-6.
In the Know (Editorial). *The Times of India*; 14 December, 2004; 8: 1-2.
Information and Broadcasting. Indra Jeet Mistry. *Hindustan Times,* 6 October, 2005; 10: 4-5.
Information Law: Dead on Arrival. Maja Daruwala. *Indian Express,* 1 October, 2005; 8: 3-6.
Information: More, or Less (Editorial), *The Tribune,* 3 December, 2005; 8: 3-6.
J & K RTI: An Overview. Kulwant Singh. *Yojana* Volume 50, January 2006; 49-52.
Loss of a Right. Avinder Kejriwal. *The Times of India,* 17 August, 2006; 14: 3-6.
Making the RTI Act Effective. Mandakini Devasher. *The Tribune,* 9 October, 2005; 8: 1-2.
Money for Nothing. Ajit Bhattacharjea. *Hindustan Times,* 7 October, 2004; 8: 3-6.
New Life for Democracy. Charulata Singh. *Yojana,* Vol. 50, January, 2006; 37-38.
Not Good Enough. Richard N. Winfield & Sherrel Evans. *Combat Law,* Vol. 2, No. 2, June-July, 2003; 79-83.
Now We Know (Editorial). *Hindustan Times,* 3 December, 2005; 8: 1-2.
OTI, Not RTI (Editorial). *Financial Express,* 16 December, 2004; 6: 1-2.
Out with the Files. J.S.Verma, *The Times of India* 9 August 2006; 14: 3-5.
Passage of Right to Information Bill in Parliament: Strengthening Democracy and the Struggle against Corruption. Bharat Dogra. *Mainstream,* Vol. 43, No 22, May 2005; 4.
People Must Know (Editorial), *The Tribune,* 17 December, 2004; 12: 3-4.
Plea to Security Outfits from Purview of RTI Act (View/Counter View). *The Times of India,* 12 December, 2005; 16: 3-6.
Poverty, Information and Accountability. Amitabh Mukhopadhyay. *Yojana,* Vol. 50; January 2006; 12-15.

Power Shift. Bharat Dogra, *The Times of India*, 15 December, 2004; 1-2.
Report. *Seminar* Vol. 551, July 2005; 68-70.
Right to Information (Editorial). *The Tribune*, 14 October, 2005; 12: 1-2.
Right to Information Act 2005. *New Frontiers in Education*, Vol. 22(2), October-December 2006; 373-391.
Right to Information and Panchayati Raj Institutions. Ramesh C. Nayak. *Kurukshetra*, Vol. 53, No.11, September 2005; 46-47.
Right to Information and the Road to Heaven. Oulac Niranjan. *Economic and Political Weekly*, Vol. 40 No. 47, 19 November 2005; 4870-72.
Right to Information—An Introduction. Manish Tiwari. *Indian Railways*, Vol. 51, No. 7, October 2005; 13-17.
RTI Act is our Last Chance to Cleanse the System (Editorial). *The Times of India*, 15 August, 2006; 16: 3-5.
RTI — Aspirations and Challenges. Arvind Kejriwal. *Yojana*, Vol. 50, January 2006; 22-25.
Secret Ballots and Transparent Campaigns. Aruna Roy and Sowmtya Kidambi. *Seminar*, Vol. 551, July 2005; 27-32.
Servants of the Public who make the Public into Servants. Maja Daruwala. *Indian Express*, 20 October, 2004; 9: 1-5.
Social Audit. Amitabh Mukhopadhyay. *Seminar*, Vol. 551, July 2005; 33-36.
Spirit of Inquiry (Editorial) *The Times of India*, 7 December, 2005; 12: 1-2.
Successes and Limitations of RTI. Bharat Dogra. *Janata*, Vol. 59, No.37, 24 October, 2004; 8-9.
The Bureaucracy is Threatened by RTI Act. My objective is to ensure no one takes it as a threat. Wajahat Habibullah. *Indian Express*, 15 October, 2006; 6: 1-5.
The Challenge to Media. Sukumar Muralidharan. *Seminar*, Vol. 552, July 2005; 50-54.
The Most Powerful Right. Kiran Bedi. *The Tribune*, 27 August, 2006; 13: 3-6.
The Notion of Transparency. Shèkhar Singh, *Seminar*, Vol. 551, July 2005; 46-49.
The Power of Knowledge (Editorial). *Economic Times*, 17 December, 2004; 4: 1-2.
The Problem. *Seminar* Vol. 551, July 2005; 12-14.
The Right to Information Act 2005. *Seminar*, Vol. 551, July 2005; 65-67.
The Right not to Disclose. K.C. Mittal. *Hindustan Times*, 15 September, 2006; 8: 4-5.
The 'Missing' Link. Vrinda Grover. *Seminar*, Vol. 551, July 2005; 59-61.
Toward a Vibrant Democracy. Madhu R. Sekhar. *Yojana*, Vol. 50, January 2005; 55-58.
We want People to use RTI Act, says Habibullah, Wajahat Habibullah. *The Tribune*, 16 October, 2005; 12: 5-6.
Whistleblowers need to be Protected, Raghu Dayal, *Economic Times*, 26 December, 2006; 10: 3-6.
Wired for Change. Rahjesh Kaira. *The Times of India*, 29 January, 2004; 12: 3-4.
Wrong Information, Right Choice. Dunu Roy. *Seminar*, Vol. 551, July 2005; 55-58.

8

Right to Information and Human Right Jurisprudence

The great Upnishadic verses describe man as 'child of mortality' and his mission in life is to realize the ultimate truth. Ignorance is darkness and must be dispelled. Information is light and must be processed through consciousness. Knowledge and wisdom spring from the base of facts sensitively structured and finished. Mere jumble of information may be bewildering or misleading mess. Knowledge is power but information is fuel of knowledge. Obviously a citizen cannot achieve knowledge unless he has certain basic freedoms such as freedom of thought, freedom of information, freedom of conscience, freedom of speech and expression, freedom of locomotion and so on and so forth. These freedoms represent the basic values of life in a civilized society and have been given a place of pride in our Constitution, i.e., Fundamental Right, which are inviolable taught subject to some reasonable restrictions. These restrictions are meant to protect the national interest and to safeguard the fundamental rights of the other persons. Freedom of information has been gradually receiving acceptance and recognition the globe over.

Implication of the Term Right to Information in a Democratic Set-Up

Transparency in administration is a sure technique to minimize the abuse and misuse of administrative discretion. As knowledge is a guarantee against ignorance so is government openness a guarantee against misconduct. Openness negatives the ideas of fantastic, arbitrary and oppressive form of government action. Justice V.R. Krishna Iyer rightly said:

> "A government which reveals in secrecy in the field of people's liberty not only acts against democratic decency but buries itself with its own burial. That is writing on the wall if history was our teacher, memory our mentor and decline of liberty not our unwitting endeavour."

Truth does not dawn but is born of discussion of public affairs, which is preceded by expression of views of individuals. The raw material for formation of opinion is information. Thus the free availability of facts is essential for sound judgement of citizens and sensible participation in government. Infallibility of authority and immunity from criticism pave the way to dictatorial form of this unwanted end is promoted by closing the doors of information on public matters although the only way to responsible and responsive government is to clothe every person with a legal right to seek information whenever he desires, however, uncomfortable the disclosure of facts may be to the administrators.

To say in the spirit of a democratic world order, it is necessary that each one of us everywhere on this earth under the Sun has a right to know and a duty to shape the course of things, on a national also as on international level. The philosophy of freedom of information and open government has been well described by the U.S. House Committee on Government Operations, which approved the Freedom of Information Act, in 1966:

> "A democratic society requires an informed, intelligent electorate, and as the quantity and quality of its information varies. A danger signal to our democratic society in the United States is the fact that such a truism needs repeating . . . "

The root truth is that freedom without information is meaningless and liberty without light will perish because "all governments are obscure and invisible".

There is a burden on the government to justify secrecy. Failure on this front is bound to spell dangerous consequences. In a democracy citizens' right to know is assumed rather than guaranteed. This right is derived from the accountability and answerability of the government to the people.

'Right to know' has been given status of fundamental right by the highest Court of the land in *Judges Transfer Case (1981)*. The Apex Court held that the right to know is implicit in the right of free speech and expression guaranteed under our Constitution in Article 19(1)(a).

Right to know is also implicit in Article 19(1)(a) is natural concomitant to free press which right is deducible from fundamental right of freedom of speech and expression. In *S.P. Gupta's case,* the Apex Court also recommended change in century-old provisions of Section 123 of the Indian Evidence Act 1872 so as to be conducive to the republican form of government and the open society, which, we the people of India, have established. Section 123 relates to immunity from production of documents and was enacted to suit the needs of the empire builders.

The Supreme Court has reaffirmed this legal position in its subsequent decisions in **Reliance Petro Ltd. case** and **Secretary, Ministry of Information and Broadcasting** v. **Cricket Association., Bengal**. In **Reliance Petro's case,** the Supreme Court has observed that the right to know has reached new dimensions and urgency and is basic right which citizens of a free country aspire in the broaden horizons of the right to live in this age on our land under Article 21 of the Constitution. The people at large have a right to know in order to be able to take part in a participatory development in the industrial life. In *Secretary MIB's case* the Apex Court has given a very broad definition to the right to receive and disseminate information through any media including air waves and electronic media. Right to information is inherent in right to live as enshrined in Article 21 and freedom of speech and expression as guaranteed under Article 19(1)(a) of our Constitution. Right to information thus emanates from the fundamental right to life and fundamental freedom of speech and expression.

These freedoms guaranteed by the Constitution have to be enjoyed subject to some reasonable restrictions. But these restrictions can never outweigh and dominate the freedoms. After all what is fundamental is the freedom and not the restriction.

Under the mantle of Welfare State, the Government today is engaged in variety of activities which cannot be termed as sovereign functions of the Government. These activities do not constitute 'Affairs of the State' in strict sense. The Government, especially of a welfare state, is responsible for socio-economic development and uplift of the people, besides main routine law and order. One of the Directive Principles of the State Policy the State shall strive to promote the welfare of the people by securing and protecting as effectively as it may, a social order in which justice, social economic and political, shall inform all institutions of the national life. The State shall in particular strive to minimize the inequalities in income and endeavour to eliminate inequalities in facilities and opportunities not only amongst individuals but also amongst groups of people residing in different areas or engaged in different vocations. "In an independent, democratic and welfare state, the citizens occupy quite an important position". They are the ones who are not only being governed but also govern by way of exercising their right of franchise and electing their representatives, who in turn formulate policies in accordance with which the administrators are supposed to govern for the benefit of the society. The benefits are to be accorded to or conferred on the citizens by the administration in a manner whereby most optimum position is attained and no one is favoured or deprived of at the cost of or for favouring the other one. In such a system, it is expected of the administration to provide to all the members of the society a reasonable dignified standard of life in which there is no risks of insecurity or stagnation on the economic front. No individual should have any fear of suspicion and mistrust towards the system in his mind. This is possible only by disseminating proper information, of course, without leaking out the vital secrets. More than fifty per cent of the citizen's problems could be sorted out promptly through a proper communication between different channels in the administration.

The Government, today, is called upon to make policies on an ever increasing range of subjects, and many of these policies must necessarily impinge on the lives of the citizens. It may sometimes happen that the data made available to the policy makers is of a selective nature and even the policy-makers and their advisors may deliberately suppress certain viewpoints and favour others. Such bureaucratic habits get encouragement in an environment of secrecy; and openness in governmental work is possibly the only effective corrective to it, also raising, in the process, the quality of decision-making. Besides, openness has an educational role in as much as citizens are enabled to acquire a fuller view of the pros and cons of matters of major importance, which naturally helps in building informed public opinion, no less than goodwill for the Government.

Justice Krishna Iyer while commenting on the public functionaries remarked, "Be you ever so high, the law is above you". The public power must not hide its heart in a welfare state and open system. The normal rule in the Government of India is secrecy and openness the exception. There is the Official Secrets Act 1923 which makes unauthorized communication of information including documents, an offence punishable with imprisonment which may extend up to three years. This Act covers all documents and information and makes no distinction of kind or of degree. A blanket is thrown over everything. Nothing escapes. By secrecy system the government safeguards its reputation, buries its mistakes, manipulates its citizens, maximizes its powers and corrupts itself. In the backdrop of judgement of the Supreme Court in the *Judges' Transfer case,* the provisions of the Official Secrets Act 1923 and of Section 123 of the Evidence Act 1872 suffer from the stigma of unconstitutionality. These colonial provisions need to be "pensioned off'. In Sweden the Constitution itself contains a provision guaranteeing access to information. Even the Russian people have been voicing their concern for Glasnost and Perestroika. England, thrust of legislation is on secrecy notwithstanding enactment of Access to Personal Files Act, the Official Secrets Act 1989 enforcement in 1994 of Code of Practice on Access to Government Information. Australia and Canada have their own Freedom of Information Acts enacted in 1982 and 1986 respectively. Freedom of Information Ordinance was promulgated in Australia in 1989. The USA has enacted Freedom of Information Act 1966 and Electronic Freedom of Information Act. Denmark, the Netherlands, Germany, Norway and France have also their legislation, which provides for access to information.

Non-Aligned Movement meeting in Zimbabwe reviewed the progress of new information order and pressed for an enduring foundation for Freedom of information without Western pressure and distortions.

Referring to the right to obtain information and to publish it in U.S.A. and England, Mr. Howard Simpson, Managing Editor of the Washington Post, observed: In U.S.A. the publishers have a right to print anything. If we get hold of a State Secret, it is the editor who has the determining authority whether to hold it or print it. The government has the right to keep secrets, but if we come by it, nobody can stop us. Whereas in Britain, the press believes in national security, which means they can be told to hold a story back. They have Official Secrets Act, etc."

The judiciary in U.S.A. shares the same concern of the Congress, which is reflected in the Freedom of Information Act 1966.

Secrecy in government is fundamentally anti-democratic, perpetuating bureaucratic errors. Open discussion based on full information and debate on public issues are vital to our health.

Woodrow Wilson has rightly said, "A democratic Government ought be all outside and not inside". Unbridled freedom is not possible in our world of perils and evils designs. Truth may have to be withheld in moments when a nation's survival is in imminent danger. In Churchill's words: "In time of war, the truth is so recoups that it must be escorted by a bodyguard of lies". No state should adopt the mendacious methodology of Goebbels and mislead its subjects, whatever the crisis. However, quite often the right to information is denied and a seemingly authentic diet of official lies is served with a view to condition the minds of men and they are expected to consume government's version. Free speech is sabotaged from within by fouling the fountains of information. The bureaucracy itself is banned from telling the truth by forced statutory secrecy. Administrative secrecy relating to classified documents concerning national security and foreign policy is justified. But routine claim to secrecy or privilege by the government and public bodies may jeopardize the very survival of democracy in India because this immunity is anti-democratic. Therefore, no government should think that people must be told only that much which it thinks to be good for the people and safe for itself.

Dangers of burying the truth have been very powerfully put by *Emile Zola*: "When truth is buried underground it grows, it chokes,—it gathers such an explosive force that on the day it bursts out, it blows up everything with it".

Equally forceful are the views of Kurt Eisner, who says that the truthful information must not be withheld because: "Truth is the greatest of all national possessions. A state, a people, a system which suppresses the truth or fears to publish it, deserves to collapse".

Right to Information and Human Rights Jurisprudence

The right to information is embedded in Article 19(1)(a) of the Constitution of India and even the Universal Declaration of Human Rights recognised this right as a *sine qua non* for democracy. When journalists purvey news and information, it sometimes results in violation of another fundamental human right — the right to privacy contained in Article 21. In a large number of cases, exercise of the right to information by the majority (represented by journalists, who are supposedly the eyes and ears of the populace) infringes the right to privacy of the minority. It will become obvious from the above discussion that the Right to Information which is included in Article

19(1)(a) comes into conflict with the Right to Privacy which the Supreme Court has interpreted as coming under the umbrella of Articles 21 and 25. Hence both these rights are mutually antagonistic. Exercise of the Right to Information or the Right to Know results in invasion of privacy of citizens. We shall briefly recapitulate the international provisions made on the Right to Information and the Right to Privacy. The United Nation's declaration in 1948 declared that: "Freedom of opinion and expression, including the freedom to seek and receive and impart information and ideas through any media, regardless of frontiers" is one of the most basic human rights. It was in 1948 again that Article 12 of the Universal Declaration of Human Rights enunciated: "No one shall be subjected to arbitrary interference with his privacy, family, home or correspondence nor to attacks upon his honour and reputation. Everyone has the right to the protection of the law against such interference or attacks.

The U.N. declaration stresses on the freedom of opinion and expression. In the words reproduced above, there are no limitations placed on the right to information. Similarly, the right to privacy does not make any exception or limitation. However, the protection extended by Article 12 has to be circumscribed. It is humbly submitted that no right can be absolute. If that were so, it would degenerate into licence. The U.S. Supreme Court has laid down in *Roth* v. *United States* that the First Amendment protection which in its phraseology appears absolute, does not protect obscenity. Hence, no right is ever absolute. Similarly, Article 19(1)(a) which guarantees freedom of speech and expression also guarantees the right to information only in limited areas.

In a conflict between the right to information or the right to know *versus* the right to privacy of individuals, which right will prevail over which is to be analysed in this thesis. At the outset, it can be postulated that when an individual is a public figure, a certain amount of invasion of privacy should be tolerated. This would subject to the public figure to mental torture and expose his family and friends to unsought for publicity. To what extent the Bentamite dictum that the good of the majority should override the interests of the few will be examined. At the centre of the problem lies the issue of a public figure. The U.S. Supreme Court has defined a public figure in very wide terms. This researcher has attempted to redefine as to who constitutes a public figure. The basic concept of privacy did not evolve in the twentieth century. It goes back to 1890 when all American legal scholar, Thomas Cooley, first defined privacy as a basic right. Towards the end of the nineteenth century, two Harvard researchers, Samuel Warren and Louis Brandeis, published an article in the *Harvard Law Review.* This article first brought the concept of privacy to the notice of legal scholars, lawyers and judges. In the article, the authors argued that the right to privacy was necessary to facilitate the development of the individual. It is the individual's right to be let alone, free from unwanted publicity, where his "home was his castle". The concept of the *purdah* system in India too can be viewed as a variation of the right to privacy. Here, women were segregated and strangers were not allowed to enter a part of the homestead which was used exclusively by women. Even while leaving their homes, these women kept their faces covered by veils. These practices and customs have devolved from ancient usage and custom in India.

In **Curtis Publishing Co.** v. **Butts,** the U.S. Supreme Court held that "public figures" are persons who "often play an influential role in ordering society. As a class, these public figures have as ready access as public officials to mass media of communication, both to influence policy and to counter criticism of their views and activities". Justice Black, Douglas, Brennan and White jointed Chief Justice Warren's separate Opinion. In Curtis Publishing Co. to the extent that they held that "public figures" suing for libel must prove there was "actual malice" on the part of a journalist or media-defendants. Hence, it was not sufficient to prove that what was published was inaccurate. The court further defined who constituted a public figure: in two other cases, viz. **Wolston** v. **Readers Digest Association** and **Hutchinson** v. **Proxmire.** The definition of public figure as those who often play an influential role in ordering society is acceptable but not accurate in all circumstances. Furthermore, it is submitted that the opinion of the judges that public figures have as ready access as public officials to mass media of communication, both to influence policy and counter-criticism of their views is not accurate in all cases. To buttress this argument, one can consider the case of notorious, criminal, Charles Sobhraj. Two books have already been written on his life history. Although he has figured several times in the news columns of the national press the major national newspaper may not unstingingly permit this criminal to use their space to propagate his philosophy of life. Hence, Charles Sobhraj is an individual who interests the reading public. He "makes" news in journalistic parlance but it is submitted that he does not and should not be allowed access to the mass media to influence policy and counter criticism.

Now, the U.S. Supreme Court does not consider those convicted of crimes to constitute public figures. This dictum has been reaffirmed in several decisions. This, it is humbly submitted, is erroneous. A criminal of the stature of Charles Sobhraj evokes interest among the reading public and could indirectly influence the lives of those impressionable enough. A public figure is any individual (including a class of persons), who has the potential to influence the lives, either directly or indirectly of at least a hundred other people. By this redefinition, judges, cricketers, film-stars, cabinet ministers, university vice chancellors and others in such categories fall, within the definition of "public figures". All these classes of persons have the potential to influence the lives of at least one hundred other people, directly or indirectly.

The Supreme Court has laid down in first *Judges Transfer Case* that :

> "India and many State governments are contemplating and a few have already incorporated the Right to Information in various forms. This right will not be a privilege for any particular section of the society ideally, this is a significant step and as likely to strengthen the democratic institutions and make the functioning of the

government more transparent and accountable. The genesis of this movement can be traced to the constant tussle between the government and media where the media sought information that the government was not inclined to part with the philosophy of a "free press" and the perception that the press media is the fourth state is built on this argument. The line between official secrets and public interest has not yet been drawn at least in India."

While the government has utilised its prerogative and restricted access under the garb of official secrets, the media has occasionally challenged this and managed to get information. We may also remember that freedom of the press in India has been raised and fought on Parameters other than the intent of the media to provide Information (Newsprint and import concessions, price page schedule, etc.) to the public. The track record of the profession and the industry in an extreme situation (the internal emergency of 1975) has not been exemplary. In fact it has been documented that it was a case of the media crawling when it was asked only to bend.

The relevant point is, has the media with its privileged position and power utilised its capacity to seek information and place at before the public? Except in a few cases, the media's role in highlighting corruption and other equally important misdeeds occurred in the pursuit of Information. They have been based on selective leaks by various groups to suit their political, economic and social agenda. Such leaks have been treated and packaged in a manner that satiates the burgeoning middle class clientele.

However, it is the irony of our items that explosion of information and exclusion from information are two competing trends in our cosmos of human rights and democracy *versus* government by secrecy. The citizen's right to know the facts, the true facts about the administration of the country is one of the pillars of a democratic state. The democracy does not consist merely in people exercising their franchise once in five years to choose their rules and thereafter retire to passivity altogether indifferent to the "ruler" and the "ruled". The democracy today has a more positive content and its orchestration has to be continuous and pervasive. The people should not only cost their vote but should also exercise sound judgement on the conduct of the government and the merits of its public policies. Intelligent and rational people can fulfil this important role in a democracy only if it is an open government where there is full access to information in regard to the functions and functioning of the government.

Freedom of information is so fundamental and communication of knowledge is so critical that the democratic set up cannot be turned as democratic unless it has access to information entrenched in its structure of government. Indeed right to information is the key to democracy and development and lays the foundation upon which to build good governance transparency, accountability and participation so as to eliminate that scourge upon the poor, called corruption infects in a democratic set-up it is individuals in alienable right to participate by means of free and democratic political process in framing the society in which she or he lives.

Given this upstanding of right to information if we look at Indian scenario which has a long history of official secrecy laws due to colonial structure of governance, now can boast of a Right to Information Act which has come into existence recently, i.e., 2005. That in spite of the fact that we had right to free speak and expression enshrined in our Constitution and now we have Right to Information Act as well, the tradition of secrecy continues to be a part of structure of governance. This is enthused to be democratic form of governance.

Even the current legislation on Right to Information which has seen the light of the day after a long struggle and coactive pursuance by the civil society in India does not fit the bill of substantial democracy due to the existence of gateway provisions, lack of retrospectives, a large net of exemptions, lack a whistle blow protection, exclusion of private sector from the ambit of right to information and circuitous procedure of retrieval of information and so on.

The present research study is an attempt made to examine and answer the following questions:

- To examine the constitutional position of Right to Information related with freedom of speech and expression, freedom of press and right to life.
- To examine the response of the judiciary with regard to Right to Information.
- To analyze and evaluate the Right to Information Act 2005 and to find out whether the Act in the present form will be able to provide access to information to the citizens.
- Critically the shortcomings in the Act and examine the impediments in free flow of information.

The various issues of this multifaceted problems have been examined thoroughly in the light of statutory provisions and judicial decisions.

In a democratic country right to information can be regarded as paramount and cardinal principle of constitutional jurisprudence. Several democratic countries have enacted various rational and functional legislations towards the essential requirements to accelerate the momentum of right to information in purpose-oriented direction in Indian perspective.

END NOTES

Judges Transfer Case, *PUCL Bulletin*, December 1981.
Pandey, J.N., *Constitutional Law of India*, 42nd (ed.) (2005), Central Law Agency, Allahabad.
Singh, M.P. *Constitution of India*, 10th ed. (2001), Eastern Book Co., Lucknow.
Tiwari, Mahendra. *Freedom of Press in India : Constitutional Perspectives*, (2006). www.supremecourtcases.com

9

Significance of Right to Information and Concept of Open Government

Commenting on the benefits of Right to Information the National Commission to Review the Working of the Constitution observed:

> "Right to information can usher in many benefits, such as speedy disposal of cases, minimizing manipulative and dilatory tactics of the *babudom*, and, last but most importantly, putting a considerable check on graft and corruption."

In a democratic set-up the people have a right to know every public act and conduct discharged by their public functionaries. The right to know is necessary outcome of the concept of freedom of speech and expression. At the same time open government does not mean that the whole government transactions are to be carried out in the market place. To cover with veil of secrecy the matters relating to national safety and security is put in the general public interest. In this sense, the right to know has to be counter balanced in just and reasonable constitutional norms. Information and communication are powerful tools and have 'a potential to shape and shake social and political development of the society', 'men make their history but not as they please', said Karl Marx it depends on the quality and quantity of information supplied to them. Accordingly, in this chapter an attempt has been made to examine the parameters of freedom of information and its pitfalls in constitutional dynamics.

Significance of the Right to Information

Savoir est pouvoir (knowledge is power) is a French saying. Today information is power. *Asato mam sat gamaya* and *tamaso mam jyotir gamaya* were not merely empty words of prayer but were demands for an open mind and open world. "I regard legislation on the right to information vital weapon of the citizen against abuse of power", said V.R. Krishna Iyer. There is a wide information gap in our legal system in the matrix of various rights and freedoms enshrined in our Constitution. Article 19 confers upon every citizen a fundamental right called freedom of speech and expression. In order to meaningfully enjoy this freedom, a citizen must also have an ancillary right to secure all necessary information on matters of public interest from public authorities. Such a right is a *sine qua non* of an open, democratic, responsive and responsible polity. Such polity can throb and survive if its citizens are sufficiently informed and kept informed. The right to information will enable the citizens to criticise, comment and approve policies and programmes of the rulers. Thus in the words of V.R. Krishna Iyer: "Informational justice has a constitutional basis." Bhagwati J. in **S.P. Gupta** v. **Union of India** described democracy as a continuous process of government, an attitude and habit of mind, in which people have to play important role only "if it is open government where there is full access to information in regard to the functioning of the government". There is hardly any need to emphasise the fact that secrecy in the working of the government would tend to promote and encourage oppression, corruption and abuse of authority. Public scrutiny and public exposure of governmental processes help achieve a clean and healthy government. Such a government has to justify its trusts of policies by giving facts for and against a selected course of action. The Court pronounced: "The concept of an open government is the direct emanation from the right to know which seems to be implicit in the right of free speech and expression administration was simply an extension of the Crown's administration of its properties, when the distinction between private and public administrations was by no means clear cut". Yet we find a small and limited area of this right in the Crown Proceedings Act 1974 under which legal action against the Crown and Government departments can be initiated. Section 28(l)(i) of this Act provides that "in any civil proceedings . . . . to which Crown is a party, the Crown may be required by the court to make discovery of documents and produced those documents for inspection". It is also provided that "the Crown may be required by the court to answer interrogatories . . . ." However, the common law did not favour this right of disclosure. **Smith** v. **East India Co.** and **Beatson** v. **Skene** are noteworthy illustrations of early setbacks. In the former the court disallowed the request of disclosure of certain documents in court as it amounted to restrain the freedom of communication between the East India Company and its Board of Control. In the other case the court refused the compulsion of production of certain documents regarding a court of inquiry conducted by the Secretary of State. Lord Chancellor Kilmuier in a later case stated two grounds when such a Crown privilege for documents can be claimed: (a) the disclosure of the contents of the particular document would injure the public interest, e.g., by endangering public security, or prejudicing diplomatic relations; and (b) the document is of such a class which the public interest requires to be withheld from production. This rigid position, however, was a little liberalised in a later case in which it was held that inspection by the court of documents could not cause harm. The only requirement, in the words of Lord Wilberforce, was that "there must be a likelihood that the documents would support the case or the party seeking discovery".

Prompt and Cheap Disclosure Approach in Australia

In Australia before the enactment of Freedom of Information Act 1982, the courts did not favour production of documents possessed by state authorities. It was held that "counsels of the Crown are secret and an inquiry into the grounds upon which the advice was tendered was not allowed", however, later on courts refused to accept the conclusiveness of the executive certificate of privilege. Thereafter, the aforesaid Act was made. Its salient features were: (i) the general right to access for the public to official documents in the possession of ministers and agencies except the one that were specifically exempted; (ii) the right to correct inaccuracies; (iii) the internal law of the Commonwealth agencies to be published every year; and (iv) a proper procedure for the disposal of requests for access to documents. Thus this Act enabled prompt and cheap disclosure of information.

Transparent and Crucial Approach in U.S.A.

The founders of the American democracy did recognize fully of crucial importance of information. Perhaps the strongest statement in support of access to information was made by James Madison: "Knowledge will forever govern ignorance. And a people who mean to be their own governors, must arm themselves with the power knowledge gives. A popular government without popular information of the means of acquiring it, is but a prologue to a farce, or a tragedy, or perhaps both". Thomas Jefferson was emphatic to give the people "full information of their affairs through the channels of the public papers, and to contrive that these papers penetrate the whole mass of the people. The basis of our government being the opinion of the people the very first object should be to keep that right; and were it left to me to decide whether we should have a government without newspapers or newspapers without a government, I should not hesitate a moment to prefer the latter". Patrick Henry, who was often in disagreement with other leaders on other matters, shared their views on the necessity for an informed public opinion; said he:

> "The liberties of the people never were, or never will be, secure, when the transactions of their rulers may be concealed from them . . . . I am not an advocate for divulging indiscriminately all the operations of government, though the practices of our ancestors, in

some degree, justifies it. Such transactions as relate to military operations of affairs of great consequence, the immediate promulgation of which might defeat the interests of the community, I would not wish to be published, till the end which required their secrecy should have been affected. But to cover with the veil of secrecy the common routine of business, is an abomination in the eyes of every intelligent man."

In the United States of America, i.e., Original Freedom of Information Act (FOIA) was enacted in 1966 as an amendment to the Administrative Procedures Act. Its purpose was: "To establish a general Philosophy of full agency disclosure unless intonation is exempted under clearly delineated statutory language. The Act exempted classified material, business proprietary material, information whose release would invade personal privacy and other material whose disclosure would compromise the public interest. This Act had little effect even after several years or its enactment. So in 1974, the Act was amended and time limits were provided to respond to requests. Internal appellate machinery was provided. It also empowered courts to intervene to enforce deadlines and review agency decisions. Arbitrary and capricious wit in holding of information by officials was made punishable. Only information relating to foreign policy, defence, national security, trade secrets, personal and medical files are not allowed under the Act. At that time it was estimated that its costs will not exceed $50,000 in 1974 and $100,000 for each of the succeeding five fiscal years. But thereafter the costs have exceeded these estimates. The FOIA costs of the FBI alone have exceeded $55 million between 1974 and 1983.

By 1987, federal agencies received more than 3,75,000 FOIA requests annually and spent about $60 million a year to answer them. FOIA fees covered only about five per cent of the costs. The Department of Defence, for example, received 87,179 requests and it spent $30 million in responding to them but recovered less than $1 million as fees. Sometimes a "segregability review" of hundreds of documents had to be undertaken to determine what material should be released and what not. This sometimes required the services of highly qualified technical and security experts. It must, however, be highlighted that if there were uses of FOIA there were its abuses too to render it "much a burden as a benefit." The New York Bar Association in 1979 warned that it was not Congress' intent that the FOIA be used as a carte blanche for unrestricted access to otherwise non-public information submitted by private citizens and businesses. And yet businessmen sought information on their competitors. The one such mistaken disclosure case a corporation lost its domination of $ 450 million per year market. Besides businessmen this law has been widely exploited by lawyers for clients who used government data to fight federal investigations, spying on the competitors and discovering how strictly regulations were really enforced.

All these led to its further amendment in 1986. The Criminals also have not lagged behind in abusing FOIA. Prisoners used it to know who incriminated them. Others used it to avoid prosecution. The organised criminals in Detroit had been instructed to submit FOIA requests to identify FBI sources. They were supplied over 12,000 pages of FBI documents. From 1975 to 1981, FBI was forced to release over 60,000 pages of documents concerning an underground crime gang. Powerful persons have sought information about investigation of allegations of political corruption against them and have thereafter subtly changed their mode of operation.

The law has been used to get technical information about intelligence. The CIA was approached for information about its agents and informants. Ultimately, the Congress made "operational files" of the CIA automatically inaccessible to FOIA requests. Also "technical data having a space or military application" were protected.

The use of FOIA by news media and public interest groups has been uneven and scattered. Some have used it extensively while others have rarely done so. But the FOIA has been extensively used by litigants against federal government. It is used to supplement the legal discovery process. It is resorted to for three reasons: it is inexpensive, it has rigid time frames enforceable by law, and makes available that material which is otherwise not available.

Another adverse effect of the FOIA must not be lost sight of Government officials have now started to avoid to fully document the process by which they arrived at a given policy decision. Though "predecisional" material is exempted from the FOIA the factual information leading to a decision has to be released. Consequently, senior executives have avoided memorialising useful background information. Officials are warned to be cautious about what they write. They are ordered to destroy all draft copies after the final document is issued.

But in spite of its above pitfalls the FOIA has to stay. It provides a useful window to peep into otherwise dark governmental processes. Richard A. Guida has suggested the following amendments to the FOIA to build that window better. He warned that unless these reforms were enacted the costs of free information will counterbalance its benefits :

1. Requests for information should be limited to U.S. citizens, and to those who are not in prison or acting on behalf of prisoners.
2. All materials from criminal investigations should be exempted FOIA requests.
3. The FOIA should be changed to prohibit its use in the legal discovery process.
4. Time limits for responding to requests, particularly those seeking many documents or old material, should be substantially increased. The responding agency should be able to establish a schedule for responses which takes into account volume, age, complexity of material, necessary review time, and so on. A request for fifty documents comprising three thousand pages of classified material might face a standard response time of several months, while the current two-week deadline could continue to apply to simple requests.
5. The full cost of administering the FOIA should be borne by the users. Though the news media are now specifically exempted from FOIA fees, this exemption

should be abolished. The fees should cover search time, segregability review time, the effort required to decide whether to release material, and the cost of copying documents and mailing them to the requester.

6. The FOIA should be extended to cover congressional committees and agencies.

Parallel to the Freedom of Information Act at the federal level there is a more recent "open meetings" statute, called the Government in Sunshine Act 1976. There has been relatively little litigation under this statute. In general, the Act requires about fifty federal agencies, including major regulatory such as the Federal Communications Commission, the National Labour Relations Board, and the Securities and Exchange Commission, to hold their meetings in public. However, the Act allows closed sessions if the subject matter falls within FOIA, though there are some important differences. The Act also prescribes in detail the procedures that one must follow to hold a closed meeting. In addition to this federal Act, all fifty states and the District of Columbia have also enacted open meetings statutes. Though these statutes vary tremendously in scope, they have much in common with each other and the federal Sunshine Act.

Parameters of Freedom of Information in India

The need for giving a statutory shape to a judicially recognised and pronounced right to know needs not to be justified. The central government has acknowledged that, "free flow of information is a prerequisite for democracy" and assured the electorate that "the right to information will be enshrined in our Constitution" ! But one need, not wait for a constitutional amendment, which would require suitable political balancing to ensure adequate support in the Parliament for its passage. Even if such an amendment is contemplated it can be safely passed, it is submitted that it is not necessary. After all its incorporation in the Part III of the Constitution will be in general, broad and wide terms with attendant reasonable restrictions. Instead, it is submitted that an appropriate statute, say, Freedom of Information, may be enacted which could be passed with simple majority, unlike a constitutional amendment requiring special majority. Such a statute must provide the parameters of this freedom and make adequate provisions to avoid the pitfalls of the U.S. FOIA.

The policy underlying the U.S. FOIA has been articulated as: (i) disclosure to be the general rule, and not the exception; (ii) all individuals have equal rights of access; (iii) the burden is on the government to justify the withholding of a document and not on the person who requests it; (iv) individuals improperly denied access to documents have a right to seek injunctive relief in the courts; and (v) there should be a change in government policy and attitude.

Soli Sorabjee articulated the objectives of any legislation giving statutory shape to freedom of information as follows: (i) protection of the rights of individuals by giving citizens right to access to information about themselves held in government or other official files; (ii) the right to correct that information if it is misleading or untrue; (iii) it should ensure wider dissemination of information gathered at the public expenses on topics such as product safety, land records; health and environmental hazards, ecological data, etc.; (iv) it should throw the spot light of public scrutiny on policy formulation and administration and thereby improve the quality of decision making; and (v) access to information should be within easy reach and at affordable cost.

Within the above objectives framework a comprehensive statute delineating the parameters and defining the various components of the freedom of information should be enacted. At the same time such a contemplated statute must have adequate provisions to avoid the pitfalls and drawbacks experienced in the working of the U.S. FOIA. This will necessitate conceptual clarity on the part of the law makers. In addition to these there are complex issues of social engineering in regard to balancing and counterbalancing freedom of information *vis-à-vis* various interests, concepts and issues. Such as: freedom of speech and expression of mass media and individuals, defamation, contempt of courts, privacy, human rights, copyright, patents, trademarks, news gathering and confidentiality of source of news, national security, public law and order, internal secrecy rules of autonomous institutions and corporations, protection against catch all provision, trade secrets, official secrets, law enforcement, coverage of court proceedings, social interest litigation, activists movements; morality and public safety; communal, election, religious and violent crime and correctional matters advertising commissions of inquiry, atomic and nuclear energy defence industry and strategies, etc. Each of these areas will need re-examination and re-evaluation in the context of freedom of information.

In addition to these some very important issues will need policy decisions. For example, who should have and not have this freedom; when to have it and when not; against whom and under what circumstances; and to what extent at what costs and within how much time, machinery regarding appeals and other reliefs; whether we should have our own version of "Sunshine Act" what could be the reasonable restrictions and exemptions of this freedom, and so on. Soli Sorabjee suggested exemptions permitting government to withhold access to information in respect of the following matters:

(i) International relations and national security;
(ii) Law enforcement and prevention of crime;
(iii) Information deliberations of the government;
(iv) Information obtained in confidence from some source outside the government;
(v) Information which, if disclosed, would violate privacy of an individual;
(vi) Information, particularly of an economic nature, which if disclosed, would confer an unfair advantage on some person or subject to some person or government to an unfair disadvantage;
(vii) Information about scientific discoveries and inventions and improvements, essentially in the field of weaponry.

The Concept of Open Government

Article 74 (2) of the Constitution says that the question whether any, and if so what, advice was tendered by Ministers to the

President shall not be required into in any Court. Accordingly, the Supreme Court has held in **Davpack Systems Pvt. Ltd.** v. **India** that it is the duty of the Court to prevent disclosure where Article 74(2) is applicable. The cabinet papers are protected from disclosure not by reason of their content but because of the class to which they belong. The expression "Cabinet papers—would also include papers brought into existence for the purpose of preparing submission to the Cabinet. The notings of the officials which lead to the Cabinet note leading to the Cabinet decision also form part of the advice tendered to the President. The Court got support for this view from certain observations in **S.P. Gupta** v. **India.**

In **Bihar** v. **Kripalu Shankar,** the Supreme Court has laid down an important proposition designed to facilitate the internal working of the government. The Court has stated that nothings made by government officials in the departmental files cannot be made a ground for a proceeding for contempt of court. The Court has advanced several sound reasons for taking such a view. A government functions by taking decisions on the strength of views and suggestions expressed by various officers at different levels, ultimately resulting in a final decision by the Minister concerned. There should be no fetter on fearless and independent expression of views by officers on files coming before them, even including court orders. The expression of opinion by the officers in the internal files are for the use of the department and not for outside exposure or publicity. These internal notings are in fact privileged documents. To find officers guilty of expressing their independent opinion, even against court orders in deserving cases, would cause impediments in the smooth functioning of government. To find an action on the notes in the flies would impair the independent functioning of the civil service essential to democracy as it would hamper a fearless expression of views, by government officers. While a court can direct production of even confidential papers for it to see, there is an implied understanding that these will not be used for any other purpose.

The Court has emphasized in this connection. In democratic countries, at the present moment, the accent is on open government. Of course, there are quite a few things, which must be kept confidential in the interest of public security or national interest. Sometimes the law may impose secrecy in the interest of the individual. But then the secrecy ought not to be more than what is absolutely necessary for this area, what is necessary is to draw a balance between 'secrecy' and 'openness' with an accent on the latter. There are many reasons suggesting an open government. Participation in government by the people is regarded as an important aspect of democracy and people cannot participate unless they have information as to what is going on in the country. A modern democratic state being answerable to the people, the people are entitled to know what policies and programmes, how, and why, are being followed by the government. People have to pass verdict every five years on the performance of the government, and decide whether it should stay in office or not. People cannot exercise their choice intelligently unless they are given adequate information about the functioning of the governance. Factor justifying openness by the government is that being an activist entity, government gathers a vast arsenal of powers in a welfare state as has been described in the previous pages. These powers are used to affect economic interests and personal liberty of the individual. It is important that these powers are exercised for public good, not improperly, and for the purposes for which the powers are conferred. This objective is best ensured by giving access to the individual to governmental information and not shroud in secrecy as to how the government exercises its powers in individual cases. Since power tends to corrupt, and absolute power tends to corrupt absolutely, there is an inherent danger that the vast powers available to the executive may be used not for public good but for private gain, or for corrupt motive. It is, therefore, essential that the people have as much information about government operations as possible.

Openness in government is bound to act as a powerful check on the abuse or misuse of power by the government. It has already been emphasized earlier that there should be public consultation in the exercise of legislative powers by the government. This idea has to be made applicable to the whole gamut of governmental functioning. As Schwartz emphasizes: "Americans firmly believe in the healthy effects of publicity and have a strong antipathy to the inherent secretiveness of government agencies". In India, so far, the progress towards open government has been rather tardy. But the consciousness is there. As Bhagwati J. advised in **S.P. Gupta** v. **President of India:**

> "Open government is the new democratic culture of an open society towards which every liberal democracy is moving and our country should be no exception."

This approach is depicted by a British case **Attorney General** v. **Jonathan Cape Ltd.** An action was brought for injunction to restrain the publication of the political diaries of the late Richards Crossman who was a cabinet minister in the Labour Government of 1964 to 1970. The plea was that the publication of the diaries would reveal the cabinet secrets and infringe the principle of collective responsibility of the government. Lord Widgery CJ accepted the proposition that when a cabinet minister receives information in confidence the improper publication of such information can be restrained by the court. Collective responsibility was held to be "an established feature of the English form of government" and that "some matters leading up to a cabinet decision may be regarded as confidential". But, in the instant case, injunction was refused against publication of the materials in question as they were about ten years old and no longer required protection in public interest. The Court emphasized that it should intervene "only in the clearest of cases where the continuing confidentiality of the material can be demonstrated".

Reference may also be made in this connection to an Australian case **Commonwealth of Australia** v. **John Fairfax and Sons Ltd.** Two journalists had obtained a number of foreign office cables and memoranda covering several matters like Indonesia, East Timor, Anzus Defence Treaty. 'The government applied for an injunction to prohibit publication of the materials on the ground of breach of confidentiality. Mason J. said in this connection: "But it can scarcely be a relevant detriment to the government that publication of material concerning its actions will merely expose it to public discussion and criticism. It is unacceptable in our democratic society that there should be a restraint on the publication of information relating to the government where the only vice of that information is that it enables the public to discuss and criticise government action".

Mason J. also said: "The court will determine the government claim to confidentiality by reference to the public interest. Unless disclosure is likely to injure the public interest it will not be protected. The court will not prevent the publication of information which merely throws light on the past workings or government, even if it be not public property, so long as it does not prejudice the community in other respects. Then disclosure will itself serve the public interest in keeping the community informed and in promoting the discussion of public affairs. If, however, it appears that disclosure will be inimical to the public interest because national security, relations with foreign countries or the ordinary business of government will be prejudice disclosure and will be restrained".

There are several aspects of open government, e.g., (1) Presentation of documents by the government in the court in the course of some litigation; (2) Official Secrecy; and (3) Access to Information. People's right to know has two aspects: (i) How far government should use criminal sanction to deter free flow of information? (ii) How far government is under a positive obligation to make available, on demand, information to the people not in the prohibited category.

Presentation of Documents in the Court

This matter has already been considered earlier. It has been seen that, in course of time, the courts have loosened the government privilege not to produce unpublished documents in the court in the course of a court proceeding against it. Since the writing of the aforesaid piece, one or two aspects of the government reluctance from making public certain secret documents have come to light. These may be mentioned here.

One significant judicial pronouncement to be noted here is *Khatri.* A writ petition was brought in the Supreme Court under Act by certain under-trials for enforcement of their fundamental right under Article 21 on the allegation that they were blinded by the police officer whilst in police custody. The court called for production of certain documents by the state. The state objected to the production of these documents on the ground that they were protected by Sections 162 and 172 of the Criminal Procedure Code and that the petitions were not entitled to see them or to make any use of them in these proceedings. The Court considered the point in **Khatri** v. **Bihar.**

The Court held that Section 162 has no application in a proceeding under Article 32 or 226. Section 162 has been enacted for the benefit of the accused. A writ petition for enforcement of fundamental rights under Article 21 is neither an "inquiry" nor a "trial" in respect of any offence and so Section 162 cannot be invoked by the state. A statement made before a police officer during investigation can be produced and used in evidence in a writ petition under Article 32 provided it is relevant under the Indian Evidence Act and Section 162 cannot be urged as a bar against its production or use. Similarly, the bar placed by Section 172 operates only in an inquiry or trial for an offence and can have no application in proceedings under Article 32 or 226. Accordingly, the Court directed the production of the documents in question.

The Official Secrets Act 1923

The Official Secrets Act 1923 deals with two aspects—(i) espionage or spying activity; and (ii) disclosure of other secret official information. The former is dealt with by Section 3 and the latter by Section 5. Section 3 is not relevant for our discussion here. Section 5 is more relevant and important for our purposes. The provisions of Section 5 may be analysed under the following heads.

Persons in Possession of Official Information

The coverage of persons having possession of official information who are liable under the section is extremely wide. It includes the following:

(a) Any person in possession or control of secret official information.
(b) Any person obtaining information in contravention of this Act.
(c) Any person to whom official information has been entrusted in confidence by any person holding office under the government.
(d) Any person obtaining or having access to information owing to his holding—any office (present or past), or holding any government contract, or any person holding office under any of these persons.

Persons receiving the Information

Not only is the person communicating the information guilty of an offence under Section 5, but also the person receiving it. It applies not only, to government servants but also to all persons who have obtained the secret information in contravention of the Act. Under Section 5(2), any person to whom secret official information has been communicated in contravention of the Act, in other words, a person who is not a person being in lawful possession of the secret information commits an offence by the mere fact of receipt of the same. An offence is also committed if the person receiving secret information from a public officer further communicates it to another person.

The Secret Information

The official information covered by the section is also extremely broad. Any kind of information is covered provided it is "secret". This includes any official code, password, sketch, plan, model, article, note, document or information. The only qualification is that it should be "secret". Nowhere the word "secret" or words "official secrets" are defined in the Act. However, one thing is clear: the Act extends only to official secrets and not to secrets of a private nature. Thus, the Act extends to secrets of a ministry or department of the government, but not to an incorporated body like a university, government company, or public corporation.

In the absence of any definition in the Act, it is for the. government to decide what it should treat as secret and what not. But does the government have an unquestioned right to decide what information it would classify as secret and so keep it away from the public? Will any information classified as secret be "official secrets" and would be caught by the Act? It appears from the cases mentioned below that the government does not seem to be the sole judge of the matter and that the courts can review the decision of the government. The practice of the government is to treat an information secret, even though there may be no danger to national security or public safety or any other public interest, merely because it may embarrass the government, that is, the political party in power.

The newspaper *Blitz* published an article inviting the public to send in official secrets to the editor for which a lavish payment was promised. The question was whether such an article would fall under Section 5 (1) of the Official Secrets Act. The Bombay High Court ruled in *R.K. Karanjia* v. *Emperor* that the said Article would fall under Section 5 (1) of the Official Secrets Act. The Court said that the expression "official secrets" was nowhere defined, "but looking to the purpose and scheme of the Official Secrets Act, especially Sections 3 to 10, which create offences against the government for publication of official secrets, they have all reference to secrets of one or the other department of the Government or the State and not to any secret of a private office". A secret pertaining to any private office, e.g., University or a corporation, would not be called an official secret. The Court refused to accept the contention that the term "official secret" used in the said article included secrets of any private institution. Referring to Section 5 (1) of the Official Secrets Act, the Court characterised the provision as "very comprehensive in its nature" and "it applies not merely to Government servants but also to all persons who have obtained that secret in contravention of this Act". The invitation to the public to send official secrets would fall under Section 5 (1) as "it is really an invitation encouraging or inciting any person to commit an offence". The Court said that it was not concerned with the intention or the motive underlying the article in question "but only with the direct or indirect tendency of the words used in the article itself", and in the Court's opinion that tendency was "to encourage or incite any person to omit an offence".

In *State* v. *K. Balakrishna,* certain parts of the budget were published in a newspaper before the presentation of the budget. It was held that the budget being a secret document of the government, the reception and publication thereof fell within the mischief of Section 5 (2) and Section 5 (1) (b) of the Official Secrets Act. Although there is no written rule declaring budget papers before being presented in the legislature as secret documents, on a consideration of the views expressed in constitutional law books and the statements made by several witnesses, there can be no doubt that the budget papers are usually treated as highly confidential before these are presented to the legislature. The budget papers are "official secrets" and that it would amount to an offence under Sections 5 (2) and Section 5 (1) (b) of the Official Secrets Act to publish them before they are actually presented to the Legislature. The Court also said that it was not a mere 'technical offence' but a "serious offence which might have far reaching consequences and repercussions on the economy of the State". In **Nandlal More** v. **The State,** the Punjab High Court again considered the question of the premature leakage of budget information. This was held to be an offence under the Official Secrets Act. The Court rejected the argument that the Budget proposals cannot be regarded as "official secrets" as they have to be made public after some time. According to the Court, "the fact that on a subsequent date the budget proposals have to be made public would not detract from the secrecy of those proposals till such time as they are announced in Parliament".

The Disclosure of Secret Government Information

A literal reading of Section 5 indicated that disclosure of any kind of secret information will attract prosecution under the Act whatever be the purpose or its impact. Even if disclosure is justified in public interest the person or persons concerned will be liable to an action under the Act. Section 5(1)(a) uses blanket language by making punishable "wilful communication" of any official secret to any person, other than a person to whom he is authorised to communicate it, or a Court of Justice or a person to whom it is in the interests of the State, his duty to communicate it. There are no exceptions like communication in public interest, etc. Everything is punishable whether national security or any other interest worth protecting is endangered or not. The section gives *carte blanche* to the executive to prosecute anyone disclosing official information or, as per Section 5(2), any person voluntarily receiving such information knowing or having reasonable ground to believe that such information is being given to him in contravention of the Act.

These provisions are harsh and the only redeeming feature is that *mens rea*, or the mental element, is the necessary ingredient of an offence under the provisions, for the words used are "wilfully", "voluntarily", "knowing" or "having reasonable ground to believe". Thus a mere "leak", unless it was intentional or wilful, will not be covered by the Act. The burden is on the government to prove *mens rea* as in the case of any other offence. In a department where a matter or an information is handled by different persons it may be difficult to prove *mens rea* or fix responsibility on anyone for the leakage. This does provide some kind of safeguard to an individual against the harshness of the law threat for its use is always there. The Franks Committee has stated that Section 2 of the English Act is rarely activated in the Court room, but is seen by many as having a pervasive influence on the work and the behaviour of hundreds of thousands of people.

Government of India's Practice regarding Official Secrecy

The normal rule in the Government of India is secrecy, and openness is an exception. Government papers and documents are divided into two categories, namely, "non-classified" and "classified". Greater secrecy is to be observed in the case of the latter. The classified documents divided into four categories, namely, "top secret," "secret", "confidential" and "personal—not for publication". The "top secret" grading is given to information of a vital nature affecting national security such as military secrets, matters of high international policy, intelligence reports, etc. The "secret" marking is given to papers of information which is likely to endanger national security or cause injury to the interests or prestige of the nation or would cause serious embarrassment to the government either within the country or in its relations with foreign nations. The word "confidential" pertains to information whose disclosure would be prejudicial to the interest of the nation or given advantage to a foreign nation or even cause administrative embarrassment. "Personal—not for publication" is meant for cases where the information is fit for communication to the individual members of the public, but it is desired that the information given to an individual is not meant for publication. These are arbitrary divisions without having any legal sanction. What is marked, and how it is marked, are matters within the prerogative of the government. It is also not clear whether there is any procedure to reconsider the classification of documents. So, the initial classification lingers on long after the document has ceased to be important.

As regards "non-classified" papers, the rule is that no official is to communicate any information to anyone, which has come into his possession in the course of his official duties, unless so authorised by general or special orders.

Similarly, note portions of a file referred by one department to another are to be treated as confidential. A government servant under the civil service rules is under an obligation not to disclose to anyone including a fellow government servant any information acquired by him during the course of his official duties. This is provided by Rule 8 of the Central Civil Service (Conduct) Rules 1955. A violation of this rule will subject the civil servant to disciplinary action, apart from punishment under any other law, e.g., the Official Secrets Act 1923.

The extent of the secrecy in government will be clear from one instance. Under Article 77 of the Constitution, the President has to make rules for the more convenient transaction of the business of the Government of India and for the allocation amongst ministers of the said business. Under the article the President has framed the Transaction of Business Rules and the Government of India (Allocation of Business) Rules 1961 which are also known as the Rules of Business. The allocation rules were published till 1973 and were available to the public but these are now treated as confidential. These rules mention the items of business allotted to each ministry or department of the Government of India. The Rules of Business which provide for the exercise of powers vested in the Government of India have always been treated as confidential by the government, and are not accessible to the public. However, these rules have been supplied by the government to the courts as and when the question has arisen whether or not the power was discharged by an authorised officer. It is somewhat illogical that though the President makes these rules under the Constitution, yet they are treated as confidential without the Constitution explicitly giving any confidentiality to them. In treating these rules as confidential the government intends to cover up its own irregularities and deficiencies rather than protect, even remotely, any public interest.

There are innumerable instances when the most trivial matters are treated as secret which do not serve any interest of the nation except perhaps saving the government from embarrassment. The reports of various enquiry committees and commissions (like plane crashes or accidents) are treated as secret. Even the recommendations made by the Interdepartmental study group, set up by the Government of India in 1977, to look into the Official Secrets Act 1923, have been treated as confidential. Printed Office manuals are kept secret. This Act uses criminal sanctions to suppress communication of official secrets. There is no law as yet imposing a positive obligation on the government to supply information to an individual when he asks for it. Such laws have been passed in the U.S.A., Australia and New Zealand imposing a duty on the government to permit access to information in possession of the government within certain exceptions.

On the U.S. Freedom of Information Act 1966, Schwartz says: "Before then, the people's 'right to know' was a journalistic slogan rather than a legal right. The 1966 statute changed all this, since it gave the citizen, for the first time, a legally enforceable right of access to government files and documents. The FOIA effects a profound alteration in the position of the citizen *vis-à-vis* government. No longer is the individual seeking information from an administrative agency a mere suppliant".

General Observations

Importance of freedom of information in a democratic polity needs no justification, It is a *sine qua non* of an open government. To achieve its embodiment, a statute on the lines of reformed Freedom of Information Act of the U.S. would be a proper strategy rather than a constitutional amendment. However, its enactment is not easy. Even advanced democratic countries had such statute only recently after a prolonged experience of running an open liberal democratic polity. India must be very cautious in rushing to legislate on this freedom. There should be full and total conceptual clarity. The parameters of this freedom should be clearly defined.

The reasonable restrictions on it, and exceptions to it need careful consideration and elaborate articulation. The Indian Statute shall endeavour to keep the pitfalls and drawbacks of the U.S. FOIA at bay. A half baked enactment may kill otherwise laudable object. Let it not be a fertile ground for legal profession to litigate eternally. Besides, the costs of free information are bound to be heavy, it should be available at, an affordable cost within specified certain, definite and reasonable time limits. There should be adequate remedies against undue delay in its supply. This freedom will be meaningless if there is no adequate infrastructure of modern information technology in the form of storage and retrieval systems. At the same time care must be taken to see that freedom meant to expose government corruption itself does not become a tool to enhance governmental corruption in matters relating to supply and suppression of information. Also bureaucratic initiative and freedom in decision-making processes need not be unduly curbed. Really, the task is not that easy as it appears to be. After all information in the present age of information explosion is a very explosive matter. It needs to be handled with utmost care:

Right to Information

- To bring together citizens who have been using Right to Information to share their experiences and explain the process to those who wish to do so, and
- To discuss the problems being faced in seeking information from the government and to collectively seek solutions including approaching the Courts, if necessary.

Whistle Blower's Protection

The murder of Satyendra Dubey highlighted the need for a strong legislation on Whistle Blower's Protection. Parivartan filed a PIL in Supreme Court demanding *inter alia*:

The murder of Satyendra Dubey should be investigated by an independent agency.

The allegations of corruption made by Satyendra Dubey should also be investigated by an independent agency.

The Central Government should be directed to make necessary arrangements for the protection of such whistle blowers.

Central Government should be directed to provide suitable machinery for the people to be able to use their Right to Information.

As a result, the Central Government passed orders appointing the Chief Vigilance Commissioner (CVC) as the nodal authority for the protection of the whistle blowers. (See also Dayal Reghu; 'Whistle blowers need to be Protected, *Economic Times*, 26 December, 2006, p. 10).

Social Audit

India is a democracy. People are masters. Government exists to serve the people. It is the primary duty of any master to take a look at the accounts of the servant at regular intervals and hold the servant accountable. Social audit or public audit is a step in that direction. People use right to information to obtain details of the works carried out by a Government Department or the manner in which the money was spent on that Department. This information contained in records is compared with field reality—This is public audit or social audit and is a very important tool in the hands of the people to hold the Government accountable.

Public audits do not have any legal sanction. The findings of a public audit are not acceptable as evidence under any law. However, a public audit creates a lot of public pressure on the political establishment to take corrective steps.

What is a *Jansunwai*?

The findings of a public audit may be used in a number of manners. The findings could be presented and discussed widely in a public meeting before the entire community and stakeholders. Such public meetings have been called public hearings or *jansunwais*. The information contained in the official records is read out to the people in the meeting and the people testify before everyone, the veracity of that information. The proceedings take place in a completely transparent manner. There is also little scope for anyone to lie because all the parties are present and if anyone says anything wrong, others would be able to counter that.

Public audit and *jansunwais* together are a big leap on the road to participatory democracy. In their present form, these were first started by Mazdoor Kisan Shakti Sangathan (MKSS) of Rajasthan. MKSS has conducted several *jansunwais* in different parts of Rajasthan till now.

Parivartan conducts First Urban *Jansunwai*

In August 2002, Parivartan obtained copies of all the civil works done by MCD in Sundernagari and New Seemapuri in the previous two financial years using Delhi Right to Information Act. Sundernagari and Seemapuri are two resettlement colonies in Delhi inhabited by lower income groups. The information was segregated blockwise. There are 11 blocks in Sundernagari and 7 blocks in New Seemapuri in the next few months, Parivartan workers went to each block, collected people at street corners by singing songs and held meetings. In these Street Corner meetings, the people were told about the details of works claimed to have been done by MCD in their block and the amounts spent on each one of them. The people were shocked to hear the details—It emerged in these meetings that a number of works were half done whereas, the quality would be an issue in the rest. Site visits were also done along with the residents. This gave a fair idea of the gap between what was written on paper and what actually had happened. Such street corner meetings raised the tempers of the people and there was a strong demand for a platform where the concerns could be collectively voiced.

On 14th December, 2002, a public hearing (*jansunwai*) was organized in Sundernagari by Parivartan along with the National Campaign for People's Right to Information (NCPRI) and Mazdoor Kissan Shakti Sangathan (MKSS) of Rajasthan to discuss publicly the works audited. The public hearing was attended by almost 1,000 people including local residents of the area, journalists and eminent personalities such as Justice P.B. Sawant, Aruna Roy, Prabhash Joshi, Vinod Mehta, Bharat Dogra, Shekhar Singh, Arundhati Roy and Harsh Mander. In the public hearing, the contracts were read out and local residents testified as to whether or not the work was undertaken, and if it was undertaken whether it was done fully or was left incomplete. Out of the 68 works audited and discussed in the public hearing, calculations of estimated misappropriation of funds have been done for 64 works worth Rs 1.3 crore. In these 64 works, the total amount of embezzlement found on account of missing items! Works is approximately Rs. 70 lakh (i.e., items or works worth about Rs. 70 lakh do not physically exist at all in these 64 works).

The *Jansunwai* demonstrated the proportion of embezzlement and the urgency with which, the issue needs to be tackled. It clearly demonstrated that most of the time, it is not the inadequacy of funds but leakages, which are responsible for poor development. The effects of *Jansunwai* can be seen and analysed on five sections of society, viz. the local administration, local politicians, the people of the area, the local contractors and Delhi administration.

Findings of *Jansunwai*

Some instances of missing items discovered during public audit are as follows:

— 29 handpumps with electric motors were supposed to be installed under 10 contracts. However, residents of this area reported that only 14 handpumps had actually been put. The rest of the handpumps were not installed at all, according to the residents. Electric motors have not been installed in even a single case. Loss on account of missing public and distributed in the community before any new civil work began. Parivartan workers offered that if he agreed to this demand, Parivartan would themselves go to the public in praise of the MLA. However, he refused to accept that. According to him, estimates worth Rs. 2.5 crore were lying pending in Sundernagari and no contractor was willing to do the job, as wherever the contractors went, the people won't let the work take place till they were given copies of contracts. He said that the contractors won't part with the contracts till the work was over, as this would affect their margins. He said that he agreed that the contractors were corrupt but if the works were stopped in this manner, then the entire money would get lapsed. This position was not acceptable to Parivartan and the local people. It was made clear to him that if the contractors wanted to blackmail then they would not do the work and if they were not allowed to swindle money, then let no work take place in the area.

For the next one month, almost every work was stopped by the people of Sundernagari, till the details of works were made public by the officials. Ultimately, in the last week of March, MLA's brother came to Parivartan office and agreed to make contracts public. But he said that the contents would be read out in public and copies of contracts would be made available to the public by MLA's workers and it should not be done by Parivartan's workers. To this, Parivartan had no objection.

In the meanwhile, Delhi Government and MCD passed orders saying that copy of any contract would be made public before it was carried out.

Immediate Impact on Local Bureaucracy

The MCD Engineers in local Division office put a number of obstacles in providing information sought under the Right to Information Act. It was after a great deal of perseverance for almost four months that most of the information was obtained. Though they would always present themselves very politely and offer all cooperation verbally, but in practice, there was very little cooperation actually forthcoming before the *Jansunwai*. A few days before *Jansunwai,* Parivartan tried its level best to obtain comments of the MCD Engineers on the deficiencies found in works. They kept promising that they would go for a joint inspection of works, but they did not do that.

During *Jansunwai,* EXEN alleged that Parivartan was making false allegations against their Department. He said that Parivartan never told them about the deficiencies in works and were now creating a scene in public. However, in later stages of *Jansunwai*, he simply kept saying that he would not like to comment without visiting the sites.

After *Jansunwai*, a number of sites were jointly inspected by a team of Parivartan workers and MCD Engineers. The Engineers offered complete cooperation in these inspections. However, they offered flimsy explanations to most of the deficiencies (read complete report) of *Jansunwai* for details.

There was a marked difference in their attitude towards public after *Jansunwai*. The officials would be far more responsive and courteous in their dealings with the public of this area. Now, whenever any person from Sundernagari or New Seemapuri would call them up, they would listen to the grievance and also make efforts to act on it. Wherever required and demanded by the public, the EXEN himself would visit the spot. Whenever public stopped any work and demanded to know the contents of that contract, he would invariably send his officials to the site, who would then publicly read out all the contents of that contract.

After the *Jansunwai*, the officials realized that the public could scrutinize the records any time and it would not be easy for them to swindle funds. The officials were also quite scared of the consequences that would follow this *Jansunwai* as the detailed report of social audit had already been presented to the government.

Delhi High Court Directs Delhi Police to Book the Culprit

A detailed report of the defalcations found in social audit was submitted to the Chief Minister, Chief Secretary, MCD Commissioner, Secretary (Administrative Reforms) and anti-corruption branch of Delhi Police. However, no action was taken by them.

In the month of May 2004, on a petition filed by Parivartan, Delhi High Court directed the Delhi Police to investigate into all the allegations of corruption made by Parivartan and file its report before the metropolitan magistrate within 6 months. The Court directed that the enquiries should not be conducted by an officer below the rank of an ACP. During the hearing, MCD said that they had already carried out investigations and have found all of them baseless. But the Court observed how could the thief be made to investigate against himself.

Municipal Councillor offers Transparency in All Government Works

In the first week of June, Mr Ajit Singh Choudhary, the Municipal Councillor from Seemapuri Ward, approached us and offered total transparency in the execution of all civil works carried out in this area. He said that he had directed the Executive Engineer of this area to provide copies of estimates and sketches to Parivartan before any work started. After the completion of work, he would offer each work for inspection by public, including Parivartan. The objections to the work, if any, would be immediately rectified and only then, the payment for the work would be made.

He informed that the entire process of *Jansunwai* and the subsequent order of High Court had its impact on the contractors and the engineers of this area. According to the Councillor, after the Court order, the contractors and engineers were afraid of their works being subjected to *post mortem* later on by the public in the form of a *Jansunwai*. A *post mortem* also leaves little scope for improvement of work. Hence, the councillor offered that let the public and Parivartan find faults with the works, when the works were taking place. He would ensure that the payment is not made for any work till the objections made by the people are settled.

Delhi Government Orders

As a result of social audit and *Jansunwai*, the Delhi Government and Municipal Corporation passed certain orders to bring transparency in the award and execution of works. The following are some of the important orders:

(i) Municipal Commissioner passed an order saying that list of all the works carried out in any quarter/year in any area should be put up on the notice board of respective Ward office and on the website. The order also says that every contractor should put up a board at the site of work displaying basic details of work like name of work, contract amount, date of start, date of completion, etc. Any contractor who fails to do that should be blacklisted for a year.

(ii) Engineer-in-Chief passed an order saying that a copy of work order of any work that takes place should be displayed on the notice board of the local MCD Store in that area.

CASE STUDY—1

Ashok Gupta gets a New Electricity Connection

Ashok Gupta applied for a new electricity connection for his premises on 3.2.2001 to Delhi Vidyut Board (DVB). He was demanded a bribe. He refused to pay bribe. As a result, he was not granted electricity connection. Ashok made several visits to DVB office but none listened to his woes. In February 2002, he filed an application under the Delhi Right to Information Act. In his application, he asked for the following information:

- I had applied for a new electricity connection on 3.2.2001. Please give me the daily progress made on my application till date.
- Please give me the names and designations of the officials who were supposed to take action on my application and who have not done so.
- According to the Indian Electricity Act, an applicant should get a new connection within 30 days of application. Are these officials guilty of violating the provisions of the Electricity Act? These officials have caused mental tension to me by not providing me the said connection in time. Are these officials guilty of harassing the public?
- Does DVB plan to take any action against these officials? If yes, in how much time?
- When will I get my connection?

On 2.3.2002, he was granted a new connection. It was almost miraculous. How did this magic happen? In ordinary circumstances, such an application would have been consigned to the dustbin. But the Delhi Right to Information Act says that the salary of the official who does not provide information in time would be deducted at the rate of Rs 50 per day of default. Hence, they have to reply to this application. But it is not easy to reply to these questions. Hence, they immediately do the pending work of the applicant.

CASE STUDY—2

Look where Pune's Mayor takes her Car

Never mind the rule book of the Pune Municipal Corporation (PMC). It says that cars allotted to office-bearers have to stay within municipal limits, but the truth is that they have been going beyond limits against rules seeking solace at tourist resorts and pilgrim centres.

Using the MRTI for the second time on the use (misuse?) of official cars by elected representatives, Maj. Gen. SCM Jatar (retd.), president of Nagrik Chetna Manch, has procured shocking details of logbook entries on innumerable outstation trips made by the Mayor, Deputy Mayor, Standing Committee Chairman, Leader of the Opposition and Leader of the House in their official cars.

The total expenditure on cars was a staggering Rs. 51,02,235 from January 1 to October 31, 2003. As for the break-up of official and private use, the PIO was evasive. But going by the over half a crore rupees bill in 10 months, it was clear that the official was overstepping the power to use official car.

RTI: Right to Information Act 2005

The last forty years or so have seen the passage of freedom of information legislation in several countries beginning with the United States in 1966, Denmark and Norway in 1970, Australia and New Zealand in 1982, Canada in 1983, and Ireland in 1998, and India in 2005. There are several major reasons why the development of freedom of information legislation is a welcome trend. *First* RTI legislation breaks with the often entrenched tradition of secrecy in several countries and, in doing so, helps empower the citizen *vis-à-vis* the state, thus deepening democracy and enhancing citizen control of political processes. *Second,* more information helps citizens make better and more reasoned choices about important public policy and electoral issues, and participate in the political process more fully. *Third,* the capacity to demand information from governments is a powerful deterrent against governmental corruption and graft or plain inefficiency. In this sense, RTI legislation can be a powerful aid to the process of economic development, not just democracy.

END NOTES

Open Government is the doctrine which holds that citizens have the right to access the documents and proceeding of the government to allow for effective public oversight. In its broadest sense open government doctrine opposes *raison of etat* (reasons of the state) which tends to legitimize extensive state secrecy.

In the nineteenth century eminent liberal politicians and writers, Benthem and Mill, advocated measures that were opposed to secrecy by government.

Among recent developments is the theory of *open source governance* which advocate the application of democratic principles to enable the interested citizen to get more directly involved in the legislative process.

Official Secrets Act 1923.

10

Global Approach and Right to Information

Speaking of Global Approach we may consider various aspects as follows:

- Technology
- Human Values
- International products
- Public information
- Media education
- Transformation of services i.e. distribution of work and marketing as is done in libraries.

In the Indian context, Rabindranath Tagore was actively responsible for utilizing the reach of the Global Approach through library and educational institutions which are clearly enunciated in his Rural Reconstruction Model.

Although mention of Trust Deed of a library and a Braham Vidyalaya is made, but such institution came into existence only after 1901 'when a beginning was made by Rabindranath Tagore with the permission and approval of his father'.

'The worth of a librarian I would guage by his power of attracting and working after such circles, of acting of the intermediary for an intimacy of relationship between the reader and the library. That is to say, on him is cast the burden not only of books, but of readers as well, and maintaining of both is the test of his efficiency, of the proper discharge of his trust (Rabindranath Tagore's Address p. 1-6).

Being pulse of democracy freedom of expression available to the people in a country is the scale of measuring how much that country is democratic, free and open. It is of immense value and supreme importance for the proper functioning of a free state. In a participative and parliamentary democracy it has many roles to play and several purposes to serve. It serves not only purpose democratic government but also helps an individual realize his own individuality and self-fulfilment. It provides opportunity to a person to unfold his potentialities and to rise to maximum of which he is capable. It allows an individual to speak as he pleases as long as he does not misuse it. Appeal to reason, unfolding of truth is possible only through this freedom. It is not only necessary but indispensable element in a democratic society and popular government. Without this freedom democracy can become a label without meaning, a form without substance. Growing importance of this right is being noticed in both developed and developing countries of the world, e.g., U.S.A., Australia, Canada, South Africa, Malaysia. In this chapter an attempt has been made to look at conceptually global approach of this right, and chapter has been divided into the following subheads:

1. Comparative Account of Right to Information in Various Legal Systems,
2. Emerging Concept of Cyber Technology,
3. Salient Feature of the Information of Technology Act 2000, and
4. General Observation.

Comparative Account of Right to Information in Various Legal Systems

The immunity from disclosure, the thick wall even against truthful criticism and right to secrecy claimed by the political bureaucracy in power, on the pain of prosecution of any person seeking to peep or publish, singularly or jointly with others, marks the eclipse and end of liberty. In modern governments, whichever the country and whatever the label of its politics, tendency is growing to construct a system of secrecy. The dividing line between popular servitude and popular supremacy lies not in the voting right of every adult but in his political right to govern himself and to run self-government vicariously. The position in law in the major countries is alike although different in practicing. Description of some broad features of the law and practices prevalent in some countries would illustrate this:

Access to Information in USA

Learning the lessons of hory, the American Congress passed the Freedom of Information Act 1966 (FOIA).

FOIA provides that every citizen has the right to request access to federal agency records or information. All agencies of the United States Government are required to disclose records upon receiving a written request for them, except for those records that are protected from disclosure by the nine exemptions This right of access is enforceable in court. However, this right recognizes nine well defined exceptions contained in Section (b) which speaks that law contained in Section (a) shall not apply to the following matters:

(1) (a) specifically authorized under criteria established by an executive order to be kept secret in the interest of national defence or foreign policy; and (b) are in fact properly classified pursuant to such Executive order;
(2) related solely to the internal personnel rules and practices of an agency;
(3) specifically exempted from disclosure by statute (other than section 552b of this title), provided that such statute (a) requires that the matters be withheld from the public in such a manner as to leave no discretion on the issue, or (b) establishes particular criteria for withholding or refers to particular types of matters to be withheld;
(4) trade secrets and commercial or financial information obtained from a person and privileged or confidential;

(5) Inter-agency or intra-agency memorandum or letters which would not be available by law to a party other than an agency in litigation with agency;

(6) personal and medical files and similar files the disclosure of which would constitute a clearly unwarranted invasion of personal privacy;

(7) records or information compiled for law enforcement purposes, but only to the extent that the production of such law enforcement records or information (a) could personally be expected to interfere with enforcement proceedings, (b) would deprive a person of a right to a fair trial or an impartial adjudication, (c) could reasonably be expected to constitute an unwarranted invasion of personal privacy, (d) could reasonably be expected to disclose the identity of a confidential source including a state, local or foreign agency or authority or any private institution which furnish information on a confidential basis, and, in the case of record or information complied by criminal law enforcement authority in the course of criminal investigation or by an agency conducting a lawful national security intelligence investigation, information furnished by a confidential source, and (e) would disclose techniques and procedures for law enforcement investigations or prosecutions if such disclosures could reasonably be expected to risk circumvention of the law or (f) could reasonably be expected to endanger the life or physical safety of any individual;

(8) contained in or related to examination, operating, or condition reports prepared by, on behalf of or for the use of an agency responsible for the regulation of financial institutions; or

(9) geological and geophysical information and data, including maps, concerning wells.

Any reasonably segregable portion of a record shall be provided to any person requesting such record after deletion of the portions which are exempt.

On October 2, 1996, President Bill Clinton signed into law the Electronic Freedom of Information Act 1996 (E-FOIA, for short). E-FOIA makes it possible for the citizen to have electronic access to the Environment Protection Agency, FOIA Reading Room. The new law requires agencies to respond to an FOIA request within 20 working days (excluding holidays).

The Environment Protection Agency (EPA) regulations for implementing the FOIA are found in Title 40 of the Code of Federal Regulations, Chapter 1, Part 2. The EPA is required to provide the fullest possible disclosure of information to the public. According to Federal regulations, requests for records to EPA must be submitted in writing to the Freedom of Information Officer. Any request submitted should be commented on or before 30 days.

On 2nd October, 1996 Bill Clinton said, 'Our country was founded on democratic principles of openness and accountability and for 30 years, FOIA has supported these principles. Today this amendment refuges an important link between the United States Government and the American people to any other programme office is considered "misdirected" and may result in a delayed reply. EPA is allowed to charge fees to requesters in order to recover the direct costs of search, duplication, and review of requested records. If the total cost of the requested information is less than $ 25, the fees are waived. In some cases, fee waivers or reduction of fees are granted in the public interest, but the request for waiver must be made and justified by supporting documentation. Pressure for disclosure of information has been resisted even in America. The career civil servant is really incapable of understanding the intent of FOI. They view information as a secret capital asset. Their information is capital, and they hate to disburse their capital by releasing it. A lot of education has to be done within the agencies. One thing we might think about is enacting sanctions for illegal withholding of information. In a republic resting on the theory of an informed electorate as vital to the operation of democracy and timely information as the real currency of power, secrecy obstructs citizens' participation and so the FOI Act was enacted in the U.S. The officials feel they own their bureaus, their files and their papers and view the applicants as troublemakers. So they play it safe and adopt the attitude—'when in doubt, withhold'. The U.S. Supreme Court, in a unanimous verdict in **Richard Nixon** v. **United States** told a tense nation that presidential privilege had a short mileage *vis-à-vis* the 'right to know'. The dawn of a new jurisprudence of light was thus heralded. The Founding Fathers of the American Constitution and the farsighted judges who expounded that instrument are the forerunners of this significant sector of the world legal order.

President Johnson, in signing the Freedom of Information Act 1966 into a law had said that it entitles Americans to "all the information that the security of the nation permit". Under the Freedom of Information Act any person, not merely an affected individual but every person is entitled, who is eligible to ask for information, because what is aimed at is not merely redressal of grievances but encouragement of an informed citizenry. Disclosure is the rule and refusal the exception since the right to know is the cornerstone of citizen participation in administration. The basis of this jurisprudence was spelt out by Ramsey Clark, then Attorney General, in a memorandum (June 1967) giving the essence of the FOI law:

> *If Government is to be truly of, by, and for the people, the people must know in detail the activities of Government nothing so diminishes democracy as secrecy. Self-government, the maximum participation of the citizenry in the affairs of state, is meaningful only with an informed public. How can we govern ourselves if we know not how we govern?*

The Freedom of Information Act was not designed to increase administrative efficiency, but to guarantee the public a right to know how the Government is discharging its duty to protect the public interest. None of the abuses of power, the brutalities of the State, the corruption of public persons and parties and the crimes of terror and horror of the Mafia which go unpublished could have been known but for the people's sovereign right to know, of their deputes in parliaments and of the media.

Position in Russia formerly Soviet Russia (USSR)

During the reign of the Czars, repression was the rule. Freedom of expression was a sure route to prison. Revolts were crushed but the Great October Revolution (1917) ended this unfree era. However, dictatorship of the single party politics grew after 1917, but, to suppress differences of opinion and frown upon views not palatable to the Communist Party of the Kremlin bureaucracy. There was news monopoly for the State and the electronic media too spoke in a controlled voice. Self-criticism within the Party and the expression, guaranteed by the Constitution mitigated the authoritarian allergy for dissent to some extent.

In Russia also the Constitution guarantees right to privacy to the citizens and freedom of speech to the citizens as well as to the press. The provisions which guarantee these freedoms are as under—

Article 50

In accordance with the interests of the people and in order to strengthen and develop the socialist system, citizens of the USSR are guaranteed freedom of speech, of the press, and assembly, meetings, street processions and demonstrations.

Article 56

The privacy of citizens, and of their correspondence, telephone conversations and telegraphic communications is protected by law.

The provisions of law do not by themselves ensure human rights and freedoms. Many times the legislated text is different from the practicing. The actual performance is the true test. Justice V.R. Krishna Iyer has beautifully described the Russian printed law and the practice:

The constellation of articles, on its face, does ensure human rights and freedoms. But often times the printed text may depart from the practice in October Revolution unfolded as a crimson dawn of people's rights But sunrise, by process and sadly moved towards a sombre sunset of humanism.

The Soviet Constitution, as the provisions show, did give juridical back-up for this mental emancipation, freedom of information and majority decision in a collegium. Free from feudal domination and Czarist repression, the Soviet men and women discovered uninhibited opportunities to seek information and form one's own views. A creative Soviet decade followed. But the dialectics of a single party system and arrogance of power in the party hierarchy and state bureaucracy with a view to extirpate the kulak under the subversive capitalist generated a slow and creeping surrender of power to the party cadres. The grip of this political oligarchy and the emergence of the personality cult, the necessities of over centralisation and democratic dictatorship, the grave fears of capitalist encirclement and fascist aggression aggravated the python process of killing by degrees from dissent. The Stalinist terror was death sentence on free information, free expression and democratic pluralism. The long night that followed, the dreaded secret police syndrome, the corruption of the Party bureaucracy and the exit of freedom of criticism produced over the decades with intermittent stage, a deadening process, a stagnant society, a soul-less bureaucracy and a political system which had lost much of its creative faculties. The spirit of the Soviet people slumbered long but now and then the party did assert itself. The Soviet leader was alive but was in hiding. The decisive hour of resurrection came with a bang when Mikhail Gorbachev, in a moral spiritual quantum jump of clinical revival of a decadent policy, impacted on the Soviet people like a terrific tornado with two words—glasnost and perestroika. The open society and the dynamics of change through free expression became an epic event. This odyssey of freedom is still an ongoing process.

Glasnost stands for open criticism of the Government while perestroika demands radical departure from the obedience culture. The basic principle is that the freedom of information as an extension of freedom of speech and expression is an integral part of the rule of law. Sidney Webb in his classic work, emphasises the need for openness, thus: "When, however, the Soviet Government feels itself as secure as the British Government does, there seems no reason why popular lectures and speeches at open meetings, and discussion in cheap pamphlets and newspapers, should be any more restricted than they are in England."

Theoretically democracy postulates government by the people but how can they govern unless they have access to the information relevant to decision-making or correcting wrong policies of the government. So much secretive had been the Soviet Union that as great an event as the death of President Breznev was not released to the Soviet people until the appropriate hour. Thus it was a closed society with an information iron curtain between the 'rulers' and the 'ruled'. When the Summit Supremo of the party turns authoritarian and intolerant of dissent, then demand for intonation and open discussion becomes a risky operation. Great scientist like Shakarov, eminent writers like Boris Pasternak, and private protesters in numbers began to come into the open facing perils and asking for more democracy and functional freedom. The demand for an open society for a radical restructuring with humanist values inspiring its dynamics, was this force for the future. Their confrontation with the *status quo ante* and the suppressive and orthodox custodians and managers of the State Power was inevitable. During the tenure of President Mikhail Gorbachev several resolutions were passed during the 19th All Union Conference of the CPSU to provide for Glasnost and Perestroika. But the tragedy is that the reformer who wanted to remove the iron curtain of secrecy, was himself removed from power. And thus the stagnation syndrome and corrupt polity have suffocated the new experiment of the Great October Resolution.

Communist Philosophy of China

The People's Republic of China has adopted its Constitution and promulgated for implementation by the proclamation of the National People's Congress on December 4, 1982. Chapter

II contains 24 articles that prescribe the fundamental rights and the duties of the citizens. Provisions relevant to the present context are set down as under:

Article 3

Citizens of the People's Republic of China enjoy freedom of speech, of the press, of assembly, of association, of procession and demonstration.

Article 37

Freedom of the person of citizens of the People's Republic of China is inviolable.

No citizen may be arrested except with the approval or by decision of a people's procuratorate or by decision of a people's court, and arrests must be made by a public security organ.

Unlawful detention or deprivation or restriction of citizens' freedom of the person by other means is prohibited and unlawful search of the person of citizens is prohibited.

Article 38

The personal dignity of citizens of the People's Republic of China is inviolable insult, libel, false accusation or false incrimination directed against citizens by any means is prohibited.

Article 39

The residences of citizens of the People's Republic of China are inviolable. Unlawful search of or intrusion into, a citizen's residence is prohibited.

Existence of all these provisions shows, at least on paper and in writing that violations of fundamental rights and infringement of human rights are not possible in China but whatever be the textual matrix the practice is altogether different. Being a communistic country, China does not allow dissidents or those who have no faith in the communistic philosophy. Thus right to know is not available to the citizens of China even in this electronic age.

British Approach

The power of the British Empire was build through processes of secrecy and the colonial people's demands for open government were legislatively suppressed by England. In Britain thrust has always been on secrecy.

Keeping in view the desirability of 'openness' of government affairs in a democratic society, the Franks Committee was appointed in 1977 following the historic judgement in Biafran Secrets case. This Committee recommended repeal of Section 2 of the 1911 Act and its replacement by the Official Information Act. Section 2 of the Official Secrets Act 1911 (British) was a catch-all provision and covered every information and each person. The Thatcher Government implemented recommendations of the Franks Committee only in 1989 when the Official Secrets Act 1989 was enacted on 11 May, 1989. By this amendment rigour of the provisions of Section 2 of the Official Secret Act 1911 (British) has been diluted to some extent. Now the British Official Secrets Act can be cited as the Official Secrets Act 1911 to 1989.

In Britain, the Government's Code of Practice on Access to Government Information came into force in 1994. It applies to all departments and public sector bodies within the jurisdiction of the Parliamentary Commissioner for Administration (UK Ombudsman). According to the Government, the aims of the Code are to improve policy-making and the democratic process, to protect the interests of individuals and companies by ensuring that reasons are given for administrative decisions (subject to limited expectations) and also to support and extend the public service principles established under the Citizen's Charter.

Under the Code, the Departments are required to do five things:

(i) to publish the facts and analysis of the facts which the Government considers relevant and important in framing major policy proposals and decisions;

(ii) to publish, or otherwise make available, explanatory material on Department's dealings with the public (this includes rules, procedures, internal guidance to officials and similar administrative manuals) except where publication could prejudice matters which can be kept confidential under Part II of the Code;

(iii) to give reasons for administrative decisions;

(iv) to publish, in accordance with the Citizens Charter, full information about how public services are run, how much they cost, who is in charge and what complaints and redress procedures are available; and, where possible, comparable information about what services are being provided, what target are set, standards of service are expected and the results achieved;

(v) to release, in response to specific requests, information relating to policies, actions and decisions and other matters related to Departments' areas of responsibility.

The Code offers members of the public genuine benefits in terms of obtaining information. It is vital that departments are consistent in its interpretation. There are exemptions set out regarding information whose release might prove harmful Article by Sir William Reid, Parliamentary Commissioner for Administration in UK, Public Accountability and Open Kingdom in Public Accountability in India polity by Dr. Raj K. Nigam and should, therefore, be withheld. Where a request is refused, the person, who made the request, must be told that "he or she has a chance of a review of the case as well as the right of appeal to the Ombudsman". The Parliamentary Ombudsman ensures that the reasons for withholding informauon are justifiable, that it is not being withheld because it might cause embarrassment or for other unworthy motives.

"The Code may prove to be a step but not the whole journey." The Code and a change of culture in the minds of officials and others who must implement it, accountability.

Britain has no written Constitution and no Bill of Rights. Although secret laws have been diluted a bit by the Data Production Act 1984, the Access to Personal Files Act 1987, implementation in 1994 of the Code of Practice on Access to Government Information and amendment to Section 2 of the Official Secrets Act 1911, but the soul is soaked in jurisprudence of official non-disclosure.

Australian Trend

The Freedom of Information Act 1982 (FOIA) extends to all commonwealth government departments and most authorities. It deals with three principal matters:

(1) It requires the publication of information concerning the functions and documents of agencies and making available for inspection and purchase of certain specified documents.
(2) It provides for general access to documents of an agency and official ministerial documents, subject to a number of exceptions.
(3) The Act provides a machinery whereby a person who claims that a document of an agency or an official document of a minister contains information relating to his personal affairs that is incorrect and can seek the amendment of that information.

It is the second aspect of the FOIA in which we are interested for our present purposes.

The Act begins with the denial of the theory of official secrecy. Section 3(1) asserts the right of the Australian community to access to government information. The object of the Act is stated to be *inter alia*: "to extend as far as possible the right of the Australian community to access to official information in the possession of the Government of the

Commonwealth by . . . . creating a general right of access to information in documentary form in the possession of ministers, departments and public authorities, limited only by exceptions and exemptions necessary for the protection of essential public interests . . . ." Section 11 states the general principle that every person is to have a legally enforceable right to obtain access to official documents other than documents exempted from access under the Act. Thus, access has to be given to official documents unless the FOIA Act itself withholds the same.

A person wishing access to a document has to make a written request to the concerned body. There is no test of standing required of an applicant, nor need the show any reason for wishing to have access to a document. The body has to make a decision within 30 days. If no decision is made within the prescribed period, it would mean that the access to the document has been denied. Fees may be charged for permitting access to the documents. Under certain circumstances, access to a document may be deferred, viz., where, publication or the document in question is required by law; where the document has been prepared for presentation to a particular person or body; if the premature release of the document concerned would be contrary to the public interest; where the minister considers that the document concerned is of such general public interest that the Parliament should be informed of its contents before it is otherwise made public. A number of documents are exempt from access, e.g., documents are exempt if it would be contrary to the public interest to disclose them because disclosure could reasonably be expected to cause damage to the security, defence, or international relations of the Commonwealth. Also, documents are exempted the disclosure of which would divulge information communicated in confidence between governments. Documents are exempt if disclosure would cause damage to the Commonwealth-State relations. Other documents exempt from disclosure are: documents submitted to the cabinet for its consideration or proposed to be submitted; internal working documents revealing opinions, advice, consultation which may have taken place within a body and disclosure of which would be contrary to the public interest; documents affecting enforcement of the law and protection of public safety, e.g., endangering the life or physical safety of any person. The following documents *inter alia* are also exempt:

(1) Documents affecting financial or property interests of the Commonwealth.
(2) Documents affecting adversely the national economy. These are documents dealing with such matters as exchange rates, interest rates, borrowings by the government, etc.

FOIA provides an elaborate system for review of decisions under the Act. First, the decision denying access to a document is reviewable within the concerned body itself at a level higher than the decision-making level. If still the decision is adverse to the applicant he may seek review through an appeal to the Administrative Appeals Tribunal. Then the Ombudsman also has a role to play in this area. When a person has been denied access to a document by an agency (but not a Minister) he may complain to the Ombudsman who may investigate the action or the agency concerned. The Ombudsman then makes a report. An appeal may also be brought before the Administrative Appeals Tribunal against the refusal to grant access to a document directly in case of a decision taken by the Minister. The tribunal has a recommendatory power only in some cases and the Minister is to decide ultimately. In some cases, the Tribunal decides the matter on the same basis as the agency or the Minister could have decided it. An appeal lies to the Federal Court against a decision of the Tribunal on a question of law. The Tribunal can see the document in question where it sees it necessary to categorise the document.

Position in New Zealand

The Official Information Act 1982, represents a significant development in New Zealand Administrative Law as it is an advance towards a more open system of government. The Act seeks to make official information more freely available and regulates the manner in which official information is to be made available to members of the public. It also establishes a right for individuals to seek access to personal information held about them, and 'to request correction of that information where necessary'. There is a further provision enabling individuals to find out the reasons for any decisions made in respect of them.

The Official Information Act applies to all Central Government departments and most Central Government corporations and organisations. It also applies to Ministers of the Crown. It does not, however, apply to local organisations such as councils, education boards and hospital boards.

Briefly, the Act establishes the principle that official information is to be made available unless good reason exists under the Act for withholding it. A New Zealand citizen or permanent resident or a body incorporated in New Zealand can request for official information. A request for official information cannot be refinished because the applicant does not have a sufficient personal interest. The Act contains a number of reasons why information can be withheld, for example, to protect the privacy of natural persons, or to avoid prejudice to the maintenance of the law, or to New Zealand's security or defence or international relations, or to prevent damage to New Zealand's economy. Information can also be denied for several other reasons, e.g., to maintain "collective and individual ministerial responsibility", "political neutrality of officials".

When access to information is denied, the applicant can ask the concerned department or organisation to have the decision reviewed by another officer. The Ombudsman also has the function of reviewing decisions made under the Act. He has the power to:

(a) investigate and review any decision by which a Minister, department or organisation:

(i) refuses to make official information available to any person;

(ii) decides how, or for what charge, a request is to be granted;

(iii) imposes conditions on the use, communication or publication of information;

(iv) gives a notice refusing to confirm or deny the existence or non-existence of any information requested;

(b) investigate and review any complaint of undue delay in responding to a request for official information . . . .

Investigations under the Official Information Act are handled by the Chief Ombudsman. The Chief Ombudsman conducts his investigations and reviews under the Official Information Act in the same manner as if they were investigations under the Ombudsman Act. Full enquiries are made and the Chief Ombudsman will study, as necessary, any papers and documents relating to the complaint. Investigations are carried out in private.

If the Ombudsman forms an opinion that the request for information should not have been refused, or that the decision complained of in respect of the request was, for example, unreasonable or wrong, then he makes a report to the appropriate department or Minister or the organisation. He has authority to make such recommendations as he thinks fit. The complainant is also entitled to a copy of the Ombudsman's recommendation. The procedure then is as follows:

(a) The Minister then has 21 days in which to decide whether the Chief Ombudsman's recommendation should be accepted.

(b) If the Minister has not otherwise directed in writing within 21 days, the Minister, department or organization concerned has a public duty to observe the Chief Ombudsman's recommendation from the twenty-second day after which it was made. In other words, the Ombudsman's recommendation becomes legally binding if it is not vetoed by the concerned Minister. The Minister is to give the grounds for his veto which are then published in the Gazette and laid before Parliament.

The courts also have a significant role to play under the Act, but only after recourse to the Ombudsman. Courts can review: (i) the initial unfavourable decision by a department; Minister, or organisation; (ii) Ombudsman's unfavourable determination on at least two grounds, viz., "without jurisdiction" and "error on the police of the record"; (iii) a Minister's veto on the ground that it contains material errors of law.

The Act also provides for the preparation of the Directory of Official Information containing (a) the structure and functions of departments and organisations; (b) a general description of the kinds of documents held; (c) a list of manuals and documents containing policies, principles, rules or guidelines, in accordance with which decisions are made.

Some Other Countries

Freedom of Information Act 1986 (Manitoba-Canada) provides for a complete system of disclosure of information. There are certain exceptions dealing with such matters as cabinet prescribes. In case of denial right of appeal has also been granted.

In France the law on Freedom of Access to Administrative Documents enacted in 1978 has flourished into a legal right to access to official information. The 1978 law on the Access to Official Information of the Netherlands has grown into a legal right to Freedom of Information, Norway and Denmark have less secrecy than India. In the Scandinavian countries, there is the institution of Ombudsman to whom the Government is accountable and must give all the information asked for. The Act of 1970 in both countries, giving citizens a statutory right of access to official documents, have grown, *inter alia,* out of these existing procedures, in Sweden the Constitution itself contains a provision that all governmental information is public unless specifically exempted from the general rule. This law dates back to the year 1766 and has been, thus, in practice for more than 230 years. This clearly proves that legitimate national interest can be well protected under the condition of administrative openness.

Emerging Concept of Cyber Technology

Now-a-days the most talked about phenomenon is the Internet. Everyone wants a piece of this pie. They sell books, music, software, toys, flowers, food, cloth, cosmetics and everything you want. It is on line. It has become an effective tool in catalyzing economic and commercial activities apart from other activities.

The internet has actually military origin Engineers thought imperative to create a network of computers that would continue to function if some parts were destroyed in combat. Towards that end Internet architects created an electronic space decoupled from the geographic world. The first steps were taken in 1969. This provided researchers access to remote computing resources by linking system operated by different branches of the Military. Subsequently more steps were taken in the Internet working. Now "Internet" and "Cyberspace" have captured the attention of the scholars and other intelligent people throughout the world. The term "Internet" refers to those networks which uses TCP protocol suite to route information whereas "cyberspace" includes the broad range of non-physical places where electronic communications takes place. The current focus of the use of this mechanism has aroused more legal problems. It poses threat to the constitutional framework in the countries. In USA a debate has started regarding the state regulations which possesses threat to their federalism. Federal constitution provides Contract Clause, the full faith and credit clause and the Due Process Clause. The cyberspace has threatened the legal system in USA and the concept of new territorialism has seized the cases. In **American Libraries Association (ALA)** v. **Patika,** a Federal Court flatly ruled that the states have no jurisdiction to reach cyber law. In USA a number of commentators have seized on this issue. Some argue that the

Internet should be subjected only to consensual self-regulation. Some argue that the Internet should be regulated by National Government. Some argue that there should be uniform federal law or regulations to pre-empt state regulations governing on line trade. Some argue that there should be international regulations or conventions to regulate cyberspace. Actually this area is posing threat to trade and commerce and other fields of activities globally. The United Nations Commission on International Trade Law (UNCITRAL) adopted the *Model Law on Electronic Commerce* in 1996. The General Assembly of United Nations by its Resolution No. 51/162 dated 30th January, 1997 recommended that all States should give favourable considerations to the said Model Law when they enact or revise their laws. The Model Law provides for equal legal treatment of users of electronic communication and paper based communication.

Pursuant to a recent declaration by member countries, the World Trade Organization is likely to form a work programme to handle its work in this area including the possible creation of multilateral trade deals through the medium of electronic commerce. The WTO conference at Seattle was to focus on this issue, held on November 30, 1999, 135 nations, representing three-fourth of world population haggled over access and markets, etc. The WTO is primarily to promote the freest possible flow of trade globally. India is also a member of WTO and was participating in the discussions at Seattle. Primarily the focus was on the world's oldest and the newest industry: Agriculture and electronic commerce (e-commerce). But the conference could not make any success. So the present attentions of the world is on Agriculture and e-commerce.

Nationally in India, the scholars are focusing attention on federal regulations of cyberspace and Internet. Some argue that the e-commerce should be free from bureaucratic controls imposed by the national regulations often investment schemes are sent by e-mail as well as through posting on websites and on-line bulletin boards promising to make them rich quickly government. Others argue that there was a need to provide a legal framework for smooth conduct of electronic commerce. Sathapathy wrote an article in *Economic and Political Weekly* and focused attention on the legal framework for e-commerce. He also argued that changes in national and international law need to be made to facilitate e-commerce by recognizing paper equivalence of electronic documents and contracts. Such changes must also legally recognize digital signatures and allow accredited certification providers to authenticate the identity of a sender of an electronic document and integrity of the accompanying document and integrity of the accompanying digital signature. It is presumed that such providers from the private sector would have to be organization of repute and of high professional standards to enthuse confidence in trade, both the national and international level. There was also need to modernize penal laws to cope with the computer related frauds such as hacking malicious falsification or eraser of data, software thefts, software attacks, etc., legislation was necessary to ensure data protection and privacy. For example, two relatively new legislations "Computer Misuse Act 1990" and "Data Protection Act 1998", precisely address these issues in the U.K. hitherto not covered by criminal law. Therefore, in India also the national government felt the need to enact legal framework to facilitate e-commerce. Security related frauds alone on Internet have increased. For example, in USA the *Security and Exchange Commission* of USA had already filed 40 cases in 1998 alleging that on-line stock scams cost hundred of investors millions of dollars. On-line frauds takes various forms. Customers are emerging patterns of frauds show that younger and affluent persons, who often use the Internet for shopping and investments, more easily fall prey to on-line frauds. Internet technology makes it very easy for frauders to react a number of potential victims at very little cost. Recently it has been reported in the newspapers that out of 5 commercial transactions in USA one is fraud.

In India, Mr. D.R. Mehta, Chairman of SEBI has appointed a Committee under U.T. Mumbai, Mr. B.P. Pathak to suggest ways to introduce share trading on Internet. A senior official of SEBI told the *Times of India* that trading on the net could be allowed even if the cyber bill was not passed by the Parliament. If the bill is passed, payment could be made on the net itself.

The National Stock Exchange already has a system compatible with net trading. Other Stock Exchanges will have to upgrade their systems to joint net trading. In the new system anyone assigned a password by his broker, would be able to trade on the net. The broker will also give the net trading. The broker will also give the client an exposure limit. Similarly, *Bhartiya International* is setting up a trading office in New York at the cost of 1.5 million dollars. Similar offices are being set up in European countries. Internet market research is also increasing. Business, retail and education also fuelling the growth adding more Internet contract suppliers and foreign entries in Asia. IDC (India) will also grow. Internet subscribers would grow 130 per cent base. China, India and Southern Korea would be key regional areas of opportunity. Internet banking too is fast becoming another services channel. ICICI Bank was the first among the new private banks to launch its net banking service. Now the Bank had 48,000 trading customers. Its net is increasing day-by-day. In the meantime, Banks are setting up Website that can give information. In all the customers never had it so good.

It all requires e-commerce legislation on the following parameters:

(a) To facilitate e-commerce and governmental transactions among and within nations by validating and authorizing the use of electronic records and electronic signatures.
(b) To validate transactions through new information technologies and to promote and encourage their implementation.
(c) To promote uniformity of law relating to the use of electronic and similar technological means of effecting and performing commercial and governmental transactions.
(d) To support commercial practice.
(e) To simplify, clarify and modernize the law governing e-commerce and governmental interactions and

promote the developmental legal business infrastructure.

(f) To promote public confidence in the validity, integrity and reliability of such transactions.

(g) To minimize the incidence of forged international and unintentional alteration.

(h) To facilitate electronic filing of documents with national, state and local government agencies; promote efficient delivery of government services through reliable electronic records.

It all requires some parameters at the implementation level.

Salient Features of the Information of Technology Act 2000

The Central Government introduced the Information Technology Bill in the Parliament on 16th December, 1999 which was to form the basis for Cyber law legislation to provide the legal framework for electronic commerce (e-commerce) and to enable electronic governance in the country. The bill also sought to make consequential amendments in the Indian Penal Code 1860 (IPC) and the Indian Evidence Act 1872, the Bankers' Book Evidence Act 1891 and the Reserve Bank of India Act 1934 and for matters connected therewith. The Bill was passed by Lok Sabha on 16th May, 2000 after making some modifications got approved from Rajya Sabha on 17th May, 2000 and received the President's assent on 9th June, 2000. It has come into force with effect from 17th October, 2000. The significant parts of the Act are as follows:

(i) It provides for a regulatory regime to supervise digital signature system, essential for carrying out financial transactions through internet and other electronic modes. It also provides for the appointment of Controller and other authorities for the purposes of the Act;

(ii) To enable electronic governance, it provides the use and acceptance of electronic records and agencies making interaction between citizen and government easy;

(iii) It also provides to create civil and criminal liabilities for contravention of the Act;

(iv) It also provides to publish an electronic gazette or official gazette where all regulations, rules, orders, bye-laws and notifications can be accessed over internet;

(v) It also makes illegal tempering with computer documents and publishing obscene information in electronic form;

(vi) It empowers the Controller to decrypt any coded information and direct any agency to intercept any information transmitted through any computer network;

(vii) It also provides for penalties. If any person without permission of the owner or any other person who is incharge of a computer, computer system or computer network:

(a) accesses or secures access to such computer, computer-system or computer network;

(b) downloads, copies or extracts any data, computer data base or information from such computer, computer system or computer network including information or data held or stored in any removable storage medium;

(c) introduces or causes to be introduced any computer contaminant or computer virus into any computer, computer system or computer network;

(d) damages or causes to be damaged any computer, computer system or computer network, data computer data base or any other program residing in such computer, computer system or computer network;

(e) disrupts or causes disruption of any computer, computer system or computer network;

(f) denies or causes the denial of access to any person authorized to access any computer, computer system or computer network by any means;

(g) provides any assistance to any person to facilitate access to a computer, computer system or computer network in contravention of the provisions of this Act, rules or regulations made thereunder; and

(h) charges the services availed of by a person to the account of another person by tampering with or manipulating any computer, computer system, or computer network, he shall be liable to pay damages by way of compensation not exceeding rupees one crore to the person so affected. It also provides for penalty for failure to furnish information, return, etc., to the Controller of the certifying authority;

(viii) It provides for the establishment of Adjudicatory authorities and the appellate authorities;

(ix) It also provides penalties for offences, e.g., tampering with computer source and documents hacking, etc., and for contraventions committed outside India but involving a computer or networks located in India; and it also provides that any Police Officer not below the rank of a Dy. Superintendent is empowered to search and arrest without warrant any person for violating the provisions of the Act. It also provides for confiscation of any computer system floppies, compact disks, tape drivers or any other accessories, etc.;

(x) It also provides for the constitution of a committee called Cyber Regulation Advisory Committee; and

(xi) The Act shall have overriding effect.

First and foremost, trust. When consumers and producers engage in a transaction, they seldom think about it, yet it is the principal force underpinning digital transactions. What matters is authenticity: that the parties to the deal are who they claim to be, that the cash is 'good; and the receipt genuine, the goods are what they were claimed to be security and privacy: that the data underlying the transaction is protected against hacking; integrity: the message received is the same as the one sent; guarantee: the message sent is actually received by the addressed party; And lastly, no reputability: that the sender can't deny having sent the message. The real challenge lies in ensuring these by putting place systems and mechanisms which bolster trust when business is conducted between parties with no prior knowledge of or dealings with each other, and making such transactions inexpensive.

Comparison shopping would give consumer the supreme power to compare shop across several shopping males locating in different countries ultimately what has to be assured that the security, scalability and extensibility of design allow the successful marriage of commerce and technology. In sum the digital commerce would revolutionize the retailing, marketing and advertising of products.

General Observation

The concept of right to know or information has spread across the entire democratic spectrum world over. Present era may be characterised as an era of information explosion. Our lives have been taken over by information technology. It has become a vital element in the scheme of open and transparent democratic process. Growing importance of this right is being noticed in both developed and developing countries of the world, e.g., U.S.A., Australia, Canada, South Africa, Malaysia.

The right to know along with its allied concept of open government has many faces, one of them being the duty of government to supply information to the people at large unless it is of prohibited degree, i.e., relating to national security, etc.

Some of the inspiring legislations on this topic in other countries include Freedom of Information Act 1966 of U.S.A., Freedom of Information Act 1982 of Australia and Access to Information Act 1980 of Canada, which portray the merits of openness of their system and are invaluable guide to us. These enactments should catch the imagination of our legislators as also executive to catch up with the above countries so that the concept of freedom of information may reach out to the maximum areas in the government process.

END NOTES

Vishva-Bharti Annual Report (1923) The Vishva Bharti Quarterly, January 1924, p. 410.

Tagore, Rabindranath: The Function of Library—Address of the Chairman Reception Committee, All-India Library Conference, Calcutta, December 1928, Kolkata: Vishva Bharti, August 1951, p. 1-6.

Tagore, Rabindranath 'On the Edges of Time' Calcutta, Orient Longman, p. 51.

11

Positive Results and Difficulties in using RTI Act

The aim of RTI is to empower people in democratic India to ensure fairness and accountability of the government officials and elected representatives. But it will take a long time before the Right to Information Act settles down, i.e., people uses it for extracting proper information and not frivolous information which leads to waste of time for the system. In that case it becomes contravening to development of the people.

Amending the Right to Information

A Threat for Indian Democracy

Recently in the month of July 2006, the Cabinet cleared an amendment to the Right to Information (RTI), which is largely being seen as an attempt to curtail the scope of RTI and obviously this cannot be a healthy sign—as far as the democratic governance of this country is concerned. When RTI was introduced in this country the decision was not taken whimsically, it was the result of ceaseless struggle spanning over past few decades. The intention behind granting this Right to Information was to free the bureaucratic mechanism from the evils of *Babudom;* however by suggesting such amendments the government has essentially surrendered the whole ethics of RTI to the *Babus* themselves.

Information on Denying Information

Under the Right to Information (RTI) Act 2005 an Indian citizen can obtain 'information'—in any available format—relating to any government decision or policy or activity except what has been kept outside the purview by the Act itself. Under it, every public authority has the obligation to provide information and maintain records about its operations. On July 20, 2006, the Union Cabinet approved an Amendment Bill to the Right to Information Act 2005 that would exclude nothing made by officials on files related to all areas except social and development sector projects. The proposed amendments will permanently shield the bureaucracy from accountability, the disinfectant power of transparency and allow them to function in an arbitrary manner. They will also shield the corrupt and deal a body blow to the efforts of people to fight corruption and the arbitrary exercise of power. Both these amendments relate essentially to the process of decision-making. The first one is to make file notings a category of information that can be concealed. If this made an act then the bureaucracy will be able to disable the Right to Information Act as far as its own functioning is concerned. The second amendment relates to barring access to cabinet notes even after the decision making process is complete—pulling the decision-making process of cabinet decisions into a permanent black hole. For a common Indian citizen, the process of decision-making is of crucial importance. When the Right to Information announced was widely welcomed by almost everyone except the hidden beneficiaries of secrecy. There are numerous instances after the implementation of RTI—when it was observed that it actually brought fresh air into our democratic participation. However, much was going behind the scene, those who are threatened by this have waged a relentless battle behind the scenes to reverse the flow of power to the ordinary citizen.

The amendments will change the very soul of the Act so that the decision can be revealed. To put it otherwise, the slum dweller would know the decision to demolition; the contractor would get the contract but none would know the level of fairness in the decision taken. What a shame, the amendment would help only to hide the aspect of bribe and corruption. Certainly, this is not going to help ensure fairness, which is the prime motive of Right to Information.

Government must realize that RTI is meant to re-establish the missing link between the government and the governed. The people of this country has a legitimate right to know about policies that lead to foodgrain stocks being made available, or the manner in which taxpayers' money is being spent, decisions related to health and medicines, power, agricultural policy and genetic engineering and governance itself. We are representative democracy, the hundred million people of this country cannot sit in the Parliament or witness a Cabinet meeting but it is a matter of right for each and every citizen of this country to know what the possible consequences of a particular decision could be before being faced with a *fait accompli*.

Shamefully the Government declared that these amendments are aimed to "remove ambiguities and make it more effective" while exempting secretary level "file notings" from this ambit. The only exception would be file notings on social and development issues, Information and Broadcasting Minister Priya Ranjan Dasmunsi told reporters, "The amendments to the Right to Information Act 2005 will remove the ambiguities and will make its provisions more effective and progressive". Dasmunsi said, "However, the Central Information Commission (CIC) as well as Prime Minister Manmohan Singh were said to be apprehensive about it. According to government sources, the Prime Minister felt that giving access to file notings could be misused to target individual bureaucrats. The UPSC had also requested that the sensitive area of its selection process be put out of the purview of the Act".

We, at Manavadhikar Samajik Manch share the concern of the whole nation with regard to the proposed impediments on Right to Information. We demand that the Government of

India must ensure that the *babus* of this country stop playing with the spirit of Indian Democracy.

What are File Notings

Under the normal bureaucratic practice, the files/records/documents relating to any government activity move from one individual government officer to another—both vertically and horizontally in the bureaucratic hierarchy—before a decision is reached—or a policy is made. The government officers involved in any normal process can range from Lower Division Clerks to Secretary of a Ministry to the Union Minister. Normally, each time a file or document changes hands within the bureaucratic system and hierarchy, the bureaucrat handling that file makes his written remarks, observations recommendations and gives his opinion. The final outcome of any government decision is based on and is decided by these observations, recommendations, opinions or the 'file notings' by various government officer/s.

Exposure through File Notings

1. Price Waterhouse Coopers (PWC) got a consultancy contract from Delhi Government. File notings obtained under Delhi Right to Information Act revealed that PWC was at 10th position. In fact, it did not even qualify in the preliminary round. File notings revealed "how World Bank pressurized Delhi Government to bring up PWC, cancel bids, do rebidding, change selection criteria, etc., till such time as PWC got the contract". File notings also revealed how some honest officers protested but their protests were not accepted.
2. 150 *jhuggies* were razed in Mayur Vihar. DDA said no land was available to resettle them. File notings revealed that 700 plots of land had actually been developed by DDA in Kondli for resettling them. Perhaps, DDA officials wanted to sell these plots clandestinely in association with land sharks.

File Notings and Accountability

A government file has two parts : papers under consideration (PUC) and file notings. File notings contain the comments, reasons and other details pertaining to the deliberations about Paper Under Consideration (PUC). Therefore, this act as the trail of whole decision making process. Thus one can easily make out details like who agreed/disagreed with the decision, who all were a part of the decision making process, what factors were considered and what were not considered, etc. And this laid bare the whole decision making process of government bodies.

The proposed amendments will permanently shield the bureaucracy from accountability, the disinfectant owner of transparency and allow them to function in an arbitrary manner. They will also shield the corrupt and deal a body blow to the efforts of people to fight corruption and the arbitrary exercise of power.

Here is a snap shot of sonic of the many successful cases of the use of the Right to Information Act applied across a range of public services ensure that the citizens work gets done.

Official Fined Rs. 18,000 under Info Act

In the second incident of penalizing an erring officer under the Right to Information Act in Madhya Pradesh, Chief Information Commissioner (CIC) T.N. Shrivastava fined Morena District Woman and Child Development Officer (DWCDO) Sajan Aluna for failing to provide information sought under the Act within the time limit and not abiding by the appellate officer's order.

The CIC imposed the fine of Rs. 18,000 after not being satisfied with the explanation given by Mrs. Aluna, who was earlier given show cause notice on the second appeal by Mr. Balwant Singh Haihayavanshi who had sought certain information from the department on December 31, 2005.

The DWCDO rejected the application on January 8 on the ground that the applicant had been suspended after preliminary inquiry.

On an appeal, the Morena District Collector directed the DWCDO on February 8 to provide copies of the document on payment as the applicant had not sought any confidential document.

After dilly-dallying on one pretext or the other, the DWCDO allowed the applicant to deposit Rs. 1200 on March 14 to provide copies of the documents. The second appeal was made as the required documents were not supplied by April 14.

The Chief Information Commissioner found Mrs. Aluna's conduct as "unfortunate" and directed to provide the required documents within seven days.

MLA Funds

Every MLA in Delhi gets crores of rupees every year to spend on works for the development of his constituency. This is the people money. MLA as should ask the people of their constituencies before taking decisions on how this money should be spent. However, most of the time this consultation is not done and money is spent on works, which may not be of high priority for the people.

The people of Pandav Nagar wanted one street to be made. They approached their MLA with a request to get this done through the MLA fund. The MLA refused saying that my fund have already been exhausted. People applied under the Right to Information Act to know about this work sanctioned using their MLA's funds and also the balance amount, if any. They were shocked to know that hardly any work had been carried out through MLA fund and almost the entire amount was lying unused. Equipped with this information the people again approached their MLA. It was difficult for the MLA to refuse the request this time.

There is little doubt that the Right to Information (RTI) Act 2005 is one of the most important and revolutionary pieces of legislation enacted in independent India. Some would even regard it as "the most important", since no other law has the potential to change the work-culture of practically the entire Indian society; its impact is also the most widespread as it places an instrument of power in the hands of every citizen of the country irrespective of any category or classification.

The fact that the law was passed is itself little short of a miracle. One indeed wonders how our members of Parliament, who have so much to hide—notice the large number of criminal and other cases against many of them—should have voted for it to turn it into a reality. One, therefore, pauses to ponder whether they did it out of a certain compulsion or because they indeed saw its virtues.

A story was that when in 1966 the US President, Lyndon Johnson (LBJ) signed the Freedom of Information Act, he declared the noble objectives behind it. He said, he did it "with a deep sense of pride that the United States is an open society in which the people's right to know is cherished and guarded". Later, however, his Press Secretary Bill Moyers recalled:

> "What few people knew at the time is that LBJ had to be dragged kicking and screaming to the signing ceremony. He hated the very idea of the Freedom of Information Act". One wonders if this may not be true of several of our legislators. However, now that it is a reality, we shall find even those who hated it in private, swear by it in public."

The legislation when passed was greeted by two kinds of reactions. First, there were those who saw in it "a magic wand", which would substantially root out corruption which so plagues our daily life. On the other hand were those (I will not dub them as cynics) who thought that the legislation and the information commissions set up under it would go the way of several earlier acts and commissions, that, after enjoying their moment in the limelight, went into a limbo. After all, the earlier Freedom of Information Act 2002, they point out, failed to take off, and so what was there to prevent the present act going the same way?

Both these views appear to be extreme. The truth lies somewhere in between and on the users of the act, will depend which way the scales of this balance tilt. So far, the experience has been salutary. In Delhi itself, it is reported that hundreds of persons—mostly belonging to the depressed and the poor classes—have received their ration cards and electricity connections in no time by exercising their right to information and asking relevant departments reasons for the delay and names of those officials responsible for it.

Access to Information

But obviously, the legislation has not been a success all the way, and at times for the wrong reasons. One of these is that many persons view this right and the information commissions as agencies for redressal of their grievances — which they are not. Someone's pension is delayed and he feels that the RTI Commission can get his pension released. This, of course, it cannot. While the information received through the RTI Act may go a long way in setting a person's grievance, by itself, however, the commission has no powers to intervene either in a dispute or order an erring official to attend to matters he is supposed to, unless it involves providing access to the information sought for by the complainant. This point needs to be clearly understood lest the information commissions in the States and at the Centre are unnecessarily burdened with such applications which only lead to a waste of time and effort and further disappoint the applicant.

Then there may be persons who may ask for information only for the heck of it. They could at times prove to be of great nuisance. This is understandable to an extent but with a heap of useless demands and complaints, the legislation and the commissions could collapse under this onslaught. So far, these fears have proved unfounded. It is reported that Delhi, which passed the Act in 2001, has so far received some 14,000 applications/complaints. If this is so, then taking into consideration the fact that the Delhi Government has about 120 departments, this would mean a total of 116 appeals/ complaints per department over a period of five years, thus meaning less than three complaints per department per year.

This number will, of course, grow and is likely to grow steeply as awareness about the legislation spreads. Already this profile seems to be changing. The Central Information

Commission which has been in existence for about three months now, has received almost 300 cases, that is 100 cases per month: a marked step-up against the figures cited earlier. If only everyone who moved a case under the RTI Act paused for a moment to consider if it would have a serious and substantial effect on things and not for the sake of harassment to some official or some department, a lot of good would be done for both sides, that is, those seeking the information as also those responsible for making it accessible.

Come to think of it, the right to information addresses the basics. The present act has made the process of asking for information an extremely simple one. Yet, it could be surmised that if this request is couched in legalese, he/she would have a greater opportunity to get what he or she wants. Thus, a large number of requests are likely to be received in verbose, legalistic language which only would tend to delay and complicate matters. Thus, the farther the lawyers are kept away from the RTI by both the parties, the applicant and the public authority, the better it would be. On the other hand, the legal community would be among those who would most use the RTI. That, of course, is welcome.

There is one apprehension that needs to be spelt out. This involves the possibility of large-scale destruction of sensitive files and records of different government departments. It is no secret that the best way to bury an issue of corruption is by destroying files related to it. This is not difficult and seems to be resorted to liberally. A colleague in the income-tax department once told me that his office was plagued by a large number of rats which proved to be a blessing in disguise for the staff there. For monetary considerations, they would put pieces of cheese on files which threatened inconvenience to certain "important" clients, so that at night, along with the pieces of cheese, the mice nibbled the files too, which were later reported as damaged and destroyed. Who can fault this system? And in most cases, a file in any government department passes through so many hands that it is impossible to pin down the responsibility of its destruction on any individual.

What then, is there to prevent sensitive files from disappearing? The standard reply in such cases to requests for information would be "not available". It is imperative, therefore, that a committee be set up for recommending not only ways of record-management (those guidelines are there but are very old and there is not enough awareness about them in government departments) but for ways for pin-pointing responsibility and also suggesting action to be taken against erring officials. As a matter of principle, harsh action should be taken against the last three officials who have handled (and "misplaced") a sensitive file. This would make it in the interest of at least one of them to see that the file or its copy is always available. Ways have also to be found for maintenance of government data in forms other than government files.

As for agencies responsible for ensuring the availability of information on public authorities to citizens, in the three months now that the Central Information Commission has been in existence, it has so far showed little evidence of the activism.

Mixed Reaction

Given this very broad parameter, it can easily be gathered that "conceding" information is no small task, and the heat is likely to build up as time passes. On the other hand, it may not. For if the public authorities reconcile themselves to this changed atmosphere — the transition from a closed administration to an open one may be smooth. As of now, it is a mixed reaction. There are some public authorities who have without much prodding, voluntarily opened up their records for scrutiny. On the other, we have an extreme case like that of the Hindustan Aeronautics, which took the absurd position that they were not a "public authority", and hence not covered under the RTI Act. And to bolster their claim, they asked for an opinion from a local lawyer. In another case earlier, there was the case of an organisation under the Ministry of Defence which on its own decided that they were outside the purview of the RTI Act. Later much the wiser, they retracted the order.

But for the legislation to be truly effective, all three: members of the public, the public authorites and the information commission, have to play an active and meaningful role.

The government of the day has to see that the RTI Act is not weakened in any manner. If there are loopholes in the act, these must be attended to and rectified but always with a view to making it more convenient for a person to obtain information and not the other way round. Earlier defined in one sentence, which is: "To talk of amendments such as closing of file makes it impossible for any citizen of India to have access to notings or revealing names of officials to get any piece of information from any has finally died down. Our Right to Information Act is one of the most powerful Acts in the world and should remain as such.

Together with this, it is incumbent on the government—which has shown so much sagacity and courage in passing the Act—to ensure that the agencies responsible for implementing the Act are not starved of funds and facilities so that they can function to their full efficiency. There is not much evidence of this as of now. The government should realise that it is in its own interest to see that the goodwill it has earned and created by passing the Act should not turn into disappointment by weakening the implementation of it.

What is important is that for the first time in history, an instrument of great power has been placed in the hands of the ordinary citizen. He can now question bureaucratic and political masters which can go a long way in curbing corruption and making the entire administration more responsible, transparent and responsive to public needs. It would perhaps be a tragedy if the RTI and the information commissions are turned into another insignificant and ineffective cog in the giant, corrupt and apathetic wheel of our polity and administration.

Loopholes and Road Ahead : Conclusions and Suggestions

The Constitution of India as a living social document is not a strait-jacket, rather it is dynamic to bring about a new social order. When such pleas are urged in the familiar name of nationalism strong traditions or welfare overtones, the courts are on trails and must prove, that constitutional decisions are not mere rhetorical material for lip service but the obligatory essence of our cherished national ethos. A kaleidoscopic view of the jurisprudential dimensions over the years has demonstrated that the law evolves. In this evolutionary process, it has been seen that the judiciary, including the Apex Court, and the jurists have played a dynamic role in adopting the law to the needs of the time, it is a movement from status to contract; from idealism to realism; from analytical view of law to social engineering or functional approach to jurisprudence, and in short from judicial passivist to judicial activist movement.

Citizens' right to be informed freely is accepted, but the need to protect certain vital national interests is also accepted. So far secrecy has been the rule rather than exception and this trend has now to be reversed. That secrecy may be necessary in the interests of national security and sensitive diplomatic matters, police investigation, privacy of an individual, State pre-budgetary secrets, trade secrets, voluntary information sources, departmental communications, etc., is beyond doubt. Still the greatly expanding role of the modern State demands openness. Hence, a balance has to be struck. As Bhagwati J., says: "Open Government is the new democratic culture of an open society towards which every liberal democracy is moving and our country should be no exception".

In the above conflict between factors necessitating openness and those requiring secrecy, the task of the Broadcasting Corporation is very difficult when it comes to compile and publish Government information especially in absence of any well-defined statutory "Right of Access". Thus, as per the Government practice where secrecy is the rule and openness an exception,—the documents are "classified", "confidential", and "personal and not for publication". A strong regimen of statutory enactments and Rules guard the Government secrecy. The most draconian, however, is the Official Secrets Act 1923. Particularly important is Section 5 of this Act which is an "omnibus and catch all provisions covering all kinds of secret official information whatever be the effect of disclosure. Literally read, it is the "disclosure" which is punishable and not the purpose of disclosure or prejudicial effect on certain interest deserving of protection in the national interest.

The above statutory authority, however, has been rarely used, still the recommendations of the Press Council of India to replace Section 5 by a more specifically worded enactment needs to be accepted.

In a democracy active participation from any walks of society is essential. Real democracy requires three basic aspects—accurate information, equal and effective participation of all citizens in day-to-day governance and transparency and accountability on the part of those holding public office. Every action of all the wings of the Government, Executive, Legislature and Judiciary should be transparent. Transparency even at the grassroots level say Gram Panchayats is quite useful in prevention of corruption, which has spread like an epidemic.

The exercise of these rights may be subject to certain restrictions, but these shall only be such as are provided by law and are necessary, i.e., the respect of the rights or reputation of others, for the protection of national security or public order or public health or morals.

We may compare the right to freedom of speech and expression with the right to information in a way that "If the right to expression is output, the right to information is input. Without adequate and correct inputs, the output cannot be good.

The citizens and NGOs like 'Janshakti'. The Mazdoor Kisan Shakti Sangathan have started campaign for transparency in public spending and are working as a Watchdog. The right to information is required to be available not only against the State but also against the banking, insurance, finance, transport, universities, etc.

As per the Chairman of the Press Council of India, Mr. Justice P.B. Sawant, "the single most cause responsible for corruption in society was the barrier to information. It facilitates clandestine deals, arbitrary decisions, manipulations and embezzlements. Transparency in dealings with every detail exposed to the public view, should go a long way in curtailing corruption in public life. Sunlight is the best disinfectant. Access to information will prove both an effective deterrent and potent disinfectant.

In absence of the right to information and due to the Official Secrets Act, everything is secret unless otherwise specified. The right to information would convert such position into everything open unless there is a specific restriction for a valid reasons. While emphasising the need for such an Act Mr. Justice Sawant said, "In a democracy, those who manage the affairs of the society are no more than the trustees of the people, and do so, subject to their giving account of their acts of omissions and commissions whenever called upon. The access to the relevant material, having a bearing on the actions and inactions of those who govern, is a prerequisite of a participative governance".

Of course, the necessity of secrecy in some sensitive areas cannot be denied. But if in the name of national security our people are denied even information already well known to our potential enemies and their allies, then it should make us sit up and wonder. And secrecy in the matter of defence purchases involving hundreds and thousands of crores should not be permitted to be so abused as to give a handle to politicians and bureaucrats for indulging in corruption with impunity.

The first Judges case gave a lot of latitude to Government in the matter of privilege in respect of official documents. But it is gratifying to find that in **S.R. Bommai's case,** it has been held by all the nine Judges that Article 74, clause (2), prohibits the disclosure of only the ultimate advice tendered by the minister to the President but not of the documents and materials on which that advice was based. This thus allows even Cabinet papers to be disclosed to the Court. If people have easier access to the decision making processes, then much of the corruption could be controlled. The Prime Minister need not be so pessimistic about the absence of a magic wand with him to curb corruption. He needs only to implement promise to enact a law conferring the right to information, as in certain developed countries, and then see the result.

In Sweden, Canada and several other countries there are special statutes conferring the right. The statute lays down a procedure for inspection of government files. They can be inspected and copies thereof obtained, much in the same manner as we can here inspect Court records and obtain copies. The authority can no doubt reject a request, but reasons have to be given for the refusal. The refusal is subject to an appeal to the Ombudsman, an independent institution like our Lok Ayukta or Lok Pal but with much wider powers.

While we all talk of the right to information *vis-à-vis* the executive it is also for consideration whether the right should not be extended in relation to Judges, also while acting administratively. Their judicial work is of course all open and speaking, hence above board. But the Judges guard the secrecy of their administrative decisions and recommendations as jealously as any minion of the Executive. Thomas Jefferson had observed that "our Judges are as honest as other men, and not more so. They have, with others, the same passions for party. For power and the privileges of their corps". Justice Jackson once observed "judges are more often bribed by their ambition and loyalty than by money". And our own Justice Krishna Iyer has been crying hoarse that "corruption inside the institution, going by credible information circulated by whisper, is mounting."

We all know of a case in which, a Judicial Secretary of a North-Eastern State was recommended of High Court judgeship by the Chief Justice of the High Court as well as the Chief Justice of India, apart from the Ministers, even though he did not fulfil the basic, qualification of ten years judicial experience. And ex-President Venkataraman has put on record a case where the Union Law Minister's wife who had just completed the minimum 10 years at the bar was similarly recommended by the Chief Justices—In the first case the Supreme Court on its judicial side prevented the swearing in and in the second; the President himself put his foot down.

There, are thousands of advocates and judicial officers who possess the minimum eligibility. What has further to be considered is their relative merit, their character, their prejudices or freedom from them, their temperament. In the United States of America every nomination by the President for such appointment is subject to confirmation by the Senate. The Senate Judiciary Committee has been headed for umpteen years by the redoubtable Senator Edward Kennedy. It does not function on party lines at all. The candidate appears before it and may be subjected to a gruelling cross-examination. Witnesses for and against him may also be examined,—not that it is always done. As a result sometimes the President himself has withdrawn his nomination. At others, the nominee has been rejected by the Senate. Our Rajya Sabha corresponds to their Senate. Perhaps time has not yet arrived when the public here may accept a similar role being given to the Rajya Sabha. It may be some time in the future, when there is less of politicking in all our institutions. The alternative proposal for a Judicial Commission should however commend general acceptance. Whether final powers are revested in the Government; as proposed by our Law Minister or should remain with the Chief Justices, as held in the second Judges case, neither position is wholly satisfactory. The difference is only of degrees.

Another area in which the need of transparency arises was indicated in the recent remark of Justice Sawant. Justice Sawant observed in a T. V. interview that the Constitution has come to mean what the incumbent Chief Justice of India wants it to mean. He was alluding to the Chiefs power to pick and choose judges to man the Constitution Benches. In the United States the Chief Justice has no such power, as all the Judges must sit to decide each and every case. There the Chief Justice is sometimes in a minority while in our country he is always in a majority. This situation could perhaps be remedied by establishing some convention about the composition of Constitution Benches. For instance, it may consist of only the senior most judges, or something like that. What is required is the Introduction of greater transparency and the elimination of secret subjectivity in the matter.

It will indeed be a good thing if our judiciary takes the lead in introducing greater transparency accountability and objectivity in its own working while enforcing it against the executive.

Transparency or right to know covers the demand of the public to be authentically informed about the functioning of the government. Every politically alert person desires to play a part in the direction of the affairs of the community. Thereby he realizes his identity and feels he is a public contributory to social welfare A system where man matters is one where every man affects the world around him. To quote Dr. Arnold,

> "The desire to take part in the affairs of Government is the highest desire of a well-regulated mind."

A voice of protest is, indeed, the essence of progress of a nation. George Bernard Shaw has beautifully described the man responsible for progress of the world:

> "The reasonable man adapts himself to the world, the unreasonable one persists in trying to adapt the world to him. Therefore, all progress depends on the unreasonable man."

A culture of individual action, political conscience and public spirit is the basis for the success of a democracy. This human potential which is essential for social development can be ignited only through intellectual alertness and access to information. Even a Parliamentary Opposition cannot effectively debate unless it has the reach to truth and the readiness to use it.

Democracy becomes a delusion and elections an illusion if freedom of opinion and expression and opportunity for the citizenry to walk in and pick up all facts relevant to public interest, are not a reality. Information without communication is social suffocation. A free society ceases to exist when the state engages itself in interception of thought and detention of truth in transit and then legitimizes this violation by legislative or executive means. Such sinister designs of the state must be opposed tooth and nail. President Roosevelt said more than 50 years back, that, "we would rather die on our feet than live on our knees".

Right to information and communication of news and views has been a burning topic during the last several decades. The great countries of the world, whether democracies or communists, have been providing access to information to their subjects. Even the United Nations has recognized Freedom of Information as basic right. Article 19 of the Universal Declaration of Human Rights 1948 coupled with Article 19 of the International Covenant on Civil and Political Rights 1966 guarantee freedom of opinion and expression including freedom to seek, service and import information and ideas through any media regardless of frontiers. Mr. Amadon Mahtar M'Bow, Director General of UNESCO had set up in 1971 an International Commission for the study of world communication problems. Mr. Sean MacBride headed that Commission. Report of the Sean MacBride Commission titled "Many Voices comprehensive study of the New World, One World" Information is and Communication Order. Foreword to the MacBride Report by Mr. A.M. M'Bow, Director General of UNESCO, a distinguished statesman shows that communication is at the heart of all social intercourse.

The question is why and what information and communication is needed? The answer is simple, so that every person may be well informed to judge for himself the issues that affect his life, his national destiny and international unity. The UNESCO Declaration 1978 recognises, "exercise of freedom of opinion, expression, and information, as an integral part of human rights and fundamental freedoms". Knowledge is power. Knowledge is yet another name for information. Knowledge always governs ignorance and people who desire to be their own masters must equip themselves with the power that knowledge gives.

To quote Justice Krishna Iyer:

> "It is edifying to drink deep from that undefiled well of public law an elixir to cure the jaundice of secrecy which

afflicts the *corpus juris* of many countries including Bharat."

And President Madison of USA remarked:

"The diffusion of knowledge is the only guardian of true liberty."

Justice Holmes reiterated the same point when he said, that the best guarantee for the triumph of good reasoning in a free society lies in preserving the 'free trade of ideas'. 'Knowledge is power' and a little knowledge is a dangerous thing. Fair access to information which affects the public weal, should be made possible by enactment of the law. Easy concealment of such information as 'classified secret' or otherwise by the administration should be made impossible.

Thus freedom to know, without which other freedoms become fragile or futile is, therefore, fundamental to the basic rights.

Freedom of information is a means to an end. The citizens are entitled, as of right to know all the information that does not threaten the security of the nation. The description of the debased power is not a peculiar American syndrome as reflected in Watergate scandal involving President Richard Nixon (1973) and Clinton-Monica Lewinsky. Sex-and-Lies probe (Zippergate) of 1998 involving President Bill Clinton. They can be found in Asia, Africa, Europe and Latin America as well. The top man in power is no different from the U.S. President's cocooned life style. In India a large number of top politicians are involved in one or the other criminal case. Former Prime Minister P.V. Narsimha Rao, former Cabinet Ministers Capt. Satish Sharma, Bhajan Lal, Buta Singh and Shiela Kaul are facing criminal trials in corruption cases. Bofors case and St. Kitts forgery cases are still being investigated. Sons of a former Prime Minister and a Cabinet Minister are involved in fertilizer scandal. A former Chief Minister of Bihar Laloo Prasad Yadav is facing prosecution in Rs. 850 crore Fodder scam. Sushil Sharma, a former President of Delhi Pradesh

Youth Congress (I) is behind the bars and facing trial in the infamous Tandoor case, Telgi Stamp scam. To know the various shady deals and deeds of our "rulers" we must have access to information so that we may decide for ourselves who should be our "ruler" and who not and why so.

Another reason for access to information is the various deals of the government. The functioning of the multi-national companies is shrouded in secrecy. The **Bhopal Gas tragedy** might have been averted or controlled in time, had the people around been aware of the deadly affects of the gas leakage. The world's largest industrial disaster would not have taken place in such magnitude if necessary information had been provided to the people residing in the vicinity of the gas plant. And it is shame for the successive Central and State governments who have failed to pay the compensation to the victims even 13 years after the tragedy. The actual reasons are veiled in secrecy and the citizens are entitled to know the same.

Big dams on Tehri and Narmada have been planned but the politicians and technocrats of 4 States have not only refused to face techno-economic facts but have also been altogether indifferent to the resettlement of ousters. They have also not shown sufficient regard for the environment and in case of Tehri, to the possible seismic dangers as well. The people of Gujarat were taken for a nebulous ride that the water of Narmada would irrigate all regions of the State and convert it into a rich paradise.

It is a sad commentary on the state of affairs that in case of Tehri, the Indian official engineers swore by the original safety designs and the height of the dam, till the Russians came on the scene and found it compelling to revise the designs and height. There had been a total lack of sensitivity to the public opinion, the lives and the interests of the local people. In mid 1998, the Gujarat State Government declared the World Commissioner of Dams to be a *persona non grata* (an unwelcome person). Thereupon the Central Government had advised the World Commissioner not to visit India to inspect the Narmada Sagar Dam. Why is the government shy of getting the technical aspect of the dam examined? Medha Patker, an eminent social worker is spear-heading the Narmada Bachao Andolan while Sunder Lal Bahuguna is struggling with the government for review of the designs and height of the Tehri Dam.

Whatever the ultimate fate of the Narmada Dam and Tehri Dam, the immediate beneficiaries have been the politicians, technocrats and contractors. Participation in development has been catapulted away by the vested interests to fill up their own coffers. The people are entitled to know about the dangers, if any in the construction of Tehri Dam and Narmada Dam Roles of the vested interests also need to be probed.

The Delhi government has been planning to construct a **dumping ground** for disposal of radiation and hospital waste near Najafgarh without informing the local residents about the hazards of the same. On coming to know of the plan of the government, the local residents have started an agitation for relocation of the site. Had the government informed the affected public well in advance by publication of all the relevant information, then the local residents and the Delhi Administration could have sorted out the problems at the very outset. Concealment of information by the State not only hampers the development works but also increases the cost manifold, which ultimately the common man has to bear. There is absolutely no logic in the government hiding its intentions from the people.

A healthy society must have a good appetite for enquiry and information and willingness to question the decision-makers. Right to information being integral to fundamental freedoms, the custodians of information should not resist disclosure of information. After all information imperialism is ultimately good neither for the 'governed' nor for the 'governors'. A democracy cannot function unless the people are permitted to know the working of the State's instrumentalities including the legislature and the judicature. Culture of open society and legacy of free information alone can build a free nation. Shady secrecy is a treachery since an enlightened and informed citizenry is the *sine qua non* of a true democracy. The hunger of power explodes when nefarious machinations to destroy the openness and democracy are exposed. Indian experience is the emergency excesses when people struck back and voted powerful Indira Gandhi out of power. In America, President Nixon had to resign in the face of Watergate scandal.

Denial of right to know and suppression of truth cannot be generally justified Plea of Thomas Jefferson for an informed people educated to discuss state policies is relevant even now. He says:

> "Every government degenerates when trusted to the rulers of the people alone. The people themselves, therefore, are its only safe depositories. And to render even them safe, their minds must be improved to a certain degree. This indeed is not all that necessary, though it may be essentially necessary. An amendment of our Constitution must here come in aid of the public education. The influence over government must be shared among all the people. If every individual which composes their mass, participates in the ultimate authority, the government will be safe."

Indian scene has been well described by Justice V.R. Krishna Iyer:

> "If forty years after freedom, Indian poverty, disease and squalor make quantum jumps in physical terms, whichever the Party or Coalition that governs, one of the major reasons is our informational bankruptcy and submissive literacy leading to what may be called the claque-clique-quack syndrome. People will suffer as underlings until they learn that power is their's."

Clive Ponting, a brilliant British Civil Servant, divulged the truth on the Belgrano affair to a Parliamentary Committee and was prosecuted for it by the Thatcher Government. In his book, *Clive Ponting* stresses the need for freedom of information:

> "Freedom of Information would open up the decision taking process. It would enable ordinary people and

small, often local, pressure groups to obtain access to important information affecting their own futures With this information they will be able to challenge and question the decisions that are being taken elsewhere inside the bureaucracy whether in White Hall or closer to home in the Town Halls. Genuine democracy is not a matter of simply voting once every four or five years for an MP and local councillor and then allowing the elected politicians a relatively free hand, in conjunction with the bureaucracy and important vested interests, to take whatever decisions they think best or most politically advantageous Genuine democracy is participation in decision taking It involves a whole public debate about policy before decisions are taken and not afterwards."

Naturally governments find life easier if they are able to debate policy questions in private, listen to those interest groups they find congenial or which are very powerful and then take decision that maximizes their own political advantage. But is this the best way of taking decisions from the point of view of the 'governed'? The answer has to be 'No'. In a democracy ordinary citizens should have the right to participate in the decisions that affect their ordinary everyday life.

If the level of secrecy is to be pushed to the top of the political agenda, we need to know why it is so important and what intangible benefits might flow from radical change. Based on my own experience in White Hall, I believe that there are two basic and linked reasons why FOI is important. First, its implementation would improve the quality of decision taking in White Hall by improving the flow and range of information. Second, FOI is about "Right to Know'. It is statement about where real power in a democratic society ought to lie. We must ask ourselves whether that right should, in effect, be restricted to the upper echelons in White Hall and the establishment or whether it should be diffused much more widely in society. Why should information be restricted to what government chooses to make available to those they govern? Surely a self-confident democracy can and should believe in a wide and well-informed public debate.

In my view, claustrophobic decision-taking in White Hall will continue to produce disastrous results simply because it precludes genuine open debate and as a consequence, powerful vested interests with access to the levers of power in White Hall can exercise undue influence at the expenses of the broader aspects of the public interest. While the decision-taking process remains deliberately shrouded in mystery, the vital process of learning from past mistakes does not take place . . . .

If people were better informed and so more able to influence the decision-taking process then this would bring about a major change in the way in which British democracy works. To White Hall this is not an attractive proposition. Information is power. Take away the exclusive right of White Hall to control information and its power is reduced and that of the ordinary individual increased. Top civil servants tend naturally to subscribe to the view that closed government is national government.

Therefore, independent informational institutions and channels must exist if the citizen is to defend himself through his right to know. Money power manipulates democracy where politics can be purchased and people drugged without compunction. It is imperative that right to information should be guaranteed even against industrial tycoons. The developing countries require this more because they are more vulnerable and ignorant as the tragedies inflicted by the Union Carbide Gas leakage and Oleum Gas leakage cases demonstrate. The suppression of corporate information claimed truth as casualty through disinformation. It is not possible for the public even to make available fact for judicial autopsy. The importance of greater access to corporate information is essential because a giant can affect the quality of life and of environment more than other comparable instrumentalities. If right to know the corporate information is stifled then the capitalists and the manufacturers together would become masters of the government.

The freedom of Press is vital to transparency in administration and an informed citizenry. Historically the newspapers are the information lungs of society and to suppress the newspapers is to suffocate people's free speech. But history also reminds us that there are grave dangers to people's right to information from the media itself. It is a fallacy to imagine that the press is always the guardian of information. Quite often it plays reverse role also. While governmental control of the media is totalitarian, the tycoon's control can be strangling and multi-nationals may tend to destabilize progressive stand. A Special Committee of the Canadian Senate identified some journalist decrease areas. Of those, the profit making and socially restrictive tendencies of the media can be serious maladies.

Notwithstanding these and many other identical factors, Pandit Jawahar Lal Nehru and many other great visionaries advocated the need for freedom of press. *Young India* was Gandhiji's weapon and Nehru founded *National Herald*. True to his tradition the first Prime Minister of India, Jawaharlal Nehru stressed:

> "I would rather have a completely free press with all the dangers involved in the wrong use of that freedom than a suppressed or regulated press."

Similarly, Thomas Jefferson has supported the need for freedom of press. He says:

> "If I had to choose between having a government without newspaper on the one hand and newspapers without a government on the other hand, I would have no hesitation in preferring the latter."

The American Constitution is more than two century old. First amendment exalts the freedom of press as of inviolable value. The Indian position practically is the same in law though different in fact. But the British lag behind. It must be remembered that freedom of the press is only an expanded expression of the freedom of information of the common man. The Fourth Estate, as the press is known, exposes, investigates, assembles, organizes argumentatively and presents descriptively all material, which helps the masses know and understand the problems of the government and doings of the ministers and bureaucrats. Since the press acts for the public in fulfilment of its right to know, its freedom is broadened and deserves higher protection. The press is *pro bono* public, engaged in the risky operation of collecting news and views and difficult data from sensitive and secret areas for the fulfilment of people's informational right. Special consideration is, therefore, necessary for access of press to information because of its strategic role in mobilization of public opinion.

The risks of the journalist profession are many. Prosecution for piracy of official secrets, defamation of persons, spreading of disharmony of violation of censorship laws plus more severe penalties under penal laws relating to national security and the like. Secrecy laws measures demand from the reporter courage and resourcefulness and a dedication to the democracy of truthful politics.

Communication of information is necessary so that every person may judge for himself the issues that affect his life, his national destiny and the international unity. In this background, the international informational order has a vital nexus with international economic order. Within the national frontiers, fundamental freedoms become essential to the free flow of information. Freedom to association and other fundamental freedoms are meaningless if there is suppression of freedom of expression.

Information and communication are powerful tools and have a potential to shape and shake social and political developments of the society. 'Men make their history, but not as they please,' said Karl Marx. It depends on the quality and quantity of information supplied to them.

United States of America, Australia and some European countries have statutory law providing for access to information. In India we do not have any law specifically providing for right to information but the Supreme Court of India, considered one of the most powerful courts in the world, has discovered this right as emanating from Article 19(1)(a) and Article 21 of the Constitution which guarantee freedom of speech and expression and right to life. The Indian Supreme Court has accorded status of fundamental right to the right to know. Important pronouncements of the Supreme Court of India in the cases of **State of Uttar Pradesh** v. **Raj Narayan** (1975), **Maneka Gandhi** v. **Union of India** (1978), **S.P. Gupta** v. **Union of India** (1982), **Reliance Petro Ltd.** v. **Indian Express** (1989), **Secretary, Ministry of Information and Broadcasting** v. **Cricket Association, Bengal** (1995), **Sheela Barse** v. **State of Maharashtra** (1997), **State** v. **Charita** AIR (1999), **Union of India** v. **Association for Democratic Reforms** (2002), **People Union for Civil Liberties** v. **Union of India** (2003), **Sarbjeet Roy** v. **DERC** (2006) are not worthy in this context, in shaping and Chiselling the Right to Information in India and has led to many State Governments in passing the Right to Information Acts. The States of Tamil Nadu, Goa, Madhya Pradesh and Rajasthan, Mahrashtra, Karnataka, Delhi, Assam and Jammu & Kashmir went ahead to enact their own laws relating to Right to Information without waiting indefinitely for Central legislation in this respect.

In 1989, Prime Minister V.P. Singh said in his broadcast to the nation, "we will have to increase access to information. If the government functions in full public view, wrong doing will be minimized. To this end, Official Secret Act will be amended and we will make the functioning more transparent. Right to Information will be enshrined in our Constitution".

In the 1990's a people's movement led by the Mazdoor Kisan Shakti Sangathan (MKSS) highlighted the significance of the right of information for rural poor in a series of struggles and public hearings. Subsequently the MKSS and other social activists cooperated with the ongoing efforts to prepare a Draft of Right to Information Bill. These effort, involving several senior journalists, lawyers, officials and other experts, were coordinated by the Press Council of India. The Council Chairman Justice P.B. Sawant handed over the Draft of Right to Information Bill, 1996 to the Government of India in September-October 1996. Around the same time the tremendous potential of the right to information was amply demonstrated in successful experiments in Bilaspur division of Madhya Pradesh. At the conference of chief secretaries an agreement was reached on them need for an early enactment of a Right to Information law.

On January 2, 1997, the government appointed a working group of Right to Information and promotion of open and transparent government. This group, also known as the H.D. Shourie Committee submitted its report in May. This report included a Draft Freedom of Information Bill 1997. So the Central Government has two Bills under its consideration, one submitted by the Press Council of India and another submitted by the H.D. Shourie Committee. The Press Council Bill promises to be a broader and more effective piece of legislation as it doesn't give too many exemptions and leaves little room for delaying tactics. It also clearly provides penalty for deliberate delay in providing information or providing false information. For over two years now the government both the incumbent one led by Mr. Atal Behari Vajpayee and its predecessor, the United Front government, have been expressing their commitment to introducing in Parliament legislation relating to the Right to Information. The Freedom of Information Bill 2000 was introduced in the Parliament on 25th July, 2000 after intense debate the Bill finally passed in 2002.

The doomed FOI Act led to sustained pressure for a better National RTI enactment. The first draft of the Right to Information Bill was presented in Parliament on 22nd December, 2004. After intense debate more than one hundred amendments to the draft bill were made between December 2004 and 15 June, 2005, when the Bill finally passed. The Act came into effect on 31 October, 2005. The RTI 2005 is facing turbulence from the bureaucracy even before it celebrates its first birthday. A powerful lobby of the bureaucracy has apparently been successful in prevailing over the collision Government. The Centre and convinced it to amend the law. But luckily the UPA Government has withdrawn the proposed amendment to the Right to Information Act 2005 aimed at exempting file notings from public access.

Finally, we have to ask ourselves—do we have the wisdom, commitment, and ability to return to the basic postulates of democracy? Can common sense rule our actions where we go back to the original ideas? Audits meant reading out aloud and obtaining a peoples verification. The sixth standard definition of democracy, by the people, for the people, with the people, is a clear and simple statement of participation. The talisman for the right to information movement should be to provide the facts and look for ways through which citizens can use those facts to confront the centres of power. Only then it can begin to realize its potential to become a tool of empowerment for every citizen.

Suggestions

The Right to Information Act 2005 is a landmark piece of legislation. If implemented well, it could be a major step towards more accountable and transparent government. However, it is imperative to recognise that the road to implementation is a long one and there will be many hurdles and roadblocks yet. With proper governmental support and a willingness to adapt, it is a golden opportunity for India to end the culture of governmental secrecy and fulfil its potential as a truly great democracy. And for the better implementation of this Act I humbly submit the following suggestions:

Suggestion 1: The need for the allocation of additional funds by the Government for implementing the Act.

The demand for information under the RTI Act is likely to increase with the passage of time. The application fees, etc., prescribed by the Department of Personnel and Training are not enough to cover the cost involved in furnishing the information. Hence, it is logical if the Government allocates special funds for the purpose, particularly in case of autonomous organizations.

Suggestion 2: The need for the sanction of additional posts by the Government for implementing the Act.

The existing staff would not be able to cater to the anticipated demand for information at all levels, as the time limits prescribed in the act are a practical constraint for the PIOs. To add to this, the failure to adhere to the time limits makes the PIOs liable to pay the penalty which may go up to Rs. 25,000. The PIOs are required to furnish information sought under the Act in addition to their normal work. The normal work may include many important items of work which the PIOs have to accomplish in the best interest of the organization. The existing staff would not be able to take proper care of the interest of the organization, when with a view to avoid the penalty, they give priority to the applications received under the Act over other work of the organization. To strike the right balance between the work relating to the RTI Act and the normal work, additional staff would be needed. This is extremely important in an organisation like Doordarshan which is operating on less than its sanctioned strength and even new plan projects are being commissioned without the staff complement, by diversion.

***Suggestion 3*:** The need for the conduct of training programmes by the Department of Personnel & Training for the proper implementation of the Act.

While the Act mentions the broad guidelines for the disclosure of information, in order to ensure that the concerned officers follow them properly. Department of Personnel & Training, being the Nodal Department, should consider conducting training programmes. There may not be uniformity in approach if the training programmes are conducted by different Ministries/Departments.

***Suggestion 4*:** The need to devise a mechanism for curbing the frivolous requests for information.

It is utmost necessary to handle frivolous demands of information, as otherwise the RTI Act would be abused and fail to achieve the purpose for which it has been enacted. The following suggestions are made in this regard:

After seeking suggestions from all Ministries/ Departments, broad guidelines should be issued by Department of Personnel and Training as to what constitutes a frivolous demand of information.

Instructions may be issued by the said department to the effect that the only action that needs to be taken on a frivolous demand of information is to intimate the applicant that his/her demand for information is frivolous.

In case such an applicant prefers an appeal against the rejection of his/her demand for information and the appeal is dismissed, the Act should provide for the imposition of penalty on him/her.

The authority competent to impose penalty should be the commission and the penalty should be as severe as it is at present for the PIOs who either fail to furnish or furnish late the information which is not prohibited by the Act.

***Suggestion 5*:** The need to curb the abuse of the Act in the types of cases explained below:

1. Under the Act, many persons are seeking the information, pertaining to several issues in a single application. For example, in Doordarshan, an individual sought information on as many as 32 points, concerning more than one office. The same individual simultaneously submitted another application seeking information on 22 points. The information sought in the two applications was in addition to what had been sought by her in other 4 applications, submitted 15 days back. This caused an unfair addition to the workload of an already heavily loaded officer.
2. In another case, an individual sought enormous data from the concerned PIO of this Directorate. The concerned officer and the staff had to attend the office on holidays in order to compile within the time-limit the enormous data, which could be accommodated in 2,661 pages, 39 floppies and one CD. The individual was asked to deposit the requisite fee of Rs. 7,372, as per the scale prescribed by Department of Personnel and Training. Initially he did not respond. Later he took the plea that the application fee of Rs. 10 covers all the costs, hence nothing is payable by him. While, this Directorate will clarify the correct position to him, it is

doubtful that he will eventually pay the requisite money and obtain the pages, floppies and CD specially prepared at his request.

3. Many applicants are using the Act to seek not pure information, but the views of the PIO, interpretation of Rules and judgement of the PIO on the actions/ decisions of some other officer, usually his seniors. The fear psychosis caused by the Act amongst the PIOs with the provision of penalty in place, forces the PIOs even to reply such queries. But this is not proper. Nobody should be allowed the liberty to seek the views/ judgements/interpretations of the PIO, who is usually not senior enough to pronounce views, etc., on the relevant rules or the decisions/actions taken by senior officers. The applicants are at liberty to seek the copies of relevant orders, rules etc. But as regards the appropriateness of any decision/action or the interpretation of rules, etc., they should take their own view and seek administrative/legal remedies, if not satisfied with the decision action of the concerned officer.
4. While there should be clear-cut directions to reject the type of applications mentioned in para 1 and 3 above, there should be a provision for imposing penalty in the type of cases mentioned in para 2 above.

Some Other Suggestions

- *Strong Pro-disclosure Requirements*: This should include provisions requiring agencies to publicise details of their programmes by electronic means, maintain and organize records to render them accessible to the public, create an index of all records for public use, and publish all materials relating to agency rules, guidelines, operations, procedures, and performance.
- *Publicising the RTI Act* by making a guide for its use available in every government office, including post-offices, and transmitting information about how to use

the Act by radio and television in order to reach remote areas.

- *Making the Act Partially Retrospective*: The extent of retrospectively depends on the capacity of the government to organize its records to meet public demands for information beforehand, but a period of three or five years seems appropriate.
- *Gateway Provisions should be removed* : The Act should not contain any 'gateway' provisions that can be used as excuses to deny requests for information except for the case of overly broad ones in which case the Information Officer should be required to help narrow the request to make it more manageable. So gateway provision should be removed.
- *Urgent Requests*: The Act should contain a provision to allow for urgent requests in cases involving life and liberty that should be responded to immediately and in any event, within not more than 48 hours, so the Act should be amended.
- *A Two-Tiered Fee Structure*: Fees for copying, search time and review time should be charged from commercial requests only, other applicants should be required to pay only copying costs. Fee should be completely waived for non-commercial requesters if the request is in the public interest or on grounds of financial hardship.
- *Exemptions should be narrowly defined*: Class exemptions should be permitted only for cabinet documents, information already published and readily available at a reasonable price and information that is due to be published within a period of 90 days. All other exemptions should be subject to a relatively stringent test that would require the government to show that substantial harm would result from disclosure, not merely ordinary harm. There should be no provision for the creation of new exemptions, except by amendment, and no clauses, such as the one in the Shourie Bill that allows the government to exempt any

record that it feels would not serve public interests. The use of certificates to shield particular records from being disclosed should be completely eschewed.

- *Appeals should be heard by an independent and specialized body* competent to hear cases relating to information. The first rung of external appeals should be heard by an Information Commissioner followed by recourse to an Information Tribunal and/or the High Court on points of law. The information Commissioner should also act as a mediator in disputes involving agencies and requesters. External mediation by the Information Commissioner should be allowed to proceed alongside an internal appeal to the head of an agency, but an internal appeal should be a pre-requisite for any formal external appeal in order to discourage litigation and give agencies an opportunity to reconsider. Internal appeals should be decided within 30 days of being filed after which the requester should automatically have the right to appeal to the Information Commissioner. Plaintiffs should have the right to hire professional legal or other assistance for internal and external appeals; and the costs of any appeal should be awarded against the government, even if the government wins the case, if the appeal involves an important principle of law, is deemed to be in the public interest, or contributes to transparency and accountability in government.
- *Creating an Institutional Advocate for RTI*: Any RTI law in India will need an institutional advocate to monitor compliance with the law, report to Parliament, receive feedback from agencies and requesters, make suggestions for further reforms and foster support for Right to Information. This advocacy function should not be combined with a judicial one, such as the power to hear and decide appeals, although it could be merged with a mediating function. The idea of creating National and State Councils for Information that could fulfil this role is a good one, if this involves too much expense or administrative complexity, the Information

Commissioners role could be limited to mediating and advocacy, as in the case of Canada, with formal external appeals being heard by an Information Tribunal and then by the High Court.

- *Whistle Blower Protection* is an absolute must for India given the high levels of corruption and mismanagement that plague administration and governance. This should be introduced either as part of an RTI. Private companies should be subject to the RTI in so far as their activities affect the public domain. The government should be able to release commercial information normally considered exempt in cases where there is a threat to the life and safety of an individual or the public, a public health hazard, or a significant environmental risk. In addition, the government should be allowed to release such information on the basis of a simple public interest test. Finally, companies should be required to provide information about their products and processes that might have implications for public safety, health, or the environment. There should be no burden on companies to release information that has no direct bearing on the public.
- *Penalities are necessary to enforce RTI Laws*. Agencies that delay providing information beyond the stipulated period, including extensions if appropriate, should forfeit the right to collect fees for such information. Prison terms and/or fines should be imposed on those who wilfully destroy or alter records to prevent their disclosures, are found to have acted capriciously and arbitrarily in refusing to divulge records, a few to obstruct investigations carried out by authorities vested with hearing appeals and ensuring compliance with RTI legislation.
- *Repeal of the Official Secrets Act and Reform of the Conduct Rules of the Government of India*: The exemptions provided by RTI legislation should be sufficient to meet the need for secrecy in government at certain times in

certain areas, while also preserving the foundations of a well informed democratic society. The passage of RTI legislation thus makes the OSA irrelevant. To retain both statues would be to create serious confusion that would inevitably have to addressed by the Courts. The Conduct Rules should also be reformed to make it an obligation for government servants to release information consistent with any RTI law in effect.

- *Regarding Appointment of Commissioner*: For the appointment of persons as Information Commissioners, it is necessary to keeping in mind the following criteria:
    - ◆ The person should be competent when it comes to judicial matters; so a person who have served as a judge, or practiced as an advocate will be very effective.
    - ◆ The person appointed should also be honest, and implement the law. Just because a journalist, or retired judge has been appointed, none can be sure of fair and unbiased results. In fact, the performance of the information commissions in states where journalists, retired judges and others have been appointed is at par with the performance of other state information commissioners, manned by retired bureaucrats.
- It will be very nice if a list of RTI activists mail IDs and contact numbers is prepared for the better interest of the poor/needy people.
- RTI applications should be allowed through information kiosks/ICT centres such as CIC, Drishtee Kiosks, e-Seva Kiosks, e-choupal, etc., set up by government and private parties across India for a small fee which goes to operator of the kiosk and these kiosk operators should also be authorized to collect government fees for RTI application. These kiosks can then submit these applications to nearest RTI office in bulk along with fees. This can really help reach RTI all across India as we already have more than 25,000 kiosks even in the remotest part of India and in next 2 years

no of kiosks will cross 1,00,000. Even the answers can be distributed back through these kiosks.

The access to information is the life line of a progressive society and, therefore, free flow of information must not be obstructed so that every willing citizen gets an opportunity to participate in shaping the destiny of his nation. An open government is a clean government while a secretive government is an unresponsive government and thus an irresponsible government. Informational bankruptcy of the citizen is complete antithesis of a democracy. Therefore, in the larger interest of the Indian public, we must reverse this retreat with courage.

END NOTE

- Belgrano Affair. Clive Ponting case confirmed the arrogance of British government. The Ponting case arose from the sinking of Argentine Cruiser *General Belgrano* by HMS *Conqueror* during the Falklands War. The sinking was the most controversial episode of the war, not only because it lost 386 lives but because it occured when diplomatic efforts to settle the conflict were at delicate stage. The version of events given by both Press and Parliament by Thatcher Government were misleading.
- Canadian Journalism Foundation.
- See: www.parivartan.com
- Whistle Blowers must be Protected *The Hindu,* 29th Oct, 2011, p. 11.
- Whistle Blower Act in India. www.indiadivision2020.com
- Whistle Blower Act coming soon—Prime Minister Manmohan Singh in *The Times of India,* 14 Oct. 2011, 'The government would soon bring the Whistle Blowers Act to protect those using the Right to Information (RTI) Act.

ANNEXURES

ANNEXURE-I

Goa, One of the Pioneers in RTI, but Loopholes Remain

PANJIM, December 15—Goa has the second-oldest Right to Information Act in the country (second to Tamil Nadu). But an analysis undertaken for the Commonwealth Human Rights Initiative in New Delhi suggests that a lot remains to be improved in this renegated piece of legislation.

Under this law, Goa does not allow for *suo moto* declaration of information, the time-limit taken to provide the information is a lengthy, i.e., 30 days, and there is no internal appeal provided for in the case of faulty decision.

This came out during a UNDP workshop on being held at Aguada on December 15-16, and emerged from comparative studies of different Right to Information laws passed in India.

Goa's Right to Information Act, passed in 1997, allows for obtaining of certified copies of documents or records, inspection of records, notes and extracts, inspection of public works, taking samples from material of public work.

Initially, there was a lot of enthusiasm about the transparency this law could bring in. But later on, as bureaucrats allegedly found loopholes on how to block the flow of information sought by the citizen, there was a diminishing interest in the law.

Ironically, even incumbent Chief Minister Manohar Parrikar was himself one of those who made good use of the Right to Information Act, to dig out ammunition against his then opponents.

Goa's law ensures transparency only in the government sector and that too, not all government funded bodies, but only those competent authorities who have been notified under the law.

Goa's law applies also to private bodies executing work for, on behalf of or as authorised by the government. The Commonwealth initiative suggests that private bodies affecting the public must be covered.

There are six exemptions, on which grounds the Goa government can refuse information to its citizen. But, this analysis points out that information that can be given to the State legislature should also be available to the citizen.

In contrast, the controversial Tamil Nadu legislation has 22 exemptions and two additional "broad exemptions" under which information can be denied. States like Rajasthan, Karnataka, Delhi, Maharashtra, Madhya Pradesh and the Central law have between 7 to 10 exemptions each.

Each Right to Information application in Goa costs Rs. 100 plus the fee of photocopying—at two rupees a page. The Commonwealth initiative suggests that the fees should be waived when likely to cause financial hardship, or if the information is sought in public interest.

Government authorities can take 30 days to accept or refuse RTI applications. The Commonwealth Initiative suggests shorter time limits for refusal.

It says an "independent forum for appeal (is) essential. Also coupling appeal and penalties (on officials for not giving the information) together, makes the process more transparent and efficient".

There are no provisions for publicizing the Act, contrary to the suggestion of there being mandatory publicity. Likewise, Goa has no provisions for the mandatory training and orientation of government personnel.

Goa's State Council which oversees this Act has been meeting infrequently, and also faced charges that an earlier more-representative body was replaced by one which had some nominees close to the powers that be.

ANNEXURE-II

Panjab University, Chandigarh

List of Public Information Officers and Assistant Public Information Officers

The following officers have been designated as Public Information Officers (PIOs) and Assistant Public Information Officers (APIOs) and also Appellate Authority for the purpose with their telephone numbers indicated against each, from whom the public can seek information in writing on a proforma and on payment of requisite fee during office hours on working days as per procedure laid down in the Right to Information Act 2005.

Panjab University RTI Handbook

A. All teaching departments
Professor S.K. Kulkarni, — PIO 0172-2541156
Dean University Instruction

B. All affiliated colleges
Dean College Development Council — PIO 0172-2541943
D.R. (Colleges) — APIO 0172-2541202

C. Students Related Information
(i) Dean Students Welfare (Boys) — PIO 0172-2541596
Student Welfare (Boys Hostels)
(ii) Dean Students Welfare (Girls) — PIO 0172-2541596
Students Welfare(Girls Hostels)

D. Examination Related Information
Controller of Examination — PIO 0172-2541825
(i) D.R. (Secrecy) — APIO 0172-2541667
(ii) D.R.(Exams) — APIO 0172-2541066

E. All matters concerning administration
(Establishment, Accounts, General Administration, Construction, Maintenance, Horticulture & Health)
Finance & Development Officer — PIO 0172-2541850

(i) Chief Medical Officer APIO 0172-2541722
(for matters concerning health)
(ii) D.R. (Estt) APIO 0172-2534820
(for matters concerning establishment)
(iii) D.R. (R&S) APIO 0172-2541275
(for matters concerning registration and store)
(iv) Executive Engineer-I APIO 0172-2534354
(for matters concerning construction, maintenance and horticulture)
(v) D.R. (General) APIO 0172-2540385
(for matters concerning general administration)

F. For Information Relating Sports, Youth Welfare & N.S.S.

(i) Professor S. K. Kulkarni APIO 0172-2541156
Director Sports
(ii) Professor Naval Kishore APIO 0172-2534033
Professor-in-charge Sports
(iii) Professor S.M Kant APIO 0172-2784448
Director Youth Welfare
(iv) Dr.(Mrs) Dolly APIO 0172-2534035
Dy.Director Campus Sports

G. For General Information

Shri Sanjiv Tewari APIO 0172-2541054
Director Public Relations

Appellate Authority for all University matters:

1. Professor R.C. Sobti 0172-2541945
Vice-Chancellor
2. Professor S.S. Bari 0172-2541716
Registrar

Keeping in view the transfers/retirements, etc., of some Officers who have been appointed as PIOs and APIOs, the Vice Chancellor has issued standing instructions that in case of any change of PIO/APIO occurring due to transfer, retirement, change, etc., the person taking over the assignment would automatically replace him/her.

Details of Fees payable for seeking information under RTI Act 2005

The requisite fee for seeking information must be deposited in cash under the Proper Fee code as given below. If the payments being made by DD or Bankers cheque, the fee code must be mentioned at the back of the DD/BC along with other particulars. Fee code : M 0100

The fee details are as given below:

1. A request for obtaining information under sub-section (1) of Section 6, shall be accompanied by an application fee of rupees (Rs. 10) by way of cash against proper receipt or by demand draft or bankers cheque in favour of the Registrar, P.U., Chandigarh and payable at Chandigarh only.
2. For providing the information under sub-section (1) of Section 7, the fee shall be charged by way of cash against proper receipt or by demand draft or bankers cheque in favour of the Registrar, Panjab University, Chandigarh and payable at Chandigarh only at the following rates:

   (a) rupees two for each page (in A-4 or A-3 size paper) created or copied;
   (b) actual charge or cost price of a copy in larger size paper; and
   (c) for inspection of records, no fee for the first hour; and a fee of rupees ten for each half an hour (or fraction thereof) thereafter.

3. For providing the information under sub-section (5) of Section 7, the fee shall be charged by way of cash against proper receipt or by demand draft or bankers cheque in favour of the Registrar, Panjab University, Chandigarh and payable at Chandigarh at the following rates:

   (a) for information required in diskette or floppy rupees fifty per diskette or floppy; and
   (b) for information required in printed form at the price fixed for such publication or rupees two per page of photocopy for extracts from the publication.

PANJAB UNIVERSITY, CHANDIGARH

PROFORMA FOR SEEKING INFORMATION UNDER THE RIGHT OF INFORMATION ACT (RTI ACT)

1. Name of the Applicant in full (Capital Letters)
2. Father's Name
3. Current Postal Address
4. Telephone No. (O) (R) ________
5. Fax No.
6. Mobile No.
7. E-mail
8. (a) Details of information required:

   (b) If it relates to Examination and/or results, also indicate.

Name of the candidate/ Father's Name	*Examination Appeared/ Passed*	*Class*	*Year/Session/ Semester of Passing*	*Regn. No.*	*Roll No.*

9. Requisite fee have been paid vide Receipt No.______________ dated ______________(Original or Photocopy of receipt for Rs.______________ enclosed).

Payment shall be received only by way of cash at the Panjab University, S.B.I. Fee Counter, Sector 14, Panjab University, Chandigarh or Bank Draft/Banker's Cheque drawn on any scheduled commercial Bank in favour of Registrar, Panjab University, Chandigarh payable at Chandigarh. No Money Orders or personal cheques shall be accepted under any circumstances. I hereby solemnly declare that the aforesaid particulars mentioned are correct to the best of my knowledge and belief.

(Full signature)

Date: Address:

Place:

ACKNOWLEDGEMENT PROFORMA

For Office Use:

Date of Receipt Draft/University Receipt/ Bankers Cheque No.___________Date Amount__________

Signature of Receiving Official

DETAILS OF FEES PAYABLE FOR SEEKING INFORMATION UNDER RTI ACT 2005

The requisite fee for seeking information must be deposited in cash under the Proper Fee code as given below. If the payments being made by DD or Bankers cheque, the fee code must be mentioned at the back of the DD/BC along with other particulars. Fee Code M 0100

The fee details are as given below:

1. A request for obtaining information under sub-section (1) of Section 6, shall be accompanied by an application fee of rupees (Rs. 10) by way of cash against proper receipt or by demand draft or bankers cheque in favour of the Registrar, Panjab University, Chandigarh and payable at Chandigarh only.
2. For providing the information under sub-section (1) of Section 7, the fee shall be charged by way of cash against proper receipt or by demand draft or bankers cheque in favour of the Registrar, Panjab University, Chandigarh and payable at Chandigarh only at the following rates:
   (a) rupees two for each page (in A-4 or A-3 size paper) created or copied;
   (b) actual charge or cost price of a copy in larger size paper; and
   (c) for inspection of records, no fee for the first hour; and a fee of rupees ten for each half an hour (or fraction thereof) thereafter.
3. For providing the information under sub-section (5) of Section 7, the fee shall be charged by way of cash against proper receipt or by demand draft or bankers cheque in favour of the Registrar, Panjab University, Chandigarh and payable at Chandigarh at the following rates:
   (a) for information required in diskette or floppy rupees fifty per diskette or floppy; and
   (b) for information required in printed form at the price fixed for such publication or rupees two per page of photocopy for extracts from the publication.

News in TOI, Chandigarh, indicating concern on People regarding RTI

Chandigarh; The fight against the UT administration increasing the fee for filing an RTI application from Rs. 10 to Rs. 50 has intensified further with several human rights activists getting together to oppose the decision.

On Friday a press conference was held by activists to raise their voice against the move, claiming that the hike has been brought about to make it difficult for the common man to obtain information. Vowing not to give up, Hemant Goswami of Burning Brain Society, even declared, "We will obtain information under the provisions of Section 76 of the Indian Evidence Act 1872, and not pay even Rs. 10 now, leave aside paying Rs. 50."

The activists said that it was only with the coming of RTI that the democracy became truly participative, but with this move the administration was trying to hide information from the common man. "The very objective of the RTI Act was to make the public servants accountable and this move of fee hike clearly goes against the purpose", added Kamal Anand of People for Transparency.

Accusing the bureaucracy of corruption, the activists further added that the intention of Parliament was to encourage more and more people to use RTI so that corruption in government could be contained and transparency be enforced. Hitender Jain, another civil rights activist, said, "The fee cannot be fixed arbitrarily. It has to be reasonable and there has to be some rationale behind the fee hike".

Goswami further claimed that they would make all possible efforts to mobilize people against the decision and may even think of legal action, if needed.

Meanwhile, with social activists' spirited move to oppose the move tooth and nail, some officials in the administration too expressed displeasure against the move. While a senior official condemned the fee hike saying it was an unwarranted and hasty decision, another official reportedly expressed his anger for not taken into confidence before finalising the decision.

In fact, this sudden development has come just days after the twin RTI controversies involving the UT Administrator and Home Secretary. While the UT Administrator's office had to face much media criticism for not appointing any CPIO to answer RTI queries, the Home Secretary had to face the music for spending enormous State funds on his oft-repeated foreign tours.

Info Chief brings More Bodies under RTI

The Central Information Commission (CIC) has brought private and deemed universities and those private bodies, which have received land on concession from the government under the ambit of the Right to Information (RTI) Act.

The CIC observed that any private body constituted through a notification under an Act of Parliament or those which receive any form of concessions from the government are covered under RTI.

"Deemed universities gets its status by virtue of a notification used by the Central Government under the UGC Act. Therefore, all deemed universities are public authorities as defined under the RTI Act", said Central Information Commissioner Shailesh Gandhi. The order came while allowing an RTI appeal by Mumbai's Mahavir Chopda on fee reimbursement. Gandhi asked a private university, Narsee Monjee Institute of Management Studies, to provide information sought by April 20 free of cost.

Bibliography

References and Notes

A Decade of Measuring the Quality of Governance.

A Fight For 'Right To Know', Aruna Roy and Others, *Yojana,* Vol. 50, January 2006, 2-8.

A New Era. Prakash Kardaley, *Seminar,* Vol. 551, July 2005, 17-23.

Access, Diversity and Representation, Kalpana Kannabiran, *Yojana,* Vol. 50, January 2006, 17-20.

On Knowing the Price of Everything and the Value of Nothing. New Press, pp. 277. ISBN 1565849817, Buchanan, James M. *Politics without Romance.*

Addressing The Digital Underside, Sucheta Dalal, *Financial Express,* 14 August 2006, 3-6.

Administrative Stagnancy and Public Indifference, V.R. Shenoy, *Janata,* Vol. 60, No. 27, 31 July 2005, 7-8.

Allport, G.W. (1989). "Attitude", in Murchison, C. (Ed.), A Handbook of Social Psychology, Clark University Press, 798-844.

Ambedkar, B.R. (1936). *Annihiliation of Caste,* Jalandhar, Bheem Patrika Publication.

Ambedkar, B.R. (1950). *Mr. Gandhi and the Emancipation of Unknowables,* Jalandhar : Patrika Publication.

Ambedkar, *A Critical Study,* New Delhi; People's Publishing House.

Ambrose, David (1999). "Judicial Response to the Right to Information in India", *Delhi Law Review,* Vol. XXI, 1999, p. 71.

Anu Kumar (2003). *Into Change News and Features,* June.

Arora, N.D. and Awasthy, S.S. (2007), *Political Theory and Political Thought,* New Delhi: Har-Anand Publications.

As regards the Rule of Law in China, see Five Years of China's WTO Membership. EU and US Perspectives on China's Compliance with Transparency Commitments and the Transitional Review Mechanism, Legal Issues of Economic Integration, Kluwer Law. *International,* Volume 33, Number 3, pp. 267-270, " 2006, Paolo Farah.

Ashton, Batoness, "The Campaign for Freedom of Information", Association for Democratic Reforms *v.* Union of India, AIR 2001, Del 126, 137.

Bacher, Christian (2007). *Capitalism, Ethics and the Paradoxon of Self-exploitation,* Grin Verlag, p. 2

Baisantry, D.K. and W. Ambedkar, *The Total Revolutionary,* New Delhi, Segment Book Distributors.

Banisar, David (2002), "Freedom of Information and Access to Government Records around the World", July 2, 2002.

Barkataky, Rahul and Kharat, Vinod (2004). "ICT for the Masses—A Comparative Study of e-governance Initiatives in India", MITPA Technology Foundation, New Delhi, December 2004.

Bedi, Kiran (2006). "The Most Powerful Right." *The Tribune,* 27 August 2006, p. 13.

Benda-Beckmann, Keebet Von, (2001), The Contexts of Law, Paper presented at XIII International Conference of Commission on Folk Law and Legal Pluralism, Nepal.

Bethesda, M.D. (2007). "Growing Older in America: The Health and Retirement Study", National Institute on Ageing, National Institutes of Health.

Betrus, A.K. (2003). "Individualized Instruction", *Encyclopaedia of Education,* 2 ed., J.W. Gutherie (ed.), Macmillan Reference. Amit Bhaduri, "Guarantee Employment and the Right to Information", *Economic and Political Weekly,* Vol. 40, No. 4, 22 January 2005, pp. 267-69.

Bhandare, Murlidhar, C. (1991). Dr. B.R. Ambedkar", in Lok Sabha Secretariat (eds.), *Eminent Parliamentarians,* Monograph Series—Dr. B.R. Ambedkar—New Delhi: Government of India.

Bhattacharjea, Ajit (2004). "Money for Nothing", *The Hindustan Times,* 7 October 2004, p. 8. (2006), "Hide and Seek", *The*

Hindustan Times, 7 August 2006, p. 8. (2006), "Telling Tales", *The Hindustan Times*, 29 August, (2005), "From Freedom to Right", *Seminar*, Vol. 551, July 2005.

Bohm-Bawerk, Eugen von (1890). *Capital and Interest: A Critical History of Economical Theory*. London: Macmillan & Co.

Bottomore, Tom (1985). *Theories of Modern Capitalism*.

Boundaries of Disclosure. (Editorial), *Financial Express*, 20 April, 2006, p. 6.

Mistry, Indra J. (2006), Breaking the Bureaucratic Mould. *Yojana*, Vol. 50, January 2006; 9-11. 6

Chandra, Ramesh and Mittra, Sangh (2003), *The Ambedkar Era*, New Delhi, Commonwealth.

Changing Discourse. Sowmya Sivakumar and Eric Kerbart, *Seminar*, Vol. 551, July 2005; 50-54.

Changing Governance Forever. Shekhar Singh & Mishra Singh. *Yojana*, Vol. 50, January 2006, 33-35.

Chanock, M. (1982). Making Customary Law Men, Women and Courts in Northern Rhodesia, in *African Women and Law—Historical Perspectives* (ed.), M.J. Hary and M. Wright, Boston, Boston University, pp. 63-67.

Charulata Singh (2006). "New Life for Democracy", *Yojana*, Vol. 50, January 2006, pp. 37-38.

Chitkara, M.G. (2002). *Dr. Ambedkar and Social Justice*, New Delhi; A.P.H. Publishing Corporation, Choudhary, Kameshwar (2000), "Ambedkar's Vision of Development of the Dalits in India", *Ambedkar Journal of Social Development and Justice*, Vol. VIII.

Coase, Ronald (1974). *The Lighthouse in Economics*.

Craven, R.G., Marsh, M.W. and Debus, R.L. (1991). *Journal of Educational Psychology*, Vol. 83, No. 1, University of Sydney, Sydney, Australia, pp. 17-27.

Dalal, Sucheta (2006). "Addressing The Digital Underside", *Financial Express*, 14 August 2006, pp. 3-6.

Daruwala, Maja (2004). "Servants of the Public who make the Public into Servants", *Indian Express*, 20 October, 2004, p. 9.

Dayal, Raghu (2006). "Whistleblowers need to be Protected", *Economic Times*, 26 December 2006, p. 10.

De George, Richard T. (1986), *Business Ethics*, p. 104.

De Soto, Hernando (2000). *The Mystery of Capital: Why Capitalism Triumphs in the West and Fails Everywhere Else*. New York: Basic Books. ISBN 0-465-01614-6.

Demsetz, Harold (1969). *Information and Efficiency*.

Devasher, Manadakini (2005), "Making the RTI Act Effective", *The Tribune*, 9 October 2005, p. 8, col. 1-2.

Dewinder Singh (2006). "Implementation of RTI Act, 2005: Some National and International Experiences", *AIR*, Journal Section, pp. 99-103.

Dheera Kandelwal and K.K. Khandelwal : A Commentary and Digest on The Right to Information Act, 20.05. Dogra, Bharat (2004) "Power Shift", *Times of India*, 15 December 2004, p. 4.

Doctor, H. Adi (WJ). *Political Thinkers of Modern India*, New Delhi: Mittal Publications.

Dogra, Bharat (2004). "Successes and Limitations of RTI", *Janata*, Vol. 59, No. 37, 24 October 2004, pp. 8-9.

Dogra, Bharat (2005) "Passage of Right to Information Bill in Parliament: Strengthening Democracy and the Struggle against Corruption", *Mainstream*, Vol. 43, No. 22, May 2005, p. 4.

Doraiswamy, P.K. (2003). "RTI Act-Panacea of Paper Tiger?", *The Hindu*, 20 May 2003.

Emdeni, C.S., "Documents Privileged in Public Interest'", CLVI *Law Quarterly Review*, pp. 476-79.

Emerson, Thomas (1963). "Towards a General Theory of First Amendment", *The Yale Law Journal*, Vol. 72, pp. 877-956.

Enhancing Administrative Transparency and Accountability through Right to Information/*IIPA Newsletter*, July 2007.

Federal Reserve Bank of Kansas City' (2004). "Global Demographic Change: Economic Impacts and Policy Challenges", *Symposium Proceedings*, August 26-28.

Fitzpatrick, P (1983). *Law Plurality and Underdevelopment in Legality, Ideology and the State*, edited by D. Sugarmann, London, Academic Press, pp. 159-182.

Friedman, Milton (1982). *Capitalism and Freedom*, University of Chicago Press Fulcher.

Galbraith, J.K. (1952). *American Capitalism; Concept of Countervailing Power,* eighth edition (1993) by Translation Publishers, New Brunswick, New Jersey (on find published by Hasishton Miffin Boston 1952).

Gandhi, Shailesh (2005). "Right to Information : Path to Swaraj", *The Hindu,* 7 October, p. 10.

Ghurye, G.S. (1998). *Caste and Race in India,* Bombay: Popular Prakashan, 1998.

Global Trends on the Right to Information; A Survey of South Asia, *CHRI,* July 2001.

Good, C.V. (1959). *Dictionary of Education,* McGraw Hills Company, New York.

Gore, M.S. (1993). *The Social Context of an Ideology Ambedkar's Political and Social Thought,* Sage Publications, New Delhi.

Gothoskar, Sujathe and Kanhere, Vijay (1992) "Asserting Right to Information", *Economic and Political Weekly,* June 27, 1992.

Governance Matters VI: Governance Indicators for 1996-2006, Governance Reform for Visions India.

Greater Access to Official Information and Continuing Conflicts of Interest Key to Continuing Corruption, *Transparency International,* Berlin/London, December 1998.

Gruber, J. and Wise, D.A. (eds.) (1999). *Social Security and Retirement around the World,* University of Chicago Press, Chicago.

Gruber, J. and Wise, D.A. (eds.) (2004). *Social Security Programs and Retirement around the World,* Micro Estimation, University of Chicago Press, Chicago.

Gurstein, Michael and Parminder Jeet Singh (2006). "E-Govonline", *Net Magazine,* August 2006.

Handbook on Right to Information, Assam Administrative Staff College, Assam, p. 28.

H. Doucouliagos and M. Ulubasoglu (2006), *Democracy and Economic Growth: A Meta-Analysis".* School of Accounting, Economics and Finance Deakin University, Australia.

Habibullah, Wajahat (2006), "The Bureaucracy is Threatened by RTI Act My objective is to ensure no one takes it as a threat", *Indian Express,* 15 Oct. 2006, p. 6, col. 1-5.

Habibullah, Wajahat (2006). "We want People to use RTI Act, says Habibullah", Wajahat Habibullah, *The Tribune.* 16 October 2005, p. 12.

Harvey, David (1990). *The Political-Economic Transformation of Late Twentieth Century Capitalism.* Cambridge, MA: Blackwell Publishers. ISBN 0-631-16294-1.

Hayek, Friedrich A. (1963). *Capitalism and the Historians.* Chicago: University of Chicago Press.

Hayek, Friedrich A. (1975). *The Pure Theory of Capital.* Chicago: University of Chicago Press. ISBN 0-226-3208 1-2.

Heibroner, Robert L (1965). *Understanding Macroeconomics,* Prentice, 1984.

Heilbroner, Robert L. (1966). *The Limits of American Capitalism,* Academy Library.

Heilbroner, Robert L. (1987). *Economics Explained,* Simon and Schuster.

Hermalin, A. ed. (2002) *The Well-Being of the Elderly in Asia: A Four-Country Comparative Study,* University of Michigan Press, Ann Arbor.

ICT Policies and e-strategies in the Asia Pacific—A Critical of the Way Forward, UNDP-APDIP, 2004.

IIPO special study report on Right to Information; A Boon for direct Democracy, *Monthly Public Opinion Surveys,* Vol. 53, No, 3, December 2007.

Information Literacy Meeting of Experts. [Prague, the Czech Republic, September 20-23. 2003]: Report of a meeting sponsored by the US National Commission on Libraries and Information Sciences (NCLIS).

Information Technology and Open Government, Office of Information Commissioner, Canada.

International Covenant of Civil and Political Right-1966, Article 9 (2).

International Monetary Fund, (2006). "The Economics of Demographics", *Finance and Development,* September 2006.

Interview with Ramesh Inder Singh, Chief Information Commissioner, the Punjab Information Commission, 'Can't be held to Ransom by Street Protests' in *Hindustan Times,* 30 December, 2010.

Jain, M.P. (2005). *Indian Constitutional Law,* 5th Edn., Reprint 2005.

Jain, Rachana and Gupta, Madhu, "Right to Information: To Generate Awareness", University. *News,* Vol. 44, No. 39.

James (2004). *Capitalism,* Oxford University Press, USA.

Janus, Symonides (ed), *Human Rights: New Dimensions and Challenges,* Dartmouth, Ashgate, England, 1988, p. 102.

Jatava, D.R. (1997). *Social Philosophy of B.R. Ambedkar,* New Delhi, Rawat Publications.

Jondhale, S. and Beltz, J. (eds.) (2004). *Reconstructing the World: B.R. Ambedkar and Buddhism in India,* New Delhi: Oxford University Press.

Joseph Raz, The Rule of Law and Its Virtue (1977). *The Law Quantity Review,* VA-93, P-195(1977).

Josephson, Matthew, *The Money Lords: The Great Finance Capitalists,* 1925-1950, New York, Weybright and Talley, 1972.

Judith N. Shklar (1987). "Political Theory and the Rule of Law", in Hutchinson and Monahan (eds.), *The Rule of Law. Ideal orideologyfroronto*: Carswell, 1987) p.1. Fora discussion of Shklar's view, see J. Waldron (2002) "Is the Rule of Law an Essentially Contested Concept? (in Florida)", in Law 85 *Philosophy,* Vol. 21/2, 2002. See also the entry on "essentially contested concept".

Kaira, Rajesh (2004). "Wired for Change," *The Times of India,* 29 January, 2004, p. 12.

Kannabiran, Kalpana (2005). "Expanding the Public Domain", *Seminar,* Vol. 551, July 2005, pp. 37-40.

Kannabiran, Kalpana (2006). "Access, Diversity and Representation", *Yojana,* Vol. 50, Jan. 2006; pp. 17-20.

Kathyayini, Chamaraj (2006). "Exercising the Right to Seek Information", *Yojana,* Vol. 50, January 2006, p. 21.

Kaushik, P.D. (2004). "E-Government Initiative in India", Agenda for Improving Governance Academic Foundation, Debroy Bibek (ed.), New Delhi, 2004.

Kejriwal, Arvind (2006), "RTI—Aspirations and Challenges", *Yojana,* Vol. 50, Jan. 2006, pp. 22-25.

Kejriwal, Arvind (2006), "Loss of a Right", *The Times of India,* 17 August 2006, p. 14.

Kemp, D.R. (1994), "An Overview of Mental Health Policy from an International Perspective", *International Handbook on Mental Health Policy,* Kemp, D.R. (ed.), Greenwood Press, London, 1994.

Kinsella, K. and Velkoff, V.A. (2001), "An Aging World: 2001", National Institute on Aging and U.S. Census Bureau, Washington, DC.

Kochhar, Sameer and Dhanjal, Gurusharan (2005), "E-Governance Report Card", *Yojana,* Vol. 49, New Delhi, August 2005.

Kshirsagar, R.K. (1992), *Political Thought of Dr. Babasaheb Ambedkar,* New Delhi:

Kulwant Singh (2006), "J & K RTI: An Overview"; *Yojana,* Vol. 50, January 2006, pp. 49-52.

Lash, Scott and Urry, John (2000), Capitalism. In Nicholas Abercrornbie, S. Hill & BS Turner (Eds.), The Penguin (Dictionary of Sociology) (4th ed.), pp. 36-40.

Laycock and Munro (I960), *Encyclopedia of Educational Research,* 3rd ed., MacMillan Co., New York.

Lokhande, G.S. (1977), *Bhimrao Ambedkar : A Study in Social Democracy,* Sterling Publishers Private Ltd., New Delhi.

Lopez, A.D.; Mothers, C.D.; Ezzati, M.; Jamison, D.T.; Murray, C.J.L. (eds.) (2006), *Global Burden of Disease and Risk Factors,* The World Bank Group, Washington, DC, Iyer, V.R. Krishna (1989), "An Open Letter to Prime Minister V.P. Singh".

Madhav, Srinivas, *Right to Information—A Vaccine Against Corruption,* Centre for Good Governance Andhra Pradesh.

Marx, Karl (1886), *Capital: A Critical Analysis of Capitalist Production.*

Mathur, B.P., *Right to Information : A Transparent Governance.*

Mehta, Ved (1961), *Gandhism is not Easily Copied,* The New York Times Company.

Micheal, James (1996), "Freedom of Official Information", OSCE Office for Democratic Institutions and Human Rights, *Bulletin,* Vol. 5:1, pp. 1-21.

Mises, Ludwig von (1998), *Human Action: A Treatise on Economics.* Scholars Edition.

Mistry, Indra Jeet (2006), "Breaking the Bureaucratic Mould", *Yojana*, Vol. 50, January 2006, pp. 9-11.

Mittal, K.C. (2006), "The Right not to Disclose", *Hindustan Times*, 15 September 2006, p. 8.

Mohammad, Taj and Ephroz, Khan Noor (1997), "Caste System in Hindu Society," Mohammad Shabbir (ed.), *B.R. Ambedkar: Study in Law and Society*, New Delhi, Rawat Publications.

Mohapatra, Satyanarayan (2006), "The Right to Information Bill—A Landmark Legislation", *Orissa Review*, February-March 2006.

Monroe, W.S. (1950), *Encyclopedia of Education Research*, MacMillan Co., New York.

Moore, S.F. (1978), *Law as Process*, London, Routledge and Kegan Paul.

Mowli, V. Chandra (1990) B.R. Ambedkar: *Man and His Vision*, New Delhi: Sterling Publishers Private Limited.

Nijalingappa (1991) "Dr. B.R. Ambedkar," in Lok Sabha Secretariat, (ed.), Eminent Parliamentarians, Monograph Series—*Dr. B.R. Ambedkar*, New Delhi: Government of India.

Mukhopadhyay, Amitabh (2005), "Social Audit", *Seminar*, Vol. 551, July 2005, pp. 33-36.

Mukhopadhyay, Amitabh (2006), "Poverty, Information and Accountability", *Yojana*, Vol. 50, January 2006, pp. 12-15,

Muralidharan, Sukumar (2005), "The Challenge to Media", *Seminar*, Vol. 552, July 2005, pp. 50-54.

Narain, Yogendra (2005), Transparency and Accountability in Public Governance, *Mainstream*, July, pp. 21-29.

National Research Council (2001), *Preparing for an Aging World: The Case for Cross-National Research*, National Academy Press, Washington, DC.

Nayak, Ramesh C. (2005), "Right to Information and Panchayati Raj Institutions", *Kurukshetra*, Vol. 53, No. 11, September 2005, pp. 46-47.

Nayak, Venkatesh and Reshmi Mitra, 'RTI, The Most Precious Right', *The Sunday Tribune*, Jalandhar, 30 September, 2007.

Nim, Hoti Lal (1969) *Thoughts on Dr. Ambedkar*, New Delhi, Print Service.

Niranjan, Oulac (2005), "Right to Information and the Road to Heaven", *Economic and Political Weekly*, Vol. 40.

Norberg, Johan (2001), *In Defense of Global Capitalism*. Washington, DC: Cato Institute. ISBN 978-1-93-086547-1.

Obrinsky, Mark (1983), *Profit Theory and Capitalism*. University of Pennsylvania Press, pp. p.l. http: / /www. questia. corn/ PM.

Organisation for Economic Cooperation and Development (OECD) (2007) "Disability Trends among Elderly People: Re-Assessing the Evidence in 12 OECD Countries", Directorate for Employment, Labour and Social Affairs, *Interim Report*, Paris, France.

Our Right to Information. A Guide for Citizens on the Right to Information Act, 2005, Action for Good Governance and Networking in India (AGNI).

Pantham, Thomas and Deutsch, K.L. (ed.) (1986), *Political Thought in Modern India*, New Delhi, Sage Publications.

Parthasarthy, Dr. Swami, (2007), 'Corporate Governance', talk delivered at ICSSR complex, Panjab University, 10th August.

Plea to Security Outfits from Purview of RTI Act (View/ Counter View) *The Times of India*, 12 December 2005, p. 16.

Preamble of the Right to Information Act, 2005.

Proceedings of Regional Seminar on Right to Information, Media Information and Communication Centre of India, The International Centre, Goa and Friedrichebert Stiftung-India, 29-30, June 2007.

Proceedings of the National Academy of Sciences: 2001, p. 98, 6354-59.

Pruthi, Raj Kumar (2006), *Manual of Right to Information Act*, New Delhi, Pentagon Press, pp. 1-61.

Rajasekhariah, A.M. (1989), *B.R. Ambedkar—The Quest, or Social Justice*, New Delhi: Uppal Publishing House.

Ram, Nandu (1995), *Beyond Ambedkar: Essays on Dalits in India*, Delhi; Har-Anand Publications.

Ramanathan, Rames (2004), *Right to Information or Disclosure?*, August 2004.

Rand, Ayn (1986), *Capitalism: The Unknown Ideal*. Signet.

Rao, D.S. Prakasa, "Social Justice Through Constitutionalism," in Mohammad Shabbir (ed.), *B.R. Ambedkar : Study in Law and Society,* New Delhi: Rawalpindi Publications.

Ravikumar, K. Bangalore University, AIR 2005, Karnataka. 21.

Reliance Petrochemicals Ltd. *v.* Indian Express, AIR 1989 SC 190: (1988), 4 SCC 592.

Ray, B.N. (1999), *Tradition (in) Innovation in Indian Political Thought,* New Delhi, Ajanta Books International.

Reisman, George (1996), *Capitalism: A Treatise on Economics.* Ottawa, Illinois: Jameson Books. ISBN 0-915463-73-3.

Report of Seminar on UNDP and the Right to Information, Oslo Governance Centre, Oslo, Norway, 22-23 May, 2006.

Resnick, Stephen (1987). *Knowledge & Class: A Marxian critique of Political Economy.* Chicago: University of Chicago Press.

Right to Information Act, 2005.

Right to Information Act, 2005, *New Frontiers in Education,* Vol. 22, No. 2, October-December 2006, pp. 373-91.

Right to Information, Master Key to Good Governance, First Report of the Second Administrative Reforms Commission, Government of India, June 2006, p. 44.

Rostow, W. W. (1960), *The Stages of Economic Growth: A Non-Communist Manifesto.* Cambridge: Cambridge University Press.

Roy and Others (2006), "A Fight for 'Right to Know", *Yojana,* Vol. 50, January 2006, pp. 2-8.

Roy, A. and Dey, N., "The Right To Information: Facilitating People's Participation and State Accountability", *UNDP.*

Roy, Aruna (2006), "An Act Disabling an Act", *The Indian Express,* 14 August, p. 13.

Roy, Aruna and Kidambi, Sowmtya (2005), "Secret Ballots and Transparent Campaigns", *Seminar,* Vol. 551, July 2005, pp. 27-32.

Roy, Aruna and S. Mahawal (2006), "Exempt File Noting from RTI Ambit." *The Economic Times,* 28 July 2006, p. 12, col. 4-5.

Roy, Aruna and Suramurthy, R. (2006), "File Noting must be shown to Public", *The Tribune,* 30 July 2006, p. 8, col. 3-6.

Roy, Ehmu (2005), "Wrong Information, Right Choice" *Seminar*, Vol. 551, July 2005, pp. 55-58.

RTI Act is our Last Chance to Cleanse the System (Editorial) *The Times of India*, 15 August 2006, p. 16, col. 3-5.

Ryder, Rodney D. (2006), "Right to Information Law Policy and Practice", Wadhwa Publications, New Delhi, pp. 101-115

Ryder, Rodney D. (2006), *"Right to Information—Your Access to Public"*.

S.P. Gupta v. *President of India*, AIR 1982 Supreme Court, p. 149.

S.P. Gupta v. *Union of India*, AIR 1982, Supreme Court, p. 248.

Sarabjit Kaur (2004), "Right to Know in a Democratic Republic", *National Capital Law Journal*, Vol. IX, New Delhi.

Sastry, Trilochan (2005), "Disclosure Norms", Seminar, Vol. 551, July 2005, pp. 24-26.

Sathe, S.P., (1998), *Administrative Law*, 505-507, Bombay.

Schumpeter, J. A. (1983), Capitalism, Socialism, and Democracy.

Scott, John (1997), Corporate Business and Capitalist Classes.

Secretary, Ministry of Information and Broadcasting, *Government of India* v. *Cricket Association of Bengal*, AIR 1995, Supreme Court, p. 1236.

Section (8) Right to Information Act, 2005, *Exempted Information.*

Section Article 39(0), *The Indian Constitution.*

Sekhar, Madhu R. (2005), "Toward a Vibrant Democracy", *Yojana*, Vol. 50, January 2005, pp. 55-58.

Seldon, Arthur (2007). *Capitalism: A Condensed Version.* London: Institute of Economic Affairs.

Seliam, A.N. (2002), *"ICTs in support of Human Rights, Democracy and Good Governance"*, International Telecommunication Union; August 2002.

Seminar. Vol. 551, July 2005, pp. 68-70. Right to Information (Editorial) *The Tribune*, 14 October 2005, p. 12.

Sengupta, Mausumi and Singh, Ram Gopal (2001), *Social Philosophy of Dr. B.R. Ambedkar.*

Sennett, Richard (2006), *The Culture of the New Capitalism.*

Shabbir, Mohammad (ed.) (1997), *B.R. Ambedkar: Study in Law and Society*, New Delhi: Rawat Publications.

Shah, Ghanshyam (1985) *Caste, Conflict and Reservation*, New Delhi: Ajanta Publications (ed.) (2001), *Dalit Identity and Politics*, New Delhi: Sage Publication, IBSM.

Shakir, Moin (1980) *Politics of Minorities*, Ajanta Publications, New Delhi.

Sharma, P. (2007), "RTI Act Unearths Illegal Construction", Sunday *Times of India*, August 26, 2007.

Sharma, R.A. (2003) *Fundamental of Educational Psychology*, Surya Publication, Meerut.

Sharma, Sarbjit and Gopal Krishan (2007), "Implementing Information Regime", *The Hindustan Times*, December 23, 2007.

Shekhar Singh (2005), "The Notion of Transparency", *Seminar*, Vol. 551, July 2005, pp. 46-49.

Shekhar Singh and Misha Singh (2006), "Changing Governance Forever", *Yojana*, Vol. 50, January 2006, pp. 33-35.

Shenoy, V.R. (2005), "Administrative Stagnancy and Public Indifference", *Janata*, Vol. 60, No. 27, 31 July 2005, pp. 7-8.

Singh, Harjinder, ed. (1997), *Caste among Non-Hindus in India*, New Delhi, National Publishing House.

Singh, Surendra (1997), "Dr. Ambedkar's Contribution to Social Justice," Mohammad Shabbir (ed.), *B.R. Ambedkar: Study in Law and Society*, New Delhi: Rawat Publications.

Smith, Adam (1976), *An Inquiry into the Nature and Causes of the Wealth of Nations*.

Sowmya, Sivakumar and Kerbart, Eric (2005), "Changing Discourse", *Seminar*, Vol. 551, July 2005, pp. 50-54.

Strange, Susan (1986), Casino Capitalism.

Stromberg, Joseph (2001), The Role of State Monopoly Capitalism in the American Empire (http://mises.org/jls) *Journal of Libertarian Studies*.

Sukumaran, K. (2006) "File-Notings Important", *The Times of India*, 24 August, 2006, p. 12.

Sunderam, Karthik (2004), "Right to Information and Democracy", *Journal of Symbiosis Law College*, Vol. IV, September, pp. 104-08.

Symonides, Janus (1998), Human Rights, New Dimensions and Challenges, Ashgate, UK.

The Problem, *Seminar*. Vol. 551, Jul. 2005, pp. 12-14.

The Right to Information Act 2005, *Seminar* Vol. 551, July 2005.

The Rule of Law, Lecture Recording—Centre for Public Law.

Thurstone, L.L. and Chave, E: (1999) *Measurement of Attitudes*, University of Chicago Press, Chicago.

Tiwari, Manish (2005), "Right to Information—An Introduction" *Indian Railways*, Vol. 51, No. 7, October 2005, pp. 13-17.

Travers, Robert M.W., *Educational Psychology*, MacMillan Co., New York.

Tripathi, M.N. (1991), "The U.N. General Assembly way back in 1946 has recognized Right to Information as a Fundamental Right".

UNESCO's Recommendations on Promotion and Use of Multilingualism and Universal Access to Cyber Space.

Universal Declaration of Human Rights, Article 19.

Vakil, A.K. (1985), *Reservation Policy and Scheduled Castes in India*, New Delhi, Ashish.

Varma, V.P. (1996), *Modern Indian Political Thought*, Agra: Lakshmi Narain Agarwal, Educational Publishers.

Venkat, V. (2007) "RT1 Act should be better implemented". *The Times of India*, August 25, 2007.

Venugopal, Justice, P. (1992), Social Justice and Reservation, p. 2, 1990, as cited in M.N. Javaraiah, *Dr Ambedkar: Father of the Constitution of India*, Mysore: Siddhartha Grantha Maala.

Verma, J.S. (2006), "Out with the Files", *The Times of India*.

Virendra Kumar, (2006), "Don't Dilute RTI Act, Please", *The Tribune*, 6 August 2006, p. 13.

Wadia, Angela, *Global Sourcebook on Right to Information*.

Wallerstein, Immanuel. *The Modern World System*.

Weber, Max (1926), *The Protestant Ethic and the Spirit of Capitalism*.

Weeramantry. Judge Christopher G. (1997), *Justice Without Frontiers: Furthering Human Rights*, Brill Publishers, 132 & 135, ISBN 9041102418.

Whalen, Charles J. (ed) (1996), *Political Economy for the 21st Century: Contemporary Views on the Trend of Economics*, ME Sharpe, INC, USA.

Winfield, Richard N. and Evans, Sherrel (2003), "Not Good Enough", *Combat Law*, Vol. 2, No. 2, June-July 2003. pp. 79-83.

Wolf, Eric (1982), *Europe and the People Without History*.

Wood, Ellen Meiksins (2002), *The Origins of Capitalism: A Longer View*. London: Verso.

Woodman, G.R. (1998), Ideological Combat and Social Observation: Recent Debate about Legal Pluralism, *Journal of Legal Pluralism*, 42: 21—59.

Working Group on Right to Information and Promotion of Open and Transparent Government, Report of Ministry of Personnel, Public Grievances and Pensions, New Delhi, para 2.1, 1997.

World Health Organization (1984), *Mental Health Care in Developing Country: A Critical Appraisal of Research Findings*, WHO, Technical Report Series. No. 698, Geneva.

World Health Organization (1998), *Supporting Governments and Policy-makers*, WHO, Division of Mental Health and Prevention of Substance Abuse, Geneva.

World Health Organization (2001), Mental Health: New Understanding, New Hope, WHO, World Health Report-2001, Geneva.

Yadav, K.C., (2000), *From Periphery to Centre Stage*, New Delhi: Manohar Publishers and Distributors.

Yilmaz, Bulrnt (1998), The Right to Information: Is it possible for Developing Countries?, 64 IFLA General Conference, August 16-August 21, 1998.

Zeiliot, Eleanor (1992), *From Untouchables to Dalit*, New Delhi: Manohar Publication.

CASES

AIR 1973, Supreme Court case, p. 1461.

AIR 1986, Supreme Court case, p. 515.

Ackerman, Frank; Lisa Heinzerling (August 24, 2005). Priceless.

Ahmedabad Municipal Corporation *v.* Nawab Khan Gulab Khan (1997), 11 SCC 121 (para 10) : AIR 1997 SC 152.

Ameeroonisa Begum *v.* Mahbooh Begum, 1953 SCR 404 (416) AIR 1953 SC 91; A.R. Antulay *v.* R.S. Nayak, AIR 1988 SC 1531 : (1988) 2 SCC 602.

Ashok Leyland Ltd. *v.* Union of India, (1997) 9 SCC 30 (para 20).

Atlas Cycle Co. *v.* Workmen, 1962 Supp. (3) SCR 89 {104} : AIR 1962 SC 1100; *Cf.* State of Orissa *v.* Bhupendra Kumar Base, 1962 Supp. (2) SCR 380 {392} : AIR 1962 SC 945.

B.C. Chaturvedi *v.* Union of India, (1995) 6 SCC 749, (para 24): AIR 1996 SC 484.

Babu Ram *v.* State of U.P., (1995) 2 SCC 689, (para 37).

Babulal Amthalal Mehta *v.* Collector of Customs, Calcutta, (1957) SCR 1110(722) AIR 1957 SC 877; Krishna A.S. *v.* State of Madras, 1957 SCR 399 (414) : AIR 1957 SC 297.

Baburao *v.* State of Bombay Housing Board, 1954 SCR. 572; Ameeroonisa Begum *v.* Mahboob Begum, 1953 SCR 404 : AIR 1953 SC 91; Suraj Mall *v.* Biswanath, AIR 1953 SC 545; Stale of W.B. *v.* Anwar Ali Sarkar, 1952 SCR 284: AIR 1952 SC 75; Ramkrishna Dalmia *v.* Tendolkar Justice S.R., AIR 1958 SC 538 : 1959 SCR 279: Casebook, p. 99; State of A.P. *v.* Nalla Raja Reddy, 1967 (3) SCR 28 [44}: AIR 1967 SC 1458.

Balaji M.R. *v.* State of Mysore, AIR 1963 SC 649 (664) : 1963 Supp. (1) SCR 439.

Bending Before Babus (Editorial), *The Times of India,* 25 July, 2006 14; 1-2.

Bennett Coleman *v.* Union of India, AIR 1973 SC 60.

Boundaries of Disclosure (Editorial) *Financial Express,* 20 April, 2006; 6; 1-2.

Budhan Choudhry *v.* State of Bihar, 1955 (1) SCR 1045 [1049} : AIR 1955 SC 191; Hanif *v.* State of Bihar, AIR 1958 SC 731; Harakchand Ratanchand Banlhia *v.* Union of India, (1969) 2 SCC 166 : AIR 1970 SC 1453; Pathumma *v.* State of Kerala, AIR 1978 SC 771 (para 41) : (1978) 2 SCC 1 ; Babu Ram *v.* State of U.P., (1995) 2 SCC 689 (para 37).

Budhan Chowdhry *v.* State of Bihar, 1955 (1) SCR 1045 (1049): AIR 1955 SC 191.

Calcutta Iron Merchants' Association *v.* Commissioner of Commercial Taxes, (1996) 7 SCC 537 (para 7): AIR 1996 SC 3166.

Central Board of Secondary Education *v.* Nikhil Gulati, (1998) 3 SCC 5: AIR 1998 SC 1205.

Devadasan T. *v.* Union of India, AIR 1964 SC 179 (780) : 1964 (4) SCR 680.

Dirty Harrys (Editorial). *The Times of India,* 30 August 2005, p. 8: 1-2 47; 19 Nov. 2005, pp. 4870-72.

Disclosure Norms. Trilochan Sastry. Seminar, Vol. 551, July 2005; 24-26.

Don't Dilute RTI Act, Please. Virendra Kumar. *The Tribune,* 6 August 2006, 13:13-16.

———, (2005) "Inform and Broadcast", *The Hindustan Times,* 6 October 2005, p. 10.

Garg R.K. *v.* Union of India, AIR 1981 SC 2138 (para 17) : (1981) 4 SCC 676 C.B. (Bearer bond case).

Garg R.K. *v.* Union of India, AIR 1981 SC 2138 (para 17) : (1981) 4 SCC 676 C.B. (Bearer bond case).

General Manager, Southern Railway *v.* Rangachari, 1962 (2) SCR 586 : AIR 1962 SC 36.

Giri V.V. *v.* Dora Suri D., AIR 1959 SC 13!8 [1325} : 1960 (1) SCR 426.

Grover, India (2005) "The Missing Link", Seminar, Vol. 551, July 2005, pp. 59-61.

Growth pegged at 8.1 per cent as a result of big push from manufacturing sector and borrowing services sector. *The Hindu,* 8 February, 2006, p. 1.

Harbilas Rai Bansal *v.* State of Punjab, (1996) 1 SCC 1, (paras 1, 12 and 13) : AIR 1996 SC 857, following Gian Devi Anand *v.* Jeevan Kumar, (1985) 2 SCC 683.

High Court of Judicature at Bombay *v.* Shimh Kumar Rangrao Patil, (1907) 6 SCC 339 (para 13)

Houchins *v.* KQED, Inc., 438 U.S.I. 16 (1978) the U.S. Supreme Court.

In the Know (Editorial), *The Times of India,* December 2004, p. 8.

Information: More, or Less—(Editorial) *The Tribune,* 3 Dec. 2005, p. 8.

J.K. Industries Ltd. *v.* Chief Injector of Factories & Boilers, (1996) 6 SCC 665 (para 39).

Jagdish Lal *v.* State of Haryana, (1997) 6 SCC 538 (para 14) : AIR 1997 SC 2366.

Jagdish Dajiba *v.* Accountant General, AIR 1958 Born. 283 : 60. Born. LR. 241.

Jayantilal Ratanchand Shah *v.* Reserve Bank of India, (1996) 9 SCC 650 (para 10): AIR 1997 SC 370.

Kanhere/Bombay High Court, 7 October 1986 (W.P. 2733 of 1986) and Supreme Court.

Kardaley, Prakash (2005), "A New Era", *Seminar*, Vol. 551, July 2005, pp. 17-23.

Kedar Nath Bajoria *v.* State of W.B., AIR 1953 SC 404 : 1954 Cri LJ 1679 : 1954 SCR 30; P.B. Roy *v.* Union of India, (1972) 3 SCC 432 : AIR 1972 SC 908.

Kedar Nath Bajoria *v.* State of W.B., AIR 1953 SC 404 : 1954 Cri LJ 1679 : 1954 SCR 30; P.B. Roy *v.* Union of India, (1972) 3 SCC 432 : AIR 1972 SC 908.

Kedar Nath Bajoria *v.* State of W.B., AIR 1953 SC 404 ; 1954 Cri IJ 1679 : 1954 SCR 30; P.B. Roy *v.* Union of India, (1972) 3 SCC 432 : AIR 1972 SC 908.

Khagesh Kumar *v.* Inspector General of Registration, 1995 Supp. (4) SCC 182, (para 19) : AIR 1996 SC 417.

L.I.C. of India *v.* Consumer Education & Research Centre, (1995) 5 SCC 482, (para 27) : AIR i995 SC 1811.

M.I. Builders Pvt. Ltd. *v.* Radhey Shyam Saku, (1999) 6 SCC 464 (paras 69, 71, 72, 73, 74, 80 and 81) : AIR 1999 SC 2468.

Mafatlal Industries Ltd. *v.* Union of India, (1997) 5 SCC 536 (para 88).

Malpe Vishwanath Acharya *v.* State of Maharashtra, (1998) 2 SCC 1 (paras 20-27) : AIR 1998 SC 602.

Malpe Vishwanath Acharya *v.* State of Maharashtra, (1998) 2 SCC 1 : AIR 1998 SC 602.

Malpe Vishwanath Acharya *v.* State of Maharashtra, (I998) 2 SCC 1 (paras 29 and 30) : AIR I998 SC 602.

Mohan Dutt Sharma *v.* Chief Justice, Punjab and Haryana High Court, (1997) 8 SCC 445 (paras 9-12) : AIR 1997 SC 3094.

Mohd. Riazul Usman Gum *v.* District & Sessions Judge, Nagpur. (2000) 2 SCC 606 (para 13) : AIR 2000 SC 919.

Moulin Rouge Private Ltd. *v.* Commercial Tax Officer, (1998) 1 SCC 70 (para 10) : AIR 1998 SC 218.

Now We Know (Editorial) *Hindustan Times*, 3 December 2005, p. 8.

OTI, not RTL (Editorial), *Financial Express*, 16 December 2004, p. 6.

P.V. Sundara Rajan *v.* Union of India, (2000) 4 SCC 469 (para 14).

P.K. Ghosh *v.* J.G. Rajput, (1995) 6 SCC 744, (para10): AIR 1996 SC 513.

Parents Association *v.* Union of India, (2000) 2 SCC 657 (paras 26, 29 and 30) : AIR 2000 SC 845.

People Must Know, (Editorial), *The Tribune*, 17 December 2004, p. 12

Rajkishore *v.* State of U.P., AIR 1954 All 343.

Ram Beti *v.* District Panchayat Raj Adhikari, (1998) 1 SCC 680 (paras 6 and 7) : AIR 1998 SC 1222.

Ram Prasad Narayan Sahi *v.* State of Bihar, AIR 1953 SC 215: 1953 SCR 1129.

Ramkrishna Dalmia *v.* Tendolkar Justice S.R., 1959 SCR 279: AIR 1958 SC 538; Govindlalji Maharaj *v.* State of Rajasthan 1964 (I) SCR 561 [618} : AIR 1963 SC 1638; State of J. and K. *v.* Golam Md. Bakshi, AIR 1967 SC 122 (131): 1966 Supp. SCR 401; Birakishore Deb *v.* State of Orissa, (1964) 7 SCR 32 (41) : AIR 1964 SC 1501; Mittal S.P. *v.* Union of India, AIR 1983 SC 1 (para 165) : (1983) 1 SCC 51; Lachhman Dass *v.* State of Punjab, AIR 1963 SC 222 : 1963 (2) SCR 353 ; Food Corporation of India *v.* State of Kerala, (1997) 3 SCC 410 (para 33) : AIR 1997 SC 1252.

Ramkrishna Dalmia *v.* Tendolkar Justice S.R., 1959 SCR 279 : AIR 1958 SC 538; Govindlalji Maharaj *v.* State of Rajasthan, 1964 (1) SCR 561 (618) : AIR 1963 SC 1638; State of J & K. *v.* Golam Md. Bakshi, AIR 1967 SC 122 (131) : 1966 Supp. SCR 401; Birakishore Deb *v.* State of Orissa, (1964) 7 SCR 32 (41) AIR 1964 SC 1501; Mittal S.P. *v.* Union of India, AIR 1983 SC 1 (para 165) : (1983) 1 SCC 51; Lachhman Dass *v.* State of Punjab, AIR 1963 SC 222 : 1963 (2) SCR 353; Reddy D.S. *v.* Chancellor Osmania University, 1967 (2) SCR 214 (2.97) : AIR 1967 SC 1305; Ry. Board *v.* Observer Publications, (1972) I S.C.W.R. 696 (705) AIR 1972 SC 1792.

Ramkrishna Dalmia *v.* Tendolkar Justice S.R., AIR 1958 SC 538: 1959 SCR 279: Casebook, p. 99.

Ramkrishna Dalmia *v.* Tendolkar Justice S.R., AIR 1958 SC 538: 1959 SCR 279: Casebook, p. 99; State of A.P. *v.* Nalla Raja Reddy, 1967 (3) SCR 28 [44} : AIR 1967 SC 1458.

Ramkrishna Dalmia *v.* Tendolkar Justice S.R., AJR 1958 SC 538: 1959 SCR 279: Casebook, p. 99.

Ravi Paul *v.* Union of India, (1995) 3 SCC 300, (para 24). Also see. Bhagat Singh *v.* Stale of Haryana, (1996) 8 SCC 649 (para 10).

Re Special Courts Bill, AIR 1979 SC 478 (508-10) : 1979 (1) SCC 380.

Roopchand Adlakha *v.* D.D.A., AIR 1989 SC 307 : (1989) 1 Supp. SCC 116.

S.B. International Ltd. *v.* Asstt. Director General of Foreign Trade, (1996) 1 SCC 439, (para 9) : AIR 1996 SC 2921. Sainik Motors (M/s.) *v.* State of Rajasthan, AIR 1961 SC 1480 (1486): 1962 (1) SCR 517.

Secunderabad Hyderabad Hotel Owners' Association *v.* Hyderabad Municipal Corporation, Hyderabad, (1999) 2 SCC 274 (paras 16 and 17) : AIR 1999 SC 635.

Sorabjee, Soli J. (1986), "Enforcing the Right to Know", 1:6 *Lex Et Juris*, 10 1986.

Spirit of Inquiry (Editorial), *The Times of India*, 7 December 2005, p. 12; August 2006, p. 14.

Sri Divi Kodandarama Saram *v.* State of A.P., (1997) 6 SCC 189.

State of A.P. *v.* Madawar, G.C., AIR 1955 SC 493 : 1955 (1) SCR 599. Also see State of T.N. *v.* Ananthi Ammal, AIR 1995 SC 2114, (paras 6 and 7) : (1995) 1 SCC 519.

State of Kerala *v.* Aravind Ramakant Modawdakar, (1999) 7 SCC 400 (paras 6 and 9) : AIR 1999 SC 2970. State of Bihar *v.* Sachchidanand Kishore Prasad Sinha, (1995) 3 SCC 86, (para 14) ; AIR 1995 SC 885.

State of Bihar *v.* Subhash Singh, (1997) 4 SCC 430 (para 3) : AIR 1997 SC 1390.

State of Kerala *v.* Roshana T.P. Kumari, (1979) 1 SCC 572 (para 15) : AIR 1979 SC 765; State of J. & K. *v.* Triloki Nath Khosa, (1974) 1 SCC 19 [42] : AIR 1974 SC 1.

State of M.P. *v.* Madawar G.C., AIR 1955 SC 493 : 1955 (1) SCR 599; Sam Lal Bharti *v.* State of Punjab, AIR 1988 SC 485 (para 5) : (1988) 1 SCC 366; Prabhakaran Nair *v.* State of T.N., AIR 1987 SC 2117 : (1987) 4 SCC 238. Also see State of T.N. *v.* Ananthi Ammal, AIR 1995 SC 2114, (paras 6 and 7): (1995) 1 SCC 519.

State of M.P. *v.* Madawar, G.C., AIR 1955 SC 493 : 1955 (1) SCR 599. Also see State of T.N. *v.* Ananthi Ammal, AIR 1995 SCSI 14, (paras 6 and 7) : (1995) I SCC 519.

State of M.P. *v.* Ram Krishna Balothia, (1995) 3 SCC 221, (paras 6 and 10) : AIR 1995 SC 1198.

State of M.P. *v.* Shakri Khan, (1996) 8 SCC 648 (para 3) : AIR 1996 SC 2247.

State of Rajasthan *v.* Manohar Singhji, 1954 SCR 996 : AIR 1954 SC 297; Motor General Traders *v.* State of A.P., AIR 1984 SC 121 (710):(1984) 1 SCC 222; Rattan Arya *v.* State of T.N., AIR 1986 SC 1444 (para 4) : (1986) 3 SCC 385.

State of U.P. *v.* Roadways Ministerial Staff Association, U.P., (1996) 9 SCC 479 (para 5) : AIR 1996 SC 3415.

State of Uttar Pradesh *v.* Raj Narain, AIR 1975 SC 865, 884 : (1975) 4 SCC 428.

State of W.B. *v.* Anwar Ali Sarkar, 1952 SCR 284 [320} : AIR 1952 SC 75, Mukherjee.; Sakhawat Ali *v.* State of Orissa, 1955 (1) SCR 1004 : AIR 1955 SC 166.

State of W.B. *v.* Anwar Ali Sarkar, (1952) SCR 284 [320) : AIR 1952 SC 75, Mukherjea, J.; Budhan Choudhry *v.* State of Bihar, 1955 (1) SCR 1045 [1049} : AIR 1955 SC 191.

Style (Dress Ltd.) *v.* Union Territory, Chandigarh, (1999) 7 SCC 89 (para 12). Also see A. P. Aggarwal *v.* Government of NCT of Delhi, (2000) 1 SCC 600 (para 12) : AIR 2000 SC 205.

Style (Dress Ltd.) *v.* Union Territory, Chandigarh, (1999) 7 SCC 89 (para 10).

Style (Dress Ltd.) *v.* Union Territory, Chandigarh, (1999) 7 SCC 89 (para 9).

Sub-Inspector Rooplal *v.* Lt. Governor, (2000) 1 SCC 644 (para 23).

Supreme Court case 4, 1973, p. 225.

Supreme Court case 4, 1975, p. 428.
Supreme Court case 2, 1995, p. 161.
Supreme Court Judgement 1, 1997, p. 697.
Supreme Court case 4, 1997, p. 306.
Supreme Court case suppl., 1981, p. 87.
Supreme Court case, 1982, p. 149
Suraj Maliv. Biswanath, AIR 1953 SC 545, Slate of W.W. *v.* Anwar Ali Sarkar, 1952 SCR 284 : AIR 1952 SC 75.
Suraj Mall *v.* Biswanath, AIR 1953 SC 545; State of W.B. *v.* Anwar Ali Sarkar, 1952 SCR 284 : AIR 1952 SC 75.
The Hindu, November 28, 2007.
The Hindu, 7 October, p. 10
———, (2006) "RTI will Improve Governance", *The Tribune,* 10 October, p. 13, (paras 12, 13, 14 and 16).
The Power of Knowledge (Editorial), *Economic Times,* 17 December 2004, p. 4.
The Sunday Tribune, Chandigarh, June 26, 2005, p. 2.
The Times of India, New Delhi, July 15, 2005, p. 9.
The Times of India, August 31, 2007.
The Tribune, Chandigarh, June 5, 2005, p. 1.
Union of India *v.* Association for Democratic Reforms, JT 2002(4) 501, Chap. XIX, Sec. D (b).
Union of India *v.* Indian Charge Chrome, (1999) 7 SCC 314 (paras 13 and 14).
V.P. Malik (Dr.) *v.* Union of India, (1996) 1 SCC 456. (para 4) ; AIR 1996 SC 1048.
Venkateswara Theatre *v.* State of A.P., AIR 1993 SC 1947 (para 19): (1993) 3 SCC 677; Khandige Sham Bhat *v.* A.I.T.O., AIR 1963 SC 591 [594] : 1963 (3) SCR 809.
Yusuf Abdul Aziz *v.* State of Bombay, 1954 SCR 930 : AIR 1954 SC 321.

Websites

http://indiankanoon.org.
supremecourtofindia.nic.in

INDEX